The Dry Fly
New Angles

Gary LaFontaine

Choosing the right fly for the moment

Illustrations by Gretchen Grayum

Black and white photographs by R. Valentine Atkinson
and others

THE LYONS PRESS
Guilford, Connecticut
An imprint of The Globe Pequot Press

To Heather
my daughter and best friend

Everyone undoubtedly gets tired of me bragging about her. I'm not saying that she's perfect, but I've raised her, and her flaws amazingly are my flaws. Somehow as parents we tend to be very tolerant of these.

————————————————

Preface

Why does a Frenchman kiss a lady's hand? He has to start somewhere.
In either seduction or fly fishing it's silly to proceed without a plan.
This is my book of plans for choosing a dry fly or emerger
(no one is clamoring for me to write a book on seduction).

Gary LaFontaine

The Lyons Press is an imprint of The Globe Pequot Press

Previously published by Greycliff Publishing Company

Printed in the United States of America

10 9 8 7 6 5 4 3 2 1

Library of Congress Cataloging-in-Publication Data is available on file.

Acknowledgments

The Royal "We"—

Frequently, I'll use "we" instead of "I" when referring to an idea. That's simply a grateful bow to all the friends who end up being more than fishing buddies on my projects. They are the workers.

Who are they? They are trout bums. They have to be; the research is no weekend affair. They don't have steady jobs or regular family obligations.

The people who worked on *The Dry Fly* are, for the most part, different than the ones who worked on *Caddisflies*. That's because most trout bums do grow up, gain responsible employment, and get married. On *Caddisflies* the leading helpers were Ken Thompson and Graham Marsh. On *The Dry Fly* they were Tory Stosich and (again) Graham Marsh. These people get paid, but the money ends up being much less than minimum wage. We call it a stipend (often, these fishing bums are also graduate students in aquatic entomology or fisheries biology).

The worst mistake I could have made after the success of *Caddisflies* was to rush another book into print. The research done for *Caddisflies*, as research usually does, created as many questions as answers. *The Dry Fly* was built on those new mysteries—it just took a while to solve the tougher ones.

A magazine editor asked me, "How come it took so long to write this new book."

"I don't do sequels," I explained.

Graham Marsh may successfully resist the temptation and never grow up— thank God!

Tory Stosich has reluctantly passed through the trout bum phase, recently entering medical school.

He reminded me of myself when I was younger— as I told him, "We could really be jerks."

He has read the first draft of this book and admits to the quotes. They were my favorites because he often blurted out things that I had become too diplomatic to say. People like us really don't get less opinionated as we get older, we just learn to hide it better.

Tom Poole was the other member of the diving team. His ability to define the problem kept us devising new methods of underwater observation.

Bill Seeples, who taught us all how to scuba dive, continually gave us advice and monitored our dives for safety.

Paul Dodds, Ron Pedale, David Dunne, and Jennifer Koenig (who I wrote about in *Challenge of the Trout* when she was eleven) have been our main workers over the past four summers.

Other people who have generously given their time are Gordon Traynor, Ernie Motichka, Taylor Lee, Marc Brannon, Burl Kinne, David Bohleen, Chuck Parke, Winfield DeLorme, Robert Zachary, Peter Ingraldi, Richard DePratu, and Howard Miner, Jr.

There are talented fly tyers who provide patterns by the dozen for our testing: Ted Marchiano (who makes me look like the amateur tyer that I am with his gifts of #20 Wulffs, Humpies, and Irresistibles), Larry Duckwall (who ties such splendid Quill Gordons), Ervin Eid (a master of both No Hackles and Compara

Duns), Larry Rohrman (terrestrials—including every type of grasshopper imaginable), Bernard Stinger, Jeffery Matelich, and Doug Rekers.

All of my new flies, even after underwater observation, go to groups of fly fishing friends, who will work them hard on a variety of waters and provide a careful analysis on the strengths and weaknesses of a pattern: Denny Nops, Thad Maliszewski, Marvin Craik, Wayne Huft, Gene Mize, Kathy Mohrenweiser, Jeff Kienow, and Glen and Sally Putnam.

Kelly Reinoehl, Pat Sadowski, and Brad Hanton were high school fly tyers who came on our diving expeditions and whipped up any improbable concoction that we could think of testing.

Tobin Wiesz assisted on the close up photography for this book.

Hal Patman, Will Eaton, Graydon Fenn, Justin Carre, Bill Redmann, Allan Kostick, and Jearold Reither showed me their favorite fishing waters and shared ideas on local flies.

Ralph Manns and Doug Hannon answered my questions and pointed me towards research materials on the effect of Solunar Periods.

Carl Wyman was the mathematician who worked out the probability formulas for us for the experiments on Solunar Periods.

A major part of this book is the series of radio telemetry studies on rivers across the country. Those findings not only gave birth to many of the theories about imitation and attraction, but through the careful recordings of so many situations they corroborated those ideas. The credit goes to the people who so carefully adhered to the "structure" of these experiments— John B. Soprepena, David Whitt, Norman Capdeville, Ed Volinkaty, James VanKrevelen, W. J. Witts, Henning Penttila, Terry Rothman, and Chris Kincheloe.

There were people who spent hours in canvas blinds along rivers observing trout—Mark Welnel, Myron Bastian, Pat Pannetier, and Jon H. Jourdonnais.

Brester Zahm, who is already working on the original research for one of my future books, *Bass*, observed and helped on all of the trout studies.

James Fenner is the physicist who so generously answered all of my questions about the physical properties of light (and who was one of my readers for the finished manuscript).

Dr. William Vessie, my fishing partner in Deer Lodge, has the uncanny knack for knowing when I'm about to go crazy with paperwork and insists that we go to one of his beautiful, "secret" spots (and he also was one of my readers for the finished manuscript). He is a superb fly fisherman, not only because of his intellect but because of an intense drive to never stop learning about the sport. With his years of experience (Jimmy Deren taught him how to tie a Double Fan Wing Royal Coachman) he has been a great resource for me right here in Deer Lodge to bounce ideas off of.

Paul Schullery and George Grant answered my questions on the history of fly fishing (I make no claim of being an historian).

Wayne Hadley, the state Fish, Wildlife and Parks biologist for the Deer Lodge area, listens to my questions and with his answers opens up areas and possibilities that I had not even thought of.

Nick Lyons, of Lyons & Burford Publishers, is the great editor and publisher of fly fishing books. The fly fishing world should be grateful to him, not only for bringing so many original books (including *Caddisflies*) to us, but also for rescuing classic works on our sport from oblivion. *Trout Magazine*, in their thirtieth anniversary issue, published a list by reviewer Robert Berls of the best fifteen books of the last thirty years (there have been hundreds published). Twelve of those books are currently in print from Lyons and Burford. Nick always gave me his time for *The Dry Fly* when I called for advice or encouragement. He has great knowledge, experience, and wisdom and he shares it with everyone.

David Engerbretson, Eric Peper, Ken Parkany, and Dan Abrams are the other people who I call up when there is anything to discuss about fly fishing, business, or life (it's strange how all three have gotten so intertwined).

Stan and Glenda Bradshaw are my partners in Greycliff Publishing Company. They are also my friends (and have been since college); and it has been fun watching them going daffy with me putting this book together. (Will this be as much fun once we know what we are doing?)

Robert Ince and John Roberts work hard at keeping me in touch with the world of fly fishing in the United Kingdom.

The people at Umpqua Feather Merchants (Dennis Black, Bill Black, and the entire crew) produce, distribute, and publicize my original flies incredibly well—it didn't take me long to find out that the greatest idea for a pattern would quickly die if the fly wasn't available in shops.

Jack Dennis just might be the most creative individual that I have ever met in any field. He puts me in his great video productions, makes me part of the "Travelling Fly Fishermen" seminars, and finds places for me in his incredible "One Fly Contest" every year. This reminds me of a story about Jimmy Stewart, the actor. He had so much faith in a particular producer that when the man approached him about starring in a movie, Jimmy Stewart accepted the part without even seeing a script, "If you want me to do a movie about a six foot, imaginary rabbit, I think it's a great idea." Whatever Jack suggests, I'll do. His touch is magic.

Mike Lawson is also part of the "Travelling Fly Fisherman Seminars." On planes, in hotel rooms, and at meals my thoughts just tend to pop out totally unrelated to the occasion or activity. Mike gives great responses, with so many original ideas, to all of my ramblings. This book has changed between the first and last drafts, and is more complete on many points of dry fly choice, because of him.

Dick Fryhover and Harry Ramsay have been my most important teachers in fly fishing. Dick taught me how to fish western trout streams, tie flies, and guide—all in one summer. My approach to fly fishing, even twenty years later, shows the wonderful influence of his ideas about trout.

Harry Ramsay's strong opinions on books (more than even his on-stream advice) had to effect me. He certainly preferred the older English authors, but he grudgingly acknowledged American writers such as John Atherton, George LaBranche, and his personal favorite, Sid Gordon. He used to say that *How To Fish From Top to Bottom* was "some of the best thinking and some the worst writing all wrapped up in one package."

My books, based as they are on research, wouldn't be possible without all of this help from all of these friends.

The Dry Fly
New Angles

Contents

What flies are in my boxes? It's a fair question. This is my selection at the moment. It evolves slowly and steadily. Old patterns fade from favor; new flies are added to my selection.

My boxes are divided into major dry fly categories.

Some boxes are small; some are large.

*The dry fly on a line following the "My Fly Box" headings
was drawn by Michael Korn.*

"Trying to imagine what goes on in the fish's brain is a dangerous proceeding, and one wholly unbecoming to a scientist, but it is permissible to a layman, and any layman who did try it might not be far wrong."

The Life Story of the Fish
by Brian Curtis

The ideas in *The Dry Fly* apply only to dry flies (unless the text is specifically mentioning subsurface phenomena). Wet flies are viewed by trout according to different natural laws and the problems of imitation and attraction are different.

The experiments for *The Dry Fly* were done on brown trout, rainbow trout, and cutthroat trout in streams (where food usually moves to trout). They are probably relevant for brook trout in running water. They might be relevant for smallmouth bass in running water. How well they fit stillwater habitats (where trout usually move to the food) cannot be answered without further studies.

Chapter 1

Why Flies Fail

Scattered throughout my fly boxes are plenty of one-time wonders, flies that possessed some unexplainable magic once but never before or after seduced anything of note. Clean them out? Forfeit the chance of their ever becoming two-time wonders? Some do. Not me.

Many anglers, myself included, are obsessed with successful flies. It is possible to come up with so many different reasons for the triumphs of certain patterns that it's a wonder a trout is able to decide at all whether to accept or reject a fly. The answer to this puzzle is that all of those reasons might be valid, but a trout—at any given moment—needs only one.

When a big fish rises like this on the Fall River (California), the angler starts hunting for a pattern that will satisfy that trout's expectations.

Since flies succeed for any one of a hundred reasons, the way to pad the odds is by carrying a large assortment of feathered frauds. This explains why there are so many different patterns. Any creation, somewhere or sometime, is going to fool a fish.

The smartest way to decide which pattern to tie on, therefore, is not to ask why a fly succeeds in a given situation, but why it fails. After all, there are dozens of reasons why a trout might respond to a dry fly, but there's only one *major* reason why the fish won't respond.

Underwater it's possible to see fish focus on a fly and then either select or reject an imitation. The surprise of these observations is that trout will also clearly reject a natural insect, breaking off a rise because of some odd action or obscured view.

My fishing partner, Tom Poole, noticed this while snorkeling downstream on his back and studying emerging mayflies. "It's the wind," he said. "When it pushes the dun across the current, the fish breaks off. That's what I think is happening."

Over the next few weeks we tested his theory by catching Big Hole River trout during mayfly hatches on both calm and windy days. We sampled the stomach contents of the fish by pumping and discovered a difference in their feeding pattern:

Calm days—	Duns=44%	Emergent Nymphs=56%
Windy days—	Duns=27%	Emergent Nymphs=73%

The wind made mayfly duns, fully emerged on the surface, a much less attractive target. Since mayflies rode so high anytime, with their bodies barely touching the surface, any riffling of the water by the wind obscured the trout's view of the insect. The wind, especially a swirling, gusty one, also pushed the insect unpredictably, further discouraging rising trout.

All of the members of our diving group witnessed this phenomenon underwater, and to this day we will use a damp, emergent mayfly imitation instead of a dry fly under windy conditions.

More importantly we started thinking about the failures, and not just the successes, of our fly pattern experiments.

It is not only the angler's fly that gets refused. When naturals, especially mayflies, get blown out of their current lanes, the trout after a few bad experiences start ignoring the insects on the surface.

The trial and error method is slow at times, but underwater it's not terribly difficult to devise new and better imitations. The tyer who has to look at the insect in his hand and wonder how his matching fly looks to a trout is guessing wildly. The only way he can confirm the effectiveness of his creation is to fish it, and although he has no way of understanding what's really happening when his fly drifts over a trout, he's forced to judge the pattern on the basis of random experiences. It takes a lot of angling experiences to confirm or repudiate the worth of a new innovation.

The process is mercifully quicker with underwater observation. The imitation drifts overhead mixed in with the naturals, and comparisons are obvious. Once an approximate match is concocted it's tested during a hatch in full view of the diver, the rising trout either accepting or rejecting the fly.

The most damning action is not when a fish notices a fly, tilts up on his fins and prepares to take, and then refuses it. That at least indicates a partial success. The worst insult happens when the fly passes over the feeding window of trout after trout and they never show that initial interest.

The secret to success lies in pinpointing the characteristic that a trout looks for first in an insect. Any changes in the fly after that are just refinements based on trial-and-error, the fish the final arbiter.

The youngest member of our diving group, Tory Stosich, in a remnant of California pop culture, called this process a "no-brainer." Who cared about cause, he said, when the effect was so obvious and definitive?

It was one of those summer evenings in the Big Hole valley. The main door was left open at the bar, only the screening keeping the mosquitoes and gnats out. In the smokey din of the Wise River Club, with the monster moths outside fluttering against the window over our table, Tory Stosich, Tom Poole, Graham Marsh, and I drank beers with two Big Hole guides, call them Buck and Duke, and listened to them tell us which flies really worked on the river.

My advantage in the discussion was my float-trip guiding experience. I understood why attractor patterns cast from a moving boat were effective choices even on the Big Hole. My underwater work may have been linked entirely to imitations, but the days spent rowing the river left room in my angling philosophy for bright, non-specific flies, too.

Even Tom and Graham accepted the worth of attractors on certain types of water. Tory, however, had no such patience with Wulffs, Trudes, and Renegades, "Those flies stink," he said.

Who hated Tory more that summer? Duke, who was quick to anger, and scowled openly, or the easy going Buck, who seemed much more dangerous, even without a glaring face, when he just stopped smiling and nodding?

Tom added, "What we're saying is that you don't use attractors during the salmon fly hatch, do you? So why flog out a Royal Wulff during a mayfly or caddisfly hatch, when the water is lower and the fishing is tougher?"

The talk, even with the blare of the jukebox, was pulling in a circle of guides and fishermen, some dragging over chairs and some standing. "You're right," Duke said amiably.

"Right," Buck said. "That's why Duke and I were hoping you'd test his mayfly against my mayfly, and tell us which one was best."

The anglers, not a single one of them surprised by his challenge, were hovering over us. Were they all staring at me? And why did Graham have his arm around my neck, pulling me towards him as he said in my ear, "What do we do when both patterns fail? Do you think it's going to be any fault of the flies?"

Tory was holding the two test flies in his palm. "It's the fish that make the decision. Not us."

Where was my escape? "Look," I said, "We can't do it unless all four of us agree."

Tory said, "We'll do it."

Those flies stink? Not really. There are imitationists who are offended by the very idea of flies like the fore-and-aft Renegade (shades of Halford?).

Tom said, "I guess."

Graham, ever indecisive, shrugged and stood up. Heading towards the back of the bar to find the restroom, he paused in front of the two doors, one marked "Setter" and the other "Pointer," and never did pick one. Instead, he came right back to the table. "Why not?"

Those moths, bashing the windowpane trying to reach the electric glow of the bulbs, were no sillier that the four divers intent on flunking the overdressed mayfly imitations tied by two of the most popular guides on the river.

"Tie the flies with some orange in the body," I told them.

"Those mayflies," Duke said, "don't have any orange color."

"No orange, no contest," I said. "The flies won't work in the Abutment Pool without orange. And don't ask me why, because we don't know."

The next day at 10:00 A.M. some of the bar crowd gathered on the gravel of our large pool. Graham and Tom set up identical outfits; they would be testing the flies—not Duke and Buck. They knew the water and the fish, and their skills, superbly polished, were very even. Tory and I would be underwater.

Duke's fly had a mink hair tail, a body of deer hair fibers spread along the shank and bound down with a ribbing of monofilament, a heavy collar wrap of hackle, and no wings. The bottom of the hackle was clipped in a *V*.

Buck had few of Duke's tying skills. His fly was rougher, looking too indelicate for the size 16 hook. The tail was split, two bunches of deer hair veering off the back. The body was wrapped yarn, which was much too bulky. The moose hair wings would have been lost in the hackle if they hadn't been so absurdly oversized. The hackle itself was a combination, one feather a good grizzly cock and the other, at the face, a longer, soft grouse.

Before we dove I told them, "Those flies look like they'd work on faster water. This pool is different."

Buck grinned, "I've caught lots of trout from this pool on my fly."

The hatch of Small Western Red Quills (*Rhithrogena undulata*) was building, fish already queuing up along that foam line between the swift main current and the slowly eddying backwater. Tory and I swam under the trout, spooking a few but settling on the bottom without disturbing the main string.

Once we were in place, the fishermen began working the tail of the 100-yard pool, alternating five casts each. They both took small fish below us, but even on those indiscriminate tiddlers one pattern was eliciting more strikes. In the better water, with the flies drifting over us, Buck's fly hooked the first nice fish—a 14-inch rainbow.

Tory, who never stopped motioning with his hands even underwater, sat speechless as the trout fought. "Don't worry," he'd told me, "both flies will flop and we'll be out of the water in ten minutes."

Buck's fly didn't flop. Duke's did, catching only one small trout. The score wasn't tallied on fish hooked, but rather on what we could see underwater. When a fly drifted through a trout's window it scored a possible;

when a trout began rising to the fly it scored a probable; and when the trout completed the rise, taking the fly, it scored an acceptable. It didn't matter whether the fish was hooked or landed.

	Possible	Probable	Acceptable
Duke's fly	12	3	1
Buck's fly	8	6	2

Six of the eight fish that could have noticed Buck's fly did, an incredible rate with so many naturals on the surface. Four of these six trout, after committing to the fly, abruptly broke off the rise—clear refusals. Something unnatural about the pattern was attracting attention as it entered the trout's window, but either that feature or another was repelling the fish up close. Still, any fly fisherman would be happy to catch a third of the rising trout he covered with good drifts.

Tory's first words when we surfaced were, "There's something special about that rabbit-eared thing of Buck's."

Duke didn't like that. "Maybe Graham wasn't fishing mine as well," he said.

I tried to explain, cutting off Tory's answer, "That had nothing to do with it. We can see any mistakes by the fisherman. There were just a lot more fish interested in Buck's fly."

"What was wrong with mine?" Duke demanded.

"I don't know. Neither fly really looked like the natural to me."

This time Tory was too fast for us. "We don't worry about failures," he said. "We just throw them away."

To this day in the Big Hole country Duke won't give me more than a passing nod, and he tells everybody that I don't know a good fly from a bad one. About that I readily admit he's correct. I'm not sure that there's any such thing as a bad fly. Too many oddball creations work for me at strange times, and I have no idea why. Yet, I can usually discover the main reason for failure when a fly doesn't work.

There is a pecking order of rising trout in the foam line. Day after day they line up the same way to feed on a hatch.

Usually, it's the angler and not the fly that fails. But fly fishing can never be a game of presentation versus fly choice. Even the beginner, who drifts his fly badly over trout time after time, still needs the right pattern when he gets that lucky float.

It's rare that only one fly will fool trout. Even during hatches there are different patterns, all within a range of acceptability, that will work with varying degrees of success. Nevertheless, a fly that isn't presented correctly has very little chance. That is what makes me a presentationist.

Presume that the angler does everything perfectly, and then ask why a fly fails?

Why imitations fail

A trout rising rhythmically to insects in a stream works within a well-defined feeding territory established by current lines. He doesn't necessarily hold in the exact center of that area; he may move a foot and a half to his right but only a foot to his left to take naturals, and he ignores any insects outside that territory during regular, selective feeding. The fish moves into faster currents on either side to take food, but he's reluctant to pass completely through them.

The surface insect appears not all at once to the selectively feeding trout, but as a series of characteristics. The first visible manifestation of a floating insect is the indentations it makes on the surface film. The weight of the creature presses a clearly visible pattern, each reverse pimple bright on the silvery underside of the meniscus (the rubbery skin of the stream).

The trout notices the light pattern well before he ever sees the insect. To a fish, this distinctive pattern is more of a hint, an advertisement of what's to follow, than a characteristic. The light pattern by itself triggers only awareness, not recognition, and a trout doesn't respond selectively to the pattern alone (but he does respond to the general impression).

It's the first strong visual characteristic, the one triggering the trout's decision to take a natural or an imitation, that is crucial. This feature varies even with different stages of the same insect, such as a mayfly, and the matching fly must have it.

The trout sees an emerging mayfly nymph, half in and half out of the water, as a subsurface food form. The fish can see it clearly from a greater distance than it sees the light pattern of the adult on the surface. In other words, the emerging insect itself is visible and not the distorted image of the floating dun.

The fully emerged dun is not visible all at once; it appears bit by bit—with the wings, upright and tall, poking over the edge of the trout's window as the insect rides downstream. This is why the trout "keys" so strongly on the adult mayfly's wings.

The egg-laying mayfly spinner, once its wings droop and settle flush on the surface, has no vertical features, nothing standing up that can materialize like disconnected spires in the trout's field of vision. Those clear wings spread out on the water, however, becoming iridescent as actual air bubbles collect

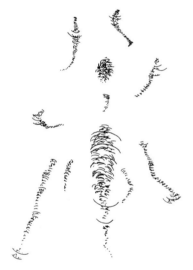

Trout do not key selectively on the imprint pattern of an insect, but those silvery, reverse pimples on the surface film do alert the fish to an approaching item. Underwater, these pimples glow with the color of the ambient light. In the evening, the walls of these dots shimmer with an intense orange. It doesn't matter what the colors of the natural insect (or the matching fly) are—it is the light, not the color of the object, that lends the color.

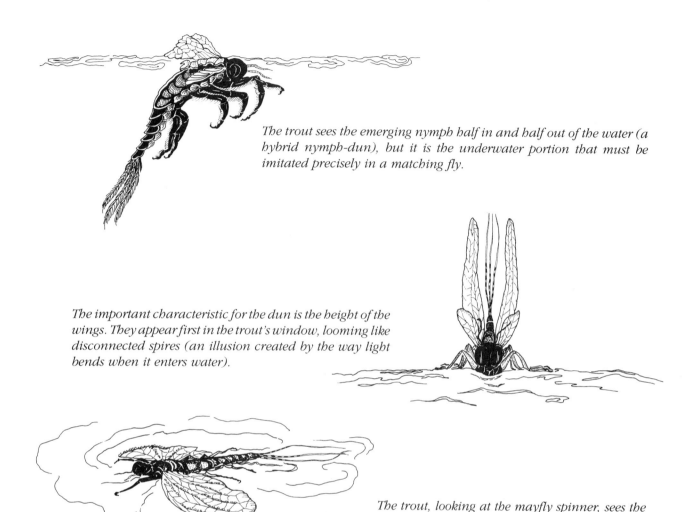

The trout sees the emerging nymph half in and half out of the water (a hybrid nymph-dun), but it is the underwater portion that must be imitated precisely in a matching fly.

The important characteristic for the dun is the height of the wings. They appear first in the trout's window, looming like disconnected spires (an illusion created by the way light bends when it enters water).

The trout, looking at the mayfly spinner, sees the bright, iridescent wings. Those sparkling appendages dominate the image—and the imitation of the spinner has to have them.

in the pleats and create a prismatic effect. A trout sipping spinners gauges the insect by the width and brightness of those wings.

It's possible to guess at the triggering characteristic of any dead-drift insect, not just mayflies, by watching how it floats on the water. If any part of the insect, including its legs if they are large enough or active enough, breaks through the surface film this trait is noticed first. When an insect floats on the surface film without breaking through, any tall, upright feature will be noticed first. When an insect without upright parts rests on the surface film, trout notice the widest feature, whatever it may be, first.

In fast water the initial triggering characteristic is usually the only important feature for the trout. The fish, spotting the insect or fly passing overhead, has to rise quickly through the water column. The decision is made with simple recognition—there is not enough time between the impulse to rise and the actual take for the trout to study the food item.

When do other aspects of the natural or artificial become important? The correlation is simple—the slower the current, the more critical the secondary features. A selectively feeding trout still decides to rise when he sees the triggering characteristic, but as he tilts up, or worse, drifts back downstream under the fly, he expects a certain shape, size, and color. If something that's supposed to be there isn't, he breaks off the rise with one of those maddening, last moment refusals.

By early June the Pale Morning Dun (*Ephemerella inermis*) begins hatching on the Henry's Fork in Idaho. Through July it emerges with other mayflies—the Brown Drake (*Ephemera simulans*), the Gray Drake (*Siphlonurus occidentalis*), and the Small Western Green Drake (*Ephemerella flavinea*)—and each day the trout feed on the sequence of hatches. Still, when there is overlap, the fish prefer the Pale Mornings over the larger insects because there are so many more of them available.

Other mayfly hatches dwindle in late July, but the Dun appears every morning (a little earlier maybe on clear, warm days) through August. The larger rainbows of the Fork become progressively more selective, locking into the picture expected with this mayfly. They (as the English say) "get the color."

At these times, the trout start snubbing even good presentations, turning away at the last moment with a whirl, a bulge forming under the fly with the refusal. The pods of rainbows, conditioned by midsummer to ignore the flailing antics of anglers, continue feeding but uncannily detect any imitation among the naturals.

The trout goes through stages when he studies a drifting fly. The entire rise sequence can develop into a maddening, drop back period of close inspection and, all too often, refusal.

Mike Lawson enjoys stalking the sippers that feed on the Pale Morning Dun hatch on the Railroad Ranch section of the Henry's Fork.

Most fly fishermen conclude that their imitation must be too large for these educated fish. They make a critical mistake, changing from a size 16 to a size 18 or 20. Then they fool only the occasional stray. They may also try various dun imitation styles—a Thorax, No-Hackle, Paradun, or Compar-adun—never realizing how close they were with their original, size 16 pattern.

Many Fork regulars avoid the dilemma of dry fly imitation by changing to floating and emerging nymphs once trout reach the fussy stage with Pale Mornings. This solution never seems right to me, not when trout are actually taking adults; nymphing at these times may be an admission that a favorite dry fly style is inadequate, but it works.

The relationship between size and color is the real problem with the effectiveness of dry flies. Any light fly, such as the pale gray Morning Dun, wears an aura of brightness when it's backlit that makes it appear larger. The size 16 Pale Morning, for example, ends up looking like a size 14.

The canny Henry's Fork angler determines by the refusals that something is amiss, assumes correctly that it is overall size, and switches to a smaller fly. The problem is that by doing so he inadvertently reduces the height of the wings—the triggering characteristic—and thus diminishes the effectiveness of the imitation.

When an angler stands in the middle of the Henry's Fork on a windless morning in late July, voices carrying clearly over the flats, even the private mutterings of frustrated fly fishermen, are audible. If he catches a few trout, some other anger is sure to shout, "Mister, what are you using?"

The Pale Morning Dun is my favorite hatch on the Henry's Fork, especially in the last weeks of the emergence. My answer? "A size 18 with the wings of a size 14."

Why do imitations fail? Trout either overlook the fly because it lacks the appropriate triggering characteristic or they refuse it because it lacks the right combination of secondary characteristics. Failure has little to do with matching the insect; an imitation fails when, distorted by the surface film, it can't match the trout's perception of that insect's characteristics.

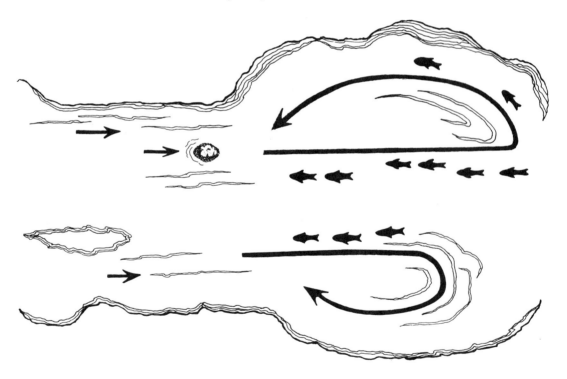

The large, deep Abutment Pool on the Big Hole River, just below Wise River, is a "dining room" for more than a hundred trout. They stack up under the foam lines during a hatch, fish arranged by order of dominance. The main current, rushing white water at the head of the pool, is so swift that no fish rise steadily there. Instead, the surface feeders hold in the creases on either side, between the main current and the reverse flows of the two backwaters.

When and why attractors fail

As Tory said about Wulffs, Trudes, and Renegades, "Those flies stink."

That judgement applies only during hatches to our diving area on the Big Hole. The river squeezes through a slot of boulders, splashing into a churn of whitewater, and then spreads out into an oval expanse. Between the main current and the 50-foot cliff of orange limestone the spill-off spins in a backwater. Trout either stack up between the main flow and the reverse current of one of the eddies, feeding on insects carried down the chute, or they cruise the large backwater, picking up cripples.

Does the "showing them something different" theory ever work in this pool? An occasional rising trout will break off a feeding pattern and move for the oddball attractor. This happens once in a while in fast water, but seldom in slower flows.

There are other fish, even during a hatch, that don't rise. They notice the insects, and see the feeding activity of other trout, but typically they hold in areas unsuited to surface feeding—places where the opportunity for bottom feeding is superb.

The Abutment Pool's heavier head waters, still bubbly from the white-water churning, hold some of the best trout. These fish are generally nymph feeders, however, so it takes a large insect to entice them to rise. They watch the emerging and adult insects accumulating on the surface, but are reluctant to move to another feeding lie or rise from their home position.

These fish are much more responsive to attractor patterns during the hatch than are regularly rising trout. It's not a matter of fish getting the urge

A trout feeding on nymphs "might" suddenly rise to an attractive dry fly, especially if the size of the pattern matches the roughness and speed of the current. A trout, aware of everything within the scope of his vision, is more likely to come up for an attractor fly than a somber imitation. The fish is also much more likely to respond to a fly on the surface if the pattern fortuitously floats overhead when there is a lull, a momentary absence, of drifting nymphs for him to feed on. (The angler would have no way of predicting such a lull—this is a tendency that the divers saw underwater.)

for something different, the "strawberries and cream" theory, but rather of non-rising trout responding to a combination of feeding readiness and a curiosity about a larger object.

Since the reluctant trout are often the bigger ones, they are worth teasing to the surface. The secret is to ignore rising fish during the hatch and drift attractors off the feeding line. If a river slopes into deeper water and trout are coming to the surface from a depth of two and a half feet, the angler should work the fly further out, over the three- to four-foot depth. If a chute churns into a pool, and trout are rising ten feet down from the head, he should drift the fly over the rougher upper water.

This off-line tactic of fishing attractors during a hatch works much better than scatter casting. It's not an approach that will yield more trout than skillful hatch-matching, but it's a way to avoid the problems of selectivity and catch bigger trout on the dry fly. It's either an admission of inadequacy, or a preference for catching larger fish.

It is a mistake to think of an attractor pattern as anything other than a food form. To a fish, it must appear to be something to eat—maybe an oddity, because of size, shape, color, or brightness—but it must still be recognizable as prey that may occur in the trout's environment.

R. Valentine Atkinson

When trout are already rising steadily, they don't want "variety." It is not the time for attractors. There are nearly a hundred large mayflies (Hexagenia limbata) *in this picture, and no other food item—all of the insects came from a stomach sampling of one trout. All of them were eaten in one hour of feeding.*

Attractors work consistently on only one group of trout. They are ineffective for fish that are already feeding steadily on the surface, even when the feeding isn't selective, and fail as completely as any other dry fly on trout lying unresponsive on the bottom. Attractor patterns do excite fish, however, that are willing, even anxious, to rise but haven't focussed on targets. Curiosity is high in this group, and a curious trout will take the oddball fly quicker than a specific or a general imitation.

Tory saw that clearly one bright noon in the Abutment Pool. From underwater he watched us cast, one with a size 16 Elk Hair Caddis and the other with a size 16 Lime Trude. The same number of trout started to rise for the Elk Hair as for the Trude, but drag usually set in before they could reach the Caddis. The trout came faster for the garish green of the Lime Trude, and twice as many fish struck the attractor.

Tory discovered one of the secrets of attractors after a few moments, and decided to test his idea by watching how fast the fish moved to the fly. He popped up, "Try different sizes with the Trude."

The size 18 and even the size 20 Lime Trudes worked slightly better than the size 16, drawing fewer last-second "turn-aways." Sizes 14, 12, 10 and 8 (in order of increasing futility) fared worse on our test in the Abutment Pool.

We moved from the pool into the hissing white water above it, and ran through the sizes again. Sizes 4, 6, and 8 all pulled midday trout out of the rapids, the size 6 the most effective. All of the smaller fly sizes failed to catch anything.

Too few fly fishermen realize that the key with attractors is to tease the fish without insulting them. The sizes most anglers carry—12 and 14—are precisely the most useless ones on a trout stream.

Why do attractors fail? An oddball fly with strange size, color, shape, brightness, or any combination of those traits fails if the idiosyncrasies are either too subtle or too exaggerated. The best way to experiment on a trout stream is to avoid the average in any aspect of the fly and match the degree of absurdity to the clarity, depth, and speed of the water.

Why a dry fly succeeds

Every imitation should have a touch of natural exaggeration; every attractor should have a basic realism. The fact that the surface film obscures a dry fly means that attraction with the dead-drift presentation on flowing waters is not only possible but, to some extent, necessary.

A trout, feeding discriminately or indiscriminately, always has expectations as he picks food from the surface. If there's no steady drift of insects, he searches (not actually moving, but inspecting the drift), curious about everything passing overhead, and looks for characteristics separating living, edible, items from flotsam. During a hatch, a fish focuses on a more rigid set of visible cues.

Think of these characteristics as a series of links. That's how a trout sees the fly—one link after another appearing for a moment in his field of vision. When a critical link fails to define the fly as edible, the fish ignores or refuses it.

That's why a fly fails. Why does a fly succeed, not just moderately but beyond all expectations? It's a combination of reasons. First of all, none of the important characteristics is missing (guaranteeing average success); second, one of the major characteristics, exaggerated in some way, like an oversize link in a chain, rivets the trout's attention and hastens the strike.

Imitation or attractor, it makes no difference. The key is to *stretch* reality without *breaking* it.

My Fly Box

Two-Winged Fly (Diptera)
Imitations

Blue Bottle (14-20)
(the fly resembles the common housefly, but it simulates a lot of aquatic true flies—including the biting Blackfly)

Buzz Ball (10-14)
(my imitation for a cluster of adult midges)

Daddy Long Legs (8-12)
(an English imitation for the adult cranefly)

Griffith's Gnat (18-24)
(for matching the adult midge)

Reed Smut (20-26)
(little specks of fluff in the fly box; main color variations are the Black Reed Smut, Olive Reed Smut, Gray Reed Smut, and Red Reed Smut—superbly simple to tie)

Comments:

This is a small but comprehensive selection for meeting Diptera situations. The main insect fly fishermen are going to encounter is the midge (remembering that the pupae are almost always going to be more important that the adults).

The Griffith's Gnat mimics high riding, active adults. The Reed Smut, floating flush in the film, resembles drowned adults. The Buzz Ball works when trout are smashing the clusters of midges that float down the stream, a few hundred insects gathered in a vibrating clump. Any standard pattern can be tied in appropriate sizes to match adult midges (for example, a size 20 Adams). It's important to carry a wide range of sizes and colors for selective situations.

[See the Emergers fly box for a series imitating the midge pupa.]

Chapter 2

Why Anglers Fail

Harry Ramsay's secret must have been in my mind all those years; he never called it a secret, or even called it important, so if anyone had asked me, until that day on the Wise River in Montana, to tell them about it, his secret of catching trout would have been a boyhood wisp lost in my memories.

The incident on the Wise River was so odd, and yet so convincing, that it deserves a full listing of witnesses. At least this clash of philosophies was convincing to me. Did my fellow anglers ever see this day of fishing as proof of a particular philosophy in approaching trout? Or did they dismiss it as an aberration of trout behavior, a mass underwater psychosis? There were no goats and there were no heroes (certainly not me); just anglers controlled by circumstances before them.

None of us were guiding a float trip that day and there were no rafts to load and shuttle, so there was more time than usual to putter around before we took the clients wading on the Wise River. Galen Wilkins and I worked inside the shop, gathering flies. Meanwhile, Phil Wright, owner of the Compleat Fly Fisher, was at the casting pond giving basic instruction to the beginners in the group. A great casting teacher, Phil could have anyone laying out forty feet of fly line in a half hour.

I knew that I was in for trouble when Phil walked across the yard, grinning at me, his arm over Tad Hilliard's shoulder. "Gary, you keep saying that a fly fisherman doesn't need to know how to cast to catch trout. So you're going to take Tad today."

I cornered Phil alone as soon as possible, "What do you mean, he can't cast? Can he get the line out twenty feet?"

I don't remember seeing Phil any happier that summer. "Not even ten feet," he said.

It was going to be one of those humbling days. Phil and Galen were going to take Tad's mother, Joy Hilliard, one of the finest fly fishers anywhere and one of my favorites for floating the Big Hole, and the two young adults who had mastered the casting lessons. All five of them, guides as well as clients, would be fishing that afternoon.

After a picnic lunch on the banks of the Wise River, Tad and I left the others and wandered upstream. After all, why would we want their whoops over every hooked trout disturbing our efforts? Tad was feeling gloomy enough. "I just can't get the line out," he said. "How am I going to catch anything?"

No one catches fish without confidence. It would be better to fail enthusiastically. It was time for a promise. "You're not going to catch anything, Tad. You're going to catch everything. Phil was right, I say it all the time, 'You don't need to know how to cast to catch trout.' You do what I say and you're going to fool every fish in this stream."

Did I believe it? Sometimes my speeches are so great that they even convince me. That's not a sign of intelligence. Even when Tad tried his first cast, and the line collapsed in a jumble at the water's edge, it didn't bother me. There was no way I was going to be able to teach him to cast, not if Phil couldn't, but there were other ways to help him show the fly to the trout.

Harry Ramsay had his Commandments of Stealth (the first nine building up to the Tenth, his secret). He preferred not to wade at all, but if he had to move in the stream he was very careful about not "pushing" a bow wave of water. The Fourth Commandment emphasized lifting the foot, pointing the toes downwards, and sliding the foot into the water.

It was one of those lingering, warm afternoons of late summer. The misnamed Wise River, not really a river at all but a stream, ran small, low, and clear at the end of a dry season. The ragged growths of trees, a mix of pines and hardwoods, threw irregular blocks of shade on the water, which tumbled in rocky chutes from pool to pool. I asked Tad when he spooked a fish, "Do you really think that that trout can't see you?"

Rather than worry about what Tad couldn't do, it was important to find out what he could do. His best presentation was a soft roll that flipped the fly line five to seven feet out, the leader falling in overlapping coils on the surface.

We snuck along the stream, using any boulder, shrub, or spindly tree trunk to hide behind. What else could we do, perched only five feet over the water? Tad talked in whispers, and maybe I should have told him that we didn't need to, but it fit the mood of the hunt.

I whooped when he hooked and landed his first trout. He had missed a half dozen strikes before mastering a technique of raising the rod and

R. Valentine Atkinson

The angler has to forget a lifetime of people telling him to "stand up straight." One way for him to sneak along a trout stream is to lower his profile by hunching over. He keeps in this stoop for most of the day.

pulling with the line hand at the same time, allowing him to set the hook with so much slack on the water.

Tad insisted that we take turns, one trout apiece, as we moved upstream. Maybe at first I was the teacher, pointing out the slots and obstructions in the runs and the ledges and slants of the pools. Tad was so close to the fish we were catching, able to see every movement of the flashing rises, that my instructions became unnecessary before we'd covered a hundred yards of the river.

Tad may not have been physically coordinated, a sixteen-year-old growing too fast, but he was an observant and intelligent naturalist. He knew exactly where he wanted to drift his fly, and by dangling it, rolling it, or just feeding it down on a current, he found ways to show it to the trout. In the early pools he hooked two or three smaller fish; later he caught eight from one boulder-sided hole, his fly never more than ten feet past the rod tip.

Tad's increasing skill with a short line helped him nail a large trout in that big pool. He didn't know how to give line, however; it hadn't been necessary even for the thirteen- and fourteen-inch fish. He just tilted backwards to gain more lift, the rod bending disastrously. The trout couldn't go down and it wouldn't come up, so the whole fight happened in ripping circles a foot under the surface. Tad landed the eighteen-inch brook trout long before it was completely tired.

The others were gone before we arrived at the picnic area, so we drove the second vehicle down the gravel road. Nothing was going to bother us. Not even the numbers of fish the others caught could diminish our day. We'd see them at the house and they'd tell us about their fishing and we'd tell them about ours.

They were still in the yard, unloading the van, when we parked next to the shop. We walked across, we two buddies, and hollered a bit too much. We were tired of whispering.

Joy asked Tad, "Did you catch anything?"

"Mom, we caught fifty of them. We stopped exactly at fifty."

"He got an eighteen-inch brook trout," I added.

Phil seemed confused, "What flies did you use?"

"All of them," I said.

No one said anything else. Was this a "sandbag" set up by Phil? Were they going to stand there looking surprised and embarrassed until I asked them how many they'd caught? Then would all five of them laugh and tell us about the hundreds of trout they'd landed that afternoon, making our catch seem paltry? I wasn't going to ask them how many trout they'd caught.

Joy's son-in-law, Roger, didn't wait for the question. "Joy caught a nine-inch rainbow."

That was their entire catch for the five of them and, embarrassed, I didn't know what to say. "What flies did you use?"

"All of them," Roger answered.

There were no heroes and there were no goats, but there never was a truer story.

My pretensions of being the hero ended quickly enough, just two weeks later. It was my day off, a day to fish alone, and the thought of the trout on the Wise River made my choice of where to go an easy one.

The conditions were the same. The autumn rains hadn't begun yet in the western mountains, and the Wise River ran low and clear. That didn't bother me. I was smugly confident that I'd take more than a single nine-inch rainbow.

I did, but not much more. In the first pool, where Tad and I had taken four nice trout, I caught but one small brookie. Even in the best holes I took only one fish, or sometimes none at all.

I gave up on the long and delicate presentations and started travelling upstream faster, as if by hitting only the honey spots I could turn the miles of failure into a triumph.

The miles didn't make the angling day any more successful.

Many times, moving and casting quickly, a style I call "hot spotting," works if the trout are bold and anxious to rise. It shouldn't be confused with long distance casts and careful floats. Hot spotting is only an oddity, not a major strategy—a ploy to try when trout are in a particular mood.

The method failed this day. Farther upstream from my car than I'd ever gone on the Wise River, on a dark pool curling deep against a pepper-stone cliff, it came to me that my declaration was wrong. It wasn't true that "You don't need to know how to cast to catch trout."

That would have made me the hero. If Tad and I had fished a ridiculously short line on purpose, creeping and poking by choice, that would have made us both heroes. We were, instead, the lucky beneficiaries of Tad's casting problems—his troubles had made me resurrect my old boyhood poaching skills.

Actually, you do need to know how to cast to catch trout, but more importantly you need to know when not to use those skills to their fullest (and that's 99 percent of the time on a trout stream).

No one knows how *not* to cast anymore.

To this day I've never fished that pool by the pepper-stone cliff; it is too perfect to flog and spoil for the one trout it might give up to my long-line casting.

It was time to remember the lessons that Harry Ramsay taught me on Mill Brook.

My problem was pride. Two to three hours an evening on the practice pond at the Compleat Fly Fisher had destroyed the slow, wide loop line arcs of my boyhood style, a sloppy casting form that limited me to twenty- to thirty-foot throws. In two years, with Phil Wright's excellent instruction on the dynamics of power, my maximum casting distances stretched out to well over a hundred feet with a shooting head. Even my short casts became quicker.

One winter, on the White River, Hal Patman took me near the dam at Bull Shoals for what he called "mile away" trout. He drove an old station wagon, the worn shock absorbers making the car sway on the corners and bounce on the hills. Hal parked near the boat rental dock. As we started to unload the back of the vehicle, he stopped suddenly and asked me, "Gary, can you double haul?"

I puffed up, "Of course, I can."

So I carried twice as much as he did down to the boat.

The ability to throw a long line helped me in saltwater, on bass lakes, and even with streamers on trout rivers. It was a skill that belonged in my full assortment of presentations. But for dry flies?

My fishing logs, so detailed, didn't lie. My abilities with dry flies were deteriorating; over the past few years my catches on familiar waters, with the same flies and techniques, had shrunk steadily. My catches hadn't changed much on the smallest streams, those trickles with brook trout and cutthroat trout where an angler crept along by picking the pockets, but on the large rivers the catch total for hours fished was down by at least one-third.

The following May gave me a chance to take my fishing logs from 1957 back to Connecticut. A weekend entry for that year recorded not fishing days, but "watching days"—two days secluded along Salmon Brook with binoculars observing a procession of fly fishermen.

My problem was pride. No one cheered the fifteen-foot cast on the platform. The game was to throw a high-speed, tight-loop line, with a quick haul on both the backward and forward strokes. With practice every evening it became easy to put an entire weight-forward line out on the water. It was hard for me to separate the casting games from the reality of dry fly fishing. My catches in most situations dropped in number. The straight line on the water, and the numerous current bands the long cast crossed, made drag inevitable.

The original notes were research for an article Harry Ramsay was writing for the Windsor Rod and Gun Club newsletter. The piece compared techniques of fly fishermen over forty-years-old with those of younger anglers. The study, nineteen hours of watching fly fishermen that weekend, was a bust—there were not enough younger fly fishermen, just one hopeless angler who lacked any technique whatsoever, to make a comparison.

Now, twenty-five years later, the notes were going to be used to compare fly fishermen of two different eras. Most of those older anglers in 1957 had covered the stream, in the words of the log:

> beautifully, with very similar casting patterns, working the lower water left to right, moving up *carefully* to hit the right slot. Maybe they fished too much straight upstream against that bank, because they couldn't get back into the tree limbs, but they drifted their flies tight. Two men, one fishing a streamer and the other a dry fly, cast from across the stream, into the bank, and the dry fly fisherman caught more than anyone else from the slot that weekend, three trout. Another dry fly fisherman did better than anyone else at the head of the pool by staying in the water and wading very deep. He was only casting a few feet. Everyone else walked around on the meadow bank to fish the head.

The notes never gave distances for the casts, but the maps for the eight older anglers had *X's* marked for casting positions showing that they were usually within twenty-five feet of the target. They had, on average, caught 1.1 trout each from this Salmon Brook pool. At least half of the fish, even though this was before the catch-and-release philosophy became familiar, were returned immediately.

By 1982 the original pool was gone, or changed beyond recognition. There was a similar spot upstream, roughly the same dimensions and configuration, and it held a fine stock of trout. A clump of bushes on a nearby hill provided a perfect place for observing a parade of modern anglers.

One difference in 1982 was that there were many more anglers: in roughly nineteen hours of weekend observation, I studied a total of twenty-one fly fishermen. They all affected the natural feeding activity, putting most of the trout down for twenty minutes. Some luckless fishermen, entering the pool on the heels of the last flogger, never had the chance to cast to a receptive target. Not one person sat and rested the water before beginning to fish.

Dry fly anglers in 1957 had averaged forty-two casts, while the 1982 dry fly fishermen made only twenty-four casts on average over their pool. The casting positions also differed for the groups, the past fishermen throwing less than twenty-five feet and the present ones throwing more than thirty-five feet. The dry fly men in 1982, nineteen out of twenty-one, caught a total of eight trout. The two nymph fishermen among them did better, one catching two trout and the other three.

My fishing logs didn't lie. It wasn't just me.

A general assessment of the average 1980s angler? Certainly there are many individuals with outstanding skills, phenomenal anglers who can consistently catch trout under the toughest conditions. There are pockets of these modern masters, linked to notable waters—the Battenkill (Vermont), the AuSable (Michigan), the Henry's Fork (Idaho), and the Fall River (California)—but these are not the average fly fishermen in America. For the most part, the average dry fly angler today is not quite as good as his counterpart of the 1950s.

The disparity between good and poor anglers today shows up most in dry fly skills. This truth is obscured, however, by how modern fly fishermen look on the stream. They come out of fly fishing schools with excellent casting technique. Whoosh, whoosh, the line goes back and forth, maybe a few too many times, and drops prettily on the water, giving the impression that the angler has a plan of attack. Actually, there's often no understanding about trout behind the random drifts of the fly.

Tad Hilliard, in one afternoon on the Wise River, probably gained more knowledge about trout behavior than most beginners do in years. When Tad crept over a fish, he would say, "That one's not looking up. He's going to have to see the fly four or five times."

This deterioration of angling skills is only true with dry flies. Nymphs? The average nymph fisherman now is better than at any time in fly fishing history. Anyone working a nymph can't be effected by long-line casting methods. He has to keep his presentations in close so that he can control line and detect strikes. Streamers? With streamers, long casts are a benefit, as long as accuracy isn't too important. A minnow imitation is a searcher, and it should cover as much water as possible. Streamer fishermen are better than ever. Classic wet flies? It's a dead art in this country, but even in the 1950s there were only a few old anglers, remnants of the pre-World War II golden era of wet fly fishing, practicing it.

Why the Angler Fails with a Dry Fly

Before World War II, and even for a few years after, a boy learned to fish streams with bait—not just worms, but with big creatures like crawfish, leeches, and minnows, and with small creatures like nymphs, and Japanese beetles, and grasshoppers. The best way to work the bait in moving water was to let it tumble with the current. That made a baitcasting reel, which needed a heavy weight to pull out line, impractical for drifting bait naturally. At least regular casting was impossible. Many of us pulled off loops of line from the reel and, with an underhand toss, gently plopped the bait, weighted with a small split shot, fifteen feet at most up a riffle.

Bait could be fished with a fly rod also, but the cast couldn't be far and the stroke had to be very soft to keep the bait on the hook. The fly rod, for those of us who mastered the rudimentary skills, was better than the bait casting rod because it was longer and allowed more line control.

Generation after generation learned to fish bait in streams at close distances. They used bait casting rods, fly rods, or cane poles. If they ever

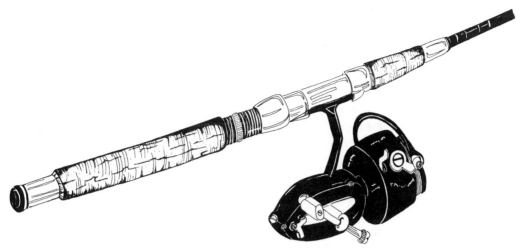

The fact that most people learn to fish with a spinning rod now means that "stream-craft" isn't a part of those early years. Who needs to learn how to spot and approach trout? Open the bail, snap the wrist, and flick the lure or bait far out into the river.

progressed to regular fly fishing, either on cold-water or warm-water streams, they took their stalking, fish spotting, and water reading skills with them.

No books, videos, or audios could teach those skills—there was a fundamental difference between seeing and not seeing. That actual awareness of what was happening in the water a few feet ahead of the angler could only be developed with practice.

Is there any doubt why the generation that learned after the 1950s never mastered stream skills? The new angler never had to practice. His first fishing pole was a spinning rod. He flipped the bail, flicked his wrist, and zing, fifty to sixty feet of monofilament peeled off the fixed spool. The lure or bait landed so far away that the fisherman never had to look down to see what he was doing to the water or the fish at his feet.

A spinning rod is so easy to use that it raises even the most hopeless beginner to a level of acceptable mediocrity. A lure reeled steadily across the flow isn't the most efficient way to fool fish, but, like the streamer dredged often enough through a river with long casts, it covers enough water to catch something eventually.

Naturally, as a boy, I adopted spinning methods, not so much for chucking lures but for drifting bait. With even the lightest split shot the rod could toss any bait out, and yet the small weight wouldn't pin the worm to the bottom if there was a current.

A favorite bait fishing trick worked perfectly with a spinning rod. On the Housatonic River, one of my Connecticut haunts, the water lay almost slack in the Garbage Hole when the upstream turbines weren't pumping. Spin fishermen would lob out worms with heavy sinkers and let their bait sit for hours on the bottom. That wasn't the way to fish the river. They never bothered to learn how to use their amazingly versatile new toys.

I'd lash a sugar cube or two on the line with a rubber band. That gave me enough weight to put a small angleworm, not a nightcrawler, into the trickle of water still coming in at the head of the pool. The sugar would dissolve by the time the worm tumbled into the pool, and there the weightless worm would drift slowly over the bottom with the feeble flow, taunting trout to distraction. One worm angler would yell at every one of my hookups, "He's catching all my fish."

That was when I was eight. By the time I was nine I was using a fly rod and dry flies for nearly all of my trout fishing in streams. Most of that fishing was as a poacher on the private club waters of the Windsor Rod and Gun Club on Mill Brook.

My method was the poacher's creep. It involved no casting; as a matter of fact, casting a dry fly would have been impossible for me. Who could have imagined fishing a dry fly without lead on the leader? Not me.

Fly fishermen who were club members would fish dry flies without split shot. Hearing them coming, I'd fade back into the woods but stay close enough to watch them fish through. They caught trout, but their casting with dry flies never impressed me as a great method. It would have been impractical anyway for a poacher, who couldn't stand out there in the middle of the stream.

Fly fishing has been perverted by the dominance of spin fishing. Fly casting instructors make sure that their students can cast forty or fifty feet, with the line laying out straight on the pond or pool, and only then will they let them onto the river. Those distances are spin fishing distances—they've never had any relevance to dry fly fishing. Maybe fishermen who grew up with that perspective, lulled by the simplicity of casting far with a spinning rod, wouldn't be satisfied with shorter presentations.

To attract new converts to fly fishing, instructors keep saying how easy it is to learn. They're only talking about the casting mechanics. In this way they ignore the need for stream awareness, which isn't easy and which can't be taught, only practiced, and they bring their pupils to an acceptable level of mediocrity as quickly as possible. So many beginners never progress beyond this point.

Distance casting is a matter of pride.

Micro-drag, the variation between the speed of the fly and the speed of the current, can be invisible to the angler, but the trout seldom misses it.

There are three major reasons (and a multitude of minor ones) why the angler fails with a dry fly: he drags the fly, he frightens the trout, or he fishes the wrong pattern.

Long casts ruin dry fly presentation by creating more opportunities for drag. No one, no matter how skillful, can fish a dry fly better at forty feet than at twenty feet. The varying current speeds simply stretch that extra line taut enough to tug the fly off its natural drift.

There are two types of drag. One is obvious—when the line pulls tight at the end of the drift and the fly wakes across the surface. Usually, the angler then simply picks up and recasts the fly.

The other type, micro-drag, is more subtle. The fly moves almost imperceptibly. If the cast is longer than fifteen feet the angler can't see his fly well enough to detect micro-drag, but it's there. Bet on it—especially if the cast is the tight-loop, straight-line style prescribed by modern instruction.

This helped doom five very adept casters to one nine-inch rainbow that day on the Wise River. The effect wouldn't have been as disastrous on rougher water, but the whole stream was so low and clear that there wasn't enough depth in the riffles for the trout. They were stacked up in the glassy pools, which magnified the unnatural movements of the fly. Those fishermen covered hundreds of trout that day and fooled only one.

Why aren't nymph fishermen, like dry fly anglers, affected by micro-drag? The deep nymph dances with the underwater forces naturally, tugged and pulled so much that little movements don't hurt its chances. Even the emergent nymph, fished flush in the film, is pinned by the viscosity of the water. It's only the dry fly, sitting on top where it can respond instantly to any whim of the leader or even to a puff of wind catching its upright wings, that demands adherence to natural drift lanes.

Micro-drag, except with dapping techniques, can't be entirely prevented during dead-drift presentations. Correct casting form and proper leader design, however, mitigates its effect. The cast has to be "sloppy," line falling in curls, curves, and clumps on the water. This slack can be dropped intentionally—the angler throwing curve casts, check casts, S casts or puddle casts, or it can be created by accident—the angler waving the rod with a wide or mistimed power stroke that dumps loose line on the currents.

Even the messiest piles of slack line on the water won't prevent micro-drag if the leader isn't designed to drift the fly freely. The tippet, the last eighteen to thirty-six inches, is critical because it must be so limp that it collapses. A piece of one-pound test spinning line reacts correctly. Will it "turn the fly over" and look pretty on the water? No, but only a soft nylon tippet allows the fly to move freely with the current.

There is no knotless leader like this on any fly shop wall. Every commercial leader tapers down with roughly the standard formula: 60

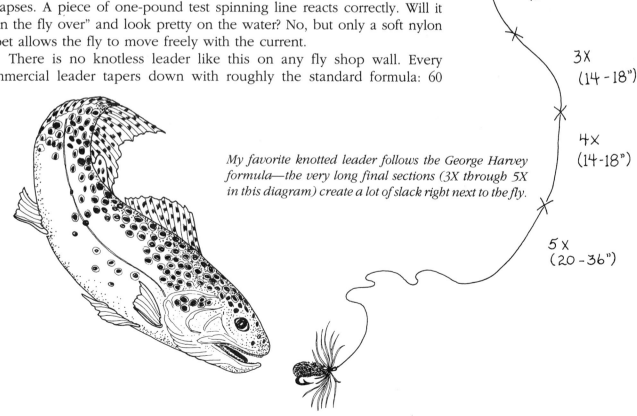

My favorite knotted leader follows the George Harvey formula—the very long final sections (3X through 5X in this diagram) create a lot of slack right next to the fly.

.017
(15")

.015
(15")

.013
(15")

.011
(12")

2X
(12")

3X
(14-18")

4X
(14-18")

5X
(20-36")

percent butt, 20 percent taper, and 20 percent tippet, using stiff nylon to guarantee that the fly rolls out nicely. Any angler more interested in fooling trout than in appearance has to tie his own leaders with extra long, soft tippets.

By cutting back on his casting range a fly fisherman controls drag, but suddenly he's much closer to the fish he's trying to catch. There's a dilemma—he loses his false security when he's no longer popping casts out (actually, he was probably scaring as many trout at forty feet as at twenty). In tight, he sees fish flushing under his boots.

To overcome his uneasiness the angler must shift his visual skill away from the spinning-rod distances of boyhood to shorter, practical dry-fly distances. Changing the focus of his eyes, from far out (where he can only see the surface) to his feet (where he can see through the water and spot the fish he's casting for) takes practice.

The fisherman's problem is that there are two perceptions possible when he looks at the water, the clearly visible reflections on the surface and the vague shapes below it. Those perceptions are superimposed upon each other in nature and the brain can only attend to one at a time.

The brain, of course, attends first to the sharpest perception unless it is trained to see through and beyond it. This is exactly the principle behind an optical illusion (two possible perceptions). The viewer, with practice, can alternate back and forth between both. The angler, likewise, can see either the surface or the bottom with practice. When he can focus at will on one or the other reality, he starts developing stream awareness.

Why can some fishermen see trout better than others? Maybe it is because they are color blind. Eighty out of every thousand men and five out of every thousand women are either partially or totally so.

Color blindness is an evolutionary adaptation. Color-blind hunters are better at picking out movement against a cluttered background of vegetation—among primitive men in hunter-gatherer societies this would have been an advantage in survival. The military discovered during World War II that color-blind soldiers were not fooled by camouflage (which tricked those with normal vision).

It's logical, therefore, to wonder about color-blind anglers. Are they as easily confused by the double image of glare or the natural camouflage of trout? They shouldn't be.

Anyone who is color blind will probably agree with this and anyone who isn't will almost certainly disagree. Since training and practice are as important as "natural talent," however, no one should doubt that they can learn to see trout well enough to successfully stalk them.

The angler should be able to catch any actively feeding trout he can see if he doesn't spook it first.

Harry Ramsey, the old caretaker at the Windsor Rod and Gun Club, was my first fishing teacher in life. He never really taught me fly fishing, not the normal, stand-and-cast style. Dick Fryhover, who taught me how to fly fish, tie western flies, and guide all in one summer after my move to Montana, was my major instructor in technique. Many other fly fishermen added to my education. Phil Wright taught me how to cast for distance, a valuable skill in many fly fishing situations; Galen Wilkins of Deer Lodge, taught me the Outrigger Method of nymphing, with lead spaced on the leader (in the winters we exercised the trout, whitefish, and even suckers of our local rivers mightily with this ploy).

But Harry Ramsey was my first teacher. He did not like children; it's doubtful that he even liked me. He lived alone in one of those two-story, white shingle houses near the Farmington River in that area of Windsor (the first town in Connecticut) with the oldest homes, some of them museums with brass plaques out front. The magical part of the house for me was the upstairs, with its shooting and fishing rooms, and its library of floor-to-ceiling angling books.

He invited me to his house a few times a year to use his collection. His first words when he opened the door were always, "Go wash your hands before you touch my books."

His last words, when he came up to the library to send me home, were always, "I said you could read my books, not memorize them."

Harry Ramsay really had no one to talk to about the literature of fly fishing because no one else had read as much as he had (especially of the English works). So he let me use his library; in effect he was training someone to argue with over tactics and strategies. For any opinion of mine he had a quote from a book with a contradictory view.

The English books were on the shelves, arranged alphabetically by author. The late nineteenth- and early twentieth-century writers were my favorites—Dunne, Halford, Mottram, Skues, and Taverner. The American books were in an unsorted jumble on a cherry wood table in the far corner of the room. Harry, without knowing it, taught me my English bias.

He also taught me his secret, this time knowingly, of stalking. He used his skills as a woodsman to hunt for me along Mill Brook, and when he caught me poaching the club water he always lectured me for an hour, mad at me not for poaching (which he didn't care about), but for getting caught.

He found me easily enough the first time, his gruff voice coming across the stream, "Do you really think that that trout can't see you?"

He scared me badly, but it was always clear to me why I didn't run— from the first words we were talking about fishing. "I've caught some," I said.

"I saw you."

"I just want to fish."

"Well, you can fish if I catch you, because I'm the one guarding this water, but you can't fish if any of the members catch you because then they'll raise hell with me. You understand?"

No member ever caught me, even though they would pass within a few feet of my hiding spot in the heavy undergrowth of the oak forest. Harry found me three times, all in the first year-and-a-half, and never afterwards. "I caught you," he'd say, "Now you owe me a favor."

The first time the favor was mopping and waxing the club house floor. The second time it was helping stock the stream with hatchery fish. The third time, almost a year after he'd found me playing a big brown trout on Poison Ivy Pool, the favor was a fishing contest.

One of the members had brought a guest, an expert in the opinion of the club; or, at least, the man was a good enough talker and a good enough caster to make an impression. Maybe this bothered Harry, who was bothered easily enough by anyone usurping his glory. Maybe not, though; maybe Harry really didn't like the fly fishing ideas the man was promoting. The basic angling philosophy of the man no doubt was repugnant to him.

He picked someone, me, with a totally different fishing style than the visitor. The idea of a fishing competition didn't bother me. Why should it? I was a child, and competing in any game, whether it was basketball on a school ground or trout fishing on a stream, was for fun. Only adults didn't compete for fun.

Harry had told the members that, to be fair to a visitor who didn't know the water, he'd bring in someone who hadn't fished Mill Brook before either. That was also why he selected me, the unknown poacher.

The visitor started on the L pool above the club house, walking across the lawn to the tail out and false casting as he waded in. He drifted flies left, right, and middle; his casts hit the head of the hole, thirty feet upstream, and every nook of both banks. He performed to the constant exclamations and compliments of the membership, but by the time his fifteen minutes were up he hadn't caught a single trout.

Even Harry, though, said, "Pretty."

Some of the members had smiled at me when I came that morning. My dress probably was comical: baggy khaki pants, old green sweater, floppy gray hat, and black camouflage grease under my eyes that made me look like a "night fighter" advertisement. It was how Harry had taught me to dress.

Not that their comments about my old clothes or my decrepit tackle had bothered me or made me doubt the outcome of the contest. I had Harry's secret—and as far as I know I was the only one he'd ever taught it to; in my lifetime of fly fishing I've never seen anyone else who understood it as fully as he.

My pool was Muskrat Bend, and I disappeared into the woods to approach on the left side. Most of the members didn't know where I was until Harry pointed at my position. "He's fishing," he said.

The lead split shot thirty-six inches up the leader protected the dangling fly from those stray puffs of wind and made it possible to "place" the fly exactly. The leader and fly were lowered or swung over the target current. Then, quickly, as the fly touched down, the tip of the old glass rod was dropped right above it, creating slack in the leader between the lead shots and the fly. The rod followed the drift lane, allowing a perfect float as long as ten feet. This was the way to dap a dry fly.

Every one of my movements was slow, a careful rhythm that took time but never wasted it. The trout came quickly enough. The first position gave me two fish: a ten-inch rainbow that was usual for the brook and a splendid twelve-inch brown, a trout that hadn't been born with his wildness but had been in the stream long enough to learn it.

The visitor cried out, "That ain't fly fishing." He quit the contest after the third set of pools. Some members apparently agreed, leaving with him, but most stayed with Harry—and Harry was happy again.

Harry started his lecture, "In Walton's day they didn't even have reels. This sport has been going to pot ever since."

There are diagrams in books showing exactly what trout can see outside of the water. The calculations, with the angle figured to the degree, prove that a fish has blind spots behind and below him. Lines illustrating how light rays bend when they enter the water demonstrate how much an angler has to lower his profile to hide from a trout.

Harry Ramsay taught me that facts could be true and still be worthless, even dangerous. "That's crap," he'd say. "A trout always knows you're there. Every time. Not some of the time or most of the time, but all of the time. It doesn't matter if you're behind him, on the side of him, or in front of him. If you're trying to catch him, he senses you."

It was hard for me not to believe the books, *his* books. "So what can I do?"

"You can't hide," Harry would finish. "Hell, even a hatchery fish knows you're there. The difference is that he's glad to see you."

I had never seen anyone fish a dry fly without lead weight on the leader until I spotted a club member casting one day. My approach was to lower the fly onto the water, creating slack, and drift my pattern repeatedly over the currents right in front of me.

Harry proved this to me one afternoon on Mill Brook. He'd have me spot trout for him, and then with his woodsman's skills and his gentle presentations he would cast for the fish. No matter what angle Harry approached from, or whether it was from the bank or from the water, a trout showed nervousness—usually even before the first cast.

During the summers Harry hunted me on Mill Brook. He never caught me in the last three-and-a-half years, however, because he raised my senses to such a high level. It wasn't necessary for me to look or listen for another person; like a soldier in jungle combat my awareness picked up subtler signs, and that instinctive wariness, which never shut off, couldn't miss an interloper as blatant as a man. Still, to me it was just a game.

It is so easy to forget that fishing is not a game to the trout. The angler is just one more possible predator in a dangerous world—a world in which the trout possesses senses so much keener than his human adversary. The fisherman's only advantage is that he's not trying to grab the fish directly. There's a distance between the hunter and his quarry that helps the man mask his intentions. The trout, nevertheless, knows that something unnatural is intruding into his world.

The fisherman has two chances to catch his trout. In the first moments of his approach there is a window of twenty or thirty seconds when a feeding fish is so reluctant to stop, even though he's aware that there's something approaching, that he will still take a fly. The trick is to keep a distance—at least thirty feet—and accurately present the fly quickly to a particular trout. It is not a scatter-cast method.

As effective as it is at times, this technique also ruins any chance to take more than one fish from a single spot. The fisherman has to keep moving upstream, outrunning the havoc caused by such a boisterous approach. This method, called hot spotting, doesn't work with the dry fly unless the fish is actively looking for food on the surface. It's not a subtle, teasing approach, but a way to pick the ripest fruits.

The only other chance to catch sophisticated trout in such numbers and size is Harry's secret. "They're going to know you're there, so the only way you're going to fool them is by looking like nothing dangerous," he would say.

There's always movement around a trout stream. Most of it doesn't scare fish, causing a moment of concern at most and then the trout settles back into his feeding rhythm. The fisherman can't hide completely, but he can blend into that easy motion of a trout stream.

Harry caught most of his fish after he had settled into his casting position for at least five minutes. No one ever lulled trout better than Harry—every cast was so rhythmic and gentle that repetition inspired familiarity. Within minutes after being disturbed, the fish were back on their feeding stations. They knew Harry was there, but with the need or desire to feed they gladly ignored him. First the small trout, which Harry would cast near and never catch, would start to rise and then the larger ones would come and force them out.

Too many fly fishermen never give fish a chance to ignore them. They blunder into the river, scattering long casts that occasionally put the fly over a willing fish (the proverbial acorn). They pick up and lay down the line hurriedly, and if they catch nothing they give up and slog away just before the smaller fish timidly start feeding.

Don't these anglers realize that it's almost impossible (there's no quibbling on this) to work a pool properly without using a roll cast pickup, not a straight pickup, after every drift? The only other options are retrieving the line or letting it carry far below the fish and then picking it up, but doing this every time is inefficient. Lifting the line off the water with an immediate backcast sends a spray of droplets over the surface that spooks trout. It's a disturbance they never learn to ignore.

This is the way actions can be divided (into threatening and non-threatening ones). There are threatening actions that trout, no matter how hungry, cannot ignore. Grinding or stomping the feet, sending bow waves ahead, slapping the line on the water, dragging the fly in a wake over risers, and ripping away half finished casts all unsettle most trout so much that they never return to surface feeding.

Those same fish may begin working on subsurface nymphs—another advantage in casting sunken flies. Trout feel safer and feed sooner, even with the commotion, when they're in deep water. Dry fly fishing, on the other hand, requires more respect for the natural wariness of trout.

The reason for donning drab clothes and using inconspicuous tackle is not complete deception. The movement of getting into position and casting to the target exposes an angler to trout. The fly fisherman could stand in the

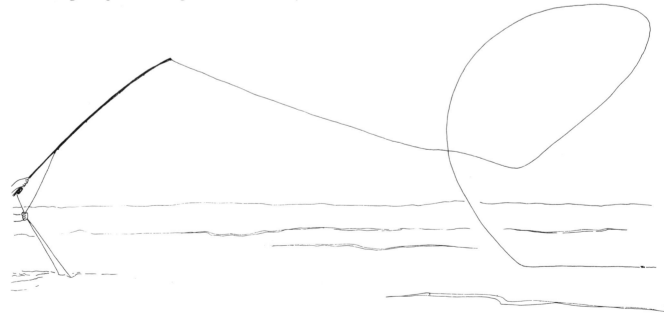

Harry's Seventh Commandment of Stealth revolved around completing the presentation. He used a roll cast pickup to flick the fly easily into the air; with this technique there was no cut on the surface or spray of droplets on the water to keep the trout edgy.

R. Valentine Atkinson

Drab clothing, such as a shirt in camouflage coloration, is not an affectation on the trout stream. It allows the angler to blend in with the natural scenery.

stream decorated like a Christmas tree, with snowy fringe, tinsel wrap, and blinking lights, and fish would gladly feed at his feet if he stayed forever frozen in one place. He cannot stay frozen and cast; he can only blend as well as possible into the environment.

The dark clothes in grays, greens, and browns are only part of the costume. What good is it worrying about cloth, a natural material, if anything at all sends metallic flashes over the water? Nothing bothers trout more. The most offensive items are ones the angler never thinks about—a ring on his finger, the shiny rim of his eyeglasses, the chain around his neck or the glittering watch band on his wrist. They should be removed before fishing, along with any metal trinkets dangling from his vest.

If his attire doesn't curse a fly fisherman's chances, his equipment will. The fly rod itself is, of course, necessary. At the same time even a perfectly finished rod, waving violently in the sky, puts down risers. There are no perfectly finished rods available to fly fishermen.

This has been known for a long time, at least since 1653:

"His rod or cane, made
dark for being seen.
The less to fear the wary
fish withal."

Secrets of Angling, by John Dennys, was the rarest book in Harry's library. He showed me the above passage one day to explain why he painted all of his bamboo rods, Paynes and Leonards mostly, a flat battleship gray.

To make a perfect stalking rod the fly fisherman has to start with a blank, preferably with slower, softer action than one of the popular fast designs, finish it a flat gray instead of a glossy polish, and fit it with non-reflective guides and reel seat instead of bright metallic ones. He should also ignore the absurd line rating, advocating a line weight that balances the rod with thirty-foot casts and leaves the angler forty feet (counting a ten-foot leader) away from his target. Instead, he should put on a line one to three sizes heavier.

Decent, dull fly reels that aren't hand mirrors flashing warning codes to the trout are available. The angler must pay less than $20 for one (this bothers a lot of fly fishermen). My favorites includes a model from England that costs $11 and one imported from the Orient that sells in mass catalogs for about the same amount. Fill a reel up with backing and a brown, grey, or green double taper line, not a garish white or orange one.

The angler tries to be as obscure as possible. Standing at attention in the middle of the stream, of course, isn't the way to accomplish this. Actually, it's best not to wade at all; that automatically makes the angler more menacing to a fish. On shore the fly fisherman can use bushes or rocks to hide behind—an effective tactic that no one seems to ever try. He can also use "broken" water and in-stream obstructions very effectively, too. If he approaches the fish from the side or the front, he should crouch down or kneel, lowering his profile, and cast sidearm if possible to make the rod less threatening.

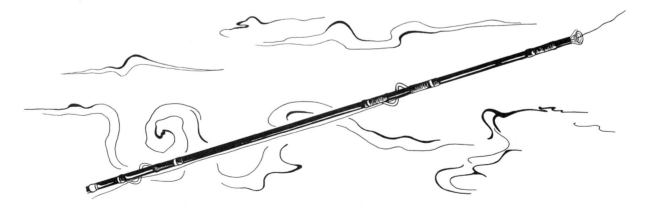

The angler who has just paid many hundreds of dollars for a shiny new rod has a dilemma—does he want to look pretty or does he want to catch trout? If he chooses the latter there is still a way for him to get his money's worth out of the rod. Right in the shop, right after paying for the rod, he can take a piece of steel wool and lightly rub the shaft, removing all glare. The look on the shop owner's face will surely be worth the price of the rod.

Even all of this stealth doesn't fool a trout completely. It just helps the fish do what he wants to do—forget as quickly as possible about an activity that apparently has nothing to do with him and go back to feeding. The trick is still the gentle and patterned movements that reinforce, rather than disturb, this sense of security.

That's what Tad and I were forced to do on the Wise River—blend into the environment and present the fly gently to specific holds. We could have done it with ten- to fifteen-foot casts if he had had the skill to throw line even that short distance. Dapping and dibbling the fly proved not only adequate but, in some spots on the river, even superior.

When fly fishing began all presentations were made at these close distances. The artificials were not dry flies, of course, but they were worked so near the surface that any strike would have been very visible to the angler. Fly fishing was a gentle game of showing the fraud to specific fish or specific holds.

Available equipment shaped early techniques. Reels didn't become widely popular until the early 1800s. References to floating flies in books like Leonard Mascall's *A Booke of Fishing with Hooke and Line* (1590) and Thomas Barker's *The Art of Angling* (1651), long before reels made longer casts possible, may not have been fully formed codifications of a dry fly art but they describe a type of sight fishing with surface flies that involved stalking the prey.

The development of reels specifically for fly fishing, heavier lines, and more castable- and faster-action rods gave birth to an entirely different dry fly strategy in the 1800s. The alternative to creeping in close to the trout was presenting the fly "fine and far off." With great casting skill the angler dropped a fly, attached to a long, delicate leader, onto the water, sometimes to a rising fish and sometimes not. He achieved "obscurity," making himself look like nothing to the trout, by depending entirely on the separation, the space between himself and the fish, and if the cast itself didn't spook the trout he successfully masked his intentions. Fifty-, sixty-, or even seventy-foot presentations were not impossible.

Here's where the pride comes into dry fly fishing: what tremendous physical talents the angler needs for this tactic! The fly has to travel a long distance; it has to fall accurately; and it has to drift on the water as far as possible without drag.

Advantages of "fine and far off"
The term "fine and far off" comes from Charles Cotton, but since he was fishing without a reel, it is doubtful that "far" meant the distances easily achieved with modern equipment.
  • The angler can reach trout that can't be approached by wading (for example, because the water is too deep).

- It doesn't demand "stream awareness." The angler does have to read the water, but he doesn't have to spend a lot of time learning how to spot and stalk trout.
- The physical skills it does require can be taught on a casting pond.
- The distance from the trout obscures the angler (but the cast still has to drop lightly).

Disadvantages of "fine and far off"
- It requires great casting distance and accuracy.
- It gives the angler a false sense of security.
- Micro-drag is a problem (one that cannot be completely solved).

The push that's made "fine and far off" the dominant strategy in dry fly fishing may have come from the casting instructors and the tackle manufacturers. It's human nature for teachers to emphasize what students can learn quickly (casting skills) and ignore what they can't learn at all away from the water (stream awareness). Naturally, the tackle makers produce beautiful and bright equipment that they can sell, even if it makes it difficult for the user to get close to the trout. Another, perhaps more difficult hurdle to fishing close, is the spin fishing foundation so many modern anglers bring with them to fly fishing.

What's wrong with fishing "fine and far off?" Even when practiced by a master it's inefficient. The long cast itself takes more time than a shorter one, there's always more chance it will land badly, and it can never be as effective as the shorter presentation because of those unavoidable problems with micro-drag. A forty-foot cast crosses so many bands of current that the maximum drag-free drift is roughly five feet. A twenty-foot cast, where it's not only easier to drop initial slack on the currents but to control and mend line, can drift drag free for ten to fifteen feet. The fly simply spends more time looking natural on the water.

My own fishing logs, always detailed, now divide all fish caught on dry flies in moving waters into five presentation categories. It's clear, when compared to that slump period from 1980 to 1982, that the balance has changed.

	1980	1987
Dapping	2%	5%
Fine and Far Off	42%	11%
Gentle and Close	10%	40%
Hot Spotting	21%	18%
Active Presentations	25%	26%

The dapping category increased so much because now it's typical for me to try to catch the first trout or two, even on large rivers, by dangling the fly instead of casting it. This is my way to set a certain attitude, to orient myself to close water instead of far water, before the serious fishing. It helps prepare me, too, for situations later in the day where dapping might be the best or only tactic for catching a particular fish.

The dry fly slump broke in 1983, more than a year after my day on the Wise River with Tad. By reversing the emphasis on presentation, from my new "fine and far off" technique back to the older stalking methods, the catches recouped that one-third loss and even a little bit more.

It was important for me to keep practicing Harry's secret. The pattern of rhythmical and gentle casting had to be continued for at least five minutes, until the fall and float of the fly, leader, and line became an accepted part of the environment. Then, the trout would relax and ignore the warning.

My logs, and the tally of dry fly trout, tell me quickly enough when the balance is right. When the problems with drag are solved by moving in closer, and yet the trout don't spook with the casting motion, presentation stops being the major reason for failure. Then it's time to wonder about the flies themselves, either as imitations or attractions, and try to increase the catch that "little bit more" by picking the right pattern for every moment on the stream.

If the angler fishes rhythmically and carefully, the trout relax and forget about him in roughly seven minutes. If the fisherman stays long enough, casting patiently, the trout will even edge closer, using him as "structure," and establish a feeding position within ten feet. This was Harry's Tenth Commandment of Stealth.

The Ten Commandments of Stealth

1. Stop—It is difficult to see fish while walking or wading. At every likely spot, take a moment to search for trout, not "sweeping" with the eyes, but staring at each block of the bottom. [Polarized sunglasses and small binoculars are invaluable aids.]

2. Do not wade (unless necessary)—Any commotion in the water is more threatening to the trout than a disturbance on the land. Hide behind bushes, boulders, or trees if possible.

3. Step lightly—Heavy footsteps, either on the bank or the stream bottom, send vibrations through the water. Trout can feel these through the lateral line. [Trout do not have to see the angler to know he is there.]

4. Do not "push" the water—Wade like a heron, lifting the foot and putting it back down slowly with a pointed toe. Swinging the leg forward (a Fifth Avenue stride) pushes a bow wave ahead of you that can spook an entire pool of trout.

5. Remove every bit of reflective material (especially metal)—Nothing is more unnatural on a trout stream than flashing reflections. Remove personal items, such as rings, watches, and metallic eyeglass rims, that reflect; keep those doodads, such as forceps, pin clips, and fly boxes, inside the vest; and don't use reflective tackle, such as shiny reels and bright rods.

6. Lower the profile—Stoop, kneel, or even lay flat to keep below the trout's line of sight. Often, it is impossible to stay completely hidden, but still get as low as possible—by doing so you put some moving parts of the body out of the trout's view.

7. Do not "rip" the line—The pattern floats over fish, but nothing rises to it. What then? Let the fly drift beyond the fish and then execute a roll cast pickup. This puts the line in the air without ripping the surface.

The wrong choice, lifting the line directly into a backcast, is one of the most common flaws in presentation. A sudden rain of droplets across the surface can put down everything under the shower.

8. Control drag—A dragging fly, even one deviating only slightly from the current direction and speed, makes a trout nervous and indecisive. Three or four bad drifts often make the fish stop rising even during a hatch.

Float the fly drag-free repeatedly when covering a particular fish. Anything less than perfection makes it impossible to "create a hatch" (the George LaBranche ploy for allaying suspicion and stimulating voraciousness).

9. Move slowly—Every movement, from walking in or along the stream to casting, should be slow and rhythmical (relaxed and patient?). Save the quicker movements of distance casting to more appropriate fly fishing situations.

Following the first nine rules of stealth make the final commandment, Harry Ramsay's secret, possible.

10. Relax the trout—Continue being as unobtrusive as possible, but keep fishing in a steady, easy manner for at least seven minutes (the minimum time it took a trout to forget the presence of the angler in our underwater observations). By staying in the area, but never posing a direct threat, disappear into the natural rhythms of the stream. How is it possible to lull a trout into overlooking a fisherman? A trout doesn't ponder, he reacts—and if something isn't worth reacting to, he doesn't think about it for long.

My Fly Box

Caddisfly Imitations

Bucktail Caddis (6-10)
(dark, light, orange, and
peacock variations)

Car Top Caddis (18-20)
(any small pattern in my assortment
is going to be extremely simple to
tie— this one is)

Dancing Caddis (8-10)
(the simplified version, tied on an up-
eyed, Atlantic salmon dry fly hook)

Delta Wing (14-20)

Devil Bug (8-10)

Elk Hair Caddis (12-18)
(in the past ten years this Al Troth fly
has become the most popular adult
caddis imitation in the country)

Goddard Caddis (10-14)

Hemingway Special (12-16)

Henryville (14-18)

Mink Wing Caddis (10-12)
(this is a variation of Leonard
Wright's Fluttering Caddis; the long
guard hairs from a mink are more
durable than hackle fibers)

Parkany Deer Hair Caddis (12-16)
(this fly is very compact; it plops
nicely when it hits the surface)

Poly Caddis (8-16)

Spent Partridge Caddis (16-24)
(a favorite on spring creeks)

Turkey Wing Caddis (16-20)

Walker's Red Sedge (14-16)
(this is my "motion" fly for smaller
sizes; the Mink Wing style fits the
same role in sizes 10 and 12)

Comments:

This is a large selection for a basically simple situation. The adult pattern is important as a searcher or as an imitation of an egg laying female. The adult caddisfly, unlike a mayfly, has fully developed mouth parts and can drink not only water but nectar from flowers. The insect is around the stream for days, weeks, or, in some species, months. This makes a caddis pattern a good choice as a general searcher when nothing is happening on the surface. The best type of pattern for imitating this active stage is a perky fly (the hook free of the water).

Egg layers can be divided into two dry fly categories (and, in truth, a wet, diving caddis female is more common than either). Species that carry a visible ball of eggs tend to collapse on the surface after releasing the package and they struggle feebly if at all—these include the very important Grannoms (*Brachycentrus*). Species that extrude eggs in a string do not die so easily— the females flutter and skip all over the surface.

The high riding flies in my box, such as the Mink Wing Caddis, are for searching the water or for matching the struggling egg layers (usually with a twitch presentation). The flush flies, such as the Elk Hair Caddis and the Spent Partridge Caddis, mimic the sprawled, dying females. The Goddard Caddis and the Devil Bug are bulky flies—for me they work when retrieved across a smooth surface. With a technique such as a Skitter they leave the distinctive V-wake of running caddisfly adults.

The work for *Caddisflies* meant testing many different flies. Putting so many good patterns in my boxes was like throwing mud against a wall—they stuck.

[During an actual hatch of caddisflies the Emerger, rather than a dry fly, is the suggested imitation.]

Chapter 3

A State of Mind

Remember seduction? It's not just a frivolous analogy to fly selection. What lover would decide on an approach, a plan, before assessing the mood of his beauty? Isn't the angler trying to seduce, or draw some reaction from, a trout?

So much research has focussed on how trout see objects. Questions have been answered on color perception, cone of vision, light refraction, depth perception, and binocular and monocular fields. All of that is important, but the eyes merely see. It's the brain that actually perceives. The mental state of the trout—what he's actually feeling, if anything, at the moment he decides to take a natural or an artificial—is the key to intelligent fly selection.

Some might counter this with the argument that trout don't have emotions; that their existence is nothing more than a series of unthinking reactions to the dangers and opportunities of their environment; or that it's wrong to give human characteristics to lesser creatures (anthropomorphism).

I'm not sure which bothers me more about these statements—their ignorance about the evolution and the function of the brain or their conceit (a human flaw).

It is true that basic emotions, or traits, if emotions is too flattering a word, are instinctive, not intelligent reactions, in fish. Surprise—they are instinctive, not intelligent, in humans, also. They're survival mechanisms, not thought processes, rooted in the most primitive sections of the brain.

Evolution is more a matter of accretion than radical change. It is very difficult for any organism to evolve by altering the deep fabric of life; any change there is likely to be lethal. Fundamental change can be accomplished, however, by the addition of new systems on top of old ones. This is obvious in human intrauterine development, when the fetus undergoes successive stages resembling fish, reptiles, and non-primate mammals before they become recognizably human. The fish stage even has gill slits, which are absolutely useless for the embryo.

The brain of the human fetus also develops from the inside out; from the neural chassis to the Reptilian complex to the limbic system, and, finally, to the neocortex. Eighty-five percent of the brain mass of humans consists of neocortex, or gray matter, and is the source of our reasoning ability as well as, undoubtedly, our conceit. That pride is false—it trusts somehow that the neocortex supplants those more primitive brain functions. It doesn't; in each one of us those older systems perform, to a significant extent, the same functions they do for other creatures.

It's not as if a fish is a fish and a human is a human. A fish is a fish, but a human is a fish, a reptile, a primate, and a human all in one package. Man is the amalgamation; he has not one brain but many, each corresponding to a major evolutionary step.

The neural chassis, or brain stem, is the most ancient part of the human brain. Comprised of the spinal cord, hindbrain, and midbrain, it is the basic machinery for reproduction and self-preservation, as well as for the regulation of life functions.

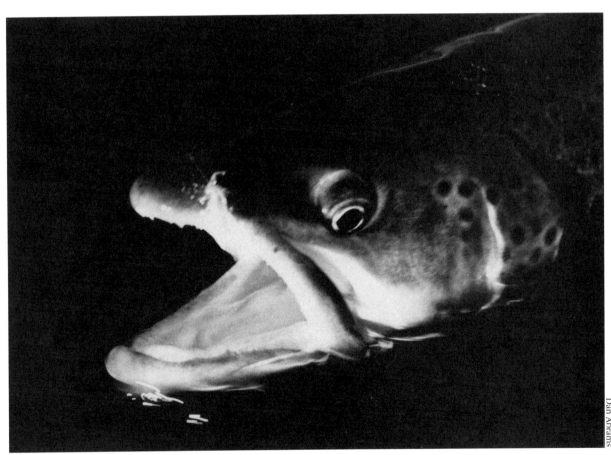

Dan Abrams

It is not the intelligence of a trout that makes it so hard for us to catch him. He is protected by a wonderful set of instincts. Those basic drives also include traits such as playfulness, curiosity, and voracity, however, and those are feelings that an angler can use to fool a trout.

In a fish the neural chassis comprises almost the whole brain, so it's there where the basic motivations for taking or rejecting an artificial fly rest. This is not speculation, or even theory based on circumstantial evidence; it's proven when scientists make incisions in the forward part of the trout's brain. The result, in the words of neuropsychologist James DeBus, is that "... even in fish, lesions of the forebrain destroy the traits of initiative and caution."

The word "initiative" might be debatable. It conjures up a trait associated with lazy, disfavored relatives. It sounds too complex for a fish. Maybe "curiosity" would have been a better word choice than "initiative," but, then, initiative was not my word in the first place.

My belief is that traits in a fish are the evolutionary forerunners of emotions in human beings, and that for every complex set of feelings in us there is a simpler corollary in the basic brain. In humans those instinctive compulsions may be amplified by the mental power of the neocortex (and thus the phrase, "the depths of emotion"), but they are no less real or demanding in a fish.

Consider, for example, feelings of parental love. It makes fathers and mothers protect and nourish their offspring until the little wretches throw off the last vestiges of childhood, roughly eighteen to twenty-four years for the females and generally never for the males of the species.

That compulsion has its seeds even in fish. It's recognizable in the instinctive care and effort a trout or salmon takes in selecting and preparing a spawning area. It's even more obvious in a bass, especially the male guardian, who protects first the eggs and then the fry with such total devotion. (Of course, after a few weeks of this a bass comes to his senses, scattering his babies and giving them a final admonition, "And if I run into any of you around the weed lanes, I'll eat you.")

Once, scuba diving in a Tennessee pond, I watched a two-pound, nesting male bass rush a marauding carp. The carp, a ten-pound fish, intent on eating the eggs, ignored the first feints and circled steadily closer to the nest. The little bass, unable to bluff the Goliath, began slamming his snout into the carp's side so hard that large, coppery scales fluttered to the gravel. For three minutes the bass butted the huge intruder. His rushes slowly lost their power, until the carp nosed among the eggs. The bass, yawing over in exhaustion, settled on the gravel next to the nest.

The traits of protectiveness (courage?) and anger (ferocity?) were so evident during the display that they were beyond denial. Afterwards, long after the carp had left, the bass poked around the nest. Would it be wrong also to give the fish the benefit of feeling more involved emotions and assume that he felt grief?

Answer as you wish. Even after the spawning season the bass in that pond, with no provocation, still attack passing carp. This must be anger amplified by memory—a very complex emotion called hate. It would even seem, by triggering an action that wastes precious energy, counterproductive to survival.

Trout, of course, are not bass. They are lower on the evolutionary scale, not quite so intelligent and not nearly so adaptable, yet they also exhibit all of the basic traits (if only as rudimentary seeds). Every one of these traits in a fish serves as a motive to strike a fly.

A Compendium of Traits
Fear

Fear is the most basic survival mechanism. It's difficult to imagine any species of animal existing for long without a healthy amount of it. Even the lion knows when to run from the hunter. The wild trout flees not just from an obvious, clearly seen predator but from any forewarning of danger, such as a shadow passing over the water. In the primitive brain the instinct to escape leaves little room for questions about the threat.

Fear, it seems, should be one reaction that always works against the angler. After all, a frightened fish never feeds. Even a slight nervousness on the part of a trout makes him much more difficult to take on a fly.

A frightening experience, however, almost always changes the trout's mood. The angler can divide the cause of the fright into two categories: an actual attacker or an unknown disturbance. The attacker might be a heron or an otter, a threat that sends a trout fleeing either for cover or deep water. That fish is spooked badly, so traumatized that he won't feed for an hour or more.

It's different when a trout is disturbed instead of frightened. The initial reaction might be the same—the fish flushes in a panicked rush. When the threat doesn't materialize, however, the confused trout returns to his regular hold.

Normally, the angler wouldn't want to stir up a fish he's trying to catch. His every action is meant to lull the target—not disorient him. The only exception is a trout that's totally inactive, immune to every blandishment. A big cannibal brown, a night feeder for the most part, needs a proverbial "kick in the pants" to make him strike a fly during the day. So does a migrating steelhead or Atlantic salmon that has stayed in a pool too many days waiting for a rise in the water level.

The ploy works because fear and anger exist as two sides of a mirror. Even in humans no one can predict the reaction, a "flight or fight" response to danger. If not scared too badly, an animal recovering from his small fright will turn angry, or at least aggressive. That's a better state of mind than lethargy in a trout.

It is possible (although the ethics are debatable) to "stone" brown trout. It's a natural trick for a fish-spotter. On my streams, lonely waters even though they are public, there is no chance of this tactic ruining another angler's fishing. It's my habit, when walking for daily exercise, to follow a stream or river. At home in Deer Lodge that means the Clark Fork or its tributary, Cottonwood Creek, both of which flow through town. When I see a large brown, one of those fish-eaters that hang sullenly back in the deep shade under the bank, I mark the spot.

Stoning a brown is nothing like stoning a salmon (or even a big rainbow trout); the latter sits out in open water and it's easy enough to drop a few small rocks on him. With a brown, the rock has to be hurled right at his head, back under the cover. Since the fish is holding deep, the stone never scares him badly.

For a trout in open water it takes a half dozen rocks, each slightly larger than a marble, to scare him without chasing him away permanently. For a bank trout a single rock, about the size of an egg, makes enough of an impact on the surface to get his attention. The angler should roll all stones in mud first; the mud dissolves in the water and somehow makes the fish susceptible to the fly much sooner.

No one can guarantee a trout's reaction to stoning. He might disappear and not return to his hold for the rest of the day, which happens often enough to make the trick a last resort. Sometimes the fish will come back and, like a fat man nervously eating peanuts, this large trout that hasn't risen to a hatch in years will start sipping small insects from the surface. The incongruous miracle (it's happened to me maybe a dozen times over the years) is enough to make a dry fly fisherman giddy. Usually, the trout settles right back into his hold, but something is different. Smaller baitfish that hovered close to the giant trout slowly slide further away.

The nervousness of those baitfish predicts the effectiveness of streamers. Any minnow imitation swum close enough to the agitated trout gets smacked. It's not like the normal strike of a feeding fish on a streamer; so often the charge and swirl seems meant more to cripple than to engulf the fraud. This artless zeal might be understandable with large imitations (size 4 through size 3/0 streamers) but the trout attack even smaller patterns—deadlier than big flies on agitated fish—by slashing at them. Also, a fast, steady swing, the faster the better, proves more aggravating that a slow, realistic presentation to these stirred-up trout.

A drag-free dry fly, no matter how perfectly it's drifted over the spot, doesn't work very well on a stoned trout that isn't already rising. A skated fly such as a Bomber or a Slider cast across stream and allowed to "wake" over the fish on a steadily swinging line (a classic Atlantic salmon presentation), though, frequently draws strikes.

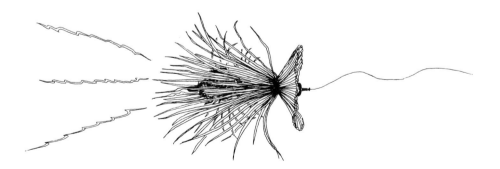

The Slider is a fly designed specifically for waking across the surface. It won't drown, even when it is hanging downstream, because the flat "face" of glued deer hair catches the water and lifts the back of the fly.

The fly fisherman has to remember always, no matter what method he chooses, that stoned trout are already half spooked. The waving of a bright rod or the flash of a line in the air, to say nothing of the upright angler himself, will surely send the fish into hiding for good. The fisherman has to stay completely out of sight and present the fly as subtly as possible.

Anger

It's debatable whether a swinging fly, cutting across the surface, is a "dry" fly. It may be on top of the water, but in truth the swiftly moving fly, obscured by the distortion of the surface film, is featureless. It's the wake that is the exciter, the trigger for aggression, and the fly is the target only because it is the source of the disturbance.

Forget anger. It has no relevance for the drifted or even the twitched dry fly because no prey on the surface aggravates or challenges a fish. A trout rises for all of those other reasons—hunger, opportunism, competitiveness, curiosity or playfulness—but there is nothing on top that he hates enough to kill randomly.

Underwater, of course, anger is a powerful trait. It's the trigger for one of my bass flies, the Tilting Sunny. School sunfish work together to steal eggs from a largemouth's nest. One of them edges closer to the male bass and lowers his head, an odd tilting maneuver. Maybe it's a challenging or a taunting signal. Whatever it is, the guardian rushes after the intruder and the other sunfish sneak in quickly to gobble a few eggs.

Months later, long after the spawn, the bass still reacts violently to the face-on tilt. The Tilting Sunny is tied with a foam tail and a deer hair back, but lead weight near the eye of the hook makes the head drop slowly downwards. The male bass rushes and grabs the fly, and if he is not hooked, spits it out and seizes it again.

Anger, amplified by spawning aggressiveness, also makes trout and salmon species strike at streamer flies. They have no great urge during the mating period to feed on minnows or to cannibalize their own kind, but they defend their spawning area against egg eaters or, worse, those precocious little jacks that try to fertilize the eggs.

In our observations, the depth of the presentation was critical in evoking an angry response—a wet fly proved most aggravating when it approached a trout at eye level. All of our surface flies, even when they were buzzed, dragged, and swung over the heads of trout, failed to incite any rage from inactive, non-spawning browns or rainbows.

Playfulness

It's easy to distinguish between playful strikes and curious strikes. A trout motivated by curiosity inspects a dry fly closely and, if it's too startling, he drifts along under it, jumps over it or swirls next to it without actually touching it. The fish wants to know what the oddball is, but at the same time innate caution keeps him from attacking it. A large purple dry fly, during the morning hours, draws curiosity responses from trout on pools or flats.

Anger is provoked mainly when one fish invades the territory of another. The result is either a warning (an agonistic display) or an actual attack on the intruder. The Tilting Sunny, one of my patterns, infuriates bass even after the spawning season.
Weight: lead wire (wrapped over the forward half of the hook shank)
Tail: foam (tied flat)
Back Spikes: deer hair
Body: wool (combed up and clipped to shape—the front of the head is cut on an exaggerated flat slant)

When a trout strikes playfully, there's no hesitation. Even a large fish may cavort like a hyperactive fingerling chasing after a fly, but there's no doubt that his intent is to grab it. The attack is playful only in the sense that the energy expended by a big trout outweighs the calories that could be gained from eating a small object.

Isn't that what play is? Nonsensical. No, nature doesn't work that way. Playfulness is no more whimsey than any other trait. The playful strike is also a survival mechanism; in this instance, it's a learning tool that teaches young predatory trout to hunt successfully.

Watch a kitten. He pounces on a grasshopper in the summer grass, and no matter how well fed he might be, he kills it. Often he kills slowly, holding the struggling insect in his mouth and testing his teeth on it. For him, hunting is a game—not drudgery—and both the chase and the killing are fun (which, in mankind, sometimes turns into a frightful legacy).

Predators as far apart on the evolutionary scale as a trout and a human share the same hunting instinct. A young animal spends more time playing the game than an older one, but even a mature animal occasionally feels like smacking or snatching something. The urge may be triggered by the memory of an activity that reminds the adult of youthful exuberance.

In his book *The Quiet Waters By*, Aylmer Tryon records an incident on Scotland's Spey:

> noticed fish rising at the tail of the pool as if they were trout being fed in a hatchery. So we dropped down in the boat to investigate and saw that they were a shoal of salmon rising at the many leaves floating down after the day's gale.

The salmon certainly weren't rising out of hunger. It couldn't have been curiosity either, since that would have been satisfied after one or two tastes of the leaves, and these fish were rising continuously. These salmon were "playing," reenacting an imprinted experience of their early times in the river.

The playfulness is triggered in trout by certain types of flies. My name for these patterns is High Profile Attractors; but the whole category can be summed up by listing my favorites—Bivisibles and Skating Spiders. These E. R. Hewitt creations, fished actively or dead drift, ride so sprightly on the surface with only the hackle tips touching, that they mimic flying insects. Trout never see these patterns clearly, only as illusions, yet these are the kind of "bugs" that young fish leap for exuberantly. Large fish that aren't feeding, just watching the top, often rise to these flies as well when more realistic floaters fail.

Curiosity

Playfulness isn't the only reason that trout take high riding flies. Sometimes there are so many flying insects dancing on the water, as with adult craneflies, that a bouncing fly *is* an imitation. On rivers with soft mud banks that are perfect habitats for the larvae of the cranefly, such as Montana's Beaverhead or the upper Clark Fork, the water at dawn appears to have an orange haze over the flats from the flitting *Tipula* adults. The fish rise quickly to gulp any

Until it is moved by the pull of the line, the Spider lays flat on the water, the hook hanging down (the fact that it gets strikes drifting along in this posture inspired me to develop a pattern called the Occasion). The Spider comes alive on the retrieve, standing on the hackle tips and skating lightly over the current lanes.

luckless insect that falls to the surface, but when they get impatient they don't wait for cripples. The trout soar out of the water in graceful arcs, snatching craneflies from the air. An orange Skating Spider pulled vigorously across the top is effective on these mornings.

Trout, even when they're not actively feeding, are curious about flies that are odd. For a fly to be odd, it should be a variation not just in what's possible but in what's probable in nature. An attractor, because of the way it looks or acts, for instance, is an improbable fly. The aberration can be in the brightness, size, shape, color or behavior of the pattern. High riding patterns certainly are odd enough to attract attention.

Why does a fish have to be curious? The answer lies both in the medium he lives in (water) and the strengths and weaknesses of his eyesight. In the trout's brain the optic lobes are, compared to the brain of a shark, tremendous in size. In the shark's brain the olfactory regions dominate. A shark feeds by smell; a trout feeds by sight. Have no doubt, the trout's ability to see is incredible, detecting details so intricate that the patterns are beyond our scrutiny.

In his classic, *The Life Story of a Fish*, Brian Curtis cites experiments with jewel-fish to demonstrate the amazing limits of eyesight:

> He has several hundred (young) at a time, each less than one-quarter of an inch long when they begin to swim, and he and his mate ride herd over their flock, driving off intruders, and picking up any stragglers in their mouths and spitting them out unharmed into the middle of the band. If you take a few of these young ones, anesthetize them until they are absolutely motionless, and lay them on the bottom of the tank, they are indistinguishable to the human eye from the sand and debris collected there, but not to the jewel. He picks them up and carries them back to where they belong. Further, there is another species of cichlid whose habits are the same, and whose young are so much like the jewel in shape, size, and marking, that they are difficult to tell apart without a microscope. If you take ten of the jewel's children away from the flock, and a moment later return to a different part of the tank five baby jewels and five of the other species, he will take them, one by one, into his mouth to carry them back to where they belong. Then, if you watch closely, you will see that each jewel is spat out into the bosom of the family, but the little strangers go into his mouth never to emerge. Instead of joining the little jewels, they become part of a big jewel. That sight is the sense which operates here, and not smell, has been demonstrated by experiments which we do not need to go into.

There have been many experiments, not quite so interesting, demonstrating the trout's visual acuity. In water, however, his ability to decipher details only functions at close range. That's why a trout has to be curious. A fish couldn't focus on a far away object underwater, even if he had the anatomical ability.

The Bivisible sits up on the numerous hackle points, never presenting a solid picture to the fish. It is my favorite "exciter" for a dead-drift presentation; the Skating Spider is my favorite for a retrieve presentation.

Once the trout becomes aware of the approaching object, he has to wait until the current carries it closer to see it very distinctly. For extremely close viewing his vision is better than human sight—he can clearly see an object within an inch of his nose (which we cannot). This is critical for a trout, for he must bring his eyes very close to whatever he eats.

In a trout, with the exception of hunger, curiosity is the most important motivating factor for taking a fly. Grasping something in his mouth is his way of testing, with taste buds inside and outside his lips, an object. That's why he might not rise the first time or even the tenth time a fly drifts perfectly over him, but often he'll get more and more curious about the "new" food item and move after a number of presentations to test it with his lips. Curiosity is the key to George LaBranche's strategy of "creating a hatch."

My boxes are filled with attractors of every color and most shapes. Some are better than others at at drawing curiosity strikes. It turns out that the "bright" flies, those tied with sparkle yarn (Antron or Creslan), such as the Clear Wing Spinner and the Emergent Sparkle Pupa, usually prove best on flat water. These two patterns were originally intended as imitations, and during hatches they are, but when no insects are around they double as attractors. Rises to them are very hurried and splashy.

One of my most effective attractor patterns on rough water is the Mohawk. This really isn't my fly. It's my daughter Heather's, but that at least makes me the grandfather. It sits so low in the water, and presents such a blocky chunk of food, that trout in riffles pounce on this strangely shaped fly avidly (for some unknown reason, it also works on slow areas of a stream).

The number one dry fly attractor, or for that matter, the second most prolific fish catcher over the years of all the hundreds of patterns in my carrying stock, is the Royal Trude. Is this a surprise? With all of my experiments in imitation, shouldn't the top fly be some sort of exact match for an insect?

Here are notes from two very different days in my fishing logs:

Aug. 4, 1986—Missouri River below Holter Dam [Montana]. Spent the morning hours, 9 to 11:30, stalking sippers during the Trico spinner fall. Caught six trout, best a 17-inch rainbow, on a Clear Wing Spinner. Great day.

July 9, 1987—Pecos River [New Mexico]. In the morning we popped the riffles. Lots of 9- to 12-inch browns and brookies on a Royal Trude. Lots. More than fifty fish before noon. Great day.

Precisely matching a hatch does not always result in large catches, especially if the trout are tough. Working the broken water with an attractor, on the other hand, frequently does turn trout "fast and furious." That's why the Royal Trude has caught more fish for me than any other dry fly. It's the one that gets tied on the most, sometimes just out of habit when nothing much is happening.

The Royal Trude succeeds on rough water because of its colors and the silhouette of the downwing. The Humpy does so well because of the bulky

The Clear Wing Spinner, in sizes that match the natural mayfly, is an imitation, but this fly also makes a very good searcher (although the large, size 10 and 12 hooks may seem odd to many anglers) on flat water. It has a duality, serving both as an imitation and an attractor, that makes it special.

shape of the body. The Renegade, even if it is tied with the stiffest feathers, settles with its body flush on the surface and attracts attention with the fore and aft hackles poking underwater. All of these time-proven flies make trout curious because of their exaggerated, improbable (if not impossible) characteristics. Yet, at the same time, they don't carry the joke too far.

Another way to take advantage of the trout's natural curiosity is to use an attractor not just as a fish catcher but as a locator. The "finder" fly can be on the far side of weird, the colors totally unnatural (try purple in the early morning and canary yellow in the afternoon). When a trout shows, swirling at but intentionally missing the pattern, the angler has him primed to strike. He quickly puts on a more realistic fly and covers the hold. More often than not this fish takes solidly.

Voracity

Curiosity is the most important motivating factor (other than hunger) for triggering a strike, at least in the number of chances it gives the angler. It is not, however, the strongest trait. From the earliest experiences as a free-swimming fingerling, a trout feeds not just to satisfy hunger. It is common to see a fish so stuffed with Salmon Flies (*Pteronarcys* stoneflies) that his belly bulges, with insects squeezing out through his gills, and yet he frequently rises once more to a fly.

What is driving that fish to strike? A trout survives by being an opportunistic feeder. There is no gray matter in his brain to let him dwell on the past or plan for the future. For stretches during the season he might settle into a daily feeding routine if food becomes available at a regular time, but even in rich spring creeks a trout is seldom so blasé that he will ignore a vulnerable bit of food during the non-feeding hours. Voracity means "greediness of appetite," and it is the strongest trait because it will make even a very reluctant trout rise to the dry fly.

Surprisingly, there are anglers who are ignorant about how trout feed. Their assumption is that a stream is like a well-stocked cafeteria, always open for business, and a trout can idle along picking up food anytime. There *are* plenty of insects in the bottom rubble of most streams, but there is a difference between being there and being vulnerable. The nymphs and larvae are well protected among the stones. A fish can grub them out, stirring up the gravel and picking up insects momentarily awash. Some fish, like the mountain whitefish (*Prosopium*) of the western rivers, are adapted for grubbing and even then there's a fearful tradeoff in energy expended. Trout, especially larger trout, that cannot feed inefficiently and survive take a greater percentage of food from the open currents.

The stream isn't a cafeteria for a trout—it's a conveyor belt. The current carries food in and on the water; sometimes the belt is empty and at other times it's filled to overflowing. The number of nymphs and larvae free in the currents depends on behavioral drift, a response to light intensity where the insects leave the safety of the bottom and ride helpless with the currents to new areas of the stream. Mayflies, stoneflies, and free-living caddisflies drift at higher rates during the night. Case-making caddisflies, sometimes with and sometimes without their cases, drift at higher rates during the day.

My major project for my college Aquatic Entomology course was measuring drift rates for the Short Horn Sedge larvae (*Glossosoma* species). This casemaker was abundant in Spring Creek, or Flathead Creek as it's named on some maps, a tributary of Montana's Jocko. At three different times during the day the pale green, size 16 larvae would by some unknown signal abandon their little turtle shell cases en masse, leaving them fastened to the rocks, and drift with the flow. All of the rainbow and brown trout in the stream would push out into the riffles, jostling for the best sites, and begin feeding on the passing banquet. Once my nets were tended there would be time for me to cast a matching nymph (this was simply a futile attempt to protect those defenseless larvae).

Most aquatic insects, including the Short Horn Sedge, end up on the surface as adults during a hatch when they rise from the bottom and emerge. Terrestrials, of course, fall to the surface; so do adult insects after mating when they return to lay their eggs.

What an easy target an insect drifting on top makes for a fish. Offer no apologies for the dry fly—for a trout, surface feeding is one of the surest ways to capture food. During the summer months on many streams 50 percent of the insects captured are taken in or on the meniscus. Even when there isn't a hatch or an egg-laying fall in progress, the trout watches the top, and if some insect drifts overhead it's difficult for him to let the prey pass. That's voracity prodding the fish to rise.

The energy expenditure of grubbing is a fearful tradeoff for a trout. In gravel-bottomed streams, where insects are the main fare, it is not worth the effort during most of the year—for example, in the autumn, after most species have hatched out, most of the nymphs and larvae left are the very small young. Grubbing is a more efficient way of feeding in slow, weedy streams. The trout can shake loose substantial food items, such as sow bugs and scuds, from the vegetation. In the slow currents, this prey is not washed out of the feeding area so quickly.

In one series of experiments, scientists (in what seems like a sadistic scheme) placed hatchery trout in a trough of flowing water. They wanted to determine how long it would take them to starve if they received no food. In an identical trough, another bunch of trout, a control group, were kept and fed a regular diet. The starved fish survived quite well, few perishing, and even took in enough nutrients from the water to grow. Nearly a third of the regularly fed fish died.

The lesson was that trout can't just feed—they have to feed efficiently. The trough was designed in such a way, with the water flowing through quickly, that feeding required energy. The trout were better off just staying out of the current and in the holding areas.

A young trout has to learn how to feed. The skill isn't instinctive. One reason hatchery fish suffer such a high mortality in streams over the winter is that they never learn how to feed efficiently on small insects (midge larvae and pupae); and they aren't smart enough to lie quietly and conserve energy.

R. Valentine Atkinson

There are diverse and abundant insect populations in rocky stretches of rivers such as the Pit in California, but the fact that nymphs and larvae are not always available helps make the rough water a good place to drift a dry fly.

They starve to death, not because they're not eating but because they're wasting too much energy trying to eat.

Wild trout achieve a balance by knowing when it's futile to feed and knowing when there are enough food items present to gather sufficient calories. They have to be voracious, not only by feeding to the point of gluttony during a heavy hatch but also, during non-feeding times, by watching for the "easy meal." The trait is a survival mechanism that prompts trout to strike even when they're not hungry. It's the strongest, most compelling urge because trout can't survive without it.

They do not live entirely on instinct. Trout are intelligent enough to take advantage of situations. This is all the more surprising considering the simple framework of their brain. They can't grub very well, but wherever there's a school of whitefish rolling and turning in a feeding mass over the bottom, there are almost always a few trout just below them. They sidle back and forth, intercepting nymphs pried free by the whitefish.

Habits like this remind me that while fish are not reasoning creatures, they are not stupid, either, in conforming to the idiosyncrasies of their environment. My angling plan is to use the trout's ability in making wise choices to predict ways of catching them—like fishing a dead drift nymph behind every visible school of whitefish.

To catch voracious fish on a surface pattern, the angler has to put on an act so convincing that the trout believes in the vulnerability of his fly. The imitation appeals to the voraciousness of a trout if it is: (1) a crippled duck, (2) a prime chunk or (3) a last bite.

A "crippled duck" is a wounded creature. The characteristic that triggers the strike in this type of fly is the sense that it is a victim, not necessarily a meal, that cannot escape. Is there a moral imperative in nature that makes predators want to kill the weak and helpless? There seems to be an instinctive need at work that goes beyond mere opportunism. Crippled flies imitate small animals, such as mice or injured minnows, and to impart the proper action the angler only has to imagine death throes interspersed with exhaustion.

A "prime chunk" is a meal, a substantial one, that any trout would be foolhardy to pass up. It must be recognizable from past feeding experiences, however; anything so large makes a trout naturally cautious. The insect, such as a grasshopper or a beetle, that drops onto the water randomly over a period of weeks becomes a marked target.

The truly voracious trout refuses to stop feeding just because the hatch has petered out. He keeps rising to stragglers and stillborns, looking for the "last bite." The memory of the emergence lingers, and even after he has abandoned his feeding area and returned to his safe hold, he will rise for an imitation matching the previous hatch.

A State of Moods

All of these traits are sublimated when a trout feeds steadily. The more selective and rhythmic the rises, the more mindless the action. One stimulus leads to one set of responses; there is no variation because variation equals

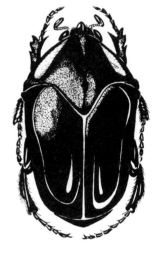

Beetles, a much more important part of the trout's diet than fly fishermen realize, are almost always prime chunks of food. Imitations make fine searching flies; they are also one of the best "hatch-breakers," patterns that trout will rise to even when they are feeding on another insect.

inefficiency. The only emotion that might be of use is the anger triggered by competition—a larger fish driving off a smaller one (agonistic behavior). This is why a streamer occasionally draws strikes during a hatch. Trying to tweak a trout's playfulness, curiosity, or voracity by using a fly that doesn't match the prevalent insect, however, is more wishful thinking than sound strategy.

Our field observations over the course of a summer on the upper Clark Fork revealed when trout begin feeding selectively, rather than randomly. A specimen of the prevalent insect species had to pass through or over the feeding window every twelve seconds for the change to occur. The selectivity might be sequential during a hatch, the trout taking a nymph deep, an emerger in the film, and an adult on the surface in that order, but the feeding was restricted to the particular species. If the insects didn't appear every twelve seconds, a trout, reluctant to break its feeding rhythm, and with little patience, would accept a different food form.

The daily feeding rhythm of the trout population revolves around these periods of abundant food. When a fish feeds on the surface he is obviously receptive to the dry fly, yet there's an opposite side to this coin—a time when no fly, much less a dry one that demands a commitment to feed, can tempt a particular trout.

It's silly for an angler, then, to ask, "What fly do I use?"

The question has to be, "What fly do I use when: a trout is inactive and not accepting natural food items?" or "when a trout is not actively feeding but is receptive to food?" or "when a trout is actually feeding?"

Of course, there's no magic formula, but a model makes answering these questions a bit easier. Picture a device with two discs. The wheels are imaginary only, mental images (shoot the first person who invents a "trout calculator"). Turn the small, inner wheel indicating fly category until it lines up with the outer wheel indicating trout mood, and the question of which pattern to use is no longer random nonsense.

The theories behind this wheel could only be verified by onstream observation. Imagine the dilemma: catching a fish on a particular pattern meant nothing unless the observers knew the activity level of the trout before he rose to the fly. There could be no guessing about it—fish had to be fixed with miniature radio tags and monitored by gauges.

These telemetry studies took more than four years—in concentrated work on the Swift (in Massachusetts by James VanKrevelen), the Tomorrow (in Minnesota by W. J. Witts), the White (in Arkansas by Henning Penttila), and the Metolius (in Oregon by Terry Rothman), as well as in many other streams, large and small, as the limited number of radio tags were shifted around the country. The individual reactions of fifty-seven trout—browns, rainbows, cutthroat, brooks, and even one bull trout (we used to know these as Dolly Varden)—were recorded with detailed descriptions.

James VanKrevelen, for example, monitored a 14-inch rainbow on the Swift River. "After his second feeding period of the day, from 9:35 A.M. to 11:09 A.M.," James reported, "he moved back into his resting area in the deeper slot. He was pretty much invisible there to observation, but the monitor showed little movement. That alone indicated no feeding activity.

The stillborn emerger, the insect that never does escape the shuck, is not particularly important during the hatch. It is after the main feeding time, when most of the insects are gone, that trout keep looking for the last few stragglers.

"Johnson Gray kept trying to bring him up to a dry fly, but nothing worked for the first hour. Now, we've caught this fish before on a nymph from the slot, but this may be one case where a dry fly won't work. Maybe he's just too deep.

"It wasn't until 3:10 P.M., when he was already starting to move and take natural nymphs, that he splashed at a size 8 Gray Double Wing (you were right about gray on an overcast day). Johnson hooked him a few casts later on a size 14 Gray Double Wing, but not before he followed and refused two drifts to the larger fly.

"We've fooled him four times now on dry flies and, even though he was a ·spring hatchery plant, in my opinion, he's getting hook smart."

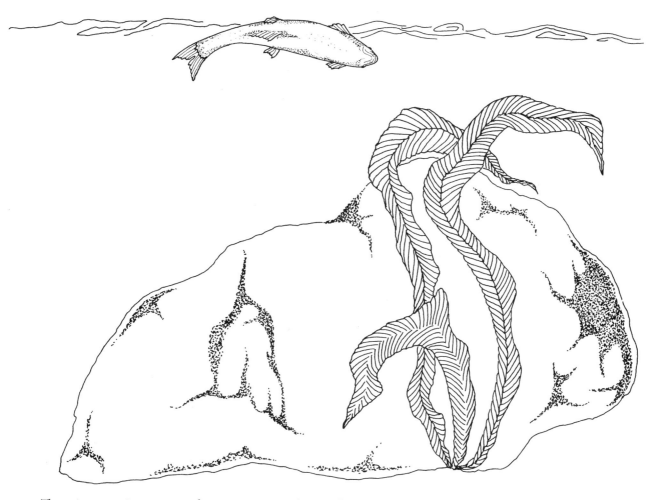

There is a certain amount of competitive greed, as well as voraciousness, that makes a trout attack an injured minnow. The idea that some other fish is going to eat such an easy meal seems to bother a predator. In experiments with crippled minnows, a single trout was likely to attack the prey, no matter what his mood or level of hunger, but often he did not "seriously" grab it. Drop a crippled minnow between two trout, however, and it is even more likely that one of them will charge the bait, grasp the minnow, and run with it.

These radio studies were combined with observation along trout streams. Our anglers didn't watch individual fish, but they studied the entire population of trout in a section of water, for weeks at a time, from canvas blinds. The telemetry readings monitored trout activity. The best of the blind observations yielded ideas on the way those activity rhythms affected the chances of fly fishermen; they hinted at which of the trout's moods the angler must appeal to at different moments.

The different levels of receptiveness

Fish do sleep. They don't have any eyelids to close, however, and when they're wired with electrodes they don't demonstrate different levels of brain activity. Yet, they enter a state of inactivity that's nearly complete. They don't respond to most outside stimuli. "They don't need to be awake to keep oxygen going through gills, just as humans don't have to be awake to breathe," writes professor David Miller, head of the developmental ethology laboratory at the University of Connecticut, in describing this stage.

This phase often happens right after heavy feeding, after the "last bite," when the simple act of digestion pulls blood to the stomach, fulfilling oxygen demands, and puts a fish in a somnolent state. The abundant hatches of large insects do this, the blizzards that leave a skim of dead nymphs and adults. It's rare for trout to have so much food.

There is not much that anglers can do with totally inactive fish. Satiated brown trout fade so far back into cover that they can't be reached with a fly. Even heaving stones at a "stuffed" fish doesn't start him feeding again. That's a tactic for indifferent or stale trout, not ones that are intent on mimicking unconsciousness.

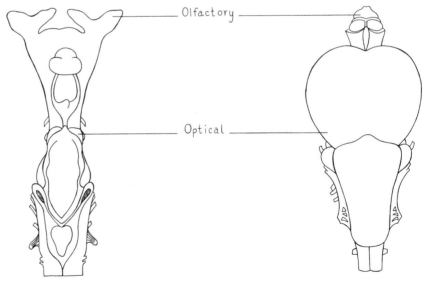

The feeding tendencies of any species of fish is largely controlled by its inherent abilities. The shark's brain, with its large development of olfactory areas, makes the shark find its food mostly by smell. The trout's brain, with its strong optical lobes, makes the trout find its food mostly by sight.

Most trout, in their daily pattern of feeding and resting, seldom shun the thought of food entirely—or of taking a proper fly. One trick that works when all others fail is to "mud" the pool (it is not an ethical trick, however, on heavily trafficked streams because of potential damage to the insect population). To do this stir up the bottom in a riffle, sending a wash of nymphs and silt into the resting area. The fish will perk up immediately and might even move out into feeding positions. The problem with mudding is that it isn't a dry fly strategy; these trout search the colored water for nymphs and are best caught on a dark pattern drifted deep.

The secret of the nymph isn't that trout prefer sunken food when they're actively foraging. Striking a surface fly, clearly outlined against the sky, promises less chance of making a feeding mistake; it's an easier target and for the sake of efficiency, the preferable one. The nymph pattern tallies such impressive totals over the course of the whole day because, when trout are not actually searching, they're still willing to take it. They will suck in nearly anything, including all kinds of inanimate drift, if it hits them in the mouth.

A variation of my boyhood sugarcube trick tempts even lethargic trout in slow pools and beaver ponds. The cubes, lashed onto the leader at the eye of the fly, pull a buoyant pattern such as a Royal Humpy to the bottom. The fly sits there until the sugar dissolves and then it wobbles to the surface.

Does a trout take umbrage? The fly hits the surface, sitting there on the smooth water for a moment. My hands quiver, because I've seen it happen too many times, and if the trick is right the trout fractures the quiet, the momentum of his take carrying him high in an off balance flight.

This strategy might offend the dry fly purist. Since I don't fish a dry fly for moral redemption, it doesn't bother me in the least. It's a desperation move that requires preparation and effort.

The angler who prefers not to fish a sunken fly can simply wait for the trout to become more receptive. They will—even before they leave their resting area they'll become more alert to food. The first trait that works for the dry fly angler—voracity—is the strongest.

The fly that represents the "prime chunk" for a given season makes a decent searching pattern. For me, in my Montana rivers, this means a Salmon Fly (*Pteronarcys californica*) early, a grasshopper in mid-summer, and a Giant Orange Sedge (*Dicosmoecus atripes*) late in the season. There's a trick with these monster flies—the angler goes even one size larger than the natural for the first few drifts over the fish. Then, even if there wasn't a splash or a refusal, he casts an imitation one size smaller than the naturals.

Ed Volinkaty spent two weeks monitoring and observing browns and rainbows in the Madison River channels above Ennis. He concentrated on two phases of activity: (1) trout that were in their last minutes in the resting areas—they would be moving to feeding stations soon, and (2) trout that had just moved onto feeding stations.

Fishermen using nymphs caught almost equal numbers of both groups. Ones casting standard dry flies, in size 14 through size 10, rose few of the trout still in the resting areas, but they hooked nearly half of the actively foraging fish. With dry grasshopper imitations fished dead-drift, the anglers caught 10

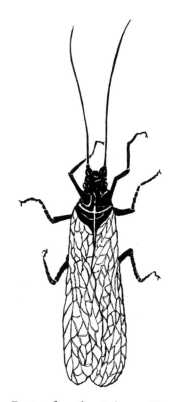

Even after the Salmon Fly hatch has gone through a stretch of river, trout remember the large adults for days. They often splash at, if not take, a matching fly.

percent of the monitored trout still in the resting areas and 30 percent of the monitored trout on the feeding stations.

The grasshoppers and other large dry flies did better than standard patterns for resting fish, but much poorer than more subtle flies for feeding fish. That disparity was frightening. It wasn't a condemnation of all dry flies— only of very large imitations meant to represent prime chunks of food. Those patterns pulled up some fish that wouldn't rise to anything else—the strong appeal to voracity—but they didn't work as well when fish were already in a feeding mood.

These problems with grasshopper imitations and other large surface flies nagged me.

When trout are inactive, and barely receptive to food, catering to their voracious tendencies might be the only hope for the dry fly. When they begin becoming more aware of surface or subsurface food, however, it's wiser to appeal to playfulness or curiosity.

Which trait I work towards, playfulness or curiosity, depends on how much water I want to cover. I can fish those Skating Spiders and Bivisibles actively, skipping them across current lanes and down runs. This is a very exaggerated motion, not meant so much to imitate as to excite. I can't do that with flies designed to pique curiosity. They are lifelike, odd enough to attract

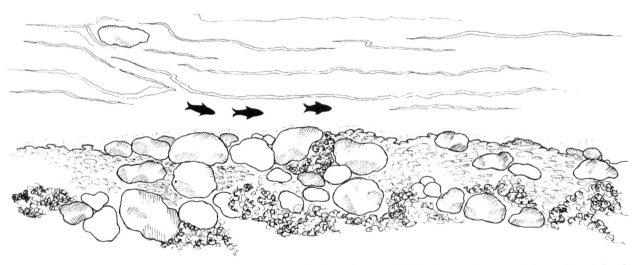

What the angler is always looking for are "mixing lanes," areas of slow, almost dead water against areas of swift flow. Where these two meet, the water mixes in a confusion of miniature eddies—and these eddies all along the mixing line hold food items for a long time. Trout usually hold on the inside edge in the slow water and pick food out of the mixing area. They will often take a fly that dallies on the calmer flow, but they will seldom rush out into the faster currents to take a fly on the outside edge. There may only be a few inches between a good line of drift and a poor line of drift for the trout.

attention but still within the realm of possibilities. Their effectiveness depends on their strangest characteristic, which might be brightness, color, size or shape.

Should the angler move an attractor? Often, it's best not to—the motion makes it impossible for the trout to study the fly, obscuring the strangeness and turning it into just another pattern.

It was obvious during my years guiding on the Madison that fishermen considered attractor patterns "scattergun" flies, ones that could be cast here and there. They're not. The truth is just the opposite. Trout that are already feeding are moving within a well defined territory; while trout that are not feeding are not moving—and they're reluctant to move. The attractor will trigger a faster reaction, but not necessarily one from farther away.

John Gantner and his fishing buddy stopped casting and we walked the raft into the bank of Madison. "Here's the current edge," I pointed, actually touching the water. "On one side you have the calm water of the shoreline and on the other you have the fast water of the river. You have to put the fly one inch inside that current edge."

They both believed me and tried to change their "general" drifts into precise ones. Only John had the skill to do it, though. In the last hours of evening he fished magnificently and caught one trout after another. His friend's drifts were usually on the outside of the current edge and, although he was using the same fly, he caught very few fish. There were only two inches difference between the drift paths of their flies, but it made all the difference to the fish.

Every method of research—scuba diving, bankside observation, and radio telemetry—showed us that attractor patterns, the most valuable dry flies for pricking curiosity, created opportunities and problems. The incidents stood as disconnected points of truth, however, because there was no unifying theory to explain trout caught or not caught.

Where were the ideas in our angling writings about attractor patterns? Balance any speculations about non-matching flies against the body of literature on imitations and it would be a lopsided comparison. It was as if bright flies such as the Royal Coachman, Humpy, or Renegade had been invented through unthinking trial-and-error flogging. And the silliest responses to their success were from imitationists trying to explain what food forms they might represent to trout.

There were two brown trout in the Jefferson River, in Montana, that we studied one July week by all three methods of observation—they were both radio tagged, a canvas blind sat above the section of stream where they lived, and scuba divers had excellent views of both fish. These trout moved into feeding areas each day at 4:30 A.M. (dawn), 10:30 A.M., 3:00 P.M., and 7:30 P.M., the foraging periods lasting roughly two hours. From 7:00 P.M. to 7:30 P.M., just before they would leave the resting areas, these trout moved to bright flies. The one under the bushes liked a Lime Trude, but the one behind the big rock in midstream would only look at a Pink Lady.

It is odd how little has really been written about patterns such as the Royal Coachman. There have been plenty of descriptions for tying instructions and some accounts of random experiences, but no one has ever given a plausible theory about why attractor flies fool trout.

Scotty Eloff laughed when a week of casting confirmed this beyond doubt, "We're all alone on this, aren't we?"

"And all we have to figure out," I said, "is why two trout, at the same time in the same stream, get curious about two different colors. If we can't, all of this work is just garbage."

What we needed was a Theory of Attraction to convince curious trout to rise consistently to bright dry flies. The fact that there wasn't one explained why thinking fly fishermen had never taken patterns such as a Royal Coachman seriously—and why no one had ever written a book called *Unselective Trout* to complement the great works on imitation.

In one way the most interesting observation technique, the canvas blind, was a failure. It didn't provide any universal answers to trout behavior. The study periods on different streams, some as long as months, simply proved that there are a great variety of behaviors.

In his famous four-year study (from 1976 to 1980) on Spruce Creek, a limestone stream in Pennsylvania, Dr. Robert Bachman recorded the actions of a wild population of brown trout. It was a landmark work because these fish were in a natural environment, not a laboratory. His findings contradicted many commonly held beliefs in fisheries biology.

The following quotes from two excellent articles in *Trout* magazine, one by Thomas Pero in the Summer 1980 issue and the other by Dr. Bachman himself in the Winter 1985 issue, recount what his studies into the behavior of trout in Spruce Creek revealed:

> (1) Except for spawning forays, each fish stays within a relatively tiny area all of its adult life.
>
> (2) Big trout are more inclined to hide during the day.
>
> (3) But what about trout moving to the tail of the pool to feed at dusk, and the biggest trout being at the head of the pool? I haven't seen much evidence to support such a contention. I see no reason why a trout should move any great distance in a stream on a daily basis.
>
> (4) The situation in regard to terrestrial insects isn't that much different either. Although feeding stations near the bank may be more profitable from this standpoint than one farther midstream, which bank and when? Which way is the wind blowing? Are stoneflies emerging or 'hoppers, Japanese beetles, ants, or crickets being blown in? In short, I doubt that the trout in a stream ever know where their next meal is coming from.

This research inspired our own efforts on various streams to duplicate Dr. Bachman's work. In the upper Clark Fork, a rich, alkaline Montana brown trout stream, we noted that:

> (1) The trout don't stay in the same lies, not for a lifetime, not for a season, not even for a month. Because of changing water levels in the river,

from the high flow of runoff to a midsummer trickle, the fish are changing both their holding areas and their feeding areas every week.

(2) Big trout in the Clark Fork, fish over sixteen inches, feed just as often as smaller ones in open water. During hatches they actually hold in shallower, more exposed areas than smaller fish.

(3) Some Clark Fork browns do drop down to the tail of the flat to feed on emerging insects—a movement of over fifty yards on our study stretch. These same fish move in pods of a dozen or more to feed on spent, egg laying insects, cruising slowly upstream next to the banks. (Dr. Bachman never noted any pods of feeding fish on Spruce Creek.)

(4) Maybe because the aquatic insect population of the Clark Fork is monotypic, the riffles supporting only net-making caddisflies, the fish lock in very strongly to the appearance and disappearance of the food source. They do seem to know where their next meal is coming from, moving to feeding lies in the upper end of the study section where the fast water delivers emergers every evening before the hatch even starts.

These fish also react like attack dogs to grasshoppers. The trout populations in the Clark Fork are incredibly high, as much as 2,500 catchable size fish-per-mile in some sections, and grasshoppers seldom drift too far. The trout seem to watch for them at certain times of the day, bolting out of holding lies in a rush to snatch the hapless hoppers before some other fish wins the prize.

*The brown trout of the upper Clark Fork live in a rich but very strange river. The residues of a century of copper mining have cemented the bottom, virtually eliminating the spaces between rocks, the interstitial habitat, where most species of stoneflies and mayflies live. Net-making caddisflies, such as the Spotted Sedge (*Hydropsyche species) and the Little Sister Sedge (*Cheumatopsyche species), dominate the insect population, and during the months of heavy hatching, from June through August, the trout do line up below riffles to "wait" for their next meal.*

Dr. Bachman discovered certain feeding and behavior patterns on Spruce Creek. My group found different feeding and behavior patterns on the upper Clark Fork. Both sets of observations were true, no matter how contradictory. They emphasized that trout respond to the demands of their environment—every stream and river is unique, with different bottom types, flow regimens, food forms, and competing populations of other fish species.

Even the work we did on the Little Blackfoot, another brown trout stream near my Deer Lodge home, revealed different habits among the fish population. Most of the trout in a 150-foot run stayed next to the bank, under heavy bushes, all day every day. Their holding lies were apparently also their feeding lies; they didn't even come out into the open to work the heavy evening hatches of mayflies, stoneflies, and caddisflies. Instead, they just sidled closer to the edge of the overhead cover. Maybe because it was such a chilly river, fed by cold springs that kept the water temperature under sixty degrees Fahrenheit even on the hottest summer days, the brown trout fed heaviest between 1:00 P.M. and 4:00 P.M. (280 feeding motions per hour).

No, the value of the intense observations didn't end up being a blueprint of trout feeding behavior in all stream habitats. The results of all the studies couldn't even make firm rules about one stream, never mind many. Among the trout there were individuals, each with his own quirks; every other fish could be resting and there would be one busily feeding (which should give the diehard flogger hope).

What the observations did show us was that trout streams have a daily rhythm—sometimes there's a lot of food and sometimes there's very little food available in or on the currents. A single pattern of abundance doesn't extend for an entire season, but there is a spring cycle, a summer cycle, and a fall cycle—weeks at a time when fish learn to expect particular food types to appear at certain hours of the day.

The late autumn cycle on the lower Clark Fork, below Missoula, offered distinct feeding opportunities. At dawn nymphs drifted at higher rates in the current and trout fed selectively on *Baetis*. Except for a few mavericks that worked throughout the morning the fish rested until 1:00 P.M., and then, on these cloudy days when the *Baetis* emergence burst out in amazing numbers, the trout all jostled into feeding areas, tolerating an unusual closeness and merrily slurping emergers and adults together until 4:00 or 5:00 P.M. when the insects stopped hatching. At dusk some trout, not as many as before, reappeared in the shallows to randomly take drifting nymphs or caddisfly emergers, these latter insects size 16 Little Tan Short Horned Sedges (*Glossosoma* species).

The oddities of this cycle were the lack of a midmorning feeding period, that activity around 10:00 A.M. when trout move into foraging holds to pick the currents generally, and the extremely long rise to the *Baetis* hatch, an extended three-hour to four-hour glut. During midsummer on this stretch of river the trout fed during six time periods, from forty-five minutes to an hour-and-a-half each, and never seemed inclined to totally refuse food, but in the fall after exhausting and stuffing themselves on the *Baetis* hatch, they were uninterested in anything.

R. Valentine Atkinson

What fly do I use? Understanding the resting-feeding cycle can help make the first choice the right one instead of a blind guess.

The prize of our observations was understanding how the daily rhythm of feeding periods affected the receptiveness of trout. There were no revelations about the population as a whole, but there were, more importantly, discoveries about the reactions of individual trout at certain points in the feeding and resting cycle.

Those discoveries answered the following questions:

• What fly do I use when a trout is inactive and not accepting natural food items?

A dry fly probably will not move the fish. A streamer might provoke a strike, or a perfectly drifted nymph might tempt him to open his mouth.

• What fly do I use when a trout is not actively feeding but receptive to food?

Trout are seldom so glutted that they won't show interest in any food. The exception usually is after long, heavy feeding on a superb hatch. If they're only mildly receptive, a fly that imitates a prime chunk of food will appeal to voraciousness. If they're almost ready to start feeding, a fly that inspires playfulness or curiosity will draw more strikes.

• What fly do I use when a trout is actually feeding?

Match the predominant food item, even if the drift is a smorgasbord of different insects and the fish are taking everything.

A fly fisherman can set up a rough timetable of the daily cycle on most streams. The main feeding period occurs during the most pleasant period of the day for that particular season, midday or early afternoon for spring or late autumn, and dawn or dusk for midsummer. Not surprisingly, this corresponds to the best water temperature and the frequency of hatches on most streams. Minor feeding periods occur before or after the major feeding time, and an angler should put roughly a two-hour resting phase on either side of the main meal period to find the minor periods. Trout don't consciously set this rhythm; the feelings of hunger and satiation simply adapt to the cycle of food availability.

The first thing a fly fisherman has to do when he gets to the river is stop and watch the water. Before he chooses a fly, whether he does it empirically, generally, or scientifically, he has to find out where he is at that moment in the daily feeding cycle. He can do that if he studies the water for rises on the surface and flashing fish below the surface. Either seeing something or seeing nothing will tell him about the mood of the trout.

My Fly Box

Cripples

Bread (6)
(tied on the Flex Hook; the first
commercially available size will be
a 24 mm., number 6)

Creature (2-8)

Injured Minnow (4-6)
(a Charley Brooks fly tied with a
goose quill)

Comments:

Each of these flies represents "meat" to a predator. They are an easy meal,
however, only when fished with a certain degree of subtlety. The fly
fisherman can start his presentation by taking a hint from the bass anglers—
let the ripples fade away before imparting any motion to the fly. It is important even on running water to let the effect of the splash, which awakens
curiosity and caution at the same time in a trout, to fade from the memory
of the fish.

Chapter 4

The Empiricist in Us All

At that time, in the early fifties, in the older Italian neighborhoods of Hartford, people like my grandparents still kept rabbits, chickens, and even lambs in backyard pens. There wasn't a supermarket on all of Garden Street.

Do you think that I was a dummy like Tony Coagglia? That fool tried to fly, flopping two squares of cardboard strapped to his arms, hoping to impress us other five-year-olds. He broke one shoulder and a collarbone, probably because he kept his swan-dive tilt right to the end, his eyes bulging bigger and bigger until he splatted on the hard-packed dirt.

After watching this, I was going to make damn sure that my feet stayed under me. I took two of my grandfather's chickens up to the second floor porch, grabbed a bird by both legs in each hand, and jumped. A rain of white feathers followed me down. The horrible squawking drowned out any yelling from the gathering of children on the ground. Those chickens flapped like mad all the way down.

It must have helped some because both the chickens and I survived the fall, unhurt by all appearances. Of course, we ate scrambled eggs every morning for the next few weeks.

My mother ran outside. She grabbed me and checked me over for bruises and cuts. Then she sat down next to me on the porch step and put her arm around my shoulder. "Boy," she said, "some people learn by making mistakes. And it's clear to me that you're going to learn a lot in your life."

It was obvious even at that age that I had what it took to be an empiricist. Most fly fishermen probably do—the basic premise of fly fishing is that there are barriers, mysteries that men can never understand, protecting the fish. Those prove too frustrating for people with the wrong temperament.

The definition of empiricism, according to the *Book of Knowledge Dictionary*, is, "the belief that experience, especially of the senses, and not theory, is the only source of knowledge."

Of course, without theories, and with no history of successful experiences, the beginner simply has to jump blindly. The early learning through trial and error ends up being a series of blunders broken only by fluke catches.

My first season flailing Mill Brook was not only without rhyme or reason, but also without success. Day after day I'd go through every fly in my meager collection, giving every one a chance. In late August, during a rain storm, a crazed nine-inch rainbow in the Blowdown Pool rushed out from a tangle of tree branches to grab a McGinty. That was my only trout of the season—he made me a fly fishermen forever.

The three main methods of deciding on a particular fly are empiricism (trial and error tempered by previous experience), generalism (actually, a denial that fly choice is very important), and naturalism (bug watching).

The thought process for each would be:

(1) Empiricism—"I'm going to use a Pink Lady because that fly worked last year at this time when the river was in this condition."

(2) Generalism—"These fish will take any fly as long as I present it properly."

(3) Naturalism—"I'm going to use a Hendrickson to match these mayfly duns that are on the water."

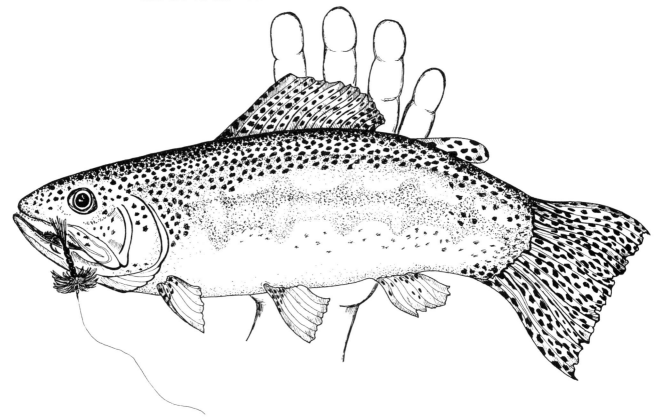

My first trout on a fly was caught on a ten cent McGinty, one of those poorly made foreign flies that used to come in an assortment of a half dozen patterns, all of them prepackaged in a plastic box. Those patterns, with webby hackles and overdressed bodies, sat flush in the film, probably mimicking drowned insects as well as better made flies.

The majority of fly fishermen are empiricists. The majority of fly fishermen are also not very good at what they do, but it is not their fault. They fish so little and their experiences are so random that when they stand there on the stream, staring into the compartments of a fly box, the choice is almost guaranteed to be a guess.

My hero (along with every other angler in our generation) is still Ray Bergman, the High Priest of the empirical school of fly choice. Most chapters in his _Trout_ are self-contained morality plays—the simple but stubborn rustic fishes through miserable conditions (water too high or too low, weather too hot or too cold, etc.) and long after everyone else has stumbled to the nearest bar in defeat, the determined flogger discovers the perfect fly or method for catching trout in awesome numbers and sizes. Of course, no one is left on the river to see him do it.

That's what always bothered me about trial and error methods. My own simple but stubborn rustic phase didn't last long. Yet, empiricism has its place—we all, even after years of fly fishing, resort to guessing. The secret of the method is using past experiences to limit possibilities to a workable number.

The Problems with Empiricism

The first thing that the empiricist has to understand is that he must carry a lot of patterns of all sizes, colors, and shapes, the odder the assortment the better. The empiricist adopts the exact opposite view from the generalist, who depends on a few flies fished skillfully. That is a denial of the importance of fly design. The empirical approach, on the contrary, is an exaltation of it.

One of my early goals was to tie every fly shown in the color plates of _Trout_ (1952 edition). That task accomplished, with enthusiasm if not skill, the next book of recipes for me was _A Fisherman's Handbook of Trout Flies_ by Donald Dubois. The thought of tying every one of the almost 6,000 patterns in that great work never even occurred to me, but it was always there as a "wish book" that could offer another oddity.

Even now, clustered around my fly tying table, are many fine recipe books: _Flies_ by J. Edson Leonard, _Fly Patterns of Yellowstone_ by Craig Mathews and John Juracek, _The Book of Fly Patterns_ by Eric Leiser, _Western Fly Tying Manual_ (both volumes) by Jack Dennis, and even an English book, _The New Illustrated Dictionary of Trout Flies_ by John Roberts.

The empiricist tries to catch trout by trial and error. His pure doggedness means that he'll never give up; he is only defeated when he runs out of time or he runs out of new flies. The latter would be a sin for the dedicated angler (maybe this explains why so many of us look more like backpackers than fishermen going to the stream).

The strict empiricist not only carries an amazing assortment of flies—he also has to fish a few favorite streams nearly every day of the season. The purpose isn't to foster a friendly familiarity, which is the way most anglers know their local streams, but instead to gain an intimacy spurred by the passion to discover every secret. Other fishermen visit waters; the empiricist lives with his.

One theory says that a fisherman is shaped by his rivers. The Letort controlled not only Vince Marinaro's angling life, but through him it beautifully infused *A Modern Dry Fly Code.* My goal has been to avoid being so strongly wed to one river. Each water has its own cure for complacency in fly fishing, humiliating any angler who tries to impose universal answers. On his home waters the empiricist can often get away with dogmatism (although it's always dangerous).

There are only a handful of rivers and streams that I could ever fish empirically. It's not only the total of days I've fished them that makes me comfortable with them but the fact that either through proximity or work (guiding) I've been on them nearly every day, in all kinds of weather, for more than one season. Yet, familiarity has never bred anything but respect for these rivers' unique complexities.

These special waters would be the Farmington River (Connecticut), my boyhood stream (1,147 angling days); the Clark Fork River (Montana), a highly alkaline and rich river near my Deer Lodge home (967 days); the Big Hole River (Montana), my favorite (901 days); the Little Blackfoot (Montana), the great grasshopper water (847 days); the Housatonic River (Connecticut), the eastern river that fishes like a western one (491 days); the Missouri River (Montana), below Holter Dam the world's largest spring creek (487 days); the Madison River (Montana), the long but fascinating riffle (460 days); Lolo Creek (Montana), not famous or even very special, except to me (283 days); the Henry's Fork (Idaho), which is both famous and special (269 days); and the Battenkill River (Vermont), where my family spent summers near Manchester (265 days). My first stream, Mill Brook in Connecticut, would also be on this list but the trout section was destroyed years ago when a golf course was built on it.

When I was fishing these waters all the time, I was able to make empirical choices. Now, however, my experiences are too faded, memories of the triumphs and not of the defeats; what good would such poorly balanced experiences do me on a river now? Empirical choices cannot be built on dreams, only on everyday reality.

How to be a better empiricist

Any angler excited by the thought of tying and carrying an endless selection of flies or fishing a local trout stream day in and day out is a born empiricist. Still, before he begins accumulating experiences, he has to understand why empirical reasoning is possible in trout fishing.

There is an artificial situation on many trout streams. It also serves as a greatly simplified example of the cyclical nature of all fisheries.

Gary LaFontaine

The Madison River, from below Quake Lake all the way to the Ennis channels, is a "fifty mile riffle." This doesn't mean that there aren't idiosyncrasies about it. Enough experiences help the angler know when, where, and how to fish this complex river. My own days on the Madison included four years of guiding, summers of sixty trips or more. The wonderful part of guiding was that days were seldom cancelled because of weather: cold or hot, still or windy, wet or dry— the clients fished hard, usually following my advice, and their successes or failures under every condition taught me something. Of course, on any day off, two or three of us guides had to rush over to the river to try out tactics and flies—we were there to catch trout, but even more so we were on the river to understand it better so that we could be even better guides.

English author John Roberts, in a 1988 letter, wrote:

> I remembered you describing on the Beaverkill River audio tape how you found out the feeding time for the hatchery fish and noted this for freshly released stock (merely to educate the rookies).
>
> When a big batch of rainbows escaped from the hatchery into one of our nearby chalk streams, I asked the riverkeeper (who also runs the stew ponds) what time they were fed. You can guess the rest. On the second day of their freedom, those trout went for the Mohawk as soon as it hit the water. As soon as one fish had hit it all the other new fish decided to surface feed too, but the only food on offer was the Mohawk. After fifteen minutes they began to get wise to it, but during the critical time 10 fish were duped.

The feeding schedule of wild trout is much more complex than that of hatchery fish, simply because one is trained by the clock and the other isn't, but both types of trout share the same dilemma—they have to wait for food. Wild trout seldom hunt anything in streams; they just let the currents deliver aquatic and terrestrial insects to them.

The empiricist isn't concerned only with the times of insect abundance, when nymphs are in the flow and adults are on the surface. He fishes so much that he needs the right fly for feeding as well as non-feeding moments. He changes his fly, or his method of presentation, until he discovers the right combination of pattern and approach.

What does he have when he catches a fish? A nugget of truth. His experience doesn't even need an explanation. All he has to do is remember every detail of the successful moment—the time of day, season, moon phase, tint of the sky, wind direction, stream color, water temperature, presence or absence of insects—and when he recognizes that moment again he'll know what fly to use.

The empirical fly fisherman doesn't ignore the hatches. He may not know the scientific, or even the common, name of an insect, but he recognizes the situation. In the same way that he experiments with patterns and approaches when nothing is hatching, he covers the rises with a variety of flies. When the trout tell him that his choice is right by hitting the pattern, he knows what to do the next day or the next season during that emergence.

Ron Pedale was a great one for mastering a hatch like this. On his home water, the Wood River in Rhode Island, he wouldn't even call an insect a mayfly or a caddisfly. Instead, he might call it the May 12th Brown or the June 5th Gray.

"What does the insect look like?" I asked him while we were waiting for a hatch.

"How do I know?"

"You mean you never even grabbed one off the water to look at it?"

He always had that smile and condescending snort that he saved for lifelong friends. "Take these flies. Don't make me embarrass you out here tonight."

He was an exquisite tyer. Sometimes a pattern looked just like it should, a recognizable match for a particular mayfly or caddisfly. Oddly, at other times, the fly appeared to be all wrong, the color, size, and even the shape clearly different than the natural on the stream.

This pattern was such an oddity. "There was a guide on the Big Hole who had a mayfly imitation that looked a bit like this," I said. "We used to call it Buck's Mess."

He waded out and started casting, "You can try your fancy flies first, if you want. You won't hurt my feelings."

Not me. Ron's fly took the better trout on the Wood, the ones that hung tight to the overgrown bank. Those fish sucked it down leisurely, like a natural, not splashily like they'd strike at an attractor. Later, the more exact imitations didn't do nearly as well.

This is why whenever an angler fishes a new area for the first time he should buy some of the "local killers." They may appear crude or even outlandish; more than likely, though, they'll just be different than his own stock of flies. They must catch trout, or they wouldn't sell. They represent the empirical consensus of the local fly fishing community, even if the reasons for their effectiveness aren't always clear.

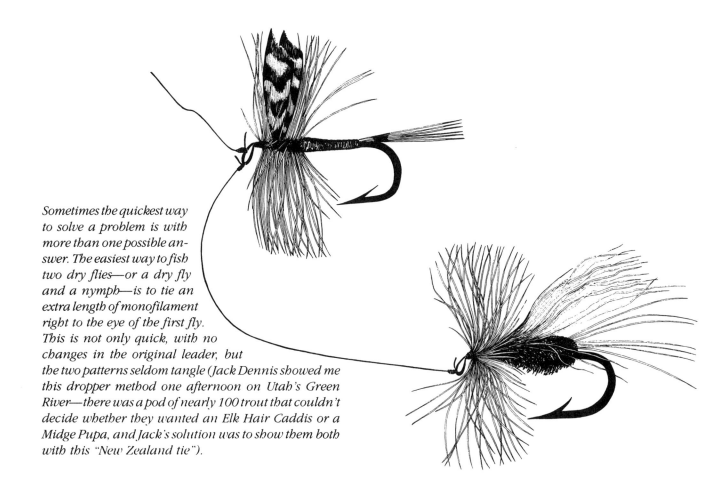

Sometimes the quickest way to solve a problem is with more than one possible answer. The easiest way to fish two dry flies—or a dry fly and a nymph—is to tie an extra length of monofilament right to the eye of the first fly. This is not only quick, with no changes in the original leader, but the two patterns seldom tangle (Jack Dennis showed me this dropper method one afternoon on Utah's Green River—there was a pod of nearly 100 trout that couldn't decide whether they wanted an Elk Hair Caddis or a Midge Pupa, and Jack's solution was to show them both with this "New Zealand tie").

The empirical fly fisherman hoards his experiences and notes certain patterns, or rhythms, which fall roughly into two types of cycles: daily and seasonal. The daily rhythms follow a 24-hour pattern. If the weather is stable, it changes little. A size 14 Foam Beetle that worked on the runs one day during the afternoon, for example, will work the next; trout do not crave diversity. However, daily rhythms aren't strong, and changes in the weather or water quickly make yesterday's experience worthless.

On the Madison River the changes in the summer wind control my choice of fly; this isn't even a conscious decision, but a pattern set from experiences through the years of midday fishing. Very little or no wind means a size 14 black ant; a breeze indicates a size 18 Jassid; a warm wind over eight miles an hour brings out a grasshopper; and if there's a gale—the type that usually accompanies the storm clouds—the fly isn't a terrestrial at all but a large Variant for bouncing on a taut' line.

Trout quickly lock into a daily rhythm. Let there be a week of copycat days and the fish become very predictable. Sometimes there's a change, not enough to affect the fish but enough to effect the insects. This sets up the mystery of the "miracle day."

The angler shows up on the river, it could be for the hundredth time or the first time on that stream, and the trout are waiting for him. They pile on his fly on every drift; presentation doesn't matter and nothing spooks them. The fishing is so spectacular, so easy, that the fly fisherman knows better than to take credit for the catch.

What happened? The dinner bell rang—the trout were hungry simply because they were used to feeding on a particularly abundant insect at a certain hour. Either the hatch or the egg-laying fall didn't come (this "missing meal" happens most with mayfly spinners; it seems as if a change in humidity can postpone the activity for hours). The trout were waiting, probably ready to sample any plausible tidbit, when the angler's fly drifted overhead.

The seasonal rhythms are much more stable and the major changes are more gradual. The empiricist in the East discovers that dark flies work well in the spring, with a steady fading of color to sulphurs and gingers and pale grays through early summer, until finally by midsummer white and cream patterns fool all species of trout consistently.

So it is on classic eastern waters with hours of hatch activity. In the bluster of opening day, the best chance for the dry fly, and a scattering of insects, is probably in the early afternoon. Week by week, as the weather warms, the hatches start a bit later each day until they finally peter out in the hottest days of August.

It might be important for me to know the "why" behind such cycles. On the Farmington why do my attractor dry flies do well on pools from 11 A.M to 1 P.M. during late May, and why do they work better on riffles from 4 P.M. to 6 P.M. during late June? The true empiricist doesn't need to know why—he only needs the body of knowledge that comes from successful moments.

If it happened once it will happen again. Fly fishermen can choose flies empirically, never even puzzling over unifying theories, because rhythms in nature are cyclical.

The odder the assortment the better it fits the empirical style of fly fishing. A strong attractor, such as the Double Wing, is as important as any imitation in the selection— with this fly, featuring a layering of colors over the tail that creates a prismatic brightness, the angler doesn't have to depend strictly on the hatches for rises.

To become a better empiricist the angler needs not only a large number of flies, but an intelligent assortment in major categories. It doesn't help him to have a hundred standard mayfly dressings in various color schemes. He needs a selection of flies that float either high or low, includes some bright and some non-reflective patterns, and feature different shapes, sizes and, finally, colors.

Prospecting empirically is a matter of refinement, like the child's game where someone tells the searcher, "You're getting warmer."

The angler floats his fly over good water. Even if he gets no reaction, the drift tells him something. He changes to a much different pattern, and maybe he gets a follow or a splash. He is getting closer to the truth.

My main dry fly categories are High-Profile Imitators, Low-Profile Imitators, High-Profile Attractors, and Low-Profile Attractors. My definition of dry flies, in the broader sense, includes a fifth type, Emergers, flies that float partly in and partly out of the water.

The profile of the fly describes how it sits on the surface film. The "low" pattern rides flush, because either its design or its weight makes the body rest right on the water. The "high" pattern sits lightly, hackle and tail holding the body above the surface.

If there are no trout rising, my first searching fly is usually a High-Profile Imitation, probably a size 14 Gray Fox Variant. Why? It has to do with the chosen water. My favorite spots are smooth runs, the streamy currents at the heads of pools and the slots against the deep bank. It's there where the surface is flat enough that any trout that flashes at the fly shows himself.

My friend, Brian Winship, does just the opposite. He starts by popping the riffles with a Low-Profile Attractor, usually a size 10 House & Lot. He reasons that even if he can't see the fish in the broken water, by covering pockets so quickly he will find any trout that are in a feeding mood.

Gray Fox Variant *Elk Hair Caddis* *Bivisible* *House & Lot*

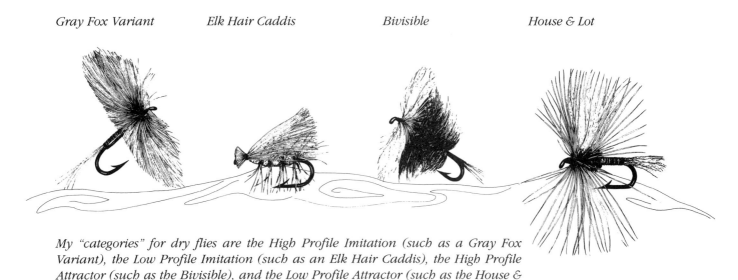

My "categories" for dry flies are the High Profile Imitation (such as a Gray Fox Variant), the Low Profile Imitation (such as an Elk Hair Caddis), the High Profile Attractor (such as the Bivisible), and the Low Profile Attractor (such as the House & Lot). The key to finding the dry fly answer on a trout stream empirically, by trial-and-error, is not to change just flies but categories.

The first fly that provokes a strike is seldom the perfect pattern. Do the trout just jump all over it? If so, then it's right. Usually, though, once the profile is working, the empirical angler still narrows the variables. Will a size 14 work better? What about a pattern with a taller wing? Or does a drab fly fit the day?

There's a way to play trial and error more efficiently. Once the profile is chosen, the angler can fish the original fly and a variation together. Every trout that strikes offers an opinion, and if one pattern is significantly more popular, the winning fly points clearly towards an empirical solution.

The miracles of empiricism

In one way empirical experiences are superior even to the carefully crafted triumphs of the finest fly fishing minds. The history of fly fishing is full of theories on what should work—and successes can be backed by brilliant arguments. But this scientific method is also limited by the boundaries of logic.

Only empiricism can find the illogical solution. The answer to an angling moment, through trial and error, isn't the child of any idea. The successful result doesn't have to fit any theory. It happened, and the explanation of why it happened doesn't have to come before or even after.

The inconsistencies, of course, drive fly fishermen like me crazy. There's always a reason that a certain fly works wonderfully. The inquisitive angler can study the trout, searching for clues in the way they react to an artificial. Or he can study the water, trying to understand the physical laws that alter the trout's perception of an object. Or, finally, he can study the insects, looking for a link between the pattern and an important food in the trout's diet. Somewhere in that triangle causation exists.

Maybe the fact that empiricists need to have such confidence, even unreasonable faith, in the value of random experience explains why some of them are superstitious souls. Most of my friends who are empiricists believe in the magic of moon phases; most of my friends who are scientists do not.

Will Eaton told us on the Esopus, "We'll want to be on the best water at 3:25 P.M. There's a major Solunar Period then."

"Solunar Period?" Tory Stosich laughed. "Do you have a voodoo doll of the trout that we can stick hooks into, too?"

Will then went out and caught more fish than either of us, working the fly magnificently from 3:25 P.M. onward. He twitched, skittered, and skated his fly with total concentration, not worrying at all about insect hatches, sunlight shifts, or water conditions (all of the things that we fussed about).

His success didn't change my skepticism. "You fished beautifully. This just happened to be one of those days when fly type didn't matter."

The experience didn't stop Tory from scoffing, either. "Trout have a cycle of feeding and not feeding. You want me to believe that a Solunar Period suddenly makes them hungry, no matter when it happens?"

What does an angler have when he catches a trout? If he'll take a moment to remember everything he can about the situation, he gains a nugget of truth that he'll be able to apply in the future to similar situations. That simple act of reflection, not just thinking about the circumstance but savoring it, plants the experience deeper in the angler's memory. Empirical learning is more complete when a person consciously dwells on sensations associated with the primary act.

Fly fishermen in England are much better empiricists (and always have been) than fly fishermen in the United States. It has to do with the English system of fee angling. Like it or not an angler there is often restricted to one stream. He belongs to an association that controls a portion of a fishery, and because of economics most of his angling days are spent on that water. Not only he but an entire membership focuses on the problems of catching trout in a particular stream; that leads, often through trial and error, to solutions.

If it's any consolation to American fly fishermen, since the early 1900s they have led the way in innovations both in tactics and fly design. These advances have come mostly from the angler-entomologists, whose work is driven by research into the habits and form of the trout's food.

English tyers, old and new, have created wet flies and dry flies with odd, unexplainable characteristics. There is little speculation now on why a particular trait should be included in the dressing—it simply is included because its effective has been proven over the years. Their patterns feature innovations as old as tinsel tags (or tips) or as new as ethafoam flotation balls. If there's a magic beyond the obvious, beyond the fact that the tinsel flash increases the visibility of the fly or that a ball of ethafoam tied in as a hump makes an emerger float in the proper position, then that's just part of the mystery.

In truth, there is an entomological reason for the effectiveness of the tag (which also explains why the right place for it is at the butt end of the pattern). It took me a long time to find it, but the fact that the tag is such a consistent feature repeated in so many standard patterns made me believe that it was more than just a tying custom.

During an emergence a mayfly, just like a caddisfly, generates air to split the outer skin. There's a difference, however. The sheath over the caddisfly pupa is transparent, and inside the air sparkles in the light. The skin over the mayfly nymph is thick chitin, and the bubble doesn't show over most of the body. The only area where it is visible is at the back of the abdomen, at the butt end. The skin there stretches from the accumulation of air, and it becomes so thin that the tail end of the nymph glows softly, looking silver in the lighter-colored insects or gold in the darker, brown-skinned insects. On old drab wet fly patterns like the Ash Fox or Bustard & Black, the tinsel tag adds the spark that makes them look very much like mayfly emergers budding at the surface.

The magic of the tinsel tag is not just its random flash; and the effectiveness of the foam emerger is not due just to its float position. These mysteries, with enough observation and speculation, can be explained by that triangle of natural causes. Many others, in spite of all the research, never fit into a neat theory and there is no danger of running out of such mysteries in fly fishing.

How much does empirical knowledge generalize?

With no prompting from me, my friends have been confirming my suspicion about brown trout. Graydon Fenn tells me that the Housatonic River

(Connecticut) browns like white flies. Wayne Anderson says that Wolf River (Wisconsin) browns like white flies. On my own upper Clark Fork (Montana) the browns like white flies. Who knows why? There seems to be absolutely no connection to any aquatic or terrestrial insect. Brown trout simply respond better everywhere to white patterns, both dry and wet, than rainbow trout or brook trout do.

There was a day in California. It was my first ever on Rush Creek in the meandering stretch between Silver and Grant Lakes, but at 7:00 in the evening, with the May light hitting the stream, it felt like I'd been there before. I have never liked that feeling—Marcel Proust, in *Remembrances of Things Past*, used the term *déja vu*, but this wasn't the Champs-Elysees and I gave into the sensation and dug through my boxes for my last Cross Special.

It was easy to pinpoint the dates of my original Connecticut memory— 1958–1959. Those were the years I bought Cross Specials from Caturna's Hardware in Windsor. There was a tiny fishing section, with a single tray of flies, in the back. Which stream, I wondered, reminded me of Rush Creek? Maybe it was Salmon Brook, where my fishing logs showed spectacular evenings with a small Cross Special, a classic eastern dry fly with drake wood duck wings, light blue dun hackle and tail, and grayish white fox fur dubbing.

The Cross Special curled next to Rush Creek's deep banks, riding the line between the slack water and the main current. It didn't have to be too close. As a matter of fact, it worked better if it drifted a foot out from the undercuts. Not all of the trout it fooled were small. Among the dozen fish in a fast two hours were a 16- and a 14-inch brown.

It is possible to cast "too close" to the bank. When a trout is tucked into an undercut, he might not notice a fly drifting tight to the grass. This happened to me on Rush Creek. My "sloppy" drifts were getting more strikes than my perfect ones against the over-hangs. The fish were willing to come out for a fly if they could see it.

Can empirical experiences generalize? They can sometimes with attractor flies. An unusual fly catches trout because some aspect of its appearance interacts with an external influence and makes a fish curious. Those external influences that affect the pattern—water speed, water depth, stream bottom configuration, type of bank cover, color of the sunlight—can be duplicated in streams thousands of miles apart. The angler seeing a river for the first time can look at a small stretch and say to himself, "That reminds me of the Such-and-Such River, and a size 14 Cross Special always works there on the pools."

Empirical knowledge does not generalize particularly well when there's an entomological basis for the feeding. So what if an angler knows the hatches on his home water? Streams that are close by may not have the same insects. Even if they do, the daily cycle is usually different, making an angler's experiences less valuable on strange rivers. A fly like a Cross Special may be an imitation of a Catskill mayfly (although I've never seen one with precisely that coloring in the East), but it's an oddity, with the contrast of brownish-yellow wing, pale gray hackle, and almost white body, that would fail as a hatch-matcher in most selective feeding situations. As a subtle attractor, on the other hand, it is valuable anywhere.

The majority of fly fishermen are empiricists. The majority of fly fishermen are not very good at choosing the right fly for the moment. The very basis for living in close proximity to *one* trout stream, the rural economy, has eroded steadily in this century. Most anglers, like everyone else, live in cities or suburbs and fish on weekends or on vacations. There are so few simple rustics anymore.

It's the blessing—or curse—of our fly fishing that there are so many fine public waters. The North American angler, with the mobility of good roads and fast cars, can easily reach many rivers in any of our trout states. Air travel extends that range—my itinerary for one ten-day period last summer included days on the Metolius (Oregon), Pere Marquette (Michigan), and Green (Utah). Situations like these force us to look for universal theories, truths that will allow us to choose the proper fly anywhere, and not for simple experiences. They make us into scientific anglers.

My Fly Box

Stonefly Imitations

Air Head (8-16)
(the most valuable all-around stonefly imitation in my selection for the heavy, mixed hatches of Plecoptera on the smaller mountain streams of the West; tied in cream, brown, and olive variations)

Bird's Stonefly (2-6)

Flex Stone (6)
(tied on the Flex Hook; the two variations, the Orange Flex Stone and the Ginger Flex Stone, imitate very large stoneflies)

Fluttering Stone
(the Orange Fluttering Stone, in sizes 2, 4, and 6, matches the Salmon Fly and the Yellow Fluttering Stone, in sizes 6, 8, 10, matches the Golden Stone)

Improved Sofa Pillow (2-6)

Jughead (2-6)

Little Olive Stonefly (14-18)

Little Yellow Stonefly (14-18)
(both the Yellow and the Olive versions are designed for mimicking the ubiquitous, midday stoneflies of summer on western rivers)

Picket Pin (8-12)

Snow Stone (16-20)
(the imitation for *Capnia*, the winter stonefly)

Stopper (8-12)
(this pattern was created by Nick Nicklas, a guide out of West Yellowstone; guides are always practical about fly design)

Comments:

The actions of adult stoneflies are usually controlled by the weather. On warm, dry days the egg-layers fly freely and bounce vigorously on the water—the females that splash on the surface to lay their eggs, such as the giant Salmon Fly (*Pteronarcys californica*), swim strongly back towards shore. On cold, damp days, however, any adult that lands on the water, by accident or intent, drifts with the current and, at most, struggles weakly.

The angler has to observe the adult stoneflies and choose his imitation to match their behavior. A high-riding, light fly, like the Fluttering Stone, mimics the active insect. A flush, heavy fly, like the Jughead, floats like the mired natural.

The importance of this difference is never more evident than during the Salmon Fly hatch. Anglers stock up on an assortment of popular imitations, but unless their guide tells them which pattern to use and why, too many fishermen chuck them randomly. The results, however, are not random—the selectivity of feeding trout to these big insects is strong, especially when the hatch has been in the area for a few days, and the wrong choice in fly style can mean spectacular failure, while at the same time the right choice is producing spectacular success.

Chapter 5

The Generalist Be Damned

(this includes me)

For most of 1974 the only pattern in my box was a Muddler Minnow. The color, and even the style, was the same for every fly, but the Muddlers were tied in a range of sizes, from size 16 all the way up to 3/0. Also, since this wasn't strictly a dry fly experiment, they could be fished unweighted or weighted, as streamers or nymphs as well as surface flies.

This wasn't a revolt against the hundreds of patterns in my normal stock (at first, the absence of all those flies caused me horrible withdrawal pains); it wasn't an extreme example of a fly fisherman embracing simplicity, either. Rather, relying on this single pattern was an experiment for discovering when fly type wasn't important to the trout. Willingly or not, it made me into a generalist.

The Muddlers meant to be fished wet were kept in a plastic bag between sheets of soaked felt, always absorbing water so that they would sink immediately. The ones for surface fishing were sprayed with Scotch Guard repellent so that they would never absorb water, but that had to be done the day before a trip (there'd be a white powder on these flies from the dried Scotch Guard).

 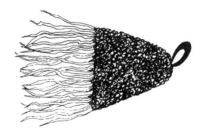 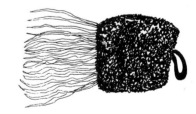

Our experiments with Muddler Minnows indicated that changing just one feature, the shape and density of the deer hair head, created patterns that performed best in different situations. The original shaggy head (Gapen style) worked well as a shallow water streamer; the denser shaved head (sculpin style) attracted by "sound" in deeper water; and the thick head (Bailey style) made the fly into a good hopper imitation.

One of my conclusions after a year was that the Muddler was a much better fly for large trout than for small trout—and this wasn't just due to the size of the pattern. It was the roughness, the shagginess, that made the fly intimidating to fish under ten inches and a tease to fish over fourteen inches.

My flies could be fished dry, but the heads were fairly sparse on them. They were patterned after samples from Dan Gapen, the son of Don Gapen, the fly's originator. This style became my favorite imitation for large, drifting nymphs, but eventually it was replaced by Muddlers with different heads for both dry fly and streamer fishing.

On the Yellowstone, when A. J. McClane first showed Dan Bailey a Muddler, his comment was, "What the hell is that thing?"

Dan must have figured out on his own that it was a grasshopper, because he made the deer hair head denser and larger and turned the pattern into a good floater. He also popularized it on rivers with trophy fish—the Muddler Minnow and big trout were soon linked forever.

Surprisingly, testing the Muddler underwater as a minnow imitation revealed that major characteristics, such as size or color, were less important traits than originally thought. Our Muddlers, with their scraggly heads, didn't fail but they didn't excel either as sculpin imitations.

The pattern's paltry performance wasn't the result of something the trout were seeing. The movement of the fly hid the shape of the head, but in our scuba diving tests below Hauser Dam on the Missouri, one style still worked better than any other. If it wasn't what the trout were seeing, it had to be what they were "feeling." A later variation, with densely packed hair shaved so that the head made a blunt front, fooled trout even before they saw it. They would spin around and hunt for that particular Muddler in the deep spill basin below the dam—others they'd merely accept.

Were there pressure waves? Was the blunt-head Muddler displacing water just like the sculpin, with trout responding to the "matching sound" of this motion? It seemed as if fish were picking up the fly through the lateral line. If so, this meant that an unseen characteristic could be as important as a visible one on sunken patterns.

My fishing experiences with the Muddler as a dry fly during the year indicated that it was a passable imitation of many things but a great imitation of nothing. As a caddisfly, stonefly, or even a grasshopper it caught trout better than non-matching patterns, but it also failed over a lot of rising fish when these insects were on the water.

The basic silhouette was so wrong for mayflies that it did poorly as a dead-drift imitation of upwings. The only hope during a hatch was to fish the fly like a streamer; then, looking like a foolish minnow swimming through the feeding territory of a trout, it sometimes drew quick, slashing strikes.

It worked best as a dead-drift dry fly when there were no hatches. As a searcher it was successful because it could look like so many things and it was acceptable to trout when they were looking for nothing. As a specific imitation, however, it was always missing something.

What it lacked, both as a wet fly and as a dry fly, was what the innovative fly tyer seeks in his imitations—not a general representation of life but of those characteristics that trout look for in a specific living organism. The fact that this characteristic might be different for every organism doomed the Muddler, not to failure but to mediocrity, in tough situations.

It wasn't that the Muddler Minnow did badly over the year. My full selection of flies would have caught more trout—but the Muddler caught at least 85 percent of that expected total. It would have caught an even higher percentage if I hadn't pressed it into situations where it would fail (thereby breaking the first rule of the generalist school).

Throughout the year there were very few situations where an imitation designed for the problem or an attractor slanted to a situation couldn't have done better than a Muddler. The type of fly and the tying style was almost always important on a trout stream.

My friends fished alongside me, patiently acting as surrogates, using the patterns that I would have used; most of them were very skillful fly fishermen and they typically caught more fish. My Muddler was never perfect, not as a dry fly, but it never flopped completely either. It never looked right but it never looked wrong, and sometimes that was enough for it to top the day.

Call me a generalist. There are a handful of patterns in my fly boxes that I use out of habit. That makes me, like many fly fishermen, someone who doesn't believe that it's necessary to think about exact flies all of the time.

The extreme view that vehemently denies the importance of fly pattern at any time might be a reaction to either the impossibility of carrying the perfect fly for every situation, or of learning the life habits of every major and minor trout food form.

One anonymous wag wrote a poem in *The Journal of the Fly Fisher's Club* (London):

> . . . I am a heretical brute
> Who does not believe
> That in order to achieve
> A dish
> Of fish . . .
> It is necessary to be an entomologist

Aren't there fly fishermen who carry only two or three patterns and catch more trout than everybody else? It's a nice story, the stubborn individualist thumbing his nose at fussy notions and outfishing everyone with just "Old Reliable."

Here's another story of a close friend, who certainly qualifies as stubborn, one of these "a few patterns is all I need" men. He was going to prove it to me on the Delaware River in New York.

As we walked along the bank there were fish rising all over the flat. He ignored them. "All of the trout in the Delaware stack up in the riffles, at the heads of the pools," he insisted. "Those are the only places worth fishing in this river."

I waved over the long flat, "What about these fish?"

"Those aren't trout."

Some of the sippers, their noses poking out on each rise, were in very close. "They're brown trout."

He kept walking towards the riffle. "It doesn't matter because it's not worth the time trying to catch them anyway."

These browns probably couldn't be caught, not on an Adams or a Henryville or even a Muddler. They were regular, selective feeders preoccupied with a hatch of small mayfly duns. They sipped a matching Compara Dun presented on a fine leader very nicely.

My friend concentrated on the riffles, skillfully fished with his pet patterns, and caught a number of those fat Delaware rainbows, at least equaling my total on the browns. So what did he prove? That he really only needed a few patterns, or that he could cope with the limitations of his fly selection?

How to be a Better Generalist

The generalist school of thought is not new—it is one side of an old battle between those who carry many flies and those who insist on the effectiveness of the few. Even these extremes are ancient arguments, threading back into wet fly history.

In the *Practical Angler*, W. C. Stewart claimed that his famous wet Spiders, fished upstream, were the only flies an angler needed to produce a suitable bag of trout. Yet here was a man who complained bitterly about the difficult stocks of fish in the river. He worked his water from sunrise until four in the afternoon, apparently with little rest, to fool his "par" of twelve pounds of trout. How many times were his three favorite patterns snubbed by discriminating fish? Maybe his catch was more a testament to his incredible endurance, a search for those scattered trout with more catholic tastes, than to skill or intelligence.

He created his own dilemma. By casting a lightly dressed fly upstream dead-drift he was mimicking an emerging insect, a stage that trout typically feed on selectively. At the same time Stewart was limiting himself to a few general patterns. He could tout his killing flies, but anglers without the stamina for twelve-hour days might disagree with him.

Everybody's list of general patterns, limited to three, would be different. My assortment of dry flies, leaving out my own creations, would have a Gray Fox Variant, a Poly Caddis, and a Crowe Beetle. Bill Vessie, my fishing partner in Deer Lodge who covers all of the same waters, listed an Elk Hair Caddis, an Adams, and a Royal Trude as his three patterns (with the footnote that if he was still living in the East, a Light Cahill would have to be in the assortment). This shows how anglers develop faith in different flies.

My patterns supply the most important aspect of searching imitations: suggestiveness. Each of them looks like a major food form, and in shape at least one or the other would mimic something that a fish has been rising to recently.

Many factors are going to effect an angler's list of favorite flies—the section of the country he lives in is going to be one of the strongest influences. The "cultural" bias of an area alone is going to put certain patterns in mind. My fishing partner, Bill Vessie, chose the Elk Hair Caddis, the Adams, and the Royal Trude as his three "must" flies. He picked these for our western Montana trout streams so that he would have a downwing (to imitate stoneflies as well as caddisflies), an upwing (to imitate mayflies), and a general attractor (for bouncing riffles). These patterns would do as well as any fly in most situations—covering maybe 90 percent of the fishing in our area.

The Gray Fox Variant (devised by Preston Jennings) is a mayfly that sits high on the surface, perched on hackle tips and tail. The body doesn't touch the water, which not only minimizes the importance of color but also means that the Gray Fox can be twitched at an appropriate moment. The Poly Caddis (developed by Gary Borger), the eminently practical caddisfly imitation, works best as an adult searcher during non-hatch times. It ends up on my cast as often as any other fly. The Crowe Beetle serves me better than a grasshopper or an ant pattern as a general terrestrial fly simply because the ubiquitous beetle is much more prevalent in the trout's diet than most fly fishermen realize; a trout's stomach isn't always jammed with them, but there are always a few in any sampling.

Let me add one of my own patterns to the selection and it would be the Emergent Sparkle Pupa or the Clear Wing Spinner. Either of them possesses the magic of Sparkle Yarn (Antron or Creslan fibers). This gives them not only brightness, but on surface flies it adds the cluster of natural air bubbles around the material. The wonder of Sparkle patterns is that they're always more than imitations—at the same time that they're matching some insect they're working as attractors to pull trout from beyond the feeding range.

How could I leave off a Royal Trude, which has caught more trout for me than any other dry fly? There should be an attractor like the Royal Trude on the list, but the three imitations are the minimum for covering the bulk of feeding activity. It would kill me to be in the middle of a heavy hatch and stand no chance.

If I could put a few more flies on the basic list one would be a Royal Trude. Then I'd add a Muddler Minnow (dry version), a Humpy, and a Wulff variation (either a Gray Wulff or a Were Wulff). An Adams wouldn't be a high

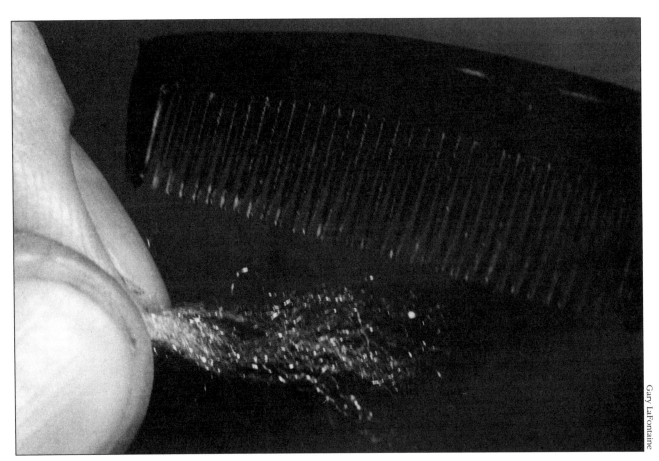

Gary LaFontaine

Patterns such as the Clear Wing Spinner and the Emergent Sparkle Pupa feature the brightness of Sparkle Yarn. This material reflects light because the individual filaments are three- or four-sided instead of round.

choice, but a Gray Coughlin, a dry fly that fills the same niche for me, would have to be there. What about some of the more recent innovations, such as a Caucci/Nastasi Compara Dun, a Stevenson Fluttering Stone, or a Mathews Sparkle Dun? My fly box would be empty without a . . . but there we go. Pretty soon I'd be right back to my indispensable carrying stock of hundreds of patterns.

"Presentation is everything," the generalist insists.

This is the extreme point of view that holds whether or not a trout takes a fly depends entirely on correct presentation; and that the pattern itself, except for general similarities, is not important even when trout are feeding on naturals.

My belief, after a year of fishing one fly in trout streams across the country, is quite the opposite: Being a practical generalist means recognizing the inadequacies of the philosophy. Then, if he wants to catch trout consistently with just a few patterns, he has to alter when, where, and how he fishes to avoid situations where his flies will do poorly—or, he has to find situations where any reasonable dry fly will work.

Maybe it's possible to devise a grading system for trout streams, the levels ranging from Chump Water to Graduate School. In some places, usually smaller, infertile streams, the fish are easy to catch, or at least easy to fool, and these waters would qualify as "chump," or if that's too derogatory for something as special as these delightful brooks, then "forgiving" or "generous" fisheries. At the other end, the Graduate School rivers don't achieve their status just because the trout in them are tough to catch—no, their fame comes because they hold large, free-rising trout that are tough to catch.

Popular myth has it that trout are naturally sophisticated in tough waters; that somehow a river breeds fussier feeders. It's not true; the fussiness is linked to the richness of the stream, but that abundance of food affects the daily state of mind of the fish and not their level of sophistication.

Tumbling mountain streams running over granite, with a paucity of hatches, are easy to understand. The trout are opportunistic feeders in these waters. Even in slower areas they don't study a natural or artificial; there's a

R. Valentine Atkinson

Trout in bouncing streams are "easy" not because they lack intelligence but because they can only watch a small patch of surface for passing food. Anything going overhead—and usually in mountain streams there isn't one dominant insect—has to be snatched quickly.

hastiness in every feeding action that precludes scrutiny. The quicker movement to the insect or fly is linked to the lesser number of food items passing through the trout's window per minute (five insects per minute seemingly the lower limit for selectivity). When those items are coming at random intervals, spaced far apart, a feeding trout automatically rises up through the water faster—call it impatience. That hastiness in infertile streams is what makes fish easier to fool most of the time.

In the opposite type of water, rich environments with stable flows and temperatures and heavy hatches (such as spring creeks and tailwater rivers) the fish are seldom desperate for food. They can slip into a daily rhythm because the insects, either during emergence or egg-laying, appear predictably and in adequate numbers. It is not a routine that trout have to think about because their daily clock, with its feeding and resting cycle, becomes attuned to it. During a hatch, with insects passing overhead so fast that a fish couldn't take them all, they rise with a regular, unhurried rhythm. This lack of haste makes them tough to fool in rich waters.

David Dunne monitored a brown trout with a radio tag in Colorado's Delores River. This was a nice fish of seventeen inches, but he never chased minnows or hunted crayfish. He was a confirmed insect feeder, rising in a

R. Valentine Atkinson

The smooth, slow flows of spring-fed fisheries such as Silver Creek in Idaho allow trout to feed selectively. The fish can sip steadily during the heavy hatches, locking onto the characteristics of a single insect species.

quiet slot of a straight, deep pool during hatches and resting in a holding lie under submerged brush otherwise. This fish exhibited two states of mind, either feeding (usually selectively) or resting (in a very non-receptive posture). He showed none of the in-between anxiousness of a trout in less-favored water.

This is what the generalist encounters in rich streams; this, and not superior intelligence on the part of the fish, explains why both general searching and attractor patterns often do poorly there. The fish are never in a mood to just randomly sample odd food forms or non-matching flies—they have an on/off switch with no intermediate stages. The only hope for the generalist is to find trout that, although they're feeding heavily on a hatch, are not rigidly selective either.

With wild trout this is not a matter of looking for "stupid" fish. The belief that species such as brook trout or cutthroat trout are not as smart as rainbow trout or, especially, brown trout is another myth. Actually, any trout has so little intelligence that whatever slight differences there might be between species plays little part, if any, in how difficult they are to fool with a fly. The habitat each species prefers, and its instinctive tendencies, not its brain power, determines catchability.

Don't believe this? Bass, of course, are much harder to catch than bluegills. In laboratory studies, however, bluegills learn new tasks much quicker, and are clearly "smarter," than bass. It's just that in natural environments, with a diet of smaller food items, bluegills feed constantly and bass don't.

The Yellowstone River, in Yellowstone National Park, hosts two distinct groups of cutthroats—resident and migratory. The fish here qualify as a joke among fly fishermen—the dumbest trout in the world. This may be true on opening day, July 15th, when anybody with almost any fly can hook fish after fish. This is when the "easy" group is in the river—spawners that come down from Yellowstone Lake each spring. By mid-July they are returning slowly to the lake, but these stillwater cutthroat, ravenous after the winter, don't know how to feed efficiently in a running water environment.

Pity the poor fly fisherman who shows up in September. The river isn't unnaturally jammed with trout. The cutthroats left in the Yellowstone are the residents. The angler has heard the stories of fifty-fish days on any fly, no matter how atrocious, but at the Sulphur Caldron the cutthroats are sipping Buffalo Gnats matched by a size 20 midge pupa imitation. These trout drift back under even a good simulation waiting for the slightest drag. The angler doesn't fool fifty fish. He leaves the river truly humbled.

The trout from the lake and the trout in the river are the same species—there is no genetic difference. Yet, in the angler's lexicon, one is incredibly dumb and the other is incredibly smart. In September, when there are only resident trout in the river, superb fly fishermen such as Mike Lawson and Bob Jacklin, who know both fisheries, claim that the Yellowstone can be tougher than the Henry's Fork.

The hatchery trout in our streams are not stupid, either, just maladapted to a new environment. After they've been in a river for a week or so, they

Ken Parkany

Are cutthroats stupid? In the Yellowstone River these fish follow a wading angler, picking up the nymphs that are stirred loose. When an angler stops moving, the trout wait for a few moments, but shortly they get impatient and begin bumping the angler's foot. That is a pretty involved thought process for a fish. They not only anticipate a food source, but are smart enough to understand what creates the drift of nymphs. Then, if it stops happening, they attempt to nudge the "agent," which is the foot, back into action.

are easy to catch. During their first few days in the stream this is not necessarily so—they've been trained to feed on pellets, and they can be selective to flies that resemble a small brown chunk. Quickly enough they get hungry, and since they don't recognize live food, they rise to anything. It is months, if ever, before they conform to the rhythm of the stream.

The generalist doesn't have to search for misfit trout, either hatchery or wild, and he doesn't have to stalk only those generous streams with undiscriminating fish. The real challenge for him is discovering areas and times, even in rivers famous for tough situations, where he can fool trout.

It's strange how the physical configuration of certain areas in a stream make fish rise faster or farther than normal. This happens not just in riffles, where current speed and broken water both help obscure the fly. There are subtler spots where general flies fool trout.

There is a deeper, meandering slot in any flat, a place with good cobble rock for holding structure. Even though the water smooths out here, however, the flow moves a bit too quickly for rising trout to hang just under the surface. These fish swim up from the bottom each time to take an insect. The initial decision to accept or reject a fly is made through all that water, and even a couple of feet is far for a nearsighted trout. Once he has risen, and expended energy, the fish often takes a fly even if it's not a perfect imitation.

The lip of the pool, where trout frequently hold in the evening to sip mayfly spinners, has a reputation for being tough water. At first glance, there seem to be obvious reasons—the trout see the fly clearly because they're close to it and the surface is smooth. Actually, the lip is an area where the fly doesn't have to be perfect. The water, as it approaches the edge, accelerates and the insect or fly speeds up slightly and trout are forced to rise faster than usual to intercept an object.

Dick Fryhover must have seen my eyes go wide the first time he showed me the huge pods of rising trout on the Missouri. He just said to me, "They're not as tough as you think."

They weren't, either. The rainbows were just under the surface next to the bank, sipping mayfly duns, but with each fish poking up every few seconds the school was competing for space as well as food, and the controlled frenzy seemed to reduce selectivity. Trout in the pod accepted an Adams—the same fly that individual fish feeding on the hatch snubbed completely.

During any warm summer rain, on canopy streams, the toughest fish turn easy. The drops beat the leaves, rivulets run in from the banks, and if the water doesn't rise too rapidly (and it won't during a soft rain) the trout often accept any dry fly. Small terrestrial patterns imitate the insects washed off the trees. This is my time to put on a dry McGinty. The Crowe Beetle would do well, also.

Except on mornings when a mist rolls off the water, dry fly fishing always seems easier at dawn, just as the light is changing. The fish feed heavily on drifting nymphs, which are free in the current because of a behavioral response to the light, but then as the day brightens the drift stops suddenly. The trout still watch for food, and in shallow areas they take dry flies (especially flush floating ones that mimic emerging insects) well.

The hatch itself is not as tough to match at the start. Trout decide to rise when the concentration of insects in and on the surface makes repetitive effort an efficient way to gather food, but at first they don't have a search pattern, a set of visual cues, firmly in mind. At the end of the hatch, when most fish have quit, there are still a few stubborn risers picking up strays, but the insects are sporadic and these fish may not be fussy, either. It's during the middle of the emergence that trout, in very rhythmic feeding, want to know the pedigree of anything floating overhead.

The value of these strategies, not just for the confirmed generalist but for the average fly fisherman, is that they're universal. If the angler gets caught on any river or stream, with no idea of what's hatching, he can still find places to fool trout with a general fly.

Why does the Generalist Approach work at all? That's simple. There may be a better fly for a particular moment, but the thinking fly fisherman has to search for it. He guesses wrong, fusses with the problem, and tries another pattern that's slightly different. While he's changing flies the generalist isn't wasting any of his angling time; his fly is on the water. The efficiency of having only three flies gives the generalist an advantage over all but the most expert empiricists and imitationists.

No, it isn't necessary to be an entomologist to catch fish, but too often a few flies aren't enough on a trout stream. It's bad enough that they won't

It's the environment, as much as anything else, that determines whether a fish will be "easy" or "hard" to catch. Even brook trout, in rich, slow water habitats, can be notoriously fussy surface feeders. Vince Marinaro, in A Modern Dry Fly Code, *writes about Big Spring Creek, "Three or four hundred feeding trout was a fair estimate of those within my view. A like amount was estimated by each of my friends, making a rough total of one thousand or more brook trout rising at the same time but rising to something that was invisible to every one of us. On comparing notes with the others at the end of the day, after the first tentative queries were warily exchanged disclosing a position that was equally embarrassing to all of us, I found that they had caught nothing and were as mystified as I was."*

be able to match the color, size, and shape of important hatches. The real limitation is the small range of behaviors that a few flies can mimic. Maybe a dozen of so carefully selected designs, each one sitting a bit differently on the water, would fit the major forms of dry fly presentation.

Generalist tactics often save me on a trout stream. What stops me from being a generalist all of the time? Even if an assortment of three flies could cover 99 percent of trout problems, it would still be the other 1 percent of the fish that would be worth catching. There's room in my box for a few, *reliable* patterns. The generalist, with nothing else, often avoids the toughest trout. This damns him to mediocrity. My large assortment often damns me to hundreds of casts, and a skunking, over one contrary fish.

That's my choice.

My Fly Box

Searcher/General Patterns

Adams (10-18)
(this is the top searcher—and general pattern—for most fly fishermen; it is not my favorite, but only because there is another fly that fills that all-around niche for me)

Carmichael's Indispensable (12-16)

Beacon Beige (14-16)

Beaverkill Red Fox (14-18)

Black Gnat (10-14)
(black is a surprisingly useful color; it provides strong contrast)

Blue Dun (16-20)
(a fly worth tying even in very small sizes; it serves as a general midge imitation in tiny versions)

Blue Upright (14-16)

Burr's Bright (14-18)
(the body is a fluorescent green)

Carrottop (14-18)
(this is a parachute fly, not my usual type of searcher, but it is a highly visible pattern that works for me when trout want a "last bite" after a general feeding period)

Cross Special (10-20)
(my main light-bodied searcher)

Cowdung (8-12)

Dark Montreal (8-12)

Female Adams (12-14)
(sometimes the butt of a different color makes a difference)

Ginger Quill (14-18)
(one of the important natural colors)

Gray Coughlin (10-22)
(this fly is the reason the Adams is not important for me; an incredibly fine general pattern, every aspect of it combining to define "bug" for the trout)

Greenwell's Glory (14-18)

Grizzly King (8-12)

Hornberg (10-16)
(this classic pattern isn't even found in many modern catalogs; that's a grievous oversight)

Housatonic Quill (12-16)
(a good fly; it's in my selection because of my lifelong affair with the namesake river)

John Storey (12-16)
(an English pattern; on my "indispensable" list of searching flies)

Leadwing Coachman (10-20)
(second only to the Gray Coughlin in my affections)

Leckford Professor (10-12)
(only in larger sizes because anything smaller is poor at hooking trout)

Mosquito (10-12)
(trout don't eat many adult mosquitoes, but they do see a range of insects with dark and light colors)

Muddler Minnow (2-16)
(this pattern could have been in other fly boxes, but for me it is a searcher)

Occasion (14-16)

Olive Quill (16-18)

Queen of the Waters (8-12)

Pheasant Tail (14-20)
(a very productive dry fly version of the famous nymph pattern)

Tantrum (14-16)

Whitcraft (12-16)

White Miller (10-14)
(this is not a moth imitation in my scheme; it's a fine searcher at dusk)

Wickham's Fancy (14-16)
(this fly rides right on the edge of being too unnatural to tempt trout)

Woodruff (12-14)

Yankee (16-18)
(this fly could just as easily be considered an attractor)

Comments:

If there is one factor for me that separates searchers from attractors it is that searching flies, at their best moments, are "familiar" representations. They are most effective when trout are actively feeding, but not taking any specific insect.

There are times when there is an abundance of food on the surface, but with so many different insects there is not a lot of any one species—this happens nearly any summer evening on bouncing, freestone streams. The successful searching fly has the general size, shape, and color of a number of the insects. It is familiar to the trout.

The easiest way to choose a particular searching fly is to key it to the season. Insects often have rough similarities at any time of year—in the spring dark colors predominate, but in the summer most hatches are light colored.

The searcher often fits what trout remember as food better than a precise imitation or an oddball attractor.

When trout are not hunting for a specific insect, the general "picture," or, in behavioral terms, the variable search pattern, is often satisfied better by the generic fly than by the imitation. Trout are not very curious, either, the feeling suppressed when they are feeding, and the generic fly is usually more acceptable than the attractor.

The major reason a searching fly fails, even when the situation is right for it, is that the fly chosen by the angler is too big (fishermen frequently make the same mistake with imitations and attractors). The pattern doesn't need to match the largest species in the hodgepodge of insects on the water.

The line separating searchers and attractors is not sharp. A pattern such as the Wickham's Fancy, with its gold tinsel body, could just as easily be placed in my attractor box. A fly from the attractor box, such as the stonefly-like Lime Trude, is a general searcher on many streams.

This searching box is so full that the lack of room makes me ruthless in culling nonproductive flies. Before anything new can be added, something old must go. So any of the patterns found in this selection fit certain situations, and season after season each one of them catches some trout.

Chapter 6

Imitation Through A Fun Glass

When is an imitation perfect? It's right when a fish moves the same distance for it, at the same speed, as he would for the natural. The precise match may look nothing like the insect to the angler, but the fly works if it has the right parts appearing in proper sequence for the trout. There is a difference between the perfect imitation and the perfect fly (the former not desirable and the latter unattainable).

There is a problem, however, with the imitationist school of fly tying: it is rattling along in a rut leading inexorably to failure. The aim is to tie a pattern that is so accurate that it looks and acts exactly like the million other insects on the water during a heavy hatch. Unfortunately, this perfect imitation reduces an angler's odds to one in a million. Such a pattern fails too often in selective situations simply because it is too good a match.

Thad Maliszewski was baffled by constant refusals one morning on the Big Horn in Montana. Everyone else was catching trout by stalking the schools of rainbows. Thad kept changing flies, coming back periodically to the little No-Hackle that was working for us, but when the fish snubbed that pattern again he would quickly knot on something different.

Thad was at the same time the best and the worst of long line casters. His skills were outstanding, every presentation dropping the fly so lightly just upstream from the rainbows that were holding mid-pool, just above the moss beds. He took the philosophy of "fine and far off" to the extreme, however, standing at least fifty feet away from the rise area. His fly never drifted far enough, not on this day when an eight- to ten-foot float was the least that these fish would tolerate.

Would any fly have made a difference? Our imitations were nearly perfect; that was the problem. The trout were rising to them in the same deliberate manner in which they fed on the real insects. Wouldn't it have been better (especially for Thad) to use a fly that made the trout hurry a bit? It's possible to do that, but then the art is not really imitation, but selective exaggeration instead.

This is imitation through a fun glass. Like the mirrors in a carnival that distort the reflection, leaving it recognizable but absurd, the fly tyer can alter certain characteristics of the artificial. The goal is, just as with a fun glass, to rivet the attention of the looker at the first glance with the odd but familiar perception.

How can skilled fly tyers, even after observing both the natural food and feeding trout carefully, create bad imitations? These innovators fail because they're basing imitations on what they are seeing and what the trout are seeing. Neither truth has much relevance.

A better way of developing new imitations is based on a trial-and-error process controlled by the reaction of the fish, not necessarily to a whole fly, but to individual parts of it. This methodology explains why so many of my patterns end up looking nothing like the natural. It doesn't matter to me what trout see; it only matters to me how they respond to the various elements of a fly.

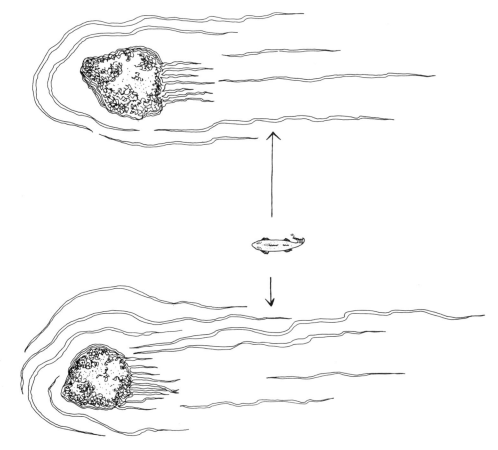

A trout has a "set" feeding territory. The boundaries are usually determined by current "barriers"—lanes to either side. His feeding area is a comfortable slot between these bands of faster water. He will range left and right, maybe six-inches one way and eighteen-inches the other, edging into a current to take food, but he is reluctant to pass through it. When is an imitation right? If he moves a certain distance for the natural, he should should move exactly the same distance for a matching fly.

A trout doesn't attack the head of a minnow—he attacts the eye of his victim. And it doesn't matter where that eye is on either the artificial or natural baitfish.

It was a minnow imitation, the Stub Wing Bucktail, that convinced me not to stick too closely to the natural scheme. Common sense, in this instance, accounted for hundreds of years of tying tradition. The weight of all this history didn't necessarily make the older flies right; basing imitations on the perceptions of man and fish actually worked against the innovators.

Should a streamer pattern have eyes? Numerous minnow imitations, from the oldest to the newest—including trout, bass, salmon, steelhead, and saltwater flies—have prominent eyes. The mere antiquity of this convention gives it validity. The effectiveness of streamers with eyes has been proven by the fishing experiences of generations of fly fishermen.

Recent research verified the importance of eyes on a minnow fly. Scientists found that the strike of larger fish, even at a fast moving minnow, wasn't general. The attacker focussed on the eye of the prey, delivering the stunning or killing blow to the vital region of the head. The eyes acted as targets on any natural baitfish or streamer pattern. A minnow imitation with eyes also drew more strikes than one without them.

Nature, through an evolutionary adaptation, protects some prey fish by putting an exaggerated, false eye on either side of the tail. When the attacker hits the non-vital target, the minnow escapes. The success of the incredible ploy stems from the fact that the attacker doesn't think about where the eye should be, but simply responds to the stimulus.

Fly tyers, recognizing the importance of eyes, have created many patterns with feather eyes, bead eyes, and doll eyes. Where do they put them? Where the eyes will also act as false decoys—at the head, as far away from the hook as possible. Without intending to, they also make flies that can escape, thereby saving untold numbers of fish the embarrassment of being towed through the water and proving a boon to anglers who like to watch gamefish harmlessly bump and flash at their streamers.

Putting eyes at the head of the fly is one of those traditions based on both what the tyer and the trout see in nature. The pattern with exaggerated eyes may get more hits, but it hooks a poor percentage of the strikers, as low as 20 percent, because the target is at the wrong end.

Eyes on a minnow imitation belong near the bend of the hook. A streamer with an eye at the back doesn't draw any more strikes than the normal-eyed fly, but there is a large increase in solid hook-ups. All streamers with eyes near the head, no matter what saltwater or freshwater species they are designed for, are mistakes based on the tyer's perception of reality.

The oddball result of underwater, trial-and-error observation is the Stub Wing Bucktail. It's not realistic in an imitative sense, but it *is* effective. The major feature is a large black and yellow eye on the bend of the hook itself.

The work with minnow eyes was going on simultaneously with our underwater testing of every well-known, American mayfly imitation. The failures and successes of those flies, although perfectly easy to observe, had no clear reason at first. The truth came to us when we applied the lessons of the streamers to dry flies, too: A predator in the distorted world of water doesn't perceive the whole insect on the surface, only the individual parts as they appear in his window of vision.

The same principles for effective fly design control both wet and dry flies. The tyer has to avoid negative characteristics, include all positive characteristics, and exaggerate the primary, or triggering, characteristic. It's not enough for an imitation to be perfect—it has to be a caricature of the natural.

The tyer doesn't have to worry too much about the negative aspects of a fly. Any trout that searches for negative traits in naturals will quickly starve to death. It takes too long. During a hatch a fish develops what is called a "search pattern." He looks only for those positive characteristics that identify the insect as the abundant food item.

Usually, a feature hurts the chances of a take only if it's so prominent that it distracts a trout. The fish is searching for drifting items that have a particular triggering characteristic, so the successful fly has to have it. Still, if there's some other trait on the imitation that is more visible than the trigger, then the fish will see that first and reject the fly.

What about the hook? It is one of those unnatural features that is insignificant enough for fish to ignore. It may not look insignificant to the angler, but no trout is going to focus on it unless he's been trained to notice it. It is possible, in some hard-fished waters, that individual trout have learned through aversive conditioning to avoid objects with hooks on them.

Another way of saying "aversive conditioning?" Catch-and-release (the way all of us in my group fish). Certainly, a trout snagged with a fly has a bad experience. After this happens a half dozen times (at least) within a short time span, he starts to associate the hook with the unpleasant occurrence. He becomes more difficult to catch on ordinary flies, not forever, but for weeks or months afterwards.

Enough experiences over the years with individual fish have convinced me that this does happen. These trout snubbed my best efforts, and I was just confidant enough to believe that neither the matching fly nor my presentation was wrong. After a quick change to a pattern with a hidden hook, most of these trout rose to my offering. All of the fish had hook scars in and around the mouth.

For anyone who fishes no-kill waters every day it might be worth watching out for the aversive phenomenon. The trick on these especially fussy trout is to switch to a fly style that obscures the hook.

Reverse hackling is one tying technique that masks the hook. The hackle is wound at the bend instead of at the head of the pattern, which provides another advantage: The concentration of hackle at the rear supports the heaviest part of the fly better than the standard method. Unfortunately, the fibers interfere with the strike unless they are soft and pliable.

The "reverse hackling" of a pattern such as the old English tie, the Leckford Professor, obscures the hook.

Another trick is turning the hook upside down, completely hiding it. This is an idea that just won't fade away and it keeps popping up in new attempts at imitation. The latest innovations, both mayfly dun patterns, include the Stalker by Hal Jannsen and the USD Paradun by John Goddard and Brian Clarke. These flies do fool critical trout, but they are delicate and, like the Reverse Hackle, they are inconsistent hookers.

At least for me they're inconsistent hookers. Rick Kuchynka, who uses USD Paraduns all the time, tells me that the solution is striking much slower than normal with upside down flies. The hook will not set unless the trout's mouth is closed; then the point hits something solid and pushes through any material. The hook won't "grab" by itself when it is sliding freely across tissue.

My daughter's Mohawk pattern flops over on its side for the first few casts, until the deer hair wicks up a bit of moisture. Maybe this "side look" disguises the hook by putting it in a different position. Lying this way, the fly has caught trout, but it is not a tactic worth encouraging in such a strange creation.

The USD mayfly by John Goddard and Brian Clarke isn't part of my regular carrying stock, but it's a convincing dun imitation. The trick with this, or any upside down fly (including my own Dancing Caddis) is to strike slowly.

Here is the dressing:
Hook: K5ST Partridge Upside-Down hook
Tails: iron-blue rooster fibers
Body: iron-blue seal's fur substitute
Wing: dark gray polypropylene yarn
Hackle: iron-blue rooster (tied parachute style)

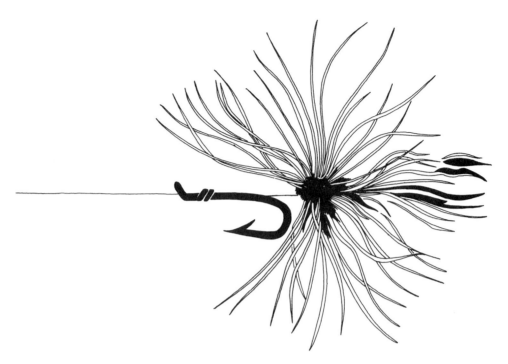

Lee Wulff "separates" the hook from the fly. This not only allows him to use bigger flies (hookless), but it increases the hooking percentage of the bare, small hook.

Lee Wulff has devised a method not for obscuring the hook, but for displacing it. Nevertheless, the result is the same. Since the hook is ahead of the fly, the trout doesn't associate it with the imitation. Wulff uses a smaller than normal hook, tying it onto the leader with a double hitch just above the fly. A size 10 fly, for example, would have a bare, size 16 hook ahead of it (the regular, size 10 hook on the fly is snipped off). This setup not only works well on educated fish but is also an incredibly efficient hooking arrangement, better even than normal flies, for less cautious trout, too.

Theories of Dry Fly Imitation

The split between the wet fly and the dry fly began in the early 1800s, with anglers increasingly and purposely casting dry flies to trout that were rising and wet flies to those that were holding. The codification of the dry fly as a separate method, however, had to wait until 1841, when G. R. P. Pulman in his *Vade Mecum of Fly Fishing for Trout* wrote, "If the wet and heavy fly be exchanged for a dry and light one, and passed in artistic style over the feeding fish, it will, *partly from the simple circumstances of its buoyancy*, be taken, in nine cases out of ten, as greedily as the living insect itself." (italics mine)

What an insight: One reason that the dry fly fooled trout, aside from shape, size, or color, was simply because it was *dry*. Pulman recognized that to imitate an insect the artificial must rest at the same level in or on the water.

This is still the most important factor in surface imitation. The profile of the fly, whether it sits lightly *on* the surface film or rides flush *in* it, takes precedence over size, color, shape, or even brightness. Why? All of those other factors vary in their effect, changing with how high or low the fly rides.

The chalk stream burst in dry fly knowledge took place in England in the decades straddling the turn of the century, not just through the published works of Frederick Halford but under the influence of anglers such as Francis Francis, William Senior, Martin Mosley, George Marryat, and Cholmondeley Pennell. How hard it must have been to follow that flowering. Where were writers like J. W. Dunne, J. C. Mottram, and Colonel Harding to find mysteries of their own? Was everything left to discover of just minor importance?

Theodore Gordon's dry flies were different from their English predecessors. Anyone who tries to diminish Gordon's role in American fly fishing should note what Harry Darbee said (quoted by A. J. McClane in his article, "Feather Merchant," in the July 1955 issue of *Field & Stream*):

> [Gordon] actually changed the anatomy of the fly. He set his wings with butts toward the rear and placed his hackles at right angles to the hook. He was smart enough to use non-absorbent materials, which made a big difference. English dry flies at that time were nothing more than modified wets. They still tied their wing butts toward the eye of the hook. I have thirty or forty of Gordon's original Quill Gordon flies. That man had a beautiful style. He tied on slightly long shank hooks, which gave his flies a real mayfly appearance.

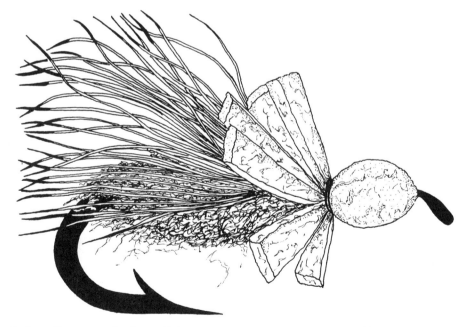

It doesn't matter whether a fisherman is trying to imitate a mayfly, a caddisfly, or a stonefly. The first aspect of imitation he must match is the "ride" of the insect. He can start by choosing a low profile pattern, such as my dry stonefly imitation, the Air Head, or a high profile pattern.

George LaBranche, not content to fish the quiet pools and runs of our freestone rivers, freed the floating fly from the restrictions of English tradition in one of the finest books ever written on presentation, *The Dry Fly and Fast Water* (1914). He wasn't even bound by the limits of imitation, stepping into the realm of attraction with his Pink Lady pattern, but his techniques worked equally well for matching rough water hatches.

Edward R. Hewitt was another great theorist, exploring fly types that not only rode on tip toes, but were designed to be fished actively (the Bivisible and the Skating Spider). He forwarded his theories in many articles and books, summing up his thoughts in *A Trout and Salmon Fisherman for Seventy-five Years*, where his dry fly advances were often overwhelmed by his groundbreaking work with nymphs. His writing ability never quite did credit to the brilliance of his ideas.

Vincent Marinaro published *A Modern Dry Fly Code* in 1950. It was centered on the limestone waters of Pennsylvania, especially the Letort; such a narrow geographic focus probably hurt early sales of the book more than any other factor. It was only after Nick Lyons rescued it and put out a new edition in 1970 that sales boomed and this, the greatest American work on the theories of dry fly design, was recognized for its universality. As stunning as it was, the information on terrestrials wasn't the major theme of the book— *A Modern Dry Fly Code* extended the concept of what a fishing season was, focussing on those summer months when everyone usually quit the streams, either by choice or by law, and in doing so discovered a new world of fly fishing problems (including terrestrials and very small mayflies).

These men stood above all others because their ideas weren't random— nothing in their writings suggested that they were fishing here and there and simply reflecting back on cause-and-effect. It was exactly the opposite: They recognized problems (the effect) and worked hard to find solutions (the cause). By doing so they each extended the limits of the dry fly—Gordon with flies designed for rougher American streams, LaBranche with techniques suited to faster waters, Hewitt with active methods of presentation, and Marinaro with solutions to the terrestrial and minutae of the summer season.

Each of these men worked with groups of fly fishing friends. On such a team only the writer receives credit, but it's impossible to pinpoint where one person's ideas end and another's begin on the trout stream. My work would be greatly diminished without Graham Marsh, who is to me what Marryat was to Halford, and without Tory Stosich and Tom Poole. Certainly, Eric Peper and Ken Parkany, brilliant thinkers on fly fishing, would be like Graham Marsh for me if they didn't insist on working at real jobs and living in places that are such a long commute to Montana.

Vincent Marinaro was a superb observer, never willing to simply lump insects or flies into general categories. Even with ants, he found differences in various types, ". . . the startling fact that in two different species of the same family, the black and the red ant, there is a tremendous variance, the former being absolutely opaque in the body and the latter glimmering and glowing as though lighted by some inner fire." (from A Modern Dry Fly Code*)*

It was Tory who listened to my ideas on imitation. After thinking about them for a week, he stopped rowing one morning as we drifted the Big Hole in my raft and said, "You and I are the only two people in the world who understand this theory of yours, and I'm not so sure about you."

American angling entomology, as opposed to regional works, burst full-grown onto the fly fishing world with one book, *Matching the Hatch* by Ernest Schwiebert. It followed and acknowledged works like *A Book of Trout Flies* by Preston Jennings and *Streamside Guide to Naturals and Their Artificials* by Art Flick, but the scope of the book, covering hatches across the country, was so much larger. Ambition alone made it a distant cousin to these earlier efforts.

Matching the Hatch strongly influenced subsequent works, especially in the area of mayflies. *Selective Trout*, by Doug Swisher and Carl Richards, and *Hatches*, by Al Caucci and Bob Nastasi, both outstanding books, not only identified many new important mayfly species for fly fishermen but also popularized no-hackle imitations for mayfly duns (the No-Hackle from

R. Valentine Atkinson

Mayfly hatches that smother the water and bring large trout to the surface can make even the most jaded angler giddy with anticipation.

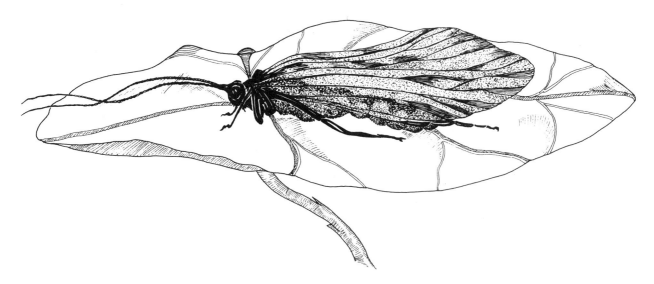

Caddisflies have been a mystery until recently—and it was easier to ignore them than to face the problems they presented on the trout stream. They have been considered inferior to mayflies not because they weren't important to trout, but because they weren't important to fly fishermen. The fact that the imitations and the tactics for fishing a caddisfly hatch were wrong made them worthless to the angler.

Selective Trout and the Compara Dun from *Hatches*). *Mayflies, the Trout and the Angler*, by Fred Arbona, Jr., and *Meeting and Fishing the Hatches*, by Charles Meck, added even more to our knowledge of important mayflies and their habits.

Caddis and the Angler, by Eric Leiser and Larry Solomon, was the first work on caddisflies. A fine effort, it deserves praise in many areas but especially for elevating caddis imitations, including older patterns like the Henryville and newer ones like the Delta Wing, to a proper place in the angler's fly selection. The authors gathered the ideas of fly fishermen across the country, fully crediting them in their book. The *Caddis and the Angler* also included my flies, the Sparkle Pupa patterns, and, although the idea had been published in magazine articles, it gave wide currency to my work on behavioral drift (and its link to nymph fishing) for the first time as well.

Is there a place for more angling entomologies of national scope? A bit. The areas of mayflies and caddisflies are crowded, but there is still room there for new revelations. The few books on stoneflies have been feeble, not because the writers are lacking but because the subject is weak (which makes one wonder whether stoneflies deserve a whole book). Gerald Almy's excellent work, *Tying and Fishing Terrestrials*, has been out of print for too long, and there have been many new flies developed for terrestrials since then. Midges (and the entire order of two-winged flies, Diptera) is the last unplowed area for the angler/entomologist; there have only been a few seeds scattered in this country, but any work on midges must by necessity focus on stillwater fisheries. That book can build on the science in the classic _Lake Fishing with a Fly_ by Ron Cordes and Randall Kaufmann.

New entomologies, rather than trying to cover the whole country, may concentrate instead on specific regions and feature carefully gathered and professionally identified insect collections, with hatch charts for individual rivers. That approach (undertaken in _Caddisflies_ on four rivers with identification by Dr. Oliver Flint of the Smithsonian), always reveals enough local anomalies to fascinate both anglers and professional entomologists. Rick Hafele and David Hughes, either individually or as a team, are wonderful researchers who have shown that they can write such entomological gems.

Any new books on fly design, even to some extent those dealing with attractors, have to be linked to entomology. Dry flies, except for Injured Minnows and such, imitate insects—the secret behind the success of any fly is what it "might" look like to a trout. This doesn't mean that fly fishermen have to puzzle over what a Royal Coachman matches (the angling version of how many angels will fit on the head of a pin), but it does mean that any fly falls into broad categories that roughly simulate particular insect stages.

New, effective imitations are not usually born at the fly tying vise. That is the last step. Yet, with too many "killer" patterns it's the first. The way to devise any fly is to study the three elements that control the feeding process. The innovator begins by puzzling over the type of water where trout are going to feed on the insects. These hydraulics control the actions of both trout

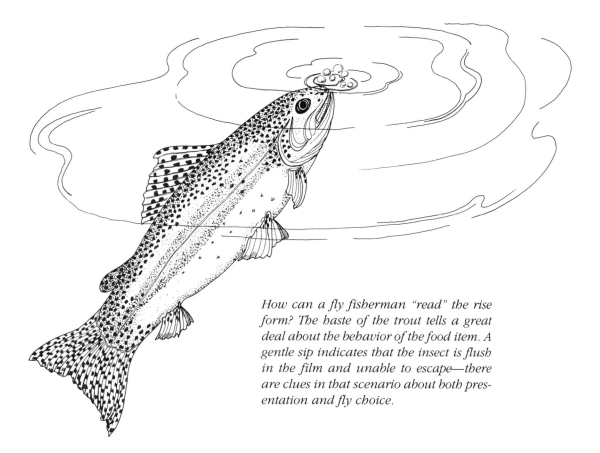

How can a fly fisherman "read" the rise form? The haste of the trout tells a great deal about the behavior of the food item. A gentle sip indicates that the insect is flush in the film and unable to escape—there are clues in that scenario about both presentation and fly choice.

and insects. The eventual imitations can end up different for a fast water species and a slow water species, even though the insects look very much alike.

Observing the trout, not generally but in minute detail over days and weeks, reveals how they react to specific food items. The rise form itself becomes an important clue to the correct method of presentation, and, as a result, to the proper fly design as well. Do trout sip insects? If so, they want the imitation helpless, pinned in the film, with a low profile like the natural.

Insect behavior, as well as form, determines what a fly is going to look like to the fish. Watching the live insect uncovers those quirks that make general catch-all patterns useless. Shouldn't the imitations of all mayfly spinners be fairly standard? Here are observations of the Small Dark Olive (*Baetis scambus*) by Robert Ince on England's Avon:

"I watched the spinners for about 1½ hours. They entered the water and as the wings folded down over the abdomen it traps a layer of air along the *entire length of the abdomen and part of the thorax.* Once under the water the spinner appeared from above to be just a small elongated tube of silver.

"Some spinners did return from below but from my observations yesterday for every twenty that went down only one came up. I have no idea whether that is usual or not. I must study this further to try and get an idea of what percentage of ovipositing *Baetis* actually return.

"I waded out of the river and sat on a stone to watch the water. In the still eddies of the extreme shallows, *Baetis* spinners lay dead. Interestingly, none of the dead females had their wings in the spent position. They were in the upright position and I supposed that these were females that had re-emerged from the river after ovipositing and then died shortly after."

Robert's close observation of *Baetis* breaks a few common beliefs about mayfly spinners, doesn't it? This is a situation, which also exists with various *Baetis* species in our country, where standard spent patterns are worthless. Maybe in part because of that, the spinner activity of *Baetis* is usually ignored by fly fishermen, even though the trout congregate at ovipositing sites and take submerged egg layers. This isn't a dry fly problem at all—a small, Olive Diving Caddis wet fly does nicely, though, mimicking the silvery appearance of the mayfly female underwater as well as it does the caddisfly.

The innovator's attempts to develop new flies can be very specific, focusing on a single species or type of insect, or it can be fairly broad, looking at a whole insect order. In either instance the effort studying water, trout, and naturals—the three points in the problem—is seldom easy or quick.

Over the years my own work has covered all major aquatic insect orders, caddisflies no more than any other. Mayflies such as the Blue Wing Olive (*Baetis* species), the Pale Morning Dun (*Ephemerella inermis*), the Eastern Green Drake (*Ephemera guttulata*), and the Ghost Fly (*Traverella albertana*),

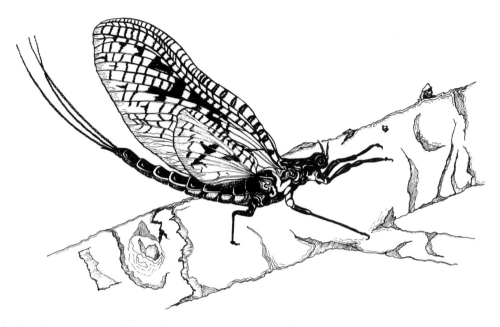

Studying, not just fishing the hatch or spinner fall, but taking the time to watch the behavior of an insect reveals its quirks. My spring months spent in pursuit of the the eastern Green Drake (Ephemera guttulata) showed me why my normal, "short-bodied" patterns were wrong. Here was one mayfly that did not lift its abdomen and tails off of the surface. The dun would give a preliminary "tap, tap, tap" on the meniscus, and then it would lay the abdomen and even the tails full out, riding for long distances in this position, as if trying to use the rear of the body as a lever to launch itself into the air.

have given me seasons of delight; among stoneflies the giant Salmon Fly (*Pteronarcys californica*) has taken up every spring since my move West; all the major caddisfly species, but especially the Spotted Sedge (*Hydropsyche* species) and the closely related Little Sister Sedge (*Cheumatopsyche* species), have fascinated me as dry fly models.

My new patterns haven't been all floating flies, or even insect imitations. There are subsurface flies like the Bristle Leech, Marabou Worm, and even the Marabou Egg Sack in my collection; and minnow patterns, a whole series based on the Stub Wing concept, are being developed through underwater observation.

How much time does it take to understand a specific food form? One piece of work, a grasshopper study, covered two and a half seasons.

Choosing the Effective Imitation

Once the angler has eliminated any negatives from his imitation, he can concentrate on the positive aspects. In selective feeding situations he knows when his fly lacks either the primary characteristic or one of those secondary characteristics by how a trout refuses it. If the fish never even inspects the fly, then it fails in the "search" phase—the trout is looking at everything that enters his window for the primary, or triggering, characteristic and he won't recognize the fly as food if he doesn't see that characteristic in the imitation. If the fish does move under the fly, acting as if he is going to take it, but finally hesitates and eventually breaks off the rise, then the triggering trait is there but one or more of the important secondary characteristics is missing.

This is the process of selection—recognition, confirmation, and acceptance. The trout recognizes an object by its primary feature, confirms its identity by the secondary feature, and accepts the fly once it displays proper behavior.

What separates the primary trait from the secondary ones is how far away the fish can see it. The moment of recognition is immediate. The trout isn't looking for minute details simply because the item is still relatively far away in most instances, but the insect has one characteristic that's more prominent, more visible to the fish than any other, and it is the one that triggers a strike. The imitation has to have it to be effective.

The act of confirmation is not sudden. The fish has, for all intents, already decided to take the fly. As he's rising under it, he expects to see the features he's been seeing on every natural—a certain color, body shape, and size—and if, upon closer inspection, the secondary characteristics are wrong, he decides the fly isn't an edible object after all.

There are feeding situations where acceptance is so prolonged that success is as much a matter of presentation as imitation. Especially when trout are holding two feet deep or more, in a flow with a smooth surface, they focus on a fly long before they rise to it. Naturally, they expect the artificial to drift drag-free all the way through their circular window of vision. They may come up for a fly slowly, and even drop back with it, not because they are being highly critical but because that is their feeding rhythm. When that bugaboo, micro-drag, makes the fly act the least bit unnatural, they will break off a rise—even if the imitation is right.

Like most fly fishermen, my main obsession over the years has been mayflies. Who could help it? Growing up in the East meant not only listening to all the talk about the classic mayflies but going on those wonderful weekend trips to famous waters in search of specific hatches. No one was just "going to the Beaverkill"—they were "going to the Beaverkill to fish the Green Drake" (or the Cahills or the March Browns).

A large part of my observation both above and under water has been of mayfly naturals and their imitations, watching not only my own patterns but all of the creative variations by other tyers, too. What a changeable insect the mayfly must be—the many dry flies to match it are so different. Through the years the disparate types have risen or fallen in favor: the softer standard dry fly of the English chalk streams, the tall Variant of Dr. William Baigent, the stiff-hackled Catskill tie of Theodore Gordon, the parachute type of William Avery Brush, the Thorax Dun of Vincent Marinaro, the No-Hackle of Doug Swisher and Carl Richards, and the Compara Dun of Al Caucci and Bob Nastasi. From England, recently, there has emerged the upside down USD Dun of John Goddard and Brian Clarke, and the intriguing Funnel Dun of Neil Patterson. New patterns muscle into the lineup so easily that either the older flies are not as good as they should be or there are niches, specific situations

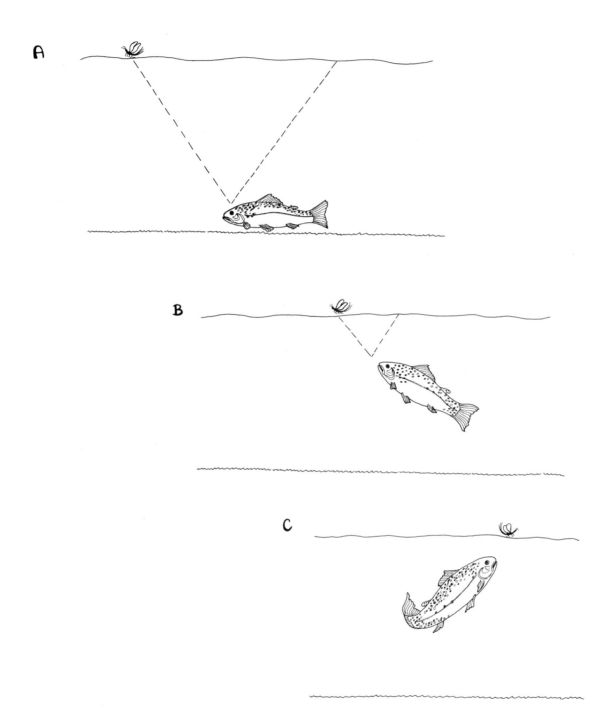

A. *The trout recognizes the insect by a primary characteristic as it enters the window of vision.*

B. *He confirms the identity of the insect by the secondary characteristics (and he is very close to the fly).*

C. *He accepts (or rejects) the insect after studying it (and the slightest drag on an artificial fly hurts chances of a take).*

or moments in the hatch, that can still be filled (for example, Craig Mathew's Sparkle Dun is an excellent, new mayfly imitation). Amazingly, all of this fly tying frenzy is just for the dun stage.

All of these patterns work to some degree during a hatch. Underwater observation, with trout responding with varying degrees of enthusiasm to old and new flies, ends up being both frustrating and fascinating—there is no clear winner. Why haven't I offered any dun imitations before? My patterns have to be distinctly better than existing imitations in the underwater testing. None of my dun flies have met that criteria.

Emerging caddisflies are just the opposite—they present a consistent picture to the trout. During a hatch all of the insects swim up to the top, hanging and drifting hesitantly under the surface film in a single, concentrated layer. They show no other "micro-stage" during emergence; they are either there, under the meniscus, or they are gone. Trout feed on caddisfly emergers still in the film so selectively because there are so few adults riding the surface.

Emerging mayflies, on the contrary, present a variable picture. There is that initial concentration just under the surface film, nymphs drifting as they struggle free of the old skin (as with caddisflies), but the process doesn't end there. The dun doesn't fly away immediately. It rides the surface while its tissue dries and stiffens internally. The float as an adult is often not only long, but dangerous. Any chop or undertow may drown a dun, leaving it sodden in the surface film.

So what is the trout seeing during the mayfly emergence? Hatching nymphs in various stages of escape, duns riding prettily on the surface, and drowned and stillborn adults awash in the film. It's a hodgepodge of images. This makes it easier for the angler to come up with a generalized imitation but almost impossible for him to create a "clear winner."

Water type and weather control where mayflies become concentrated during a hatch. One extreme—slow, smooth water on a warm day—often means more emerging nymphs are available to trout; but the other extreme—riffle water on a damp, cool day—often means that more adult mayflies are riding the surface.

Trout do feed selectively during a mayfly emergence, but sometimes it is a sequential process. They rise to various insect stages in a rhythm, taking a certain number of nymphs and then a certain number of duns; they may eat three, sip two, and repeat. The sequence differs with the water type, weather conditions, and, perhaps most importantly, with the stage of the hatch. Usually, trout eventually settle on one stage or the other. The key to catching them is finding out which one.

Emergent mayfly nymph

G. E. M. Skues, during nearly thirty-five years of angling, followed the prevailing code of the chalk streams and fished a dry fly. It wasn't until 1910 that he published his first book, *Minor Tactics of the Chalk Stream*, which contained the heretical view that rising trout could be caught on a matching nymph fished in or just below the surface (interestingly enough, Frederick Halford's main objection to such patterns was that they couldn't imitate the movement of the naturals).

It wasn't just coincidence that Skues developed his imitations of emerging mayfly nymphs on the unruffled waters of the Abbott's Barton section of the Itchen. In those slow, smooth currents the thicker and more resistant meniscus retarded the hatching efforts of all insects.

The main concentration level throughout an entire mayfly hatch on smooth streams often is just under the surface film—and this affects the feeding sequence. Trout regularly take a dozen or more nymphs to every dun on flat waters.

It can be just the opposite on a riffle. In broken water, where nymphs transform quickly into adults, there are often more insects on the surface than under it. The trout focus on the duns, rising rhythmically. Each motion during the process of recognition, confirmation, and acceptance is repeated exactly.

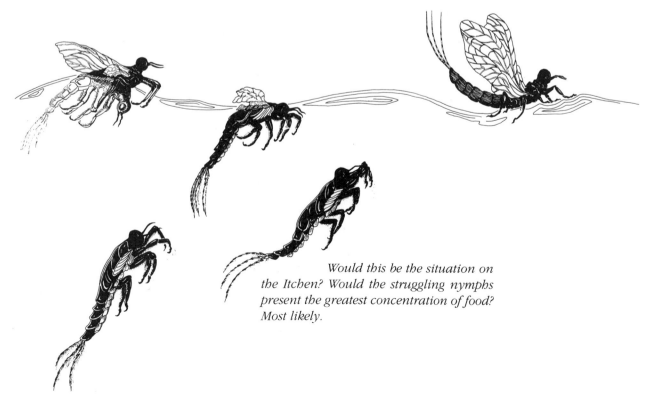

Would this be the situation on the Itchen? Would the struggling nymphs present the greatest concentration of food? Most likely.

They want the fly to ride at the same level as the natural, high and dry, so that they don't have to change the form of their rise.

Weather affects how quickly a dun's tissue hardens. Cold and wet conditions keep an insect on the surface longer. During dry and warm days with lower humidity, however, the wing muscles dry quickly, and after a flex or two, the adult flies off to the bankside foliage. More adults drown on windy days than on calm ones.

I tried to repeat a professional study done on the Fall River in California. On this flat, gentle stream biologists noted that trout took twenty emerging nymphs (some near the bottom and some in the film) for every adult during a hatch. My observations confirmed this ratio for three species of mayflies, but only at the beginning of the hatch. Even here, on the calmest of flows on a sunny morning when the adults didn't linger too long, the percentages shifted to a diet of 60 percent nymphs and 40 percent duns after the first hour.

Throughout a hatch, as the relative numbers of insects change for each stage, the feeding conforms to those rough ratios. In the beginning, nymphs dominate. On most streams enough duns collect on the surface for trout to shift strongly to true floaters by the middle of the hatch. By the end, as numbers of new recruits diminish, the luckless stillborns trapped in shucks and the drowned duns become more important.

R. Valentine Atkinson

This Fall River rainbow fell to a hatch-matching nymph.

The hatching mayfly nymph, struggling in the film, demanded a better imitation. Clearly, all of the available patterns for these emergers lacked a particular characteristic. The innovators did not, in this instance, understand the physical dynamics that alter the appearance of the natural—their flies were copies of lifeless specimens.

For many summers, Tom Poole, our mayfly fanatic, echoed my mutterings whenever we watched trout feed on emerging mayflies and hesitate at standard imitations, "Those flies are missing something?"

"But what, Tom? I can't see any trait that could be that strong."

"The trigger is the body below the surface. That's what trout are seeing first."

Sometimes we would be stumped by how to imitate a strong characteristic (it took years to find the material to match the bubble of the caddisfly pupa), but the trait itself was usually so outstanding that the basic problem was easy to identify. Not so with emerging mayflies—shape, color, size, and brightness all seemed obvious with the naturals.

With any emerger there are two sets of visual laws in effect, not one, as with the true nymph or the true dry fly. The "damp" fly is a hybrid, bridging two worlds. The good modern imitations recognize that, portraying the body hanging down and the humped back, half in and half out of the film. They work better than the simpler fur nymphs of Skues because they achieve the right balance with some type of buoyant material—closed cell foam, cork, or deer hair—on top of the thorax. They have the triggering characteristic, the abdomen hanging down, and the obvious secondary features, but the trout hesitate so clearly in the take that something is missing in all of them.

What do these flies lack? The missing trait isn't evident in the study specimens; it's not there in the naturals, either. At least, it's not there all of the time. The trait, one of the strongest secondary characteristics found in our work, only exists for ten to twenty seconds during the life of the mayfly. It so happens that this brief span coincides with the trout's selection process.

The trait was discovered by watching mayflies emerge in an aquarium. It was no ordinary aquarium, which is a limited tool for studying the appearance of an insect on the surface, but one with a partially mirrored bottom. The viewer, in our setup, looks down at the mirror and sees the underside of the emerger.

This revealed that the hatching mayfly creates an aura, not a brightness but a soft glow, as it climbs free of the nymphal skin. An insect breaks through the tough meniscus by forming a meniscus, a concentration of molecules, of its own. It floats with its back secured in the film and the skin splits along the top of the thorax. Water doesn't rush in on top of the emerger because the edges of the skin are pulled out and up by the tremendous forces of the newly created escape hole, or meniscus, spreading around it. The aura is this stretched, thin flange of skin, infused by light from the open sky and the reflection of air bubbles along the inside rim. From below it looks like the insect is wearing a halo.

Theodore Rogowski used a ball of polystyrene, encased in a nylon netting, to float a mayfly emerger nymph. The polystyrene was not translucent and did not represent the halo of the natural, but the pattern was a breakthrough in mayfly imitation.

There is one type of emerger imitation that accidently mimics this key trait—it just doesn't do it well enough. The material used to provide flotation in these patterns is ethafoam. The translucent, closed-cell foam, actually a collection of tiny white bubbles, radiates softly along the edges in sunlight.

The reputation of these flies was built empirically. No one ever stopped to consider that there might be some reason besides flotation for their success. Ethafoam, as well as polycelon and plastazote, found a place in terrestrial imitations. These flies, also, seemed extraordinarily effective.

A little ball of ethafoam on top of the mayfly emerger wasn't enough. The material, hidden above the thorax and wrapped in netting, gave only a hint of a halo. This trait had to be, if not an exaggeration, at least a match for that glowing edge of the bulging escape hole, the foam spilling over and above the sides of the body in circular flaps.

Tom Poole and Tory Stosich had to test the new flies without me the first week. They scuba dove in Utah's Green River, and after observing the fly as trout rose to it, they added the fluorescent coloring to the wing stub and actually made the foam flaps wider. Tory reported, ". . . made minor changes. The trout were taking *Baetis* emergers, and there was none of that drop back, 'what's wrong with this picture,' behavior with the new fly.

"Since the foam flaps weren't the trigger factor, they didn't make the fish 'choose' the fly over the naturals. Maybe the butt of white sparkle helped there a bit, though. With the halo there were no late refusals.

"The foam glows so nicely. I give the fly an A. You'd give it a B+, but then you're a tougher grader than I am."

For a change it was my turn to fish the fly for on-the-stream approval.

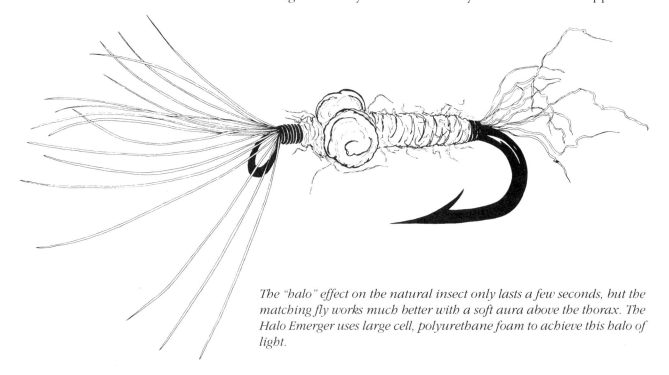

The "halo" effect on the natural insect only lasts a few seconds, but the matching fly works much better with a soft aura above the thorax. The Halo Emerger uses large cell, polyurethane foam to achieve this halo of light.

Mayfly Dun

My first idea for exaggerating the mayfly dun was to simply try a larger fly than the natural—a size 14 for an insect properly matched with a size 16, for instance. These "Big Boy" flies failed quickly and completely, but they revealed a major reason why imitations flop in selective situations.

My on-stream surveys showed that anglers instinctively choose patterns too large for the naturals. It's much better, actually, to go a size too small. At least with undersized imitations, on normal rivers, those "turn-away" refusals by trout aren't so common. The exception to this is on tainted rivers, where the water never gets crystal clear.

John Bailey says that on the Yellowstone River near his Livingston home, he casts large dry flies all summer, even when fish are rising. It's not that John doesn't enjoy using small flies; during the winter, when the river is at its lowest and clearest and midge hatches are heavy, he matches the micro-hatches. During the summer the Yellowstone, even after the runoff is over, has a green tinge. The trout in most spots hold on the bottom, rather than just under the surface, and when rising they key better on a bigger fly. A size 14 is as small as John will go, even when a summer hatch is smaller.

What surprised me, even during heavy hatches, was that there were times when, if size and color suited the trout, the design of the mayfly didn't seem critical. How could all of these different fly types in our testing work as imitations? After enough observation, it became clear that each style had strengths and weaknesses, but none was overwhelmingly superior to all of the others.

Testing the Dun Imitations

It's not the dun that most dry fly styles are imitating. They are really mimicking the intermediate stage, the nymph-dun (or, as Pete Hidy named it, the "flymph"), the adult insect struggling to pull free of the nymphal shuck. The natural is a dark skin still in water, either under or trailing behind the emerging adult, one wing or two in the process of unfolding, with the color, size, and bulk of the fresh dun partially free. It's a composite, changeable picture; but often it's the one that lasts longest during the emergence process. Any fly with its body pressed into or onto the surface matches this stage to some extent.

The Catskill Dry Fly

The best imitations of fully emerged duns may be the classic Catskill ties and the Variants. This doesn't mean that they're the best flies for catching trout during the hatch—sometimes they are and sometimes they aren't. They simply look more like the high riding duns than any other mayfly type.

When a mayfly rests on the surface, the legs and the thorax usually touch the water and the abdomen curves up into the air. The legs are not in the water, they are on it—and if one is stuck in the surface film the insect plucks it free, like a man pulling a foot out of the mud. Some mayflies keep that rear section of the body in light contact with the surface and others don't. There are many that just lift the back end up and down and tap the water repeatedly as they drift (try to imitate that).

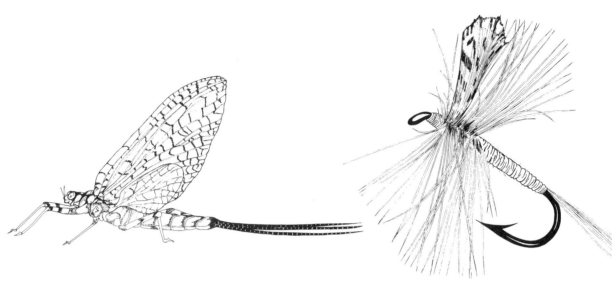

The Light Cahill is frequently used to match mayflies, the various species of Stenonema, *on the Catskill rivers, but, along with other classic eastern dry flies, such as the Quill Gordon, Light Hendrickson, Dark Hendrickson, and Red Quill, it is popular and effective on trout streams everywhere in this country.*

The closest float characteristic to this is found in the tiptoe dry fly. The hackles and the tail touch, but the body stands completely clear of the water. The elegant ride is achieved with sparse and lightweight materials, a tying style completely different from the standard, heavily dressed dry fly (typified by patterns such as the Adams and the Coachman).

No other style of dry fly has its own cult of tyers. The masters of the Catskill pattern are not only known but revered for their ability to adhere to the original concept. Walt and Winnie Dette are the legends; along with their daughter, Mary Dette Clark, they still produce flies for their shop in Roscoe, New York. Larry Duckwall, who learned directly from Elsie Darbee, and Frank Kuttner, who has the remnants of Harry Darbee's blue dun stock, along with men such as Dee Weidig, Eric Leiser, Ralph Graves, Poul Jorgenson, Terry Finger, Del Maza, Dick Talleur, Dave Brant, and Matt Vinciguerra, are inheritors of the philosophy. They know the exact techniques for creating a Catskill dry. More importantly, they are privy to the reasons behind each step in the process.

No fly tying style could attract such a following if its patterns weren't effective. These flies—including the Quill Gordon, Red Quill, Light Hendrickson, Dark Hendrickson, Light Cahill, and Dark Cahill—matched originally to the spring and early summer mayfly hatches of the Catskill rivers, are not only valuable in one region or even only in the East, but wherever there are mayflies.

Frequently, the Catskill patterns catch more trout than the modern mayfly styles. The successes are specific in our tests, not general—the high-riding flies, either Catskill or Variant types—are the best imitations roughly 20 percent of the time during hatches.

The Catskill dry flies perform well when adult duns outnumber struggling emergers on the water. The mathematics are simple: If nymphs are escaping their shucks quickly (which happens in broken water), but duns are having trouble flying (which happens on chilly and damp days), the concentration of mayflies grows heaviest above the surface film, not on it. The trout use the upwing, free adult as a search model. They take the Catskill dry fly because it matches the predominant stage of the hatch.

What are the quirks of the Quill Gordon mayfly (*Epeorus pleuralis*)? Like many other members of the Heptageniidae family, it sheds the nymphal skin underwater, not at the surface. During the first weeks of May, in the middle of the afternoon, it pops from the rough water sections of rivers like the Beaverkill. There is little hesitation at the surface film because there's no need to undress. The dun is quickly up and on the water. The adult rides the currents for a long time, drying its wings after the underwater dash, drifting down to the pools and waiting trout.

Is any other dry fly style better suited to the peculiarities of an insect? A Quill Gordon hatch isn't the place for those nymph-dun hybrid flies that lay the body in the film. There are many other hatches where adults outnumber nymphs, but with this one there is only a single level of concentration at the surface.

Matt Vinciguerra

The Beaverkill River, one of the Catskill jewels, has many mayfly hatches that are still imitated best by the sparse, classic dry fly.

It's very difficult, especially outside the Catskill region, to find properly tied Catskill dry flies for sale. Just because a pattern is named a Quill Gordon or Light Cahill, and the materials are roughly the same, doesn't mean that it is authentic. The proportions make the Catskill fly—and usually such a fly is too sparse for the tastes of beginners (which make up a large percentage of buyers). An alternative is to become an apprentice to one of the masters and learn to tie these flies according to original precepts.

The Thorax Dun

When Theodore Gordon used a stiff, high quality hackle, and tied the stem crossways onto the shank, he ended up with a sharp right-angle flare of fibers. The wings, tied in with butts toward the rear, also canted naturally forward. His fly was an exaggeration. Riding high, the upright hackle and wings combined to recreate the main triggering characteristic of the mayfly dun, but they were taller and farther forward than the real wings.

Vincent Marinaro understood the value of wings on his innovations, writing in the Introduction of *A Modern Dry Fly Code*, "If you believe as I do that the bodies of the duns are meaningless and superfluous, then with one mighty stroke you have eliminated a great deal of confusion and uncertainty. You need imitate only the wing, which is of paramount importance and which is limited to very few colors: The large blue gray group and the yellow group."

In his famous experiment, Marinaro tested the importance of wings by clipping them off live mayflies and then drifting these surgically altered examples over a feeding trout. Thirty-seven wingless mayflies passed over a steadily rising fish and he never took a single one.

For the fun of it, my friends and I devised an off-shoot of this experiment. Painting the wings of mayflies odd colors with marking pens, we expected absolutely no results—there was no theory preceding these tests. What happened? The sampling wasn't large enough to be reliable, only 242 mayflies, but the trout showed some interesting biases. Chartreuse wings worked slightly better at noon than red ones, but in the evening this preference was reversed. Also, brilliant white wings attracted a lot of attention all the time, and metallic coatings of silver and gold failed on the trout. What did all this prove? That we had a lot to learn about color.

Marinaro, so observant and so aware of the preferences of his Letort trout, created a more realistic simulation of the freshly emerged dun than the Catskill dry fly. His Thorax Dun, properly, also exaggerated the wing, in width if not in height. The large cut wings, shaped from hackle points, flared out broadly. The hackling wound in a criss-cross fashion around the wing stems, splaying fore and aft. Only two or three fibers curved up behind the fly to form the sparse tail.

Illustrations in *A Modern Dry Fly Code* shows the Thorax Dun alongside a natural mayfly, the wings of each reaching exactly the same height. If it was tied like this, however, the fly would not even match the effect of the natural feature. The cut wings have to be taller, almost one-and-a-half times the height of the real wing.

[*The above illustration appeared in* A Modern Dry Fly Code.]
What did Vincent Marinaro create with the Thorax Dun? A fly where the primary characteristic was not exaggerated; a fly where the secondary characteristics were virtually perfect. With this pattern he made an imitation exactly like the millions of naturals on the water. Is this desirable? No, except in one situation *(see caption and illustration for the No Hackle later in this chapter).*

The wings can't be a slight exaggeration. They sit in the middle of the fly, just like the real insect's wings. That is what both the trout and the tyer sees, but the fact that the wings are centered, instead of being forward like on a Catskill dry, diminishes the impact of this feature.

The Thorax Duns, in our underwater comparisons, did not fool more trout than the Catskill flies. Graham Marsh objected to the conclusion, "It's not a fair test. The pools we're diving in are deeper and faster than the Letort."

We moved to one of our Montana versions of a limestone stream, weedy and slow Poindexter Slough, and from a canvas blind on shore we watched trout react to the Thorax concept. They still didn't key on the fly, amid all the natural insects, as well as they did on the front-hackled dry. The trigger was weaker on the Thorax imitation. It did catch more fish in this type of water, though. In the slower flow, where trout settled under a fly and stared at it as they rose, the Thorax Dun got fewer late refusals than any other type of mayfly imitation.

There have been few trout stream observers in this country equal to Vincent Marinaro—he saw, and he interpreted what he saw correctly. Both his strength and his weakness was that he was limited mostly to the Letort; the fact that his concepts worked there didn't mean that his flies would be the best ones on all waters.

The Thorax Duns are valuable as more than just spring creek flies because there are micro-habitats, little pieces of any river, where trout study the secondary characteristics of an imitation. The fisherman has to be aware, however, that a Thorax Dun isn't going to attract attention as well as other types of dry flies. His drifts will have to be very precise, the pattern entering the window exactly where the trout looks for the next mayfly, and they'll have to be timed to the trout's rise rhythm. Still, once he gets the fish to look at the fly, the battle will be fairly won.

The Compara Duns and No Hackles

Marinaro was right—the body isn't critically important on patterns such as the Thorax style or the Catskill style where it is held free of the water by hackle. Nevertheless, no one ever leaves this part off these patterns. That would fly too much in the face of convention (and such a pattern would never gain commercial acceptance). But the body's color and translucence are critical secondary characteristics on damp flies that look like half nymph and half adult, especially Compara Duns and No Hackles.

For a long time No Hackles and Compara Duns shared a place in my stock. That all ended one day on the lower Clark Fork, below Missoula, during an afternoon snowstorm. John Randolph was waiting with me for the *Baetis* hatch. He asked, as the flakes fell, "You still think they're going to come at one o'clock?"

The duns started popping and the fish started rising in a big backwater under the highway bridge. There was only one place to stand on the rock rip-rapping. From that spot, one of us could make a twenty- to thirty-foot cast. The river was too deep for wading and there were no fish closer. We took turns presenting flies to the trout.

The heavy snow fall, the flat, gray light, and the chop of the water made it terribly difficult for me to see the size 18 No Hackle. We were catching one trout apiece, but I was slowing down the parade. With fruitless drifts, missed strikes, and all the fuss that I was going through to float the fly, it was taking me twice as long as John to hook a fish. There was that urgency of the *Baetis* hatch, with its definite beginning and its definite end, that made efficiency important.

I had tied equal numbers of No Hackles and Compara Duns at the beginning of the season. Yet, when I opened my box to change flies, there were no Compara Duns left. "John, do you have another one of those?"

He generously shared his flies. The Compara Dun was easy to see even at thirty feet, and the rainbows, mostly fourteen- to sixteen-inch fish, took one on nearly every drift for us. The snow stopped and then the hatch, both very suddenly. We were cold once the fishing was over.

That was the last day that I ever carried No Hackles as a regular part of my stock. The Compara Duns were more efficient flies—more durable, buoyant, and visible. This didn't mean that they were better imitations (the No Hackles, for the hundreds of trout they had caught for me over the years, still deserved respect). Many flies gained their initial popularity more by serving the fisherman, by being practical, than by pleasing trout. The underwater comparisons would tell me how good No Hackles were as mayfly imitations.

Tests revealed that the trigger on a matching No Hackle was weak when trout were selecting duns. That was no surprise—the duck quill wings slope back on the fly, reducing what's already a short wing. What *was* a revelation was how quickly this deficiency grew worse. After a few fish the quills became torn and frayed, the separate fibers laying almost straight back. The No Hackle wasn't even a nymph-dun imitation after a short while; it was a surface nymph, pure and simple.

The first person I saw use No Hackles was Barry Trapp, on Silver Creek in Idaho. "Why do you throw the fly away after every fish?" I asked.

"Trout just seem to like them fresh," he said.

Of course, any angler using No Hackles specifically as an imitation of the emerging nymph, and not the hybrid nymph-dun, wouldn't mind the frayed wings on a mangled fly. This contradiction simply illustrates how important it is for the fisherman to understand what a pattern is supposed to imitate before he casts it.

Whether it is used as a nymph or a dun, the imitation's body length is critical. Standard dry flies have tails like brushes, so thick that to a fish they look like an extension of the body. The No Hackle, a flush fly, has a cleaner silhouette. This secondary impression is strengthened when the imitation is exactly the same length as the natural insect.

The No Hackle is a plausible fly, but the Compara Dun is an absurdity. A trout would rarely, if ever, see anything like it on the surface. It has the body of the nymph trapped in the meniscus, but there, in magnificent splendor, are the fully unfolded wings of the adult fanned in a 180-degree semicircle right over the head.

It's such a magnificent absurdity, with its mismatched parts, however, that trout respond to it enthusiastically. The deer hair wing is a fine triggering feature. Underwater, it's possible to see the Compara Dun, along with two or three naturals, enter the trout's window. The fish just locks right onto the fly.

The Compara Dun's secondary characteristics are usually acceptable to trout, too. If the wing, touching the water on each side of the head bothers them, they manage to ignore it. The impression that the deer hair makes on the surface even turns this fly into a fair representation of an egg-laying mayfly spinner. The body is drab, like most mayfly imitations, but it resembles the dull skin of the nymph.

Nymph, dun, and spinner—this pattern covers all of these stages at once (working best when trout are feeding on the emerging nymph-dun hybrid). The trout look at the parts and not at the whole fly, but any mayfly using the Compara Dun as a mirror would topple over in fits of mirth.

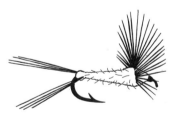

This is an absurd *imitation. That is why it appeals to me.*

The Parachute Patterns

There are always a few parachute-style dry flies in my boxes. They do a fair job fooling trout as a nymph-dun hybrid, but my favorites are used more often as spinner imitations. The only place parachute flies prove indispensable during a hatch is below heavy riffles and runs, those choppy waters that

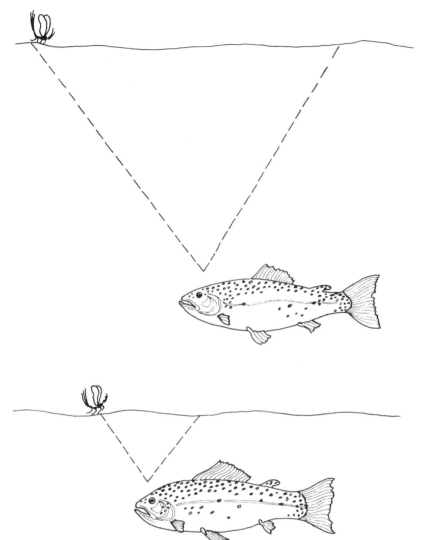

The No Hackle (a nymph dun imitation) is like the Thorax Dun (an adult imitation)— they are both "perfect imitations." They lack the exaggeration that focuses attention and raises the chances of a fly being noticed by the trout. But the secondary characteristics are so good that they do not get late refusals. These are not the best flies under ordinary circumstances, but there is one feeding situation where they catch more trout than "exaggerated" imitations. This happens in slow water when trout hold just under the surface and sip insects steadily.

Ordinarily, the triggering characteristic can be (and should be) an exaggeration because a trout sees it for the first time from a few feet away. The secondary characteristics cannot be exaggerated because when a trout looks at them he is already very close.

So why are surface sippers an exception? They are so close to the top, and their window of vision is so small, that they see even the triggering characteristic for the first time very close. Any exaggeration at such a distance is *unnatural. The No Hackles and Thorax Duns, each for its respective stage, match the mayfly precisely.*

drown the fully emerged duns. These chutes spew out the bedraggled mayflies in a downstream pool. When trout key on the drowned insects, the parachute fly, spread out on the water, does exceptionally well as a match.

The Mess

There's an interesting English pattern, the Funneldun by Neil Patterson. It looks nothing like a real mayfly—and that intrigues me. It might be the practical, easy to tie, upside down (the hook rides up) fly for hook-shy trout. Unfortunately, like every other upside down fly, it is poor at hooking fish.

Robert Ince sent me photocopies of an article about the Funneldun from an issue of the *International Flyfisher* (now defunct). I showed the pictures to Graham Marsh and told him, "This is the third time I've seen a fly hackled like that."

"It looks a little like Buck's Mess in the front, doesn't it?"

"Ron Pedale has a mayfly pattern with that kind of hackling, too."

The hackle on these innovations flares forward, forming a cup, or funnel, of fibers around the eye of the hook. There are two ways to exaggerate the wings of a mayfly—either by making the feature higher or by moving it forward. They are different enough in other ways, but on all of these strange looking flies the hackle, representing the wing tips, leans very far forward.

The original Buck's Mess frustrated us completely on the Big Hole. After two seasons of watching trout roll near it, nip it, and follow it downstream (but too often snub it), the pattern was banished until further tinkering.

It needed changes in all of its secondary characteristics. Some flaws were obvious—the yarn body was much too thick, bulging in the middle like a cigar; the moose hair wings were so long that sometimes they made the fly topple on its side; and the tail, formed by split V bunches, were heavy enough to look like two more insects hanging like little hitchhikers onto the main fly.

Even after these features were altered the Mess still wasn't right. It looked fine to me—or at least as fine as such a farfetched mayfly imitation

A spill pool dooms thousands of emerging mayfly duns to a watery death. The insects tumble over the lip, sink in the undertow, and come out drowned and bedraggled at the tail of the pool.

could look. The trout showed a lot of interest when it first entered the window, but they kept eyeing the fly suspiciously as it drifted through—sometimes taking and sometimes not.

Bam—there it went, into the oddball box with all of the other one-time wonders, where it would seldom see the light of day and then only under the most meaningless of circumstances. It stayed there for almost another year, but it was never buried too far in my thoughts.

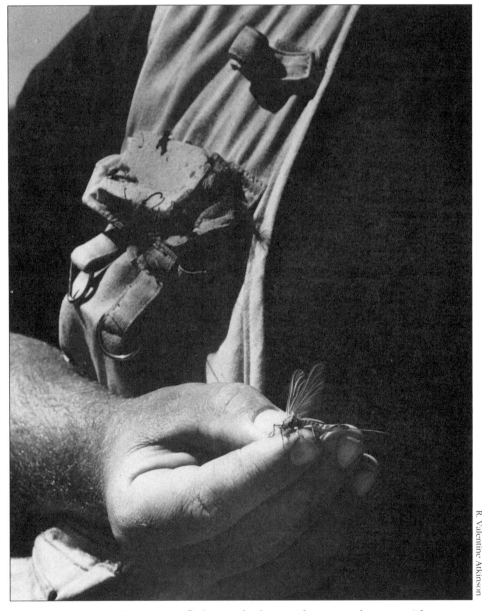

R. Valentine Atkinson

In my observations the Hex mayfly lays its body straight out on the water. This means that the fly has to match the full length of the insect. The choices for imitating large mayflies include the extended body type (not my favorite) or the Mess style.

What was wrong with that fly? It had the strongest triggering action of any imitation in our comparisons, but it also tallied the most secondary refusals. The only time a normal fly was turned down that often by selective trout was when it was at least two sizes too large.

That was the problem—it was too large. The hackle was already big enough, sticking out ahead of the fly, to change the relative size of the fly. Matching a size 14 insect with a size 14 Mess exaggerated the wing just fine. Watching it underwater, as the hackle entered the window, looming in disassociated ghastliness (like the special effects in a horror movie), made it clear why trout were fascinated with it. When the body of the fly slid into full focus in the middle of the window and the parts suddenly came together, however, it was suddenly a size 10 pattern.

There are very few mayflies in North America that demand a size 10 fly. The Hex (*Hexagenia limbata*) in the Midwest is matched with size 6 and size 4 dry flies, but a size 8 fly would be more accurate even for that monster. Other large mayflies, such as the eastern Green Drake (*Ephemera guttulata*) or the western Gray Drake (*Siphlonurus occidentalis*), are properly matched with a size 10 imitation. With these large mayflies, oddly enough, the back end of the insect does touch the water, and the abdomen should be part of the overall length of the fly. Many of these insects (including the Eastern Green Drake in my studies) lay the body out straight on the surface.

The Mess was redesigned to reflect these realities. The flaring, front feathers, a strange combination of stiff and soft hackles, were left long to exaggerate the wing. The hook was scaled down two sizes, reducing the overall length of the fly. A thorax of synthetic seal's fur was worked inside the hackle, creating not just a base but, flattened on the water, a brightness under the head as well. The tails were thinned to wisps, three split on each side, and curved up.

The body of the new fly had to be special—so right that it would mesmerize the fish, not just confirming the identity of the imitation but soothing any suspicions about the odd imprint pattern on the water, too. It had to have two features normally lacking on mayfly patterns—translucence and undercolor.

The body of the freshly emerged dun is translucent. Light passes through the skin and the tissue, and some colors of the spectrum are filtered out and those that are left are enhanced by the living, internal parts. That isn't the color that the angler sees. Even if he held up a specimen of the insect to natural sunlight, he might be looking at a male.

To a trout looking up, the males and females are clearly different for every species (this also applies to caddisflies, stoneflies, and midges on the surface). The body of the dun glows with a deep fire as light filters through it, but the females always have something inside them that the males don't— eggs. The eggs are intensely colored, ranging from green through pale yellow to an orange-red. The fish take either males or females during a hatch, but they notice the difference—the correct undercolor helps mask any other mistakes in secondary traits (it soothes suspicions).

Translucence was the problem in mayflies that so vexed J. W. Dunne. In his book, *Sunshine and the Dry Fly*, he wrote about sunshine flies. He used cellulite, a floss that dissolved when coated with celluloid varnish, forming a smooth, colored translucent body.

Did the flies work? Harold Golden, who fished them for years on English chalk streams, wrote to me, "In my opinion, yes, they caught more fish. I think that the bodies would have been even better on those no-hackle flies. Then the trout could have seen them better. They were almost worth as much trouble as they were to tie and preserve them."

The finest fly will not last if it is impractical. The cellulite bodies were not only difficult to tie; they also deteriorated very quickly in the sunlight (a grievous flaw in a sunshine fly). The materials became scarce, the floss disappearing entirely from catalogs, and the Sunshine Flies vanished from English trout streams.

The failure of the flies doesn't diminish the truth of Dunne's idea. A mayfly with a translucent body is better (especially on a fly that lies flush in the film). It's a problem that just had to wait for a new, practical material for achieving the right effect of color and translucence.

The answer for the Mess was the same material that glowed on the emerger patterns, the new closed cell foam, but it was used differently. The foam was tested on the flies in two ways—the hook shank was painted the

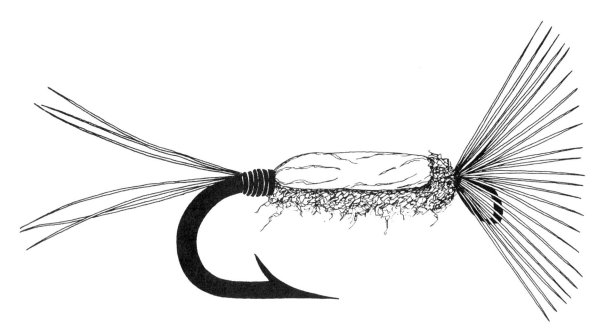

The Mess is the refinement of two earlier patterns, the very crude fly of a Big Hole River guide and the very delicate fly of Ron Pedale. Isn't it odd that this dry fly style always matches mayflies? The final version of the Mess, like its forerunners, really doesn't look like a mayfly, but it ultimately provides both the triggering characteric and the secondary characteristics that a trout wants to see in an emerging insect. It is such an excellent imitation of larger mayflies that it has replaced all of the extended body patterns in our boxes.

appropriate color (á la Dunne) and clear foam was wrapped on as a body, or the material was wrapped on and colored with a felt tip marker. The second method was easier, but either way achieved the desired effect.

The colors for the Mess correspond to the various parts of the mayfly body. The flared rooster hackle is the color of the wings, but the mallard feather in front is always a pale color. The synthetic seal substitute (Aunt Lydia's Polyester Kodel Yarn) matches the color of the thorax. The foam body is the color of the eggs in the female, not the external color of the insect's body. This results in some strange looking imitations — the Mess, for example, often has an orange body when every other fly ends up being green.

The Mess, using the information gained in the comparison testing, is designed to be the ideal mayfly imitation. Not perfect—ideal. It isn't possible to create a perfect fly, one that replaces all other imitations of a food form, because there are too many reasons that a fly succeeds.

What was the best method for exaggerating the mayfly's wings? It was the old fanwing style, the matched feathers curving outwards in splendid symmetry. These flies, too, were impractical (although in my attractor box there are still a few Fanwing Royal Coachmans). No matter how good they were—and the exaggeration was only slightly better than the Compara Dun and the Mess—they were never considered for a place in my box of mayfly imitations.

There are different styles of flies in my boxes, in many color combinations and sizes, just to imitate the mayfly dun, but it is not a confusing, hodgepodge assortment; every pattern has its purpose. There are none of the standard-tied flies, which look like miniature shaving brushes on the water, for example. These standard flies have a place elsewhere, in a box of general searching patterns, but not in my mayfly box. There are no extended-body creations, either, because for me they are poor hooking flies. The Thorax Duns and the No Hackles are left out, too, although hearing an eloquent and intelligent defense by Eric Peper for the Thorax Dun or by Mike Lawson for the No Hackle always makes me wonder about my decision. These flies are ultimately too good, their proportions too close to the live insect, thereby reducing their chances to the same odds as a natural and placing too much of a burden on presentation. My emergency tying kit for on-stream desperation, though, always holds the materials for Thorax Duns and No Hackles (the flies are for those sipping trout that hang with noses scant inches from the meniscus).

The Catskill dry flies and the Variants in my box are there for hatches that leave more duns on the water than nymph-dun hybrids struggling in it. The Compara Duns match the flush hatches, the majority of mayfly situations. Sometimes the strange imprint (the light pattern), makes this fly fail when secondary characteristics are critical, but such refusals are rare. The Mess series, tied only in size 14 or larger, is a silly looking imitation that seems to amuse and intrigue both angler and trout. It is more practical and effective for larger mayflies than the Compara Dun. The Parachute flies match

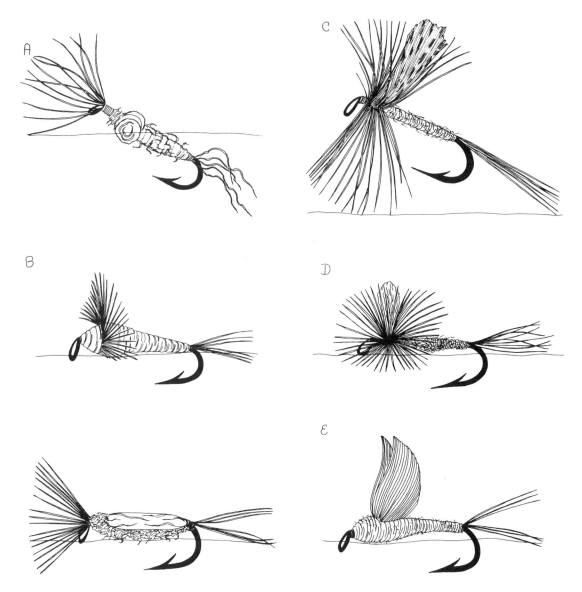

My selection of imitations for a mayfly hatch is not a hodgepodge; each "style" has a specific use.

A. The Halo Emerger hangs from the underside of the film. It's effective when trout are selectively taking emerging nymphs.

B. The Comparadun and the Mess are nymph-dun imitations. The Comparadun is good up to size 14. The Mess makes a fine match for mayflies larger than that. When is the best time for these half-in and half-out flies? When trout are feeding "sequentially," taking first a few emerging nymphs and then a few adults (or vice versa).

C. The classic Catskill patterns (and Variants) match the adult mayfly, riding perkily on the film.

D. Parachute patterns mimic drowned, bedraggled duns.

E. The "exact imitations," which lack a triggering characteristic, are saved for situations where trout hang just under the surface, when they see either emerging mayflies (the time for No Hackles) or free adults (the time for Thorax Duns) up close right away.

The advantage of the Flex Hook is the versatility of the interchangeable head. There is not just "one way" to tie the fly—different heads can be made from cork, balsa, spun deer hair, or large-cell closed foam. The fly tyer is free to have fun with the concept.

The orange light reflecting off the limestone cliff at the Abutment Pool "ruined" the picture, but this photographic mistake turned out to be an important clue for solving the Theory of Attraction.

Halo Mayfly Emerger

Shroud

Mohawk

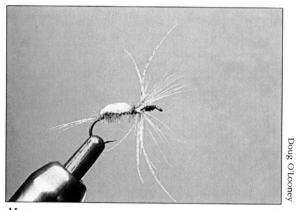

Mess

Air Head

Doug O'Looney

Double Wing

Doug O'Looney

Clear Wing Spinner

Doug O'Looney

Doug O'Looney

Occasion

drowned mayflies well. A selection of Rene Harrop's Captive Dun patterns are my alternative for stillborn and bedraggled emergers.

There's also my little box for new patterns that are promising, having proven their effectiveness in actual fishing. Flies such as the Sparkle Dun (Craig Mathews), Dumpy Butt (Chuck Tryon), and Close Carpet (George Close) don't have an exact, defined role yet, but there is no doubt that they are valuable concepts.

Mayfly Spinner

The trout was either snubbing me or my fly. "What does he want? I floated it right over his nose."

Tory Stosich was catching trout. "That's the problem," he said. "You're hitting the fish dead center with the drift."

This particular rainbow, like many trout, had a dominant eye, and preferred to feed off it in the smooth flow. He rose at a slight angle to the right, and was more likely to notice a fly drifting into that area of the window. He was so close to the surface that the window was small enough without having to divide it into sections.

That's how fussy spinner fishing gets in slow water. The presentation must be so precise, with absolutely no hint of drag, that the angler never knows whether to blame himself or his fly for failures. The sheer numbers of mayfly spinners on the water during a heavy fall add to the confusion. The "perfect" imitation is overwhelmed by naturals.

Vincent Marinaro tied two styles of no hackle spinner—one with wings partially upright, for early in the flight before the wings droop, and another with both wings spread out on the water. He noted in *A Modern Dry Fly Code*, "There is a great difference in the light patterns."

All innovations in mayfly spinners build on his observations and work. The rules never change—the fisherman studies the insects on the water to determine the wing posture of the naturals and matches the spinner with a no hackle pattern that creates the proper imprint on the surface film.

Force me to choose only one of my imitations and it would be the Clear Wing Spinner (even over the Emergent Sparkle Pupa). There is no way for me, or any other angler, to compensate for a poor fly during a heavy spinner fall. The presentation already has to be perfect—always. The Clear Wing Spinner, in the two different wing styles, in the proper size and color, competes well with the naturals for attention during those perfect drifts.

The innovation in this fly, built on Marinaro's no hackle principle, is the wing material. The hackle fibers of older patterns are dull, but the spent wings of the mayfly on the water, on the contrary, are anything but dull. Not only are they clear and shiny, but air bubbles collect in the pleats underneath them. Only the clear fibers of sparkle yarn can match—and even exceed— this brilliance. As a bonus, this material also collects air bubbles like the real mayfly.

The first thing the angler checks during a spinner fall is the "posture" of the dead insects. Are the wings flush, or is one wing still up? The fly should match the prevalent silhouette.

The alternative is the drab fly that enters the window along with a flotilla of naturals. The trout, looking up, sees all the bright wings and keys on one of the insects. He is not likely to search for a strange, hard-to-notice imitation during such a feeding glut.

A trout wants not only to rise, but, if possible, feed selectively, too. To do so he needs a certain number of insects entering his window of vision per minute, but he has a way of controlling that frequency; he can expand or shrink his window to fit the hatch.

During a heavy emergence or egg-laying fall, when fly life is plentiful, he can hold near the surface. The window can be very small and he still sees enough insects, that particular number per minute, to enable him to rise rhythmically. He feeds this way in slower water.

But what happens when the hatch is sparse? Now, to feed selectively, the trout has to drop lower. This opens the window, increasing the search area, and the trout sees more insects per minute. Typically, because the current is quieter near the bottom, he will hold right over the rocks rather than in the middle of the water column.

The trout is a graceful riser, no matter how many insects are available. Compare his feeding motion to the frantic slash, twist, and dive of a whitefish. What a contrast of evolutionary adaptation. The Rocky Mountain whitefish, with his cylindrical shape and small mouth, grubs so well on the bottom, but with this body he can't hold just under the surface and sip insects easily. Every rise starts from the floor of the stream, a reckless and inefficient dash that too often ends up in a miss. Seldom does any fish in a school rise rhythmically.

A trout looks as inept grubbing as a whitefish does rising. His body is too flat, and with the current catching it when he holds downwards, he must constantly readjust, throwing those flashes of brightness. Studies by biologists show that grubbing accounts for less than 15 percent of a trout's feeding activity in most stream environments.

Whitefish do rise and trout do grub, but with each species these seem like desperate alternatives. The very pattern of the trout's day, the cycle of resting and feeding, conforms to periods of insect abundance. Trout search for food when it's most likely, either as free-drifting nymphs or as adults, to be plentiful in the open currents.

The key to imitation is that a steadily feeding trout is always looking for something specific—he expects it to be there. Whether he snatches nymphs from the currents, plucks emergers from the underside of the film, or rises to adults riding on top of the water is determined by the relative abundance of food items at each level. At each zone he is searching for the triggering characteristic that identifies a particular stage of the insect life cycle.

The concept of a triggering characteristic can be carried to an extreme. It is wrong to put tall, exaggerated wings on a deep nymph. We know—we tried it. Reality wasn't going to limit us. Fish were feeding on adults and we wanted to see if they would accept an adult drifting near the bottom. They wouldn't take it consistently, even when it passed their noses. Take away that freedom and match the triggering characteristic to the correct feeding level, however, and there are few other impossibilities. The tyer's exaggeration of that primary trait doesn't have to be the same color, size, degree of brightness, or even in the same place as it is on the natural. It just has to be recognizable to the trout as a possible variation.

One angler politely came up to me after a morning's fishing on the Henry's Fork and asked if he could see the fly that I had been catching trout on. He looked at the Halo Emerger, my match for the Pale Morning Dun (*Ephemerella infrequens*) hatch and just shrugged, "Sometimes these rainbows do like a giggle."

Maybe they do. The way to exaggerate a triggering characteristic is to make it more visible to a fish. The only reason this primary trait can be more prominent than the real feature is because the trout searches for it when the fly is still relatively far away. He sees it, accepts it as the identifying trait of the natural, and, as he moves closer, forgets it.

The secondary characteristics, the basis for confirmation, are dangerous to exaggerate because when the trout looks for these he is very close to the fly. They have to be in balance, all of them together presenting the picture that the trout expects to see. The fact that the fly tyer's perception of reality often doesn't match that of the fish makes on-stream, trial-and-error tinkering absolutely necessary for these secondary traits—the color, size, and shape.

Let me explain what genius is in fly tying. It's the ability to see a problem and not settle for the easy and obvious solution. So often new flies are simply an evolution; and evolution is clumsy. The older way of tying the fly seldom fits the new solution.

There are three areas for the innovative tyer to study—the water, the trout, and the insect. American anglers are fortunate—they have had the

R. Valentine Atkinson

One river where the Halo Emerger was tested extensively by my friends was the Henry's Fork in Idaho. They fished it effectively during the heavy mayfly hatches of late June.

chance to read provocative dry fly books such as _Fishing Dry Flies for Trout_ (a study of water) by Art Lee; _What the Trout Said_ (a study of a trout's perceptions) by Datus C. Proper; and _Fishing the Dry Fly as a Living Insect_ (a study of insect behavior) by Leonard Wright, Jr. It is caricature in fly tying that can bring the three disciplines, and their spokesmen, together.

The angler should ultimately look at all of his imitations with a skewed eye. If they aren't a bit humorous, offbeat caricatures with a particularly noticeable feature of the natural exaggerated, distorted but still recognizable reflections of the live, original models, then they simply might be too good—tributes to tyers more interested in exact representation than success on the water.

My Fly Box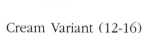

Mayfly Imitations

Black Quill (14-18)

Blue Quill (14-16)

Blue Wing Olive (16-20)
(a hackled version for
imitating _Baetis_ duns)

Captive Dun (14-20)
(a Rene Harrop creation for matching the stillborn duns)

Clear Wing Spinner (8-22)
(this series has body colors of
black, rust, cream, olive, pale gray,
reddish orange, and dark brown)

Close Carpet (12-16)

Compara Dun (14-22)
(the color designations for this
series list the wing color first and
the body color second: White, Pale
Gray/Cream, Cream/Yellow, Pale
Gray/Yellowish Olive, Slate/Olive,
Gray/Yellowish Gray, Dark Gray/
Brown, Pale Gray/Black)

Cream Variant (12-16)

Cul de Canard (12-18)
(this fly typically survives only one
fish; if the angler is a good observer, each one of those trout will
be a fine one)

Dark Cahill (12-18)

Dark Hendrickson (12-18)

Double Trike (14-16)
(this fly features two sets of wings,
simulating two Trico spinners drifting
together)

Dumpy Butt (14-16)
(a new pattern—and it truly deserves
that tag—created by Chuck Tryon)

Dun Variant (12-16)

Ginger Quill (14-20)

Gray Fox Variant (12-16)
(an indispensable pattern for me)

Light Cahill (10-16)

Light Hendrickson (12-18)

March Brown (10-16)

Meloche (16-20)
(originated by Dan Bailey for matching an August mayfly brought into his shop by Gilbert Meloche. Meloche then went back to the stream and caught the first trout for the Wall of Fame. What mayfly was it? The colors are not quite exact, but the time of year, the time of the day, the spring creek environment, and the size of the fly all point to the Pale Morning Dun.)

Mess (6-12)
(a series with White, Medium Gray/ Lime, Cream/Lime, Medium Gray/ Orange, Cream/Orange, Dark Gray/ Brown, Pale Gray/Yellowish Olive, Slate/Olive, Gray/Yellowish Gray, and Pale Gray/Black versions)

Orange Quill (16-18)
(an English pattern popularized by G. E. M. Skues)

Pale Evening Dun (14-20)

Parachute (12-24)
(the Adams Parachute, Blue Wing Olive Parachute, Light Cahill Parachute, Mahogany Parachute, Pale Morning Dun Parachute, and Para Spin are the standard color variations in my box)

Quill Gordon (12-18)
(this pattern matches a number of mayflies for me—not just *Epeorus pleuralis*)

Red Quill (14-18)

Sparkle Dun (14-20)
(this is an excellent variation of the Compara Dun; there is a trailing "shuck" of sparkle poly yarn—color variations are the same as for the Compara Dun)

Comments:

Does the angler/entomologist have to carry a lot of flies? What a strange notion. Such an idea totally misunderstands how a knowledge of the hatches on a stream changes confusion into simplicity. The naturalist, if he is supremely confident and a bit cocky, only has to take one or two patterns with him to familiar waters on any given day.

On an overcast afternoon in late September the only important insect hatching on Montana's Clark Fork below Missoula is the Blue Wing Olive (*Baetis*). A fly matching the emerging mayfly catches trout early, but on these cold, damp days the duns ride a long time and soon the rainbows and cutthroats (the latter so fat, shaped like a semicircle, that local anglers call them footballs) key on the concentration of insects truly *on* the surface. A size 16 hackled pattern, a Blue Wing Olive, is the main pattern the fisherman needs in his box.

In the 1986 edition of *Hatches* (Al Caucci and Bob Nastasi) included my new foreword. One paragraph dealt with the concept of simplicity (a central theme in that great book):

That is the force behind the entomological wave that has swept fly fishing in the last few decades. It takes so much more effort to blunder around a trout stream, flailing with nondescript patterns, in effect, guessing, than it does to observe the natural clues. There is no fun in inefficiency and ignorance; even a basic understanding of the trout's food reduces the probable angling choices to a workable number.

My carrying stock of mayfly styles is very specific. The Compara Dun (matching the nymph-dun in the act of shedding the skin) and the classic Catskill dry fly (matching the fully emerged dun) are the major patterns in the selection. The Mess series has replaced extended body flies in my stock for matching large mayflies. The Parachute type flies simulate drowned, bedraggled duns.

The Clear Wing Spinner is really indispensable for mimicking medium and small mayflies, especially the size 18 to 22 Tricos—the beauty there, with the Sparkle Yarn wings reflecting so much light, is that even the tiniest flies are highly visible to the fisherman. If some of the sizes recommended for this fly seem unusually large, on the other hand, it is because the pattern also doubles as a Searcher/Attractor in my fishing.

I always carry materials with me for tying Thorax Duns and No Hackles. Why not just pack along finished flies? I only use these "exact" patterns for the fussiest situations (for example, when trout hang inches from the surface and study every detail of the imitation). It is difficult—if not impossible—to tie up a fly months before a hatch that will precisely match a natural. Characteristics such as color and size in insects vary not only from stream to stream, but on the same stream from week to week. These secondary traits are so important on Thorax Duns and No Hackles that I like to use one of the actual mayflies hatching at the moment as an on-stream model for these flies.

My body colors for insect imitations frequently do not follow the prescribed shades. The commonly recommended colors match only the outside skin of the natural. There is an undercolor with females, an intense fire caused by the sunlight passing through the eggs inside the body. The Mess series contains four color combinations that simulate the main "undercolors"—Medium Gray/Lime and Cream/Lime for the pale green eggs and Medium Gray/Orange and Cream/Orange for the reddish-orange eggs. The way to identify the undercolor in the field is to hold the female insect up to the light and view the abdomen with a hand magnifying glass.

Chapter 7

A Grasshopper Study

A grasshopper falls with a delicious *smack!*, spreading tiny concentric waves, and it is always surprising if a trout doesn't take it immediately. It's part of our fly fishing mythology: Any grasshopper unfortunate enough to land on the stream will be attacked like a blood bait in a shark frenzy. Some grasshoppers *are* snatched down by fish at once—about one percent of them. The rest drift along for a way, and are eventually dispersed by currents to all parts of the flow; the ones not eaten escape or just sink. Drowned grasshoppers undoubtedly end up as fish food also, but fly

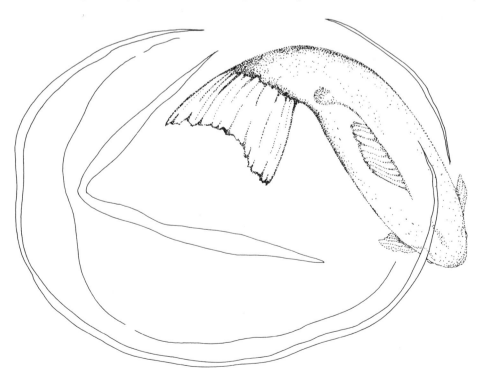

Even when he doesn't "explode" under a grasshopper, a trout usually takes it with a strong, rolling motion that makes a characteristic semicircle on the surface.

fishermen are so enthralled by the rise of a trout to a grasshopper that they generally ignore this subsurface opportunity (which might be a mistake).

What is there about the rise? Usually a trout takes a grasshopper neither frantically nor gently, but in an instantly recognizable motion—a roll that leaves a characteristic semicircle on the surface that means *hopper-feeder* to the experienced angler. The basis for this behavior might be psychological: The fish knows that the insect is helpless, which eliminates the need to rush, but at the same time he must be so reluctant to let this tempting morsel sit there that greed forces him forward. Or the reason just might be physical: To turn up and engulf it like this may be a surer way of capturing a large, buoyant insect. No dainty sip will do for a grasshopper.

But no fly fisherman ever remembers those assured, rolling takes after the season. He carries instead a picture of an eruption, the thrust of a large trout surging half out of the water, shaking spray, as it smashes a grasshopper. This happens often enough, but most strikes are not so spectacular.

Such unreal expectations are part of the paradox of hopper fishing. Maybe this is a symptom; almost everything that fly fishermen believe about this activity ends up being false.

What makes a good grasshopper day, or month, or year? What are the population dynamics of the insect?

How do trout react to a grasshopper? Do they respond the same way to the natural, or the imitation, every day? Or do they have different moods that demand different tactics?

What is the best imitation? Is any one pattern (and there are so many) significantly better than the rest?

Good Years; Poor Years

On some of my "chumming" days, as I sprawled beside a river tossing grasshoppers onto the water, the trout took almost every one of the sacrificial victims; on other days the same stream might as well have been deserted. I experienced many more poor grasshopper afternoons than good ones.

That all changed in the summer of 1984, when a bumper crop of grasshoppers hatched early and grew quickly in my Montana valley. In downtown Deer Lodge, on hot days, the insects would cluster in rows on the sides of buildings. Along the Clark Fork River it was worse; grasshoppers everywhere were jumping out of some simple herd reflex, at least one ending up on the water every few minutes.

Never before had there been a perfect day, when trout took every one of my fifty chum grasshoppers, but by mid-July that year the average had climbed to thirty-five out of fifty. On one warm afternoon near the end of the month the tally rose to forty-nine straight, every hopper gulped down before my binoculars, somewhere in the 150 yards of river before the bend. There was only a single "volunteer" left in the bottle.

The last one stared at me, a Migratory Grasshopper (as were all the others this day), dribbling brown juice onto my fingers. My usual pre-launch pep talk was losing any sincere enthusiasm; the odds were just too depressing. It was the wrong day of the wrong year for a grasshopper to be swimming.

Those trout had been nosing upstream all day, ever closer to my cover on a brushy spit. The first hoppers chummed onto the surface had made it down a tongue of current, at least until they drifted over a limestone ledge, but then a shoal of five nice fish had taken positions in the shallow water. My last few insects vanished instantly in a rush of swirls.

Maybe they were actually onto my timing, because as I hesitated, holding the final grasshopper, the trout began breaking the surface, almost pushing each other onto the bar. Here were wild, wary brown trout cavorting like hatchery fish. It wouldn't have taught me anything more to toss that last hopper to them. So I let him go in the grass. It was an act of mercy.

Nothing affects the quality of grasshopper fishing more than the abundance or scarcity of the insects. The quantity ending up in the water quickly conditions the trout; enough grasshoppers passing overhead make the fish eager, but without this chumline they quickly become leery of the best imitations and, even, of stray naturals. A grasshopper infestation along a fine stream actually reorients the fish—even in the richest waters, trout appreciate all that extra food falling continuously. They gorge throughout the summer months until they become so wedded to the midday routine of hopper feeding that little else interests them. They abandon their usual holding spots, setting up tight to grassy banks on the windward side instead.

If only those fly fishermen who dote so much on hopper fishing realized how big a difference an abundance or a scarcity of insects means to their summer angling success. There is no comparison between the sport in an infestation area and that in a depressed area. Why return blindly to the same river year after year, then, if some seasons are good and some seasons are poor for grasshoppers? Why wait for that one great year out of ten, no matter how spectacular, when nearly every season produces incredible populations of grasshoppers somewhere.

Fishermen can predict how good the grasshopper season will be along their local streams. Even in ideal regions, populations can fluctuate greatly from year to year. A boom year, of course, produces more of those outstanding hopper fishing days, but three or four years of the right conditions prime the insect population for a severe outbreak. Everyone should experience a grasshopper plague once, if only to see nature out of control.

A good year for grasshopper populations would start with (1) cool weather early in the spring to prevent premature hatching; followed by (2) several weeks of continuously warm, dry weather late in the spring, to encourage a complete hatch and to provide ideal feeding conditions. Then there must be (3) a hot summer, with enough rain for an ample food supply but with no extended damp periods that might stimulate disease; and finally (4) a mild, late autumn, ensuring maximum egg-laying time.

In those years, hopper hoards attack crops conveniently arranged in monoculture plots first, stripping everything off the stalks and leaving behind a field of skeleton sticks. Then, they clear weeds and tall grasses. Lawns are fairly safe, simply because they are clipped so short there is no shade for the insects, but the grasshoppers gnaw the bark off trees, killing them. They also eat holes in clothes hung on lines and even get inside homes, ruining curtains and more clothing.

Grasshopper flights increase when vegetation is short and midday temperatures rise above 75 degrees Fahrenheit. Under these conditions the ground surface heats up to more than 100 degrees, yet even in direct sunlight insects can find a place 40 degrees cooler simply by climbing two inches up a blade of grass. They can find a still cooler spot by seeking shade—if they can find any. In infestation years the insects feed so voraciously that they rapidly reduce both the height and density of any vegetation. Soon there's little to climb on, and no shade. Then the grasshoppers take to the air in swarms to cool off; many end up on the water.

Not all areas of the country are equally blessed (or cursed) with grasshoppers. They never become abundant in deserts because of lack of food. In areas with prolonged spells of rain, cloudiness, or even high humidity, bacterial and fungal diseases decimate the insects. They do thrive

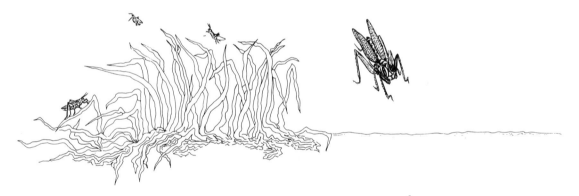

Trout fall into a rather unthinking feeding routine. They do not ordinarily seek food—they simply find the best places in a stream to wait for it. But grasshoppers are different. Trout do choose particular areas not just to wait but to hunt, and they are ready to rush towards any grasshopper that hits the water. This happens only when grasshoppers are very abundant (my observations of this "orienting" behavior were on the Clark Fork, the Big Horn, and the Yellowstone—including one amazing brown trout on the Yellowstone who would move towards the splash point while the grasshopper was still in the air).

Rick Harding

in moderately dry climates (states with an average rainfall of ten to thirty inches). While localized outbreaks can occur almost anywhere, the Midwest and Rocky Mountain regions provide ideal breeding grounds.

It isn't necessary for hopper-fishing fanatics to monitor weather conditions far and wide to find hopper hotspots for the coming season. They might consider this a small task for grand fishing; if they could locate mini-plagues, they could concentrate on the best waters within that region.

Actually, the government already does this homework. Every fall the United States Department of Agriculture sends out teams of entomologists to check grasshopper egg-laying success. They then match the egg counts with long-range weather forecasts to pinpoint probable areas of infestation for the following year. During the winter, the department publishes and distributes a hopper map (free through county extension offices) of the entire country. It might as well be a treasure map for fly fishermen interested in incredible grasshopper days.

Good Days; Poor Days

The more grasshoppers that land on the water, the more receptive the fish are. The only variation in this rule happens after a spell of ideal conditions. Then the fish keep looking for grasshoppers on the first bad day. This situation—trout lined up at the dinner table with no food being served—creates spectacular dry fly sport in the shallows, but after a few bad days, with few natural grasshoppers available, the fish move back to their usual stream-bottom haunts.

The sun controls the daily activity of grasshoppers. In early morning the insects crawl from their hiding places and position themselves broadside to it, absorbing the radiant energy. They start moving when the temperature reaches 68 to 70 degrees, remaining active until the cooler hours of dusk. Rain, or even just a thick cover of clouds, ends the fluttering and hopping for the day.

The number of grasshoppers falling on the water depends on more than temperature, however. Even when stream banks are thick with insects, four other factors affect the frequency, height, and direction of their hops and flights: stream width, wind, vegetation, and bank activity. A grasshopper in midflight is *not* out of control; it knows when it's over water, and it knows that it doesn't belong there. It usually manages to turn back or to fly across the stream to the opposite side. So anything that disrupts its control improves the grasshopper fishing.

Wind is the most important factor because it pushes the insect in one direction (out over water when the wind is blowing off the bank). On small streams a grasshopper simply flies to the safety of the other side, but on larger rivers it might not make it across; if it can't turn back, it's in trouble.

The height of the grass and brush along the banks affects the altitude of the initial jump; fishermen should look for vegetation that is waist-high, so the insects leap well up into the wind.

Finally, any streamside activity—such as a wandering cow or a hay-cutting machine—that provokes grasshoppers into quick, uncontrolled hops also scatters more of them over the water.

Grasshopper Strategies

All fly fishermen know something about grasshoppers, and this may be one reason most of us fish the imitations lazily. We all catch trout on grasshopper patterns, and at first blush these successes might even seem satisfactory. When measured against *potential* catches, however, typical hopper days are usually the least—not the most—that anglers should expect from effective mimicry.

Why? Well, few flies are cast with less forethought than grasshopper types. They are slapped down indiscriminately and drifted haphazardly at both the right times and the wrong times on waters all over the country. Amazingly, they usually catch some fish, bass as well as trout, but these minor triumphs occur because the imitations are so easy to use randomly. The occasional fish obscures the greater opportunities.

Suggest that someone use a stonefly or a caddisfly imitation, and he has questions: *when, where,* and *how?* But hand him a hopper pattern, any one of them, and he strides boldly out to meet the trout. He fishes it one way, usually with a slap-and-drift presentation, on the fringes of the good water.

Fly fishermen need to understand certain facts about grasshoppers: For one, they aren't the most abundant or even the most important terrestrials along trout streams. In wooded sections beetles provide most of the drop-in fare, and in meadow areas leafhoppers fall into the stream much more frequently (on the order of fifty to one). The ubiquitous ant also stands well ahead of the grasshopper. Often an imitation of one of these smaller insects will catch more trout than a grasshopper pattern. It is easy to recognize when this is happening. The fish roll up to that bigger fly, and maybe even nip it, but every strike ends short (call it a _curiosity refusal_).

Oddly, the time to use grasshopper imitations is during either the best or worst of summer situations; between these extremes it's often wiser to match the smaller terrestrials. Anglers instinctively recognize those ideal hopper days: The hot air, alleviated only by a gusty breeze, settles in by early morning; if nothing else, the constant crackling and buzzing sound of insects and the rustling of the grass make it an unforgettable situation. The combination of wind and high-jumping hoppers dumps a steady supply of big morsels on the water; and this, in turn, conditions the fish to look for such food. At least until appetites are somewhat dulled, greed overrules discrimination in their feeding. Perfect grasshopper conditions reduce the problems of imitating large insects.

During the middling days, not perfect but seemingly still suitable, hopper fishing usually disappoints the random caster. Either the fish are deeper, not actively on the prowl for grasshoppers, or else they are sipping those smaller terrestrials and are inclined to selectivity. Their native caution, in force whenever they aren't overanxious, makes them view the larger imitation too carefully. There are ways to disguise the fraud—if the fly is presented to the right place in the right way it can still elicit a reaction, but this is not random casting. The flogger slapping a grasshopper fly on the stream during a middling day catches the occasional fish only when he accidently does everything right.

On poor angling days, when the summer water is so warm that trout are lethargic, the _expert_ hopper fisherman still does surprisingly well—and he may be the only angler doing anything under the midday sun because he is properly imitating such a choice food item. A grasshopper is a large, helpless chunk of meat. For a trout in warm water, caught between a high metabolic rate and low energy for feeding, it represents enough temptation to make him stir. Normally that fish might sit quietly until the river cools; but although he might refuse the first pass of the fly, even the second or third, if he's teased enough he will finally rise to a grasshopper.

Different tactics not only work for different times of the year but also for different times of the day—now fishing a grasshopper imitation becomes a thinking game. It also becomes much more productive.

For an angler who wants to catch more and larger trout, even the casting strokes have to change with the situation. The basic slap cast works well only when the fish lie deep, watching the surface and reacting to the plop of natural or fake. It's not such a dangerous tactic then, but slam a fly on the head of a trout holding near the surface and the result in usually panic.

The more delicate drop cast (the fly hitting without the splash) still attracts an interested trout, and it reduces the chance of spoiling water. It's also more natural; watch a real grasshopper fall and this is obvious. The energy that a fast-turning leader imparts to a big fly makes an exaggerated

A beetle imitation may not only be the most useful "all around" terrestrial, but the most valuable fly for general searching. It is usually a better fly than a grasshopper pattern for average size fish.

crash that sometimes works splendidly, but the gentle plop produces more consistently.

It's a trade-off. Two anglers may move along a bank—one slapping with enthusiasm and the other dropping with finesse—but they won't catch trout of similar disposition. The pounder gets the ones most likely to chase a fly. These more active, less cautious feeders tend to be smaller—except when competitive fervor makes all fish move fast to a fly.

Experiences on both eastern and western rivers make me feel that the gentler approach usually works better for large fish. The fly should of course drop upstream from the trout, just at the edge of his perception. The distance should vary with the water; the rougher the surface the closer the fall, but three to four feet above the fish usually proves safe. The purpose is to alert him—no more. The drift should cover the holding spot, but a few feet above the lie the angler twitches the fly (not boisterously; it's enough to mimic the ineffective kick and struggle of the natural). Only if the imitation passes by the trout without a strike should the fisherman twitch it again.

Nothing is spoiled by such a subtle presentation. *It can be repeated*, and this may be the secret of its effectiveness. With pauses of at least thirty seconds between drifts, a hopper fly becomes a teaser. The fishing becomes a game of convincing the trout that the "hatch" is real.

The early season, when the new crop of tiny grasshoppers begins foraging, demands a patient approach for tempting reluctant fish. The trout have not seen enough grasshoppers in the spring to begin keying on them. The naturals, therefore, are just another random, unfamiliar food for possible testing. It takes a few drifts with a matching fly, and possibly some of those subtle twitches, to make fish believe (or remember) that grasshoppers are edible.

During the peak of the midsummer grasshopper frenzy, such a methodical approach wastes time. Interested fish are going to hit the first drift—they are waiting for these insects.

When a trout concentrates on grasshoppers, it feeds more by sound than by sight. The fish senses the fall of the insect and the disturbance on the surface through its lateral line, rushing from as far as ten feet to the scene. A clear view of the natural is obscured because the fish is moving, and even the roughest imitation may satisfy a trout then.

This is the day to slap the fly along the bank. Even the choice spots deserve no more than a few drifts; it's best to wade upstream, casting towards shore, showing the fly to as many fish as possible. Big and small trout both will race to the *splat!* The point now is to put the fly near those niches that hold big fish.

The late season after the first frosts can be chilly and unsettled or warm and stable—spells that can produce either spring-like or summer-like grasshopper fishing. In both scenarios, the nights become colder and the grasshopper population, after egg laying, begins to decline even with seemingly ideal weather. The productive hours for grasshopper fishing narrow daily. The unpredictable fall season develops into a game of picking and choosing the right moments for grasshopper tactics.

Grasshopper Presentation

Hopper fishing is not for the timid caster. Picking and pecking at the edges of overhanging vegetation only wastes the water. The good grasshopper caster keeps his fly in and under the streamside snags. Successful drifts pass through the tangles of branches from overhanging trees and brush, dallying momentarily on that magic inner ribbon of calm water no more than a few inches from the bank.

The art of dapping is one of the simplest and deadliest tactics for picking individual fish from tough holds. It isn't, however, an efficient way to cover a stretch of stream. Anyone who tries to catch all the bank-hangers by dapping is going to spend more time crawling than fishing. For stalking that one old warhorse barricaded in an unreachable maze of cover, however, it presents a grasshopper pattern perfectly. Instead of simply flopping the fly down immediately, it's better to touch it teasingly on the surface a few times. Then, it can be lowered for short drifts against the bank.

Fishing blind, simply covering water instead of individual fish or even individual spots, demands efficiency more than finesse. A parallel presentation, with the angler standing right on or against the bank and working upstream, divides the water into strips. Nothing fancy here—just plop and drift, letting the fly search for random trout from the bank out to the dropoff. This is not the way to reach the tougher—and in many streams, the bigger—fish, but the fly blankets a lot of water quickly, and on the right day this technique will produce the greatest number of trout.

Plopping and drifting, to be blunt, is a chump method. Unfortunately, it's the method of lazy fly fishermen everywhere for letting a good hopper pattern, so tantalizing that it works even when it's fished poorly, draw out the occasional explosive strike. It's enough for most fly fishermen.

Not for me; there is something better. Other fly fishermen must use the skip cast, but I have never actually seen anyone else do it. Someone must have written about it, too, but I have never found another description in print. Still, it's so simple and so effective that it can't be much of a mystery. It is the difference between waiting for the fish come to the fly and aggressively going after them with it. Yet, depending on the placement, the skip cast fits the mood of the fish; it can be subtle and exciting at the same time.

The *skip cast* is the most effective technique of all for presenting a grasshopper. The fisherman delivers the fly with a sidearm motion, throwing a tight loop of line at a high speed. The grasshopper hits the water at a low angle and caroms forward as far as another two feet. The skip puts the fly back under the tightest canopies or cut banks; on many rivers this is the only way to coax those retiring brown trout out during midday.

Wherever possible the angler should kneel or at least squat down in the water, for otherwise he is silhouetted against the sky or bank where any fish can see him. Kneeling not only lowers his profile, it also lets him reach farther back under overhanging obstacles.

To "skip" the fly the angler gets low to the water and casts a tight, fast loop sidearm. He needs an aerodynamic pattern (the Henry's Fork Hopper, with its bullet head, is my favorite design for this tactic). This is not a technique just for overhung banks. The "bounce" can be directed two or three feet from any holding lie—the commotion on the surface grabs the attention of any trout.

That is all there is to it. But the skip cast should be used on every delivery, in open as well as overgrown water, with soft as well as hard presentations. The initial skip might crash onto the surface, but the landing at the end of the bounce settles feebly onto the water. The effectiveness of the skip cast lies with its duality—the splash alerts the fish, but the fly itself arrives softly (the carom should never hit the trout, or the target area). This tactic works even for the shyest trout. The key is to make the bounce hit five feet (or more) away, and let the fly settle within a few feet of the fish. At such distances, this is still a delicate delivery.

Grasshopper Imitations

Grasshoppers have never been totally ignored by fly fishermen. Observant anglers always knew that the occasional grasshopper ended up in the water, and numerous (and very realistic) imitations have existed for years. Until the American obsession with them—marked by a continual flow of articles and stories—began thirty-five years ago, however, grasshoppers were just not considered an important trout food.

Such a misconception, like many others, stems from the influence of English tradition over early American fly fishermen. Not that English theorists were ignorant of grasshoppers, either: Charles Cotton, in his 1676 addition to *The Compleat Angler*, included two matching patterns.

Nevertheless, grasshoppers remained an afterthought to British anglers. As Robert Ince explained in a letter, "I have never seen a grasshopper on a stream or lake in this country. We do have them over here, but not in the tremendous quantities that I've seen in the United States. I can assure you that if grasshoppers appeared on our waters regularly, fly fishermen would design and fish effective imitations."

Why are grasshoppers uncommon in the British Isles? It's simple. Those islands are rainy and damp; grasshopper populations fall prey to diseases in such places. This is the tradition (so right for them and so wrong for us) that taught the early Catskill theorists to disregard grasshoppers.

Perhaps on those forested, freestone New York rivers these insects *deserved* only minor attention. None of the Eastern states experienced regular cycles of grasshopper hoards; occasional infestations might occur anywhere in the region, but without those widespread, periodic plagues, fly fishermen felt that they didn't need to codify a theory of grasshopper imitation (a notable exception to the general apathy about terrestrials might be a most interesting series of flies designed by Theodore Gordon "neither to sink nor float").

Paul Schullery, former director of the American Museum of Fly Fishing, emphasized to me that the place to research early fly fishing in America is not in the books, but in the sporting journals and catalogs of the era. He immediately found a grasshopper fly in the Thomas Chubb catalog (a firm that flourished in Post Mills, Vermont in the 1880s and 1890s). Even though there was no information about how to fish the pattern or even whether it was a wet or dry fly, an illustration showed a precise imitation with legs and wings.

Although mentions of grasshoppers and their imitations were scattered throughout the early periodicals, there was no serious effort in the literature to understand their niche in fly fishing. It was a glaring oversight, made all

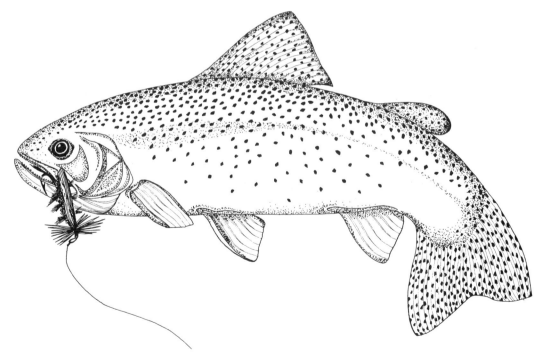

In many catalogs, the Joe's Hopper has been replaced by more exact imitations. But the old Joe's Hopper, both wet and dry, still catches trout.

the more obvious by many well-done articles in these journals about using natural grasshoppers as bait. In that more egalitarian age, when fishermen were likely to switch freely among all methods and tackle types, the grasshopper was valued more as a live lure than as a model for imitation. It was either fished crudely, dunked on the bottom with a sinker, or masterfully, drifted wet or dry (often with a fly rod) as a moving bait.

Something changed this philosophy and led to the modern popularity of grasshopper flies. It wasn't the development of new, effective imitations—that assumption would flatter modern tyers and insult past masters too much. Innovators, of course, experimented continuously with various materials: George Herter, in *Professional Fly Tying and Tackle Making Manual* (late 1930s) presented an exact, clipped deer hair imitation; Art Winnie, in the early 1940s, developed his Michigan Hopper (known now as the Joe's Hopper), a turkey wing and hackle pattern that spawned a similar variation from that region, the Cooper's Hopper; Ray Bergman, in the 1952 edition of *Trout*, included the dressing for Cooper's Hopper, although he himself favored a fore-and-aft grasshopper fly; and Vincent Marinaro, in *A Modern Dry Fly Code*, devoted part of a chapter on grasshoppers to Bill Bennett's Pontoon Hopper. It was odd that Marinaro, writing about the fussy, limestone fisheries of Pennsylvania, should tout such a clumsy, unworkable fly as the Pontoon Hopper—a pattern with a plugged, hollow quill body. Fortunately, the emphasis on grasshoppers in *A Modern Dry Fly Code* made a lasting impact on the American fly fishing scene, even as the fly faded quickly to deserved oblivion.

Those Pennsylvania creeks were different from the rushing brooks and rivers of the mountains. Instead, they meandered through meadows, their trout feeding in the spring-chilled water throughout the summer months. On such waters not only grasshoppers but many other terrestrials were finally elevated to more than an afterthought in the fly fishing scheme. The only problem was that the fish demanded effective tactics and patterns.

It was on the Letort that Ernest Schwiebert developed his grasshopper imitation. The fly, inspired by the western successes of a greased Muddler Minnow, offered a clean silhouette to the trout. Its fish appeal, along with its bouyancy and durability, made it a favorite among limestone anglers. Once the Letort Hopper proved itself on other types of trout streams, it spread across the country to rival the popularity of the Joe's Hopper.

The developments of the 1950s signaled a new age in hopper fishing. There is no other way to describe the change—even a cursory review of angling literature shows a definite break in fly fishing attitudes. Articles began to appear regularly in the magazines; most of this work simply rehashed the obvious, but the better writers began to explore grasshopper tactics seriously.

At the same time, the eastern magazines discovered the Rocky Mountain region. Grasshoppers and the semiarid West—the combination was more than just coincidence. The angling population of this country, made much more mobile by increased leisure time and better highways, flocked to the windy, range land rivers of the high country. In the dry western states, they found incredible numbers of grasshoppers.

Why? What are the prime fly fishing months on eastern trout streams? May and early June, before the grasshoppers become abundant. But what are the prime fly fishing months in the Rockies? Late July, August, and September, when the grasshoppers reach full growth. The sociological phenomenon of fly fishing travel finally made trout and grasshoppers synonymous.

The West never developed any popular grasshopper imitations of its own. There were general flies by area tyers, not specifically meant to match the insect, that served as rough copies; the Bunyon Bug (Norman Means) and the Bloody Butcher (Jack Boehme), for example, worked as midsummer floaters. Western fly fishermen adopted patterns from other areas, mainly the Joe's Hopper and the Palmer Hopper, a cork-bodied variation from the East. Maybe the greatest contribution by the West to grasshopper mimickry was Dan Bailey's alteration of the Muddler Minnow. He made a more robust version of the Don Gapen fly, with a head of densely spun deer hair, so that the Muddler could be greased and drifted on the surface as a grasshopper imitation.

George Grant, who sold sporting goods and fishing tackle for over twenty years in Butte, Montana, confirmed the dearth of original grasshopper patterns from the West. He also offered a possible explanation, "Almost all Montana anglers were wet fly men before 1950. There was very little market for any kind of dry fly." One of my pollings of fly fishermen across the country verified the modern dominance of the dry fly version of the grasshopper imitation. The Joe's Hopper still held a following among older anglers, but younger fly fishermen split their allegiance among three hair-head imitations—the Dave's Hopper, the Gartside Hopper, and the Letort Hopper.

The most interesting quirk in the poll was the devotion of a small minority of fishermen to the Joe's Hopper, fished not as a dry fly but as a wet fly. This group may have been few in number, but none of the other respondents felt as strongly about a particular pattern.

Or, to quote the scribbled note of Myron Craik, "On top even a grass bud will work at the right time. So who cares about those other flies? But underwater it's different. Tie up some weighted Joe's Hoppers and you'll see what I mean."

August was a month of fishing competition that year. This was no formal contest of any kind; instead, it was just a friendly match between myself and Denny Nops to pit the grasshopper fisherman against the nymph fisherman. As with any acceptable competition, it really wasn't important who won the days. It was a way to learn about the effectiveness of different methods at different times.

Every morning on the Little Blackfoot River, precisely at 9 A.M., the fishing started at the first pool above the Avon Bridge. On most days it was my job to work a grasshopper imitation, while Denny, a superb nymph fisherman, plied his delicate Hare's Ear or Zug Bug patterns. Occasionally we exchanged roles: Denny took over as hopper slapper while I became the nymph plopper. This worked out all right, too.

On the Little Blackfoot, an odd Montana stream that never runs warmer than 60 degrees Fahrenheit even during hot weather, the brown trout rise best during midday (breaking their night or low light feeder stereotype).

From 9 A.M. to noon the nymph easily outperformed the grasshopper or any dry fly, the tally usually standing at roughly twelve to four for the sunken pattern. At midday the grasshopper began catching up, however, until by late afternoon the floating fly had passed the nymph. Only when the bright sun left the river, at 5:30 P.M., did the nymph again start catching more fish; then, even with full-blown hatches of mayflies and caddisflies in the evening air and on the water, the nonconformist brown trout of the Little Blackfoot seldom rose to naturals or imitations.

On one of our reverse days, with me drifting a nymph along the brushy banks and through the pools, the early morning generally proceeded predictably enough (the nymph surging ahead). This one summer day bloomed even hotter than usual, 90 degrees by 10 A.M., however, and either the grasshopper activity or the warming water prompted the trout to start looking to the surface.

Now, although it wasn't important who won these friendly daily competitions, it was important who lost. Or at least how badly one fisherman lost. A tromping, which wasn't supposed to happen because the prime nymph and grasshopper hours were balanced, gave the victor too much to gloat about (not that either of us ever would—not Denny or me). The real purpose was to learn, and an overwhelming triumph could teach some important lessons; it was just that neither of us wanted to learn that badly.

So, to save my pride, it was time to tie on that weighted Joe's Hopper. A bit of saliva on the fly (a ritual critical for all nymph fishing) sank it quickly. On the third drift, with the Joe's Hopper tumbling out of a riffle and under a dragging tangle of willow branches, a brown trout—not just another of the ten- to sixteen-inch fish so abundant in the stream, but a true two-pounder—broke out of cover and into shallow water to snatch the fly. This was the largest trout of the summer on the Little Blackfoot for either of us up until that time.

The Joe's Hopper never lost ground to the surface flies in the fish count. Throughout the afternoon it not only caught as many trout, but also bigger ones. It wasn't successful just in the riffles, where the nymph usually worked best during the hot part of the day; the weighted fly drew larger fish out from the undercut roots in the slow pools, too.

As we moved upstream side by side, taking turns on the best water, Denny cocked an eyebrow after another nice trout. He asked suspiciously, "What're you using?"

"Same old stuff."

"Isn't that a hopper?"

"I like to think of it as a big, scraggly, brown and yellow nymph," I said.

"Ain't that cheating?"

"It's just a friendly match, Denny."

"Is this going to be another lesson, my friend?" he asked. "If it is, we're switching rods right now."

Ever meet a nymph fisherman who wasn't a bit touchy? Maybe staring at a line tip for hours affects the personality; or maybe only a certain character type becomes a fanatic subsurface fisherman. If they ever start using sunken terrestrial imitations—ants, bees, and caterpillars, as well as grasshoppers— those flies might eliminate the slack periods that even nymph fishermen hit, ruining any chance to keep them humble.

During the rest of that grasshopper summer the sunken Joe's Hopper performed beautifully in two versions. One fly was wrapped with lead wire, heavily weighted for bouncing the bottom; the other, wrapped only with a ribbing of copper wire, was a lighter pattern designed to drift high in the water column, less than a foot below the surface, like a freshly drowned grasshopper.

Even during the best hours for surface activity, the weighted Joe's Hopper caught as many trout as any dry imitation. It really proved itself during the mediocre and poor fishing periods, when a dry fly man had to use all of his tricks to tease a few trout to the top. The fish seemed more willing to experiment with this sunken fly, as if the drowned imitation presented less of a gamble. On a daily basis, during the so-so hours of the morning or evening—or, on a seasonal schedule, during the marginal weeks of late spring and early fall—the pattern's seeming ability to allay suspicion extended the grasshopper fishing.

Grasshoppers drown quickly enough. The currents carry them to all parts of a river; and once they are sunk, trout aren't nearly so suspicious of the large item.

Were there times when the sunken Joe's Hopper didn't work well? Large numbers of aquatic nymphs in the flow, due to a hatch or a behavioral-drift response, made the trout key on a food form with a very different appearance. At these times a Joe's Hopper suddenly became one of the worst flies to use, much less effective than a general nymph pattern. Even a dry grasshopper, which attracted stray, aggressive fish, drew more strikes than the wet fly.

Overall the weighted Joe's Hopper was still the deadliest of all grasshopper imitations. The angler wading upstream and drifting the fly naturally with the current not only caught as many or more trout than he could with any surface pattern, but he also fooled the larger ones. The biggest trout, always the most cautious, seldom rose except during a grasshopper bonanza; during the normal fishing days of summer they might ignore all surface food, but they still recognized a grasshopper well enough to accept one drifting at eye level.

Only the skip cast could make a dry fly hopper more effective than the wet version. This didn't mean that the fly was better—the *skip*, with its spray of light, added an element of attraction. Fish curious about the commotion

R. Valentine Atkinson

It is worth the effort finding a "good" grasshopper imitation for tough water. The reward, on a river like the Madison River in Yellowstone National Park, is a trout that will run hard enough and long enough to bow the rod dangerously.

searched for the source; they could find a dry fly more easily than a wet one that sank out of the search area.

It doesn't matter to most anglers how well the sunken Joe's Hopper works on their trout stream. They won't use it. These people are either unskilled at nymph tactics (and many fly fishermen fall into this category), or else they are so enamored with the fuss of a trout taking a grasshopper on top that they gladly sacrifice numbers of fish for visual excitement. The dry fly is the only choice for them. As Marvin Craik pointed out, "Even a grass bud will work at the right time."

When a trout feeds aggressively on grasshoppers, it never clearly sees a natural or an imitation. It reacts to the *splat!* of the insect, the fall that creates a shower of light streaks on the meniscus, and immediately decides to accept the object. In slow water the fish is more likely to move towards the source of the disturbance, but even in fast water it lifts up, planing higher in the current, and takes the fly indiscriminately.

The quality of the imitation does become a factor during slower fishing periods. The trout stays in his hold and waits for the current to bring him the fly, studying it for the confirmation that proves to him that it is a real food item.

In grasshopper imitations the size of the fly is important. The general silhouette, showing the ragged wing shape over the back and the legs, also has to be right for fussy trout. Color should be generally correct, usually a yellow, green, brown, or gray hue, but enough variation exists among the naturals, even within a particular species, so that exact shades are not necessary.

What is the right size or color on a given day? Those summers spent chumming live grasshoppers proved how critical these secondary factors can be. My early morning collections captured hundreds of grasshoppers of all sizes and colors, but later, on the river, the trout would take just one type overwhelmingly. They always preferred the mature specimens of the most abundant streamside species, refusing larger grasshoppers (for example, the huge, 2½-inch flying variety) and even the smaller grasshoppers of the dominant type. They also keyed on the color of the most numerous species.

The smart angler can survey the fields in the morning along a trout stream and match the most abundant grasshoppers. He may choose one of the popular imitations—the Letort Hopper, the Dave's Hopper, or the Gartside Hopper—or he may use any older or newer pattern that provides a realistic silhouette.

The Herter's Deer Hair Hopper, even though it was such an exact representation (replete with eyes, antennae, legs, wings, and shaped body) that it took considerable time to tie each one, caught plenty of trout and bass for me. It produced as well as any other surface imitation, and its durability and buoyancy made it one of my favorite grasshopper flies—a fondness intensified on the Little Tennessee River one August when it brought up my largest Eastern hopper trout, a brown of nearly four pounds.

Early in the season, in addition to one of these standard flies, a fisherman should carry the Nymph Hopper. This pattern, developed by Gerald Almy and included in his fine book, *Tying and Fishing Terrestrials*, imitates the immature grasshoppers of spring. It is nicely conceived, a simple tying procedure specifically for matching smaller insects.

During midsummer those superb, popular flies—the Letort Hopper, Dave's Hopper, and Gartside Hopper—are all ultimately failures as matches for the typical streamside hopper. It is not their fault; they simply lack one characteristic of the natural. Their very size emphasizes the rigidity of the hook shank and makes it impossible for them to mimic the constantly flexing abdomen of a struggling grasshopper.

How critical is this flaw? The total refusal of standard grasshopper flies by certain fish baffled us during our observations. These trout grabbed smaller caddisfly and mayfly imitations foolishly enough. While they selected live grasshoppers chummed to them one after another during the day, they passed up every artificial fly and even every dead grasshopper. They

A Montana stream like Armstrong Spring Creek, with stretches of grassy bank, fishes well with grasshopper imitations throughout the prime summer months.

uncannily recognized every fraud larger than size 12. On fussy days (or when grass buds failed as imitations), roughly five brown trout out of ten on the Clark Fork River ignored all rigid patterns.

This same type of refusal occurs with imitations of other large surface insects, whether the bug is a giant *Pteronarcys* Salmon Fly or a *Dicosmoecus* Giant Orange Sedge. At least with these food forms the feeding is frenzied enough to lessen the problem. Even with grasshoppers there is always some tension during the feeding, an uncertainty about this victim that drops to the surface so unexpectedly, to help a fish overlook the rigidity of the hook. During a heavy hatch of large mayflies, however, the trout establish a regular rise rhythm to the drifting duns, picking and choosing without haste, and an effective imitation of these insects is not only difficult but frequently impossible. This refusal mechanism certainly explains why fine hatches of giant mayflies, such as the eastern Green Drake (*Ephemera guttulata*) or the western Green Drake (*Ephemerella grandis*), develop reputations as disappointing fly fishing experiences.

There are only a few ways to overcome the unnatural appearance of large, dry imitations. The angler can concentrate on presentation, placing the fly in the critical area, right on the edge of a trout's awareness, where the fish is hurried into a decision. He can also impart action, even if it is delicate, that focuses attention on the movement rather than the appearance of the imitation. Or, by hitting pieces of prime holding water in a stream, where two or more trout crowd together, he can hope that competitiveness will make a fish rush the fly.

One other possible solution worth considering is a hinged hook that allows an imitation to flex in the middle. Such a fly no longer has a rigid, size 12 or larger body; the action imparted by even minute variations in the current makes the rear portion sway back and forth enticingly. This flexible hook can either be a homemade affair, with a monofilament loop on a forward shank, or, better yet, a manufactured hook with interconnecting eyes.

"Fly fishing," according to Eric Peper, "is a battle of wits against the unarmed."

It is the instincts, not the intelligence of a trout, that causes problems. It is the intelligence that creates opportunities. For me, the act of tying a fly means first identifying one of those specific problems. Why concoct new patterns at random?

My daughter, Heather, does that as a fly tyer brilliantly. Not bound by history, technique, or the practicality of what a fly is supposed to be, she creates some very strange concoctions. She tied the Mohawk that way, stacking a high, bristling block of deer hair along the top of the hook shank and wrapping a long, webby hackle at the head, and it's a deadly dry fly. She doesn't care in the least why.

A child can do that. Me? I need something more concrete. When I was studying emerging caddisfly pupae the problem, at least during underwater observation, was obviously the brightness of the air bubbles carried by the

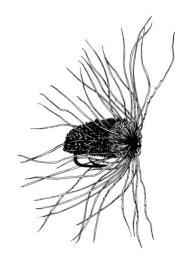

The Mohawk did not have any "justification" for existing, but on the trout stream it quickly showed what trout think of my sensibilities. To everyone's surprise—and most of all mine—it caught fish.

insects. That was something real—a concrete objective. The solution eventually was sparkle yarn (Antron or Creslan); and with a bit of tinkering on the design a new fly type, the Sparkle Pupa, was born.

With grasshoppers, I was satisfied with the popular and creative hopper imitations, especially the Dave's Hopper, Gartside Hopper, and Letort Hopper—good flies all. I had no intention of devising something new just for the sake of newness.

Maybe we should have known there would be a problem with grasshopper imitations. There is an axiom in fly tying: The larger the food item the harder it is to imitate. The reason given is that trout can supposedly detect the flaws easier on a large fly. That's poppycock. Trout have such fine eyesight that they can see every detail of the smallest fly in clear water—if trout looked for flaws, anglers would never catch them. Trout look for positives, things that are supposed to be there, and the problem with large imitations like grasshoppers is that an important positive is missing. On big artificial flies, the trout don't see that waggling movement.

Where's the break point? At what size fly do trout get suspicious? It seems that at size 10 dry flies begin to lose some of their effectiveness on clear, slow-moving waters. The problem gets worse as the fly gets larger.

The solution again was obvious—fly fishing needed a hook that would flex and bend. The difficult part was designing such a hook within the boundaries set by the manufacturing process. The efforts eventually produced a Flex Hook.

What is a Flex Hook? The front section, a shank with a hump in the middle, is detachable and designed for a deer hair, balsa, cork, plastic or foam head. It can be snapped on and off the separate rear section—the business end with a wide-gap hook for better setting.

It was interesting to compare natural grasshoppers, straight hook artificials, and Flex Hook artificials. All offerings, roughly size 8, were tossed

The Flex Hook has the following dimensions:
Size 6—

Rear section:
The rear section is a standard size 8 TMC 800B straight-eye hook. The interchangeable front section is designed to clip onto it.

Front section:
Rear Eye: an open clasp for snapping this "head" on and off the rear section
Front Eye: straight
Length of shank: 12 mm (the hump rises in the middle of the shank)
Wire diameter: .80 mm

on a riffle and allowed to drift down into the pool (and thus the "plop" couldn't affect the results).

Percentage of takes once a trout showed interest:

	Acceptances	Refusals
Natural hoppers	86%	14%
Flex Hopper	72%	28%
Basic Hopper	53%	47%

Eventually, the real boom for the Flex Hook should be as a bass bug. Think about it—a detachable head means that a popper-face cork head can be quickly replaced with a bullet-shaped foam head (or any other style and color of cork, balsa, foam, or deer hair head). For largemouth bass fishing, where the angler is searching for the right attractor, that flexibility would be very valuable, indeed.

Possibilities. Isn't that what makes fly tying fun?

The sudden awakening to terrestrial insects in this country during the 1950s provided an awareness of grasshoppers, but maybe not a full understanding of them. Maybe everything about them seemed too obvious—the fisherman only had to know that those all-too-familiar grasshoppers ended up on the water. Such an attitude precluded the type of careful thinking and research that has characterized the work on aquatic insects during the last three decades.

Fly fishermen can catch more fish with dry fly grasshopper imitations in at least four ways:

(1) Any hope for a "miracle" fly would be misguided faith. No floating grasshopper pattern is going to make a spectacular difference in the catch rate, but a properly designed hinged hook reduces the refusals to rigid imitations of all large food forms. The flexible grasshopper fly appeals to bigger trout, the added inducement of that active body overcoming the reluctant nature of these fish.

(2) A feel for the daily predatory moods of trout will let an angler tailor his grasshopper approach. When fish search the surface, hitting anything resembling a grasshopper with a rush, a fisherman can cover water quickly and pick up every aggressive feeder. But when fish rise half-heartedly, if at all, he can drum them up with teasing tactics at specific holds.

(3) Mastering the skip cast, and pounding the brushy recesses of a stream with it, will mean more trout every day for a grasshopper fisherman. Careful manipulation of the carom (a strong attraction), and the landing (a subtle attraction), manages to alert trout without frightening them.

(4) Nothing can have a greater effect on grasshopper success than a basic understanding of the year-to-year population dynamics of the insect. Any angler who is mobile enough to pick where he is going to fish should pinpoint areas of infestation. The fly fishing is always incredible somewhere in this country because of grasshopper plagues.

An angler only has to throw away the old notions of grasshopper fishing. It is still not complicated, but with new dry fly strategies, he can increase his productive hours and days on the water.

My Fly Box

Terrestrial Imitations

Cicada (4)

Cork Bug (14-16)
(tied in a wild array of colors)

Crowe Beetle (10-16)

Dave's Hopper (6-10)

Deer Hair Hornet (12-14)
(consistent only on rainy days)

Deer Hair Wooly (8-14)
(an important fly for me, not as a caterpillar representation but as an all-around, "buggy" trout finder)

Double Caterpillar (12-16)
(this fly has two hooks tied together)

Flex Hopper (6)
(any time a grasshopper imitation is larger than a size 10 hook this style provides an advantage on fussy trout)

Flying Ant (10-20)
(there are red and black versions)

Foam Ant (10-18)
(there are red and black versions)

Foam Beetle (8-18)

Foam Inch Worm (16)

Foam Spider (14-16)

Fur Ant (14-20)
(tied with red, brown, black, and white bodies)

Gartside Hopper(6-10)

Henry's Fork Hopper (4-8)
(a very aerodynamic fly; good for "skipping" under banks—the same quality makes it possible to cast accurately in a heavy wind)

Japanese Beetle (6-10)
(there are no hoards of Japanese Beetles anymore, but this Marinaro design still works fine matching large beetles)

Jassid (16-20)
(surprisingly easy to see for a small fly because of the light color of the Jungle Cock nail)

Joe's Hopper (6-12)
(the newer designs still have not replaced this pattern as my favorite grasshopper imitation)

Letort Cricket (4-10)

Letort Hopper (4-10)
(at times the slimmer silhouette of this fly appeals to critical trout)

McGinty (14-18)
(in my box these are tied like my original models—with cheap materials and sloppy techniques)

Nymph Hopper (14-16)
(this is a fly for late spring or early summer)

Spruce Moth (12-14)
(it is worth hunting for the infestations)

White Deer Hair Moth (8-12)
(this is a night fly; tied bushy like a bass bug)

Comments:

Terrestrials fall onto the water day or night. What do they look like? Almost anything. Fishermen recognise the major types of land bugs, the ants, grasshoppers, beetles, leafhoppers, and caterpillars, but any sweep with a net through the bushes along a stream captures numerous other crawlers, jumpers, and flyers that have no common name. And how do they fall on the water? They hit in total disarray, flopping and fussing on the surface. Terrestrials can look like anything.

Mike Lawson asked me once, "Have you ever noticed those little brown spiders that crawl around in the grass on the banks of the Henry's Fork? They must fall in a lot because everytime I check stomach contents on a trout there are always a few of them mixed in with the other food."

This is not to imply that fish don't feed selectively on terrestrials. They do—if ants, inchworms, spruce moths, or spiders (which are not insects but eight legged Arachnids) are falling steadily, allowing trout to establish a feeding rhythm, the fishing is just as fussy as it is during any aquatic hatch.

Maybe, as incredible as the fishing is during those blizzard dumps of terrestrials, the less spectacular but continuous fall of bugs of various kinds is even more important to anglers. Without a smattering of food items always drifting on the surface, trout would lock into a cycle of feeding and resting even more rigidly; then maybe they would not rise at all unless there was a hatch in progress. As it is, the availability of odd food items floating overhead rewards curiosity.

My terrestrial selection caters to the possibilities. The flies in my box match all of the common forms, but they also cover the colors (Cork Bugs in polka dot), sizes (a giant size 4 Cicada), and shapes (the buzz of a Foam Spider) that tempt credibility. They also reward curiosity.

Chapter 8

Large Trout with Finesse

In the autumn, watch the men on the Missouri River prepare for a day of fishing. They gather in a little knot on the stony beach below Beaver Creek. Their breath pushes out mist in the morning cold during the story telling ritual.

Why stories? Everybody has to declare how perfect the conditions are—no matter what the conditions—for a feeding spree. So everybody around the smudgy, driftwood fire tells a story about a big trout caught on a day just like this one. They sip their last cups of coffee, faces buried in the wisps. The group marches down to the river with a final burst of shouting that resembles the preparations in a football locker room more than any Waltonian musings about a fishing trip. To be sure, there is nothing lyrical about a full day standing waist deep in a strong current thrashing out long casts. These men have to forget each futile strip and retrieve as soon as it is finished. They have to believe totally in the next one.

Mal Holdstock told the newcomers, "You keep your fly deep, running that slot. You work hard enough and you're going to get a trout. This is foolproof."

Bill Seeples draped his arm around my shoulder, "Have you tested that theory out on my buddy?"

"It's his favorite game," Mal said.

Any fisherman can perfect one of the trophy-hunt methods—pounding out size 3/0 streamers with a shooting head, running weighted nymphs through heavy rips with a sinking line, and retrieving surface disturbers all night over big pools. The methods for taking super-size trout usually mean long hours casting large flies in the hope of hitting the rare moment when a giant fish decides to eat something. These trophy games demand a certain mental state (or meditative mindlessness) from anglers—and a total disregard for the odds.

My friends call me a master at the mental aspects of these large trout methods.

There's an alternative to pounding up large trout with oversized wet patterns. There is a phenomenon that happens during every hatch—the biggest insect feeders in a stream hold in spots where few anglers look for them; and these spots are not in the classic water described in every beginning manual but in the open shallows.

Large insect feeders work a hatch two ways. One feeding style, "bank sipping," is fairly well known; the other, "shelf tailing," is virtually unknown. These feeding mechanisms are entirely different, although both methods are efficient, and one is much more common (and thus more important to fly fishermen).

The bank sippers are better understood, providing challenging surface fishing on spring creeks and tailwater rivers. Why not on freestone streams? On snow- and rain-fed rivers the high flush of runoff scours a gravel edge, and in midsummer the water level drops to expose the stone borders. There are few bank sippers on freestone streams because there are few suitable banks present. On spring creeks, with their constant flow, however, there are deep slots next to the grassy overhangs.

These bankside sanctuaries give large trout the chance to sip great numbers of surface insects. The water against the bank is a buffer zone, a quiet and slow corridor that gathers insects spun off from the main current. In this protected water trout, sometimes in a pack of a dozen or more fish, hold comfortably just under the surface and, with a nodding motion, take insects from on or just under the meniscus every few seconds. The feeding in these pods is not extremely selective; individual risers are tougher to fool than trout in competitive situations.

Good rivers for bank sippers, although not rare, are uncommon enough to attract loyal followings of anglers. On any good day there are fly fishermen carefully walking the banks of the Henry's Fork, for example, searching for the best pods of rising fish. During any of the incredible hatches on that river they find groups of rainbow trout, fish between sixteen and twenty-two inches, working snug to the grass.

In contrast, no one looks for the shelf tailers anywhere. These fish are in all streams and rivers, freestone as well as spring flows. How big they are depends on the basic productivity of the water. In a sterile, bouncing stream the tailers might be nine-inch brook trout or in a rich, winding river they might be twenty-inch brown trout. Wherever they are, though, they will typically be the biggest insect feeders in that water.

Why are the bank sippers tight to the grass? Why are the shelf tailers in open water so shallow that it barely wets their backs? The same answer applies for both: the only way very large trout can afford to feed on insects is in situations providing maximum efficiency. These waters give fish easy places to hold as well as concentrations of insects.

The shelf tailers behave nothing like the bank sippers. For one thing, they usually don't feed on adult insects during a hatch. For another, although they are no more difficult to catch, they are harder for fly fishermen to believe in—a phenomenon that anglers don't recognize simply because they don't accept the possibility. These trout represent a rich lode; they are the key to

R. Valentine Atkinson

Spring creeks have stable flows for the proper stream bank habitat for bank sipping trout. Pods of large fish hold in the slower water near the grassy edge.

taking large trout with light tackle methods. Nevertheless, so few fly fishermen see them, that for most they might as well not exist.

To have shelf tailers, a river has to feature a gravel shelf. Fortunately, most streams have such shelves in abundance. Picture a bend in the river—on the outside the current accelerates and digs into the far, steep bank, but on the inside curve the water flows evenly, with weak centrifugal force, over shallow gravel or stones. This shelf slopes slowly down until it breaks sharply into deeper water.

For most of the day a shelf area fulfills the dour expectations of anglers—it is totally barren. But once a good hatch begins, the trout slide up like phantoms from the break and squeeze into the shallows. They lay exposed, even on the brightest days, sidling back and forth taking insects easily from under the film.

What bothered me for a long time about these large trout was a missing explanation. Why are they in the shallows? Why should such fish abandon the break, where hatching nymphs also drift, and come into such a perilous area to feed? The reason is efficiency—bigger fish leave the safer, deeper water because they can't gather insects quickly enough there.

Along the deep break, where rising, struggling nymphs or larvae scatter throughout the water column, the food spreads several feet from top to bottom. In the shallows, however, the nymphs concentrate top to bottom in only inches of water. It's this compression of available food that draws trout onto the shelves.

Shelves are common in most trout streams. At a bend the current is weak on the inside, the water shallowing out on a gravel slope.

On the Missouri, Paul Dodds wondered about my kneeling and creeping approach. In the rowdy spirit of the day he shouted advice, but at least this once he stayed back from the water. "Don't cast there. What are you wasting our time for?" he asked.

He never saw the fish, a seventeen-inch rainbow, working in inches of current. Maybe such an incredibly fine nymph fisherman, who could catch so many trout with blind prospecting, thought that this was a stray when it took a Halo Emerger. The fish never dissuaded him in the least from his cast-and-move routine.

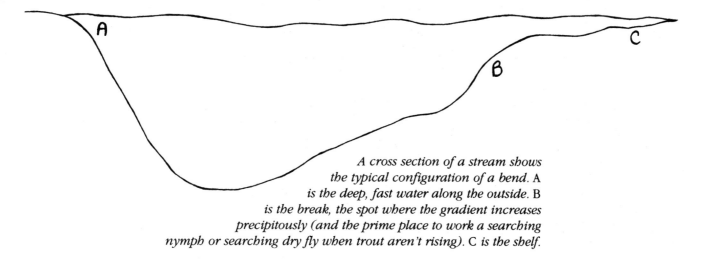

A cross section of a stream shows the typical configuration of a bend. A is the deep, fast water along the outside. B is the break, the spot where the gradient increases precipitously (and the prime place to work a searching nymph or searching dry fly when trout aren't rising). C is the shelf.

He bulled upstream, tall beside the water, flailing and wallowing enough to send every decent trout scurrying out of the shallows. He never saw them either—and what should have been a day of fifteen- to twenty-inch trout remained a day of tiddlers. On the river he caught incredible numbers of fish, but few of them were over fifteen inches. This made me feel like a seeing eye dog at a convention for the blind.

Wayne Huft found the key to breaking Paul's addiction to numbers. He changed the rules—only trout over sixteen inches counted in the day's tally. Then, when we'd come in and join the crowd at the inn each evening, and someone would ask, "How'd you do?" one of us would immediately answer, "Paul got skunked."

I was hunting the Missouri for fresh pods of bank sippers, walking the high embankment and scanning with binoculars. Normally, I would have passed the gravel flats quickly; the stretch was long, though, and I sat on the rocks for a rest, but kept searching the water out of habit. The light was right, making it easy for me to spot the large rainbows.

They were loners, each one locked onto his own lie, but at least twenty of them were on the flat. Why hadn't I seen them before? I had never searched for trout on such shallow benches before, in just inches, not feet, of water.

The problem first encountered on the Missouri baffled me for five seasons on other waters, too. The shelf feeders were on every trout stream; the only difference was that suddenly I was seeing them and not catching them—not on dry flies, anyway. I took fish easily on nymphs; once the stalk brought me close enough it was simple to flip the fly—once, twice, three times, lifting the rod high, often with only the leader touching the water. I knew that these fish were rising; the tops of their noses, their nebs, were breaking the surface softly.

Gene Mize was with me one day during a Pale Morning Dun hatch. He was a superb dry fly angler and he caught a different kind of trout, the bank sippers holding in pods, easily enough. The fly was right; the angler was performing masterfully. Why not give a fresh player a shot at the shelf trout?

Gene worked those tailers for two hours. They were so near, and bigger than any fish he'd caught all day. He really wanted them, but finally he reeled in his fly.

Once the angler starts looking for them, he spots shelf tailers everywhere, bellying up on the sloping gravel during hatches.

It ruins the day when a grown man cries. To forestall the tears, I handed him my rod, set up with a nymph. "This will make you feel better."

"You think so?" he asked.

In all our years of fishing I'd never seen him cast anything except a dry fly. It surprised me, then, when he read the strikes so well. He waded the shelf and hooked one nice rainbow after another. I was getting excited and, as is my wont, started babbling about his performance.

He turned with a sorrowful stare, a look reflecting the inner anguish of a sinner. "Fishing a nymph is like drinking prune juice," he said. "Sometimes it's necessary, but you feel sort of silly bragging about the results." He kept catching trout that day on a size 16 Pheasant Tail nymph, a rough simulation of the mottled brown Pale Morning Dun emerger, but I never saw him fall from grace by tying on another nymph after that.

Why didn't I try emergers earlier? In my experiences with rising trout the emergent stage of the insect might be preferred, sometimes by as much as four to one, but these same fish would eventually take a dry fly. When the dry fly flopped completely there was either something wrong with the imitation or the wind was pushing the pattern (which happened more with some fly styles than others).

To me, the term "dry fly" encompasses emergers. That feeling is not based on the fact that emergers are, if not exactly dry, at least damp, but on the way that trout view them—by looking up. This creates many more similarities than differences. The effective imitation still must deal with the peculiarities of the half-emerged insect—the sunken portion and the aura—but presentation remains a precise, short-line affair.

The oddity of a shelf-tailing trout is that the surface imitation usually has to be an emerger pattern. Even during a hatch, with rafts of adult insects floating over his head, a fish holds in areas where the gravel scrapes his belly and ignores anything completely on the surface.

A trout in deeper water feeds differently during a hatch, sometimes taking varying insect stages in sequence. He will pick off a nymph or two drifting deep, follow an emerger to the surface and pluck him from the underside of the film, and then rise to the top to take an adult.

In careful observations, fish tailing on the shelf ate as many as eighty-four emergent or bottom-drifting nymphs without taking an adult. There is selectivity—and then there is exclusivity. For the feeding pattern to be this rigid there had to be something limiting their choice—the adult wasn't a feeding option.

The feeding on emerging insects, rather than adults, was very rigid on the shelves. The trout were keying on the sunken portion of the insect, picking out a particular victim long before it reached the surface window.

The shelf tailers held in such shallow water that they had almost no circular window in which to see surface insects. They didn't waste effort getting under an adult perched on top of the film. Instead, they fed on emergent nymphs that they could isolate and recognize from the sunken portion dangling under the surface. They cocked up on their fins to intercept insects long before the naturals reached the window.

Answering one question didn't require a lot of underwater observation: Are there differences in the way various species of trout feed on surface insects? My early experiences on western rivers convinced me that each trout—brown, rainbow, brook, and cutthroat—had its own style of rising.

When I came to Montana to attend college I didn't know how to really fly fish. This didn't mean that I couldn't catch fish on flies; but still, I was no more a fly fisherman than Izaak Walton or Charles Cotton (and hopefully, not much less of one either). I did everything within a fifteen-foot radius of the rod tip, never actually casting or shooting line, or drifting the fly.

The man who gave me not only my basics in fly presentation but a fine grounding in how to catch large trout was Dick Fryhover (an angler of legendary skill in the Helena, Montana, area). Just watching him cover rising trout was a seminar in dry fly efficiency for me.

We played a game on float trips. One person would fish. If he missed a strike he took over the oars, and if he missed a "call" he took over the oars. What was a call? The angler had to name the species of trout and guess the size of the fish within a half inch immediately upon hook-up.

One evening on a Smith River float trip Dick correctly called the size and species of eighteen trout in a row, a feat all the more amazing because this stream contained brook, cutthroat, rainbow, and brown trout. He only hesitated once, the trill of an "r" starting before he spit out, "Cu, Cu, Cutthroat, fourteen-inches." He never even complained about the fact that it was getting damn dark out there.

The trick was that he often knew, just before he set the hook, both the size and species of the fish. The rise forms were generally the same; if one species was sipping, another species would also be sipping. The difference was in how much patience the rising trout showed at the last moment of the take. A brown trout always took flies a little slower and a little more cleanly than the others. Rainbows were more efficient than cutthroats, but both fish tended to roll or at least tilt to the side after rising. Brook trout were the splashiest, always seeming to give a final surge on the capture that rolled a hump of water. It did not seem to matter what type of water the trout were feeding in—the differences were always there.

Imagine what an advantage this gave Dick on large trout. He always stopped a moment and scanned a stream, spotting working fish up and down.

Then, like a pool player planning four or five shots ahead, he picked them off in a string. The sequence always led him in his wading path to the best trout, the winning eight ball, and this fish would always be an "easy shot."

Wayne Huft, the best in our group at catching large numbers of shelf tailers, often tallied more than a dozen trout between eighteen and twenty-two inches during a hatch on the Missouri. He had learned to be quiet about his wonderful days; if someone asked him how he had done on the river, he'd only say, "Better than I deserve."

No one should expect to become a hero to all by catching large trout with finesse. Fellow fly fishermen forgive the trophy hunter and his specialized tactics involving huge streamers or fast-sinking lines, clucking with praise over the monstrous trout, but they also understand the hours that such fish cost, and they can add, when describing this type of prowess, "But you have to be crazy to go through all that."

R. Valentine Atkinson

Any angler who stalks shelf tailers looks oddly out of place. He stands in ankle-deep water and casts onto a gravel bar that is just as shallow. (I've had people blunder up and try to help me, saying as they pointed, "The fish are out there.")

No one, however, likes to have another angler fish his home water with small flies and catch fish that he did not know were there. This is especially difficult for fly fishermen with the rudimentary talents it takes to catch good numbers of trout.

The Missouri, like all tough trout streams, is certainly no place for flailers. The weedy, insect-rich river below Holter Dam is a giant spring creek where large trout feed with decorum on hatches every suitable day. They pick nymphs from the drift, but often hold in shallow water on shelves that the angler who casts randomly usually ignores.

The potential of the Missouri, though? In an article in *Montana Outdoors*, Rod Berg, the biologist who surveyed the trout population of the river, described an evening:

> "Thousands of mayflies were emerging from the water, drying their wings, flying high into the air to mate, and falling back to the surface where scores of rainbow trout—many in the 15- to 20-inch range—were breaking the water in a feeding frenzy."

It's a paradox: some men see them and some men don't.

The shelves and to a lesser extent, the banks, are the private worlds of only a few anglers. Fishermen who stalk these areas are specialists, just like the trophy hunters who work big flies in deep and heavy water. There is nothing random about either endeavor. The typical fly fisherman, walking up the stream, doesn't have the tackle or the techniques to cover areas so deep or areas so shallow. The angler who goes out in the morning for trophy trout has nothing else in mind.

The feeders in shallow water give fly fishermen the chance to take large trout with finesse. This is the place for very light tackle, the one-weight rod and line, and the long leader tapered to at least 5X, but beyond this it's a time for specific skills. These are things that the angler after ordinary trout seldom has to do—to catch shallow water trout he has to believe in them, he has to spot them, and he has to stalk them.

It was fun just lying on the rocks, sunning with the rattlesnakes, watching Paul pick out that one splendid feeder on the shelf. "A brown, at least 20 inches," he said.

"Be more specific."

He had mastered seeing the fish and reading the rise, "21½ inches"— and when he landed it that is what it measured.

Instead of reading the water the angler has to read the trout. Instead of casting blindly in the hope of catching a lot of ordinary fish, he has to present his fly specifically to one feeder at a time. Instead of using a general fly, he has to choose one that not only mimics a certain insect but also matches a particular stage in the life cycle. The rewards in this fussy game are more large trout than the dry fly fisherman with general methods and general patterns even dreams about.

My Fly Box

Emergers

Cone (6-14)
(this mayfly emerger comes in three color variations—Chocolate Cone, Pistachio Cone, and Vanilla Cone)

EmergentSparkle Pupa (4-22)
(the four main color sets, which cover more than 80% of the hatches, are Brown/Yellow, Brown/Bright Green, Dark Gray, and Ginger)

Halo Mayfly Emerger (10-24)
(Brown, Cream, and Olive versions cover most mayfly species in the emergent phase)

Halo Midge Emerger (16-28)
(midge pupa imitations have to come in a wide variety of colors; black, brown, red, orange, green, rust, cream and purple are the main body shades)

Hare's Ear (10-18)

Klinkhamen Special (14-18)
(the use of the parachute style of hackling "hangs" the fly in the surface film—this is a fine mayfly simulation)

Olive Hare's Ear (10-18)

Comments:

My carrying stock includes emergers to match the major aquatic insect orders that pop on the surface (rather than crawl out of the stream). But the percentage of time for using emergers varies with the type of hatch: mayflies—50 percent emerger and 50 percent dry fly; midges—80 percent emerger and 20 percent dry fly; caddisflies—90 percent emerger and 10 percent dry fly. With mayflies the internal tissue is still "wet," and adults have to ride on top of the water for a period of time before they can fly away. Caddisflies and midges (both higher on the evolutionary scale than mayflies) hesitate during emergence on the underside of the surface film, struggling in each instance to escape a transparent sheath, but they don't dally long on the water once they have emerged. They are both able to fly away after a preliminary hop or two.

Whether the major concentration level is below or on the surface for mayflies depends on water and weather. A broken surface allows duns to escape the nymphal shuck quicker; cold, damp conditions keep the duns drifting longer—a strong combination of these factors means that my choice is the dry fly. The opposite combination, creating a greater concentration of half emerged nymphs, is smooth water and warm, dry weather—this tilts the balance towards an emerging nymph pattern.

My main emerger types, the Emergent Sparkle Pupa, Halo Mayfly Emerger, and Halo Midge Emerger, are visible to the trout below the surface film. At the same time, they all have parts that stick out of the water. The flies are designed to be fished dead drift, with the "upper" portions greased with floatant. These patterns are exactly like dry flies in the sense that the angler watches them drift along and sees any rise to them.

Chapter 9

Unnatural Acts

The loud "hut, hut" to pull the other team off side; the quick snap to catch the other team with extra men on the field; and the hidden ball to send the other team after the wrong man—my old football coach was a master of these techniques. He was so masterful, in fact, that league officials tried to pass rules against these tactics.

A reporter asked our coach, "Do you mean that you need to cheat to win?"

"We never cheat to win," the coach explained. "We're so bad that we cheat just to be respectable."

In my fishing, the active fly is not a minor tactic. At least 90 percent of my presentations, at some moment, include motion. Most of my casts are across and downstream. The fly's movement usually doesn't replace the dead drift; it occupies just a split second in the total presentation. This is my way not of masking but adding to the identity of the fly (either as an imitation or as an attractor). The tactic makes me respectable against even the toughest trout, even when the fly isn't quite right.

Motion has two purposes—it either alerts the fish to the fly, which means the trout is still going to scrutinize the pattern, or it obscures the fly, minimizing good qualities as well as flaws. The difference? When motion alerts, it's just an advertisement; when motion obscures, it makes the fly a moving target. Both methods offer risks as well as rewards because of that natural caution fish have about food that moves.

What is missing in every description of active presentations is the disclaimer, the other side to all the successes of the twitch. When it is used indiscriminately, the twitch interrupts as many rises as it triggers. It has to be a precise method, not a random one, because when it breaks the rhythm of a trout's rise it often sends that fish back to the bottom.

One morning, while scuba diving on the Big Hole, Bill Seeples surfaced unexpectedly. "Did you prick that trout?" he asked.

"I never touched him," I said. "You didn't see me strike, did you?"

He stared at me oddly. "He was just about to take. All of a sudden he goes down and sulks."

"All I did was twitch the fly a little."

It was strange to see phrases from my underwater research on selectivity, such as "triggering characteristic" and "exaggeration factor," actually enter the formal language of behavioral psychology.

There is one phrase, however, missing from my work, and it is so important for explaining the feeding mechanism of a trout that it makes me wonder why it took me so many years to see it. My only excuse is that during the early research any movement of the fly was dismissed as an accident.

My description of the feeding process started with the trout recognizing either the insect or the imitation as an acceptable target. What if our fishermen had twitched dry flies on purpose? Then, there would have been no missing the fact that there is a step, anytime a trout feeds, before recognition of the food. This explains both the success and the failure of the twitch presentation.

When a trout rises he focuses specifically on an insect with his wonderful close-up vision. After eating his luckless prey, he searches for

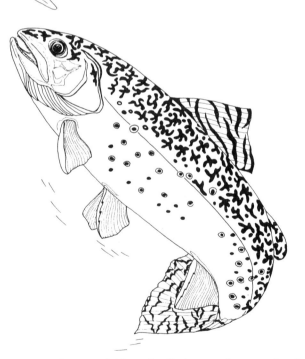

When is a twitch wrong? Move the fly just as the trout is about to take it and he will frequently break off his rise.

another victim. He looks as far ahead as possible. However, for a trout rising to take surface items, "far" is only to the edge of his window of vision. He dips his head ever so slightly, even if he's holding just under the surface, as he concentrates on that outside rim.

There isn't a clear line at the edge of the window. In *To Rise a Trout*, John Roberts describes the boundary as, "the two areas (inside and outside the window) overlap and blend in a confused prismatic zone, known as Snell's circle. There is also considerable variation in the amount of light penetrating the surface at various points. Because the light rays at the edge of the window are the most compressed, so too will be the light intensity, which on a bright, sunny day could be considerable. Around the immediate window edge there is about $4\frac{1}{2}$ times the amount of light because of the compression of light rays."

The trout, gazing at this bright, prismatic edge, waits for the next insect to slide into the window. During a heavy hatch a half dozen naturals might cross the rim, but no matter whether it's one or six the trout has to do something. Even before he tries to ascertain that an object is food, he has to separate that one piece of flotsam from the rest before he can study it.

He has to isolate the natural, not just from other insects but from every bit of debris floating on the surface, too. If the naturals are scarce or sporadic, as with terrestrials, the trout simply searches for anything edible. When he sees what is possibly an insect, he rises and confirms that the object is food. This process of visual confirmation is slow in quiet water and fast, or non-existent, in rapid currents. He selects or rejects insects in broken water, no matter how swift, too, but he does it there with the taste buds on his lips (by actually grabbing the insect or fly) and not with his eyes.

There are five perceptual processes involved in the strike of a trout—sense (by sight or sound), isolate, recognize, confirm, and accept (or reject). The trout doesn't search for food in a current—he matches passing items against his expectations. His mind locks into a pattern of selective feeding. If the naturals are abundant, entering the window of vision in bunches, then the trout must still isolate one insect from the group. The feeding motions during a heavy hatch or an egg-laying fall are different, much more rhythmic.

There's a way an angler can help a trout, even when insects are flooding overhead, single out his fly from among all of the naturals. It's a tactic based on the Isolation Principle, the missing phrase from my work. All he has to do is twitch his imitation slightly at the right spot—at the edge of the window. If the fish is watching the rim, choosing one fly from among many, his eyes lock onto any object that moves. The motion cannot be so violent that it pulls the fly too far away for the fish to follow its movement. Instead, it should be a gentle twitch, not an inch, but a quarter of an inch; sometimes a quiver is enough. A small pull on the line, not a waggle of the rod, activates the imitation. Then, the fly has to begin drifting drag free again, down into the middle of the window.

The magic of the twitch is its power to make a fly stand out among everything else on the surface. As long as the fly moves just at the edge of the trout's window of vision, it never hurts the chances of a take. The worst that can happen, if the fish isn't looking at the edge, is that it won't help.

The twitch does hurt the chances of a take if it isn't executed at the edge of the window. This is why it's not a random technique—the bad balances the good. If the fly moves once it's inside the window, as the fish rises for it, one of two things can happen—the trout may rush to grab an escaping insect (and this is not good because the fish often misses the moving target) or he may simply break off the rise.

My usual approach is to float the fly over the fish a few times totally drag free, with no movement. If that doesn't tempt a strike, it's time to twitch it, ever so gently, at the front edge of the window. This is worth trying on two or three drifts.

What if this doesn't work? Then why not try the back door? The formula is different for figuring out the rear edge of the window, since the trout has a blind spot directly behind him. The twitch has to be made just behind his eyes, as the drift clears his head and reaches his dorsal fin. The movement here has to be a lot stronger, at least an inch, to be effective. The twitch, as the fly comes skittering back into the trout's field of vision, sometimes triggers a reflexive, spin-around, fall-back rise. This technique is also more likely to put the fish down for good, so it should be saved for the last presentation.

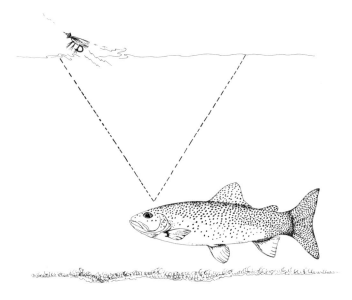

The twitch, a subtle act, is used to help a trout "isolate" the fly. The place to twitch the imitation is at the edge of the window, before a trout sees the fly clearly. The angler can calculate roughly (which is good enough) where the edge of the window is by multiplying the depth of the trout by one and a half.

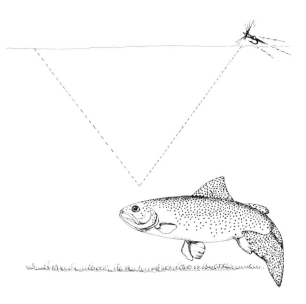

Sometimes, with a substantial twitch, just as the fly is about to leave the trout's window of vision, it is possible to trigger a reflexive rise. But this is a risky technique.

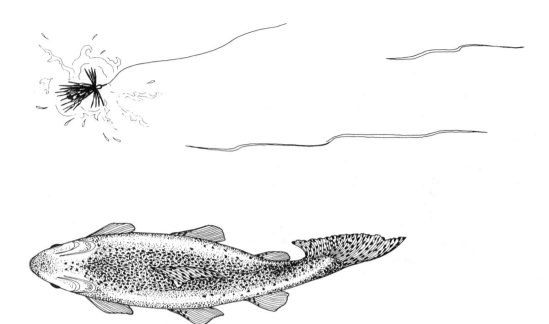

With the Reaction Method, the angler drops the fly just behind the "dominant" eye of the fish.

Even the splash of the falling fly alerts a trout. This commotion, in its ultimate form, can be even more important than the pattern itself. With one such technique, the Reaction Method, the angler studies and stalks a feeding fish, watching which eye the trout rises off of, left or right, and drops a small, chunky fly a few inches to the side (just behind the dominant eye). The trout whirls and, without clearly seeing it, snatches the pattern.

My crowning glory with this technique was six nice White River trout, each caught on the first cast with a size 14 Parkany Deer Hair Caddis. That streak was followed by a string of misses caused by inaccurate casts, each bad toss sending a large fish rushing in a prominent wake towards the middle of the river. So went the day of a home run hitter.

In subtler form, the fall of any substantial fly alerts the fish. Caddisfly species that lay eggs underwater break through the rubbery meniscus by diving from thirty feet in the air, like a bomber on a suicide mission. Even mayfly spinners often drop with a noticeable splash onto the water instead of settling lightly, maybe to shake the egg mass loose. With or without actual egg-laying activity, the splat of the fly can replace the twitch technique as an attention getter. The trick is to make the fly land the same place where the twitch would happen—at the edge of the trout's window.

The Tick Cast and Skip Cast are two active methods that depend on commotion to signal the trout. The "tick," devised by George LaBranche and called the "bounce cast" in _The Dry Fly and Fast Water_, works splendidly in certain water types. The name bounce cast is inaccurate, though, because the fly is not bouncing and landing but is barely touching the surface. The trick is to let the artificial tick the water in a series of false casts. These touches, all at the same spot, send splashes of light under the meniscus. The meniscus

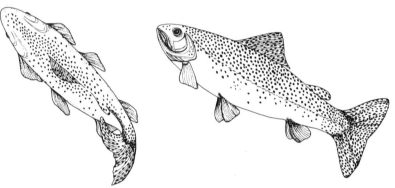

With a properly aimed false cast, the fly ticks the surface, attracting trout to the contact point.

is silver from reflected light—tap on it and that light sparks. The tactic works best if the fly doesn't break through the surface film.

The tick is most effective at the heads of pools. A classic spot like Cairns Pool on the Beaverkill, with a current tumbling through pockets and then fanning out, is a good example. When the fly hits repeatedly where more than one trout can see it, the commotion causes a general excitement among the group. They edge up, jockeying for position in their curiosity, and when the fly finally lands, more than one usually rushes for it.

The Skip Cast, the tactic that bounces the fly as far as another few feet, is my pet method for grasshoppers. The skip demands a large, not-too-air resistant fly, but it's not just a hopper technique. It's invaluable during the Salmon Fly hatch, too. A streamlined fly like Pat Barnes' Jughead bounces and gets back under the bank brush where no ordinary cast can reach, and when a western river is up, pushing into the willows, that is where huge trout wait for giant stoneflies to drop. The slap on the surface as the fly skips mimics the clumsy crash of the adult Salmon Fly.

Is it always fatal when a fly moves sideways (sudden drag)? Not if a trout is holding deep enough so that he's looking up at it. The quick jot by the fly across current lines, especially if it is followed by a drag-free drift, still alerts

The Jughead (a Pat Barnes pattern), with its bullet head, is an aerodynamic fly that skips well. That is an important characteristic when the Salmon Flies are falling from the overhanging willow branches onto the river.

the fish. Unfortunately, it also makes him suspicious of a pure dry fly. He wonders how far he is going to have to chase it if he starts to rise. He may be in the mood for a game of tag, and he may not be.

A trout usually needs assurance that the fly is coming—not going. There is one "sideways" technique that gives the proper message. A buoyant pattern fished on a floating line with a sunken leader dives underwater when the angler tugs sharply, and then it pops back to the surface. There is no stronger attraction on the surface than this movement.

One August day, with the heat over 100 degrees Fahrenheit, the fish snubbed every technique, surface or subsurface, on the big Blackfoot River. Chris Coyle rowed the raft for us, and he so badly wanted someone to catch a trout. The river was deep on this particular stretch, but in the clear water the smooth ledges were visible eight feet down. Not a fish was in sight. Still, anyone familiar with the Blackfoot knew that there were trout holding in the shade of those lava slabs.

A tug made my Deer Hair Wooly Worm swim down a few inches. Then, after it popped up and drifted dead again, a trout came up slowly through all that water to roll on it. He wasn't a big fish. None that rose to the Dive technique were that afternoon, thirteen inches the best, but for the last few miles of the float the ghostly trout of the ledges entertained us with their agonizingly long ascents.

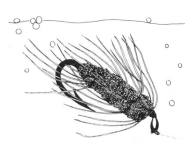

A tug on a buoyant fly makes it dive, but then it pops back to the surface. This struggling motion really tantalizes trout, pulling them up from even deep pools.

The Dive is such an indispensable tactic in my bag of tricks, working so well in deeper, slower currents, that there are two flies in my carrying stock for it—the Deer Hair Wooly Worm and Gary Borger's Poly Caddis. The Wooly is for midday searching, when nothing is rising in the pools and deep flats. The Poly Caddis, a more realistic representation of both swimming caddisfly and mayfly egg layers, doesn't pull trout up as far as the chunky Wooly but it fools more fish during random insect activity.

Movement not only triggers a response, it also obscures a fly. In many active techniques the motion is not meant to alert a fish but to tease him into striking something that he can't really see. Here, the willingness, or unwillingness, of the trout to give chase becomes the main factor in the success or failure of the tactic.

The various methods—the Skitter, the Skate, the Hang, and even the Struggle—all make a fish come after the moving fly. The artificial doesn't drift placidly after the first spasm. Its continuous movement provokes a fish to actually attack a disturbance which at best is just a vague shape.

Why is it that Atlantic salmon fishermen have always understood that with an active fly it's the sequence of presentations and not the single cast that finally hooks the fish, while trout fishermen slide and pull an active fly randomly over the water with no pattern of presentations at all? Resident trout are much more willing to chase after a dancing fly than an anadromous fish, so the angler probably believes that his active attractor, cast here and there, is doing just fine with the occasional spectacular strike. Yet, how much more successful he would be with a planned approach.

It usually won't take the proverbial thousand casts common in Atlantic salmon fishing to get a trout jumping all over a dancing fly, but the principle is the same with either fish. Unless an angler is covering a particular trout or a known lie, he should work an area of the stream in a methodical pattern of presentations.

When the trout first spots the commotion of the moving fly, those inseparable feelings of initiative and caution both work on his mind. With the second or third cast, however, his nervousness fades away; the initiative, or curiosity, is still there and he tracks the path of the fly. There is still something that keeps him from going after it when it's upstream from him—maybe it's a feeling akin to skepticism or just a reluctance to venture beyond his feeding territory. Whatever the reason, the trout's anticipation grows as the fly comes closer on each pass and finally, when the movement carries the pattern over his nose, he bolts after it.

A series of experiments clearly showed different responses to an active attractor and a passive (dead drift) attractor. Both flies were unnatural to some degree, but there was never any fear from the trout for the dead drift fly, no matter how garish it looked. If the active fly came out of nowhere and crossed over a fish on the first cast, though, he seldom chased after it. It took three or four preliminary passes, far enough away from him so the fly posed no threat, before he would tilt up slightly and wait for it.

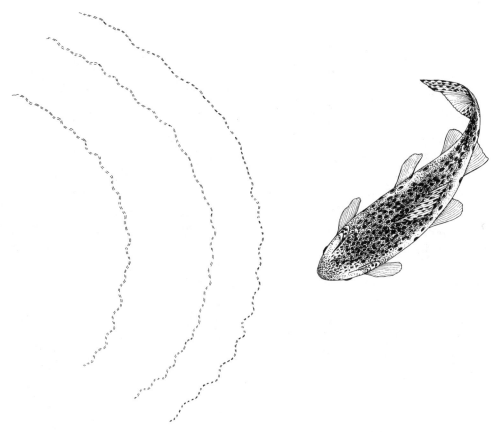

The angler casts, lets the fly swing, and then takes a step downstream. He methodically approaches the best holding water. It is this entire series of swings, even with a moving dry fly, that sets up the strike. The trout slowly loses his nervousness about the approaching object.

The Skate

My favorite skating pattern is not the classic Hewitt Spider, although that is still heavily represented in my boxes. Instead, it is Nevin Stephenson's Fluttering Stone, a fly that he created one spring on the Big Hole when we were both guiding for Phil Wright at the Compleat Fly Fisher. It was so different and so effective that it quickly became a standard stonefly imitation throughout the Rocky Mountain region.

The Fluttering Stone comes in two versions, a large orange pattern, sizes 2, 4, and 6, for the giant Salmon Fly (*Pteronarcys californica*); and a smaller yellow one, sizes 6, 8 , and 10, for the Golden Stone (*Hesperoperla pacifica*). It's this smaller pattern, the yellow Fluttering Stone, that has become my general skating fly, not just for trout during all seasons, but as a deadly bouncer for smallmouth bass as well. It has joined, if not replaced, the Skating Spider in my stock because it hooks a higher percentage of strikes.

If the trout are already feeding on active, bouncing insects—stoneflies, craneflies, caddisflies, or even some types of mayflies—there's no need to be methodical; they will take a dancing fly the first time they see it. When trout aren't rising, however, the fly should be fished in a pattern. If it is cast across or down and across, a high riding attractor like the Fluttering Stone bounces across stream as drag pulls a belly into the line. The fisherman slows or speeds up the swinging fly with mends. A mend upstream typically slows the fly down; a mend downstream typically speeds it up. One way anglers can cover all of the water is to start at the head of a pool, flat or run, and take a few steps downstream after every cast.

The Skitter

This tactic is specifically designed to match the crashing, sliding, and running frenzy of egg-laying caddisflies. A smooth lift of the rod, accompanied by a pull with the line hand, makes the fly slice the top of a pool. Oddly enough, however, it works well when big mayfly spinners, such as the Green Drake (*Ephemera guttulata*) and the Hex (*Hexagenia limbata*) are falling on the water. Even though these insects aren't that rambunctious, the line that the fly etches on the surface film separates the imitation from all of the naturals. It is also a fine searching technique as long as the fly, when it stops moving, is over good fish-holding water.

The Dancing Caddis, a fly with wing edges that leave a sharp wake of double lines on the meniscus, works as a caddisfly imitation or as a general searcher. The hook can't puncture the surface because it rides up on this pattern. The light pattern streaking across the water is more important than the details of the fly because the strike usually occurs immediately after the motion stops. This is why the lift of the rod and the strip of the line should

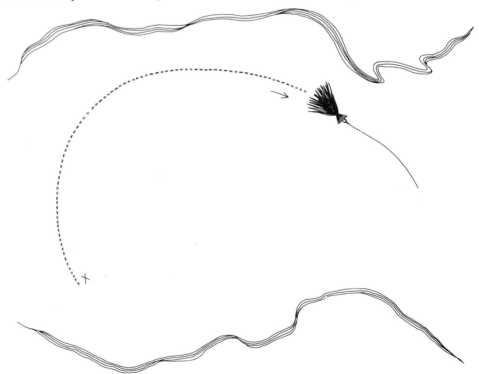

The path (dotted line) of the Skitter should start in unproductive water and end in prime water. It is the dead drift, following the motion, that draws strikes.

be smooth and not too fast; the curving line has to make trout believe that the disturbance is something worth watching.

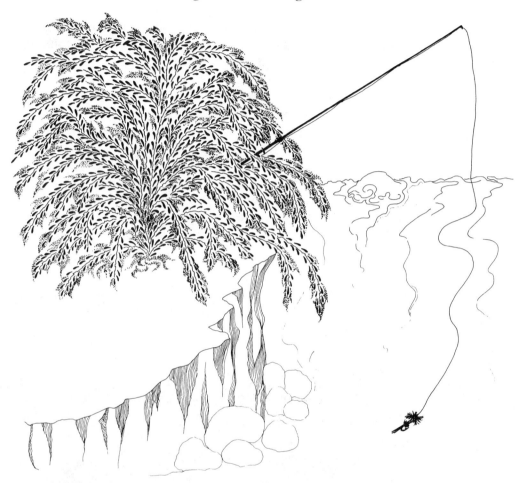

The angler shouldn't stand in the middle of the river and hold his rod straight up to "hang" a fly—that spooks the fish that might take the pattern. He should stay hidden on the bank and poke the rod out over the stream.

The Hang

With the Hang method, the fly does just that—hangs straight downstream and kicks on the surface. Like any of the active techniques it mimics the natural behavior of insects. There are females of different orders that dip their abdomens, flying in the same spot as the current strips the eggs.

My interest in the hanging fly is linked to water temperature. The rivers around Montana, for much of the summer season, are too cold early in the morning for good, dead-drift dry fly fishing. The proper use of a high-riding attractor, with the added inducement of a "guarantee" for the trout, adds another hour or two to the dry fly portion of the fishing day.

In late summer, the morning after the first frost, Bill Vessie took me and his young grandson, Dino Mills, far up to his favorite brook trout water on the Big Hole. Our fishing began at 10:00 A.M. With a Pheasant Tail Nymph,

Bill started catching trout immediately. I picked up a stray here and there, but it wasn't until 11:00 that my swinging and hanging dry fly began taking lots of fish. Dino, a very skillful angler, worked a dry fly dead drift but, even though there were small mayflies hatching, the brook trout weren't rising to naturals or artificials; and it wasn't until noon that Dino found a pod of sipping fish and, from bottom to top, fooled every one of them.

Bill took the water temperature at the start of the fishing and it was 52 degrees Fahrenheit. Normally, this wouldn't be too chilly for brook trout to rise, but it was the sudden and long drop after the first frosty night of early autumn more than the actual temperature that made the trout hug the bottom. By early afternoon, when the water was 58 degrees Fahrenheit, the fish were ready to range farther for food.

An active fly, swinging and kicking, attracts a trout with its movement, but when he's sluggish and unwilling to commit to a chase he needs assurance that the food is still going to be there when he arrives at the surface. The hang, even if it's only for twenty or thirty seconds at the end of every active swing, gives him that guarantee. The rub to the trick is that the angler has to plan the swing and the subsequent dangle so that the fly ends up in

R. Valentine Atkinson

A trout watches for crippled minnows. He wants to attack when he first sees it, but often he will just study the feeble struggles of the natural or an imitation until he is convinced that the act is real.

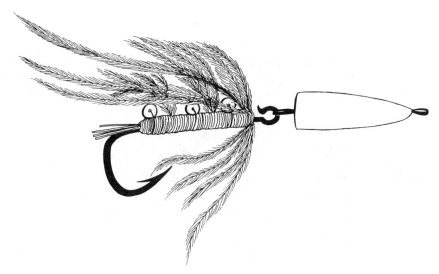

My injured minnow imitation, Bread, is tied on a Flex Hook—the bending movement makes the struggle all the more realistic.

prime water over the head of the fish, not in the shallows where a reluctant trout won't chase it. The fact that it is right over him, and looks like it is going to stay there, persuades him to rise.

The more sluggish the trout, the longer it takes to persuade him to rise. The hang is simply persuasion time. The skill that it takes to position the hang precisely over trout is what distinguishes it from the art of trolling.

The Struggle

A trout doesn't focus on a struggling, injured fry imitation either. This is true even though the fly doesn't move far or fast. The crippled minnow, with a convincing act, makes a predator attack swiftly. He is bolting forward too quickly to notice much more than size, shape, and movement. It is the movement that had better be correct.

This technique is like fishing bass bugs. It's important to let the ripples clear because the crash of such a large fly fascinates and frightens fish at the same time. Often, a trout rushes up to the edge of the slower water, but doesn't come close to the intruder. Here is where the movement has to convince the hunter, through quivers more than jerks, that this is a cripple.

My favorite fry pattern for teasing fish is one of the Flex Hook series, named simply Bread for its all white coloration. Like any of the Flex flies, it is meant to have a life of its own on even the gentlest currents. There is no long shank to handicap the imitation with a stiff appearance.

The fly also has an unusual balance. The head section, made of cork or balsa, floats high; the rear section, with three wood beads on top of the shank, bobs at an angle. This bending movement mimics an injured minnow laying on its side on the surface, flexing its body futilely.

Flies, moved vigorously over the surface, are pure attractors. Anglers accept the fact that trout have to be ready to rise to imitations, but they forget that fish have to be *willing* to move to attractors, too. They can't be forced to take a surface pattern, so recognizing the right moment is the key to fishing attractors.

That moment depends on the mood of the fish. My observations indicate five possible influences on trout mood—feeding/resting cycle (mood independent from food supply), changes in water temperature (temperature moving towards the ideal for the species), rain, circadian rhythm, and the Solunar Period (even suggesting this is controversial).

The willingness to rise to an attractor pattern is strongly connected to the feeding/resting cycle. It is during the half hour before they actually start taking food items that trout will respond quickly to an unnatural looking or behaving dry fly.

Water temperature affects the metabolism of trout. A sudden rise towards the ideal temperature range might trigger a burst of activity simply because the trout's "internal engine" is racing. Oddly enough, even when they are already feeding, trout can suddenly want attractor flies when the temperature shift is abrupt.

One morning, the same fish that had sipped Tricos fastidiously all week in Cheesman Canyon on the South Platte and wouldn't nod at a dead drift or active attractor, suddenly began ignoring the tiny mayflies and any matching pattern entirely. When the warm surface water from Cheesman Reservoir spilled over the top and down the dam, the fish went on a spree. They no longer demanded, or even wanted, small dry flies on fine tippets; those trout jumped on Variants and Skaters. A twitch was better than a dead drift and a skitter was better than a twitch. The trout were giddy (there's no better word to describe the madness).

Fly fishermen have long known about the benefits of rain. What are the possible reasons? Maybe the rain changes the water temperature, or it oxygenates the stream, or it knocks insects out of the vegetation. Probably all of these factors (and others) contribute to the effect.

F. M. Halford, in *Dry-Fly Fishing in Theory and Practice*, wrote about wet days, "the best of sport can be had; in fact, in some parts of the Test and other chalk-streams it has become almost a cant expression that the fish are always *silly* in rainy weather."

The circadian rhythm refers to the 24-hour biological clock. At dawn and dusk animals become more active (experiments show that this happens even when the light source is removed). Trout usually feed the heaviest at dawn and dusk because more nymphs and larvae are drifting free in the current (the phenomenon of behavioral drift), but they seem also to anticipate the onset of these periods. They rise to attractors especially well about an hour before dusk or dawn (the latter, of course, means night fishing).

There is another phenomenon that, at least in theory, makes fish feel good—the Solunar effect. Is this the secret of the sun/moon tables? Does gravitational influence make fish foolish with exuberance? Since these periods, major and minor, shift from day to day, they cannot work by making animals hungry all of a sudden.

Ralph Manns, a biologist who operates Fishing Information Services, found more than twenty references to the positive relationship between animal activity and solunar influences in scientific papers, including one study of guppies by Lang (1967) showing that the sensitivity of a guppy's eyes varied with the lunar cycle—especially strong evidence of lunar influence because the changes in sensitivity are involuntary reflexes.

But do Solunar Periods really affect how fish (especially trout) react to flies? There was no need for me to go through life wondering about it. This was a yes-no question that might be answerable by our three methods of observation—radio tag, streamside blind, or scuba diving.

There was another possibility—a type of test both Ralph Manns and Doug Hannon did on largemouth bass. They did their work independently on different waters during different years, fishing (and both of these superb anglers fish hard) without consulting the Solunar Tables for a season and charting the time for every bass caught. Then they went back and calculated what percentage of their catch occurred during Major and Minor periods. Doug Hannon, who has a degree in Behavioral Psychology, plotted his results like a regular experiment and found a 91 percent probability that solunar influences were positively affecting his catches of large bass (the larger the bass, the stronger the correlation). Ralph Manns discovered that 70 percent of his bass had been caught during Solunar Periods.

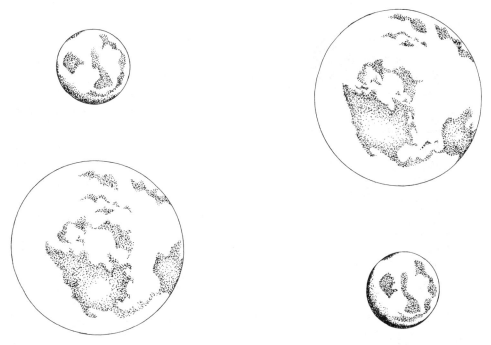

The moon directly over a spot on the planet creates a Major Solunar Period; the moon directly below a spot on the planet creates a Minor Solunar Period. Numerous experiments on saltwater and freshwater creatures demonstrate that they sense the gravitational shifts and not just the changing tides. The trout fisherman will have to decide for himself whether or not this affects his chances of success (there are no scientific experiments proving this absolutely one way or another).

Ralph also told me, "The surprise, in going back over the records, was that I hardly ever caught a fish in the hour *before* the start of a major Solunar period."

Our fishermen cast flies over radio tagged trout before, during, and after Solunar Periods. Any angler casting randomly might never know if Solunar Periods were affecting his catch rate—there were too many unknowns. For us it was possible to weigh the other major factors—prey availability, water temperature, feeding/resting cycle, and circadian rhythm—and judge how well our dry flies would have done without Solunar influences.

Whether trout were ready to feed was determined by what we jokingly called our "imaginary mood calculator." It was based on the daily rhythm of feeding and resting by any individual fish. Right after eating heavily a trout was *unlikely* to rise; after an hour or so, *maybe* he would be interested in something on the surface; and just before the next feeding cycle he would *probably* take a tempting item. Since a diver could see how frequently a fish responded to or ignored real insects over a period of time, determining mood (or feeding readiness) was not a wild guess.

The first unexpected discovery was that attractor flies seemed to work better than drab searchers or exact imitations during Solunar Periods. Even when fish were already feeding on a hatch, if the insects were small, trout often wanted bigger, active flies.

The attractors caught more than twice as many trout during a major Solunar Period than would be normally expected. During a minor Solunar Period, the success ratio was still 1 1/2 to 1. Our groups of divers, working independently and usually without the slightest idea of what they were testing (double blind experiments), all ended up with the same conclusions.

The results bothered the skeptics among us terribly. "What do we test next?" Tory Stosich, who charted one of the successful dives, wondered. "Voodoo? Astrological charts?"

It is important to understand that a Solunar Period could never guarantee that an angler is going to catch a lot of trout. This is where a fisherman misunderstands the promise of the theory. Anyone, flailing away, would have a hard time telling how much effect the Solunar influence is having on his success. What if there is a situation where trout are deep in their resting period, and the probability of them taking any fly is very low? An angler who fools a few small trout can legitimately complain about "poor fishing," but maybe he wouldn't have caught anything without a Solunar influence.

There are no conclusions here about Solunar Periods (my skepticism is legendary). The probabilities that our own experiments were accurate were in the mid-90 percent range (which sounds good to a layman, but scientists like a 99.9 percent correlation). Even if Solunar influences make fish strike bait, lures, and flies better, there are other factors in the environment to consider when choosing time, place, and strategy for a fishing day.

Fly movement cannot be random. At best it gives the angler a whole new bag of tactics to experiment with on the trout stream. The right technique stretches the effective hours for dry fly fishing. By appealing to the curiosity, playfulness, or voraciousness of a trout it makes otherwise reluctant fish strike. Even under the most marginal dry fly conditions, this movement in its various guises can help the purist give a respectable performance.

My early hesitancy over the active methods came from watching the moving fly hurt the chances of fooling trout. Underwater observation of both negative and positive effects made me want to know when, where, and how to use an active attractor. My instinct even now might be to try various attractor patterns with a dead drift first, letting some visual characteristic of the fly tweak the trout's interest, but as my understanding grows of active attractors, both new and old, they become a larger part of my fishing day.

My Fly Box

High Profile Attractors

Bivisible (10-18)
(my favorite colors are black, blue dun, brown, cree, golden badger, grizzly, and pink for the rear hackle)

Flame Thrower (6-16)
(a Variant style fly with a fluorescent hackle)

Hair Spider (12-14)
(an Al Troth pattern)

McKenzie (8-14)

Orange Asher (12-16)

Shroud (10-18)
(this fly has the marabou tail for a wet "trailer")

Skating Spider (8-16)
(tied with silver badger, blue dun, brown, grizzly, and dyed orange grizzly hackles)

The Bomber and the Slider are listed separately because they are actually "waking" flies, not really high floaters. They belong in this category because trout never do get a good look at them.

Bomber (8-14)

Slider (10-16)

Comments:
My active patterns are separated by how vigorously they get moved on the water. Often, there is no need to move Bivisibles at all. It is enough that they just look like an insect about to take flight. The tiptoe profile makes trout hurry a bit. Skating Spiders jump across current lanes—the best retrieve consists of two- or three-foot bounces interspersed with moments of dead drift float. Strikes frequently come right after the pause, just as the fly begins moving again. The Slider and the Bomber are stripped or allowed to swing as smoothly as possible so that they cut a clean line on the water.

Chapter 10

A Theory of Attraction

Bill Seeples, the ex-Navy diver who taught us all scuba, also told us the secret of studying fish. "The first thing you have to do," he said, "is watch them long enough to understand what's normal."

The problem was that the reaction of trout at certain times to certain colors wasn't always "normal." From the hastiness of the rise and the distance fish would travel to take a pattern it was obvious that they were attracted to color. But why would a color be attractive at some times and not at others?

There were two alternatives for us—we could either find the basic cause, thereby constructing a unifying Theory of Attraction (for dry flies on trout streams), or spend years testing every color under every possible natural lighting and by dogged, empirical study devise a chart for telling which color to use when. The former was a mystery, the latter an impossibility.

Imagine a person cleaning a house for years and occasionally finding pieces of a giant jigsaw puzzle. The person may save those pieces, but they're such a small part of the whole that he never even tries to put the puzzle together. He just wonders what the finished picture would look like—and that was what we were doing as we gathered bits of information about color.

Our obsession with color didn't mean that we ignored the other characteristics of the fly. Size, shape, and brightness, too, had to be part of any conclusions about the worth of attractor patterns. With attraction these traits were much simpler than with imitation—the fish weren't looking for specific traits in a fly, staring at it at close range seeking confirmation, like they would be doing during selective feeding. There was a basic duality at work in these characteristics—bright or dull (brightness), large or small (size), and tall or wide (shape)—that could be decided one way or the other. The trout's decision to accept or reject these traits depended almost completely on the type of water the fly was floating on.

Brightness

Brightness should be easy, shouldn't it? Throw sparkle yarn, or at least a seal fur substitute, on any fly and won't it have the same powers of attraction as the Emergent Sparkle Pupa? Actually, that is not true with imitations and it is not true with attractors, either. Dullness, as well as brightness, has to be specifically simulated in different situations.

The specular reflection from naturally bright materials does two things that aren't always desirable—it obscures both color and outline. This is especially detrimental on broken water, where a fly that sparkles gets lost in natural air bubbles. It is not a problem during a heavy hatch of insects, such as caddisflies, however, because at these times fish are looking for clusters of brightness. On the other hand, when trout are just sitting on the bottom and watching the surface they need color and shape to define an object.

Even on slower water, with an unruffled surface, an Emergent Sparkle Pupa isn't my only searcher. The Clear Wing Spinner in a size 10, with puffy wings of sparkling clear Antron or Creslan poking out from the sides, is also a favorite. Air bubbles collect under the wing material, turning the flush-

Dan Abrams

If there are giant Salmon Flies bouncing all over the river, then the angler can safely use size 4 attractors, also. Usually, however, such big aquatic insects are the exception.

floating imitation into a deadly attractor. At the same time, the fur of the thorax and abdomen, and even the split tail fibers, lend a solid contrast to the fly.

Brightness is a variable to play with, and so is dullness, the opposite trait. By controlling the percentage of reflectance in his attractor, the angler can choose patterns for specific water—bright flies for flat water and dull flies for rough water.

Size

Ted Marchiano sent me a dozen exquisite, size 20 Royal Wulffs. They went into my fly box, but not because they were ever going to be used. Instead, they were intended as conversation pieces for showing off to other anglers . . . not for fishing. Then, one day I tried one of them—and it was deadly business. Over the next year, the flies were lost in all the ways that flies on 6X and 7X tippets are usually lost.

Any attractor pattern stretches credibility. These flies don't need the handicap of size. Why is it, then, that the average angler typically chooses a size 12 Royal Wulff, Humpy, or Renegade. The trout, during the season, seldom get into the rhythm of eating a size 12 anything; most important insects are bigger or smaller. Take away the "giant" insects, such as the Salmon Fly, and on my streams the spring hatches average a size 14, the midsummer hatches a size 16, and the fall hatches a size 18. Trout don't live on exceptions—they live on what's available every day. If fish can see a size 16 mayfly clearly, why should a brightly colored dry fly have to be any larger? On the normal pools, riffles, and runs of a trout stream, an attractor that matches the "hatch of the day" in size, even when there isn't a hatch on at the moment, consistently outfishes the same pattern one or two sizes larger.

The only place where it is wise to exaggerate size is on rough, fast water. Then, it's the size of the fly, and not features such as color or shape, that attracts attention. The larger pattern works because it represents enough "meat" to make the trip to the surface worthwhile for a trout. Low Profile attractors in sizes 8, 6, 4, and even 2 are the effective and exciting "cheeseburger deluxe" theory of fly dressing.

A large, low profile attractor, such as a Hornberg, doesn't have to represent anything specific on rough water. It is a "meal"—and that is often enough for a trout.

Shape

In rough water it isn't merely size that controls the trout's acceptance or refusal. A fish here wants a "wide" fly. The lateral dimensions of the body, the flared hair of a downwing, or even the spread of a palmered hackle along the hook shank of a flush-floating pattern attracts this fish better than a normal upwing fly with a simple, elongated body.

A "tall" fly excites trout on the moderate currents. The mirrored bottom of the surface film in these smoother flows is tilted and warped, yet the fish can still see through a window. He especially notices an attractor pattern with upright wings. This characteristic makes them move quicker to the fly.

Flies can possess another quality—bulk, or substance—that is more nebulous than mere size, height, or width. Patterns that are bulky (or give that

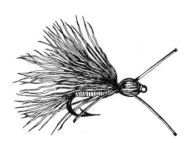

The rubber legs on a Madame X make it a "wide fly" that often works well on rough water.

impression) attract trout by promising them a substantial morsel that makes the effort of the chase worthwhile.

In the mid-1950s when the Japanese Beetles infested my area of Connecticut, a bulky-looking Vince Marinaro imitation fooled trout on any water—from trickle to large river—all summer long. The beetle populations, before the "milky disease" provided a biological weapon against them, were out of balance. A sweep of the hand over a single rose bush in our yard knocked hundreds of them onto the ground. These beetles were big and heavy, too, but the Marinaro Beetle (an enlarged version of the Jassid) only gave the illusion of bulk. It was a successful imitation because trout, looking upward, had no way of judging the depth of the pattern.

For years after the virtual disappearance of the Japanese Beetle, this fly remained one of my favorites. Without the beetles falling on the water constantly to train fish to look for such an out-sized insect, it became as much an attractor as an imitation of anything specific. It was one of those in-between flies.

I thought that I needed an attractor-imitation, rather than a straight attractor, in a low profile, flush pattern on quieter areas of the stream. My regular choices for pools and glides were the Japanese Beetle, Emergent Sparkle Pupa, or Clear Wing Spinner—and all of these flies had a connection to an insect type.

The very idea of attraction on flat water always spooked me. The years of watching trout in quiet flows showed me how they would swim up to an odd fly, but stop at the last moment and hang under it. Without a steady current to make a decision imperative, the fish frequently gave into their doubts about a flush attractor. The high-profile flies, such as Bivisibles and Variants, usually did better at fooling fish in slow water because no matter how strange the coloration, the tiptoe ride of those floaters captured the impression of life.

"Have you ever noticed how when you change dry flies you'll catch a fish right away a lot of times?" Harry Ramsay asked me once, speaking of those wonderfully sparse Catskill dry flies like the Quill Gordon and the Hendrickson. "That's because it's fresh, sitting up there so perky on the water. You have to keep your dry flies dry."

Is it possible to have a pure, low-profile attractor that works well on slow water, too? The Mohawk works—and watching it underwater it is obvious why; it has bulk both above and below the surface. I have never seen any other fly that looks so substantial for its size; a size 12 Royal Wulff, for example, doesn't appear anywhere near as bulky (or, to a trout, as meaty) as a size 12 Mohawk.

The fly projects this impression due to its weight distribution. The deer hair, not a light material, spreads out in a *V* cut that is much wider at the top than the bottom. This pushes down on the fly, which is still buoyant because of the hollow deer hair, making the Mohawk bob along with the current like a cork wearing a full backpack. It doesn't float on the surface, like any low-profile or high-profile dry fly, or hang from the surface like an emerger. Rather, it floats "in" the water.

I told Tom Poole, when we surfaced from a dive, "Sometimes it seemed like fish were searching for the fly before they ever saw it. They'd spin around and spot it as it drifted by the side of them. Maybe it was displacement. Why not? Just like the Muddler underwater. Maybe the fly was sending out pressure waves and the fish were picking them up through the lateral line."

"That's going to be hard to prove. Maybe you're right, though."

The combination of overly long hackle fibers that are forced underwater and waving, and the odd drift with the body submerged so deeply that it is visible both above and below the surface to a trout—a unique split-screen image—achieves for a Mohawk, in a much different way, the same effect as achieved by high-profile attractors. These patterns give such a strong impression of life—a high-profile pattern with its perkiness or the Mohawk with its struggling wobble—that trout notice the whole effect more than the individual characteristics of the fly.

This is exactly the opposite of what usually happens in the selection process. With most flies, the trout waits for the individual characteristics to appear, like links, one at a time. With these two types of flies, however, the fish see the whole pattern as a living insect. It is that illusion of motion, more than any actual movement, that makes them effective attractors on the slow parts of the stream.

R. Valentine Atkinson

The Mohawk worked as an attractor for me even on the slow water stretches of Hat Creek in California. Even though the fly was fished dead drift, trout rushed out from the sedges for it the same way they they would for a large, struggling terrestrial.

Choosing Characteristics for Attraction

Brightness
  Bright patterns on flat water
  Dull patterns on rough, aerated water

Size
  Pattern matched to the depth, speed,
  and turbulence of the water

Shape
  Wide patterns for rough water
  Tall patterns for moderate water
  Bulky patterns for slow water

Thoughts on Color—A Theory of Attraction
(or, to be precise, a Theory of Attraction for Dry Flies on Trout Streams)

How strange it was for me, after minimizing the importance of *exact* color in imitation, to find it so important in attraction. Some unknown factor was influencing how trout saw the color of a fly on the surface.

It was exciting to verify, or at least clarify, through underwater observation at least the first part of an old fly fishing truism, "Dark day, dark fly; bright day, bright fly."

It wasn't exactly correct; it was like one of the prophesies from the Oracle at Delphi that was broad enough to mean almost anything. The "dark" fly for a dark day in our experiments meant only a dull, earthtone color—such as brown or dark gray.

My first thought on bright colors was to follow a primary rule of attraction: The more visible a characteristic, the further it could pull fish. If the trout wanted visibility, then why not fluorescence? This started my flirtation with fluorescent colors.

Certain light waves invisible to the human eye are called ultraviolet. When these waves strike certain substances, they are changed into longer waves that are visible. Materials that convert ultraviolet light into visible waves like this are called fluorescent.

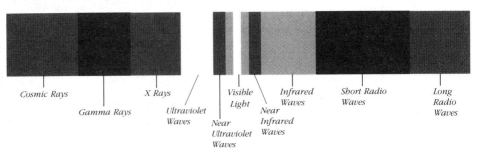

Cosmic Rays   Gamma Rays   X Rays   Ultraviolet Waves   Near Ultraviolet Waves   Visible Light   Near Infrared Waves   Infrared Waves   Short Radio Waves   Long Radio Waves

Ultraviolet light is invisible to the human eye, but it activates fluorescent materials. The colors of these materials remain intense even in dim natural light.

It was an American angler, Eugene Burns, who thought of using fluorescent materials in flies. The concept received a fair amount of publicity, enough so that not only the dyes, but also a specially manufactured floss, became available to tyers. Fly fishermen, skeptical but curious as always, tested various "bright" patterns in this country. The new flies never gained widespread acceptance here and fluorescent materials faded into oblivion.

The English, enamored of the concept, studied and wrote much more about fluorescent materials. Their literature included two books, _Fluorescent Flies_ (1964) by Joseph Keen and _The Truth about Fluorescents_ (1967) by Thomas Clegg. Undoubtedly, the "bright" flies were fished on all sorts of water in the United Kingdom. Over there the fluorescent materials never disappeared from the angling scene. Especially on stillwater fisheries, subsurface patterns with fluorescent tags, butts, and wings remained popular.

There were major differences between the American floss, Depth Ray Fire, and the English floss, Firebrand. The English material was dyed after manufacture, all of the fluorescence emanating from the surface of the nylon. The original American material was dyed during manufacture, and color was mixed in the translucent nylon. In the daylight Depth Ray Fire was much brighter than Firebrand, glowing with an internal intensity.

That extra brightness of Depth Ray Fire probably doomed any chance for fluorescent flies in America all by itself. The way that daylight fluorescence worked, absorbing ultraviolet rays and emitting strong colors even in low natural light, made it too bright on the surface of the stream. The colors went beyond what was probable, or even possible, in nature.

There's another problem with fluorescent dyes—the color that the angler sees is not real. He would have to look at every different shade for each brand of dye under a blacklight to see what is really radiating from the material. The fisherman may not know that his pink fluorescent fly is actually orange.

None of this stopped us from studying various experimental fluorescent dry flies. Some of the patterns had fluorescent wings, some had fluorescent bodies, and some fluorescent hackles. The wing colors, so emphasized on some styles of tying, made little difference on upwing flies.

George Harvey, in his article "Fluorescent Flies," in the July 1984 _Fly Fisherman Magazine_, wrote about his experiments with fluorescent wings. This work was prompted by eye problems that made it difficult for him to see normal flies. He concluded, "Body and hackle colors are essential in imitating the natural insects. However, I am now certain that wing color does not make any difference to trout."

This doesn't agree exactly with our observations (the color of upwings made a slight difference), but as long as his conclusions are referring to the wings on mayfly imitations, the difference is minor. For the hair or feather of a downwing, spreading like a carapace over the hook shank, the color is important. Sunlight filters through hair or feather fibers, creating an aura of color around the body.

Bodies of fluorescent floss or wool on a fly made a difference. During most of the day the colors neither hurt nor helped the performance of a pattern (and it didn't matter what color it was). In the low light of dusk or dawn the fluorescent brightness attracted or repelled trout, but even then the results were unpredictable.

Fluorescent hackles promised the most. The trick was to use two cock feathers, a darker of natural color and a fluorescent of pastel, wrapping them together. This muted the effect of fluorescence enough so the color enhanced the form of the fly at dusk without alarming the fish.

The trout's response still wasn't normal—a fish rose to inspect the fly, and even bump it, but often resisted the temptation to take. These were splashy refusals (classically curious), not at all like the quick, purposeful rise to a successful attractor pattern. The value of such an unnatural specter was that it aroused a trout even when it didn't catch him. The best way to fish it was as a change of pace, following the fluorescent teaser with a normal attractor fly.

The Flame Thrower, one of the experimental variations with a neon orange hackle, actually hooked enough fish—not just astounded them—to find a place in my carrying selection. It joined the only other fluorescent attractors in my stock, two Kolzer flies and Burr's Bright. The Kolzer patterns, with fluorescent yellow or orange bodies, came out of the Dan Bailey catalog. Burr's Bright, with a green fluorescent body, was given to me by the creator, Walt Burr, at one of our Connecticut Fly Fishermen's Association meetings in 1972. They have never been "regular" flies for me. They have always been oddballs—patterns to run through riffles at dusk or on dark overcast days.

In recent years many new fluorescent flies have emerged in the United Kingdom. The new creations aren't just dry flies, though—they're mostly what the English call "lures" (streamers to us) for stillwater fishing, patterns such as the Cat's Whisker and the Christmas Tree. The strong interest in these streamers indicates—as well as anything—that fluorescent materials add attractiveness underwater. Even a few inches below the surface, where ultraviolet light fades quickly, the colors are not too bright.

The Flame Thrower, with one fluorescent hackle, is tied Variant style. Two factors diminish the garishness of the fluorescense: the dark natural hackle wound through the bright one and the high riding style of the fly (it is my opinion that the "mixed hackle" wouldn't be nearly as effective on a flush floating fly).

It was a soft autumn, like New England gets sometimes, with the warm weather lingering and the trees not really wanting to turn. Still, just the days getting shorter were enough, even without frost, to make the shrubs along the swampy banks of the lower Parker River lose their green. They just hadn't decided yet what shade of red-orange they would adopt for autumn dress.

John paddled the canoe easily upstream. The bog was so bad here, where the river changed from trout stream to estuary, that in many places wading was impossible, but John made it easy to drop a fly on the riffle to the left. We talked softly and laughed softly—who knows why, but lonely rivers do that to fishermen—and even the line cut the air easily.

We were taking turns, testing various colors of the Double Wing series, and when we found the right one we started catching the nine- to thirteen-inch brown trout of the Parker quickly enough. There were no insects, but the fish rose that afternoon to an Orange Double Wing (but then they should have if the idea, the "fly on fire" theory as we called it, was true).

Something large broke the quiet. It wasn't a huge splash. It was just that any big fish rolling like that on a day with no natural rises would grab attention. The trout was there, where the riffle deepened into a run, holding like a salmon. He was so silver and large that he wasn't difficult to see.

John found solid footing and slipped across and a bit upstream of the trout; it was his turn to fish. He bit off the Double Wing and took out his box of flies for sea-run browns, tying on a Shrimp Pattern first. With a very nice touch he slid it more than a dozen times past the trout. There was no response to the dead-drift presentation. A killifish streamer imitation, swung in a steady swim made the trout turn, but he never struck or even looked at the later casts.

I commiserated with John, and told him everything that I knew about sea-run browns, which made for a short speech, "In England they call them harling. There they cast for them at night."

It wasn't night. The bugs were out much earlier than the bats. "I hate to leave him, but we can't waste the rest of the afternoon," John said.

He knotted on another size 14 Orange Double Wing, but before we paddled away to search for resident trout he made a cast to the sea-run fish. The fish moved, not really rising but turning his whole body downstream after the fly, showing a flash of his side. He moved on the fourth drift and on the fifth drift, too.

I felt myself shaking, just standing there watching, and I was bouncing so much that the flies and mosquitoes weren't landing on me. A four-pound trout in Massachusetts can do that to a fly fisherman. To me, at least—not to John, who seemed amazingly calm.

He hooked the fish on the next cast following a clean rise. Then it was me who was collected, quietly mumbling theory on how to land a trout on unsuitable tackle, and John who was bouncing, yelling, "Fella', fella'."

No doubt, this was a horse on the end of a 5X tippet—a horse with no plan. He swam and jumped wildly but never attempted to leave the run at either end. He never pushed near the reeds alongside the stream. Even though the brown trout tired steadily, he was not fully spent for a long time—and the fear was only for the fine nylon rubbing against skin and teeth.

I captured the sea-run brown in the undersized net, with a bag suited for normal eastern trout. John kissed the fish smack on the lips, and then tried to kiss me, but I parried his move. I gave him a hug. That was enough for the first date.

We released the fish and splashed out of the Parker through the silt. "You were great," John said, as we sat on the mud. "A split second before he'd move, every time, you told me what to do."

I didn't remember saying that much. I knew from past battles that I babble incoherently during moments of excitement, and that people in great need of advice often mistake that for wisdom.

Now I was shaking again, either from the chill or in my excitement over the sea-run brown. My feelings were intense not because I hadn't seen a four-pound trout, but because John Guy had never seen a four-pound trout.

"I feel like I lost my virginity," I said.

"I feel like I wet my pants."

"To each his own."

We weren't talking quietly anymore. "That fly must have been on fire," John laughed.

"Now we just have to figure out why."

The work with fluorescence had not been a total failure. It taught me not only that color had intensity, but that the intensity of any color varied throughout the day. The one thing left to find out, in lieu of testing every color under every condition, was how a fly can be vibrant one moment, literally "on fire," and dull the next.

The August day started badly for me. Two rolls of colored slide film came back that morning. My hopes had been so high for these evening pictures of Jeff Finley McRae on the Abutment Pool of the Big Hole, action shots of him playing leaping trout. "Maybe," I thought, "here's where I get the cover of a magazine."

Cover shots? They were garbage. Every element in the pictures was a garish orange; not just the limestone cliff at the back of the pool. Everything in the slide was tinged a sickly shade.

In my excitement while snapping pictures, I had forgotten what every photographer has to think about when he composes a shot—light has color. That color constantly changes. In ordinary, everyday life this is so easy to forget because the brain unconsciously compensates for the phenomenon. People seldom realize the color of the light flooding down on them, but a photograph, balanced for ordinary daylight, shows what is really there.

Later we were laying in sleeping bags, our heads outside the doors of individual tents, in a semicircle around the dying fire. The bright orange licks in the flame played in front of me.

I yelled, more a garbled shout than words, but what I was trying to say was, "I know why."

Tory Stosich was half asleep and jumped reflexively, but he understood. "You really know?" he asked.

"Yes, I know why orange flies work on the Abutment Pool. It's that limestone wall. It's what, twenty feet high? The sun always hits it in the late afternoon and the orange light reflects all over the pool. And over any fly floating on it. The orange light must do something to an orange fly that it doesn't do to a green one."

Why has there been so little fruitful speculation throughout the ages about bright flies? There have been silly, fanciful theories on what even the oddest pattern might imitate (butterflies are a recurrent theme). There have also been some theories that seemed plausible, such as the idea that certain fly colors stand out clearer against particular types of sky. Nevertheless, they all hit a quick dead end; none of them could tell anglers exactly what color fly to use at any given moment.

Intense color is a strong factor in attraction. Trout are drawn to it. Is orange intense? Sometimes it is and sometimes it isn't. And the same enigma is true for the other colors of the spectrum.

The secret is that the color of sunlight (either direct or reflected) interacts with the color of the fly. Certain combinations are intense and others are dull. All that a fly fisherman needs to do is crack the code for all possible combinations to explain the effectiveness of not only a Royal Coachman, but of any other attractor pattern.

I wrote a note to myself: "Talk to a physicist."

One found me. After a speech in Jackson, Wyoming, a man stayed to talk. He started asking the questions, but once he introduced himself as a physicist, it was my turn. He knew about the properties of light—the fact that James Fenner, Ph.D., an Assistant Professor at Auburn University, was also a fly fisherman made it easy for me to make him understand what part of his knowledge applied to attraction in flies.

Our discussion about color shattered the code.

People learn most of what they need to know about color in the first grade, when the teacher shows them how to make a color wheel. They spend the rest of their lives correctly using and responding to it in the everyday world, if they don't want to look foolish.

Visible light is a small part of the full electromagnetic spectrum. The human eye sees wavelengths from 400 nanometers (violet) to 740 nanometers (red). In order from shortest to longest, the colors visible to us are violet, blue, green, yellow, orange, and red. Trout probably see colors in the ultraviolet portion of the spectrum, also.

Red, orange, and yellow are called warm colors, while violet, blue, and green are considered cool colors. The different wavelengths create various levels of heat that can be measured with sophisticated instruments, but the terms "warm" and "cool" refer not to temperature but to the psychological impact of colors on people.

Mixing all the wavelengths creates white. The light emanating from our sun is not pure white. That collection of wavelengths is further disrupted when it hits the dust particles and water vapor of our atmosphere. As light passes through air, it breaks up and the separate colors scatter (cool colors scatter the most). The color balance of sunlight changes with the time of day, season of the year, condition of the atmosphere, and position of the planet.

Why is an object a particular color? It absorbs the wavelengths of certain parts of the spectrum, in effect capturing them, and reflects or bounces back other wavelengths. Red cloth absorbs green, blue, and violet and reflects mainly red wavelengths. Our eyes see the red rays and the object appears red.

Intensity is strongest in pure colors, and an artist knows this well—if he wants to lessen the intensity of his paint he adds a little of the complementary color. Adding a bit of red to green paint, for instance, makes the green look grayer (or less intense). There are many degrees of intensity, or value, between a pure color and gray.

Think of sunlight as a complementary color. Pour reddish light on a green fly and it's still green, but a very dull green. Pour greenish light on a red fly and it's still red, but not as intense. Both of these situations happen all of the time on the trout stream.

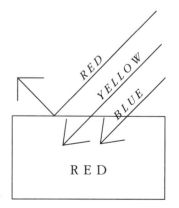

A red object absorbs the other colors of the spectrum and reflects the red wavelengths. That is why it looks red to us.

This is the combination that the fly fisherman needs to understand to select intense attractors, patterns that are "on fire." The key is how the color of the light interacts with the color of the object. It is a simple equation that adds up to intensity, or a lack of it.

Red

Red has a different type of attracting power than other colors. It is a natural exciter, both underwater and on top of the water, that fish attack instinctively because it is a reminder of blood.

Late in the afternoon, when the sun falls nearer the horizon, light travels through a much thicker layer of air than at midday. At this time, the atmospheric particles scatter the shorter wavelengths of light. On one end of the spectrum, the longer wavelengths, red and orange, come through directly; on the other end, violets and blues get bounced out of the direct beam.

Evening and dawn, if water temperatures encourage rises, are the times when red is so powerful. There are none of those cool colors pouring onto the fly and dampening its value with a subtle graying. At high noon, the color is still red, but it's a duller red. It doesn't help a dry fly attract trout then.

Orange

Direct rays aren't the only way that light reaches a fly. When the sun beats on trees and rocks standing high along a river, only parts of the light reflect onto the water. If the rocks are orange, the cool wavelengths of the spectrum are absorbed and mostly orange rays flood onto the surrounding water (and any dry fly).

The limestone cliffs of so many western rivers reflect orange light. The angler has to consider the direction of the sun, though—he cannot just flop his fly against any cliff. A wall in the shade isn't reflecting orange light, but one exposed to the sun spreads a strong glow.

We fished the Abutment Pool hard for a month, two hours in the morning and two in the evening, with orange flies. When the sun was hitting the cliff, after 4:30 P.M., various orange patterns caught almost three times as many fish as they did during the morning. Both the early and the late hours were good dry fly periods, but one of them turned out to be much more prime for orange flies in the Abutment hole.

Autumn is the best season for orange attractors. During these months in our northern latitudes, the sun's rays are warm because they come in at more of a slant. There is another reason, based on imitation, that also makes orange a hot color for fall. Most of the huge Limnephilid caddisflies that emerge at this time of year have brilliant orange bodies. In the western states the Giant Orange Sedge (*Dicosmoecus* species) rates as one of the "super hatches" on insect-rich rivers from California to Montana.

Why should any insects have orange bodies? In the fall this is protective coloration because the leaves also turn orange. In California this happens in November, and that's when the Giant Orange Sedge emerges. In Montana the trees change color in early September, and on streams such as Rock Creek, the Little Blackfoot, and the Smith, there are superb hatches in the evenings.

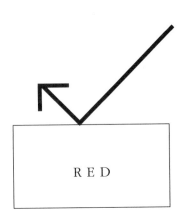

Red light hitting a red object equals intensity (and intensity equals attraction).

The orange leaves are the major reason that an orange attractor is so successful—even to the point where it is an all-day dry fly if nothing is hatching. On heavily wooded canopy rivers, orange leaves are not only alongside and above the water, but they are also floating on it when they fall. Even at midday the sunlight filters through the vegetation, bouncing from leaf to leaf, creating an orange aura among the trees.

Orange has always been a favorite color for autumn steelhead. It is not because sea-run rainbows have an inherent affinity for it. They respond to it for the same reason resident trout, of all species, do—it's fall. September and October are among the best months to use floating lines for steelhead.

Yellow

Yellow, like red, has other associations in a trout's mind that are as important as color intensity. With bright yellow, however, it is a negative instead of a positive connection. In nature pure yellow, not some weaker off-shade, is a warning mechanism. No insect wears it to be subtle, since yellow is usually an intense color.

In his book, _The Outside Story_, Robert Scammell writes about the McGinty:

> Browns often take this imitation of bee and wasp as though they expect to be stung. Often the first suggestion that there is a fish anywhere in the vicinity is one jumping crazily with the McGinty in his soon to be bee-stung lips. Three times on a recent day browns that I know I had pricked on a previous cast came to and were hooked on a McGinty. It is unusual for a brown to come again immediately after feeling the hook in other flies; it almost seems as though they find nothing unusual in being stung by a fly that looks like a bee.

It is not the bee itself that trout learn to recognize and avoid. After all, how many bees do trout see? Instead, it is the color yellow (a bright shade) that conditions them to be cautious.

This is not wild speculation. The same thing happens with a water boatman (yellow-bellied in our western species). This insect with a piercing tube gives a nasty sting. Only trout fourteen-inches or larger will feed on water boatmen on the upper Clark Fork. Apparently, smaller fish find the easy meal not worth the injury. Even big trout snatch the fly gingerly, often two or three times.

The Water Boatman has a yellow body. It can deliver a nasty sting.

The McGinty, with its bright stripes, epitomizes both the problems and opportunities of yellow in a fly. It can pull strikes from even the most sophisticated trout, but it also gets a lot of flashes and refusals. Many times, smaller fish avoid it entirely.

Bill Seeples told me about an incident where he was underwater while two friends drifted yellow dry flies over a pool of rainbow trout. The fish looked like they were playing a game of dare, rushing up and bringing their lips as close as possible to the fly without touching it. Not one of the trout took the McGinty, but they kept the game going for almost ten minutes, some fish rising four or five times. They finally settled on the bottom and ignored all subsequent drifts.

Trout do lose some of their wariness of yellow if there are consistent hatches of insects with bright yellow bodies. It helps if these insects are not poisonous and do not sting. The Yellow Sally stonefly (*Isoperla* species) and the Black Dancer caddisfly (*Mystacides* species) are two common and important trout stream hatches. When either one of these has been on the water for a few weeks the fish take not only specific imitations, but they rise better to intense yellow attractors, especially from 10 A.M. to 2 P.M.

Still, bright yellow is a color to use very sparingly in flies. Even a McGinty fishes best on rainy days on canopy streams, a time apparently when trout expect odd terrestrials to be drowned and safe to eat. Better colors, or at least those acceptable to fish in more situations, are chartreuse (a sickly yellow-green color that doesn't spook timid feeders but still works as an attractor), or the pale yellow commonly seen in many insect bodies, including classic mayflies such as the Pale Morning Dun (*Ephemerella inermis*) and the Light Cahill (*Stenonema* species).

Green

Green would not be nearly as important in flies without the misfit vegetation of this earth. Our sun gives off more yellow and green light than red or violet. Plants shouldn't really be green—efficient absorbtion depends on being the opposite color. Chlorophyll, when it is the sole photosynthetic pigment in a plant, uses the energy in the red and violet bands to create carbohydrates. At the same time, plants reflect the more plentiful green and yellow light (which is why leaves look green).

Some plants, almost as an evolutionary afterthought, have tried to make amends for this little absurdity. They have "added on" other pigments, such as carotenoids and phycobilins, which reflect red light and absorb yellow and green light. Still, even in these "red" plants, chlorophyll remains the photosynthetic engine, receiving the energy it can't produce directly from the working, accessory pigments.

Plants are like the human species in that way. They couldn't evolve by discarding their chlorophyll, the earlier development, any more than the brain could do without its primitive stages.

Why did plants develop a photosynthetic process using chlorophyll in the first place? Why didn't they just start with red pigments? Those questions inspire the theories that earth was purposely or accidently "seeded" with life in the form of single-cell plants, instead of spontaneously developing its own living organisms.

After a year back in Connecticut for school, my fishing log for 1971 contained the entry: "On streams such as the Little River and the Yantic, and even on the Housatonic, it seems like I'm using a lot more olive, lime, and green dry flies all the time this summer."

In the West green flies were important, both for imitation and attraction, but they did not dominate the fishing. On open rivers like the Madison, from the outflow of Quake Lake up to the channels below Ennis (a fifty mile stretch

On small, canopy streams the towering hardwoods filter out all colors except green from the sunlight. The leaves create a world of shade and reflected green for the trout.

mostly through grazing range) patterns with no green, such as Queen of the Waters, Blonde Humpy, and Pink Lady (with no green) caught as many trout for me as attractors with strong green attributes, such as the Lime Trude, Grizzly King, and Renegade. In retrospect, looking back at the logs, the time of day dictated success with various colors.

In the East there was no balance. My empirical bumbling always led me to green flies for searching the water. Even if there was no hatch to match, the trout on tree-lined streams responded much better to predominantly green flies.

For years this was a mystery to me—now it's not. Green is the most important color of attraction. Except for particular seasons—such as very early spring before the trees bud or autumn when the leaves change, or on open streams and rivers where trees don't tower over, or even cover, the water—green is the most effective choice.

Green is an abundant color in our sunlight anyway. Direct rays hitting a fly during the middle of the day make green colors even more intense. Under tree cover, until very late in the evening, there is enough reflected green light to overwhelm even the warm red and orange rays from the sun.

Blue

There are not many dry flies anywhere with prominent blue parts—not blue dun in its various shades, but real blue. The color is rare in insects as well as imitations, but it still has an odd, shock value in attractor patterns.

An English trout pattern called the Blue Bottle has a blue floss body. Even that is obscured by a rib of clipped black hackle. The fly represents various terrestrial insects, such as house flies, that are seldom found on the water. Nevertheless, the Blue Bottle has occasionally proved useful.

A blue fly isn't going to look bright, or intense, even under the midday sun. The blue rays, one of the shorter wavelengths, scatter from the direct sunlight high in the atmosphere (which is why the sky is blue). The only two blue flies in my carrying stock for streams, the Blue Bottle and the Yankee, seldom draw fish up from deep water like warm-colored flies can. Yet, they are sometimes successful in riffles and runs when the direct rays of sunlight disappear.

There is no direct sunlight whatsoever in the shadows. The small bit of illumination in the shade comes from weakly scattered blue rays (which is why shady areas are so much darker than open areas). There is not enough light to make any color intense, but a blue fly is brighter than any other in the shadows.

Violet

Violet is not the same as purple (which is a mixture of red and violet). Since it emits the shortest wavelengths, violet is lost in only two inches of water. That is the problem—any trout holding deeper than two inches from the surface isn't going to see this color. A trout lying under the top is sipping and, since he's undoubtedly feeding selectively, he wouldn't be interested in a violet fly unless he was taking violet insects (some emerging midge pupae are violet).

Anyone can try a simple experiment at home. Project any slide on a screen and turn the focus knob. As the picture turns fuzzy, the red, orange, and yellow areas expand; the green splotches stay the same; and the blue and violet points shrink. This diminishment demonstrates why violet and, to a certain extent, blue do not succeed as colors of attraction. Only the wavelengths as long as or longer than green on the spectrum retain enough intensity or value to interest trout holding on the bottom of a stream.

Does this mean that under certain light conditions a predominantly orange fly will catch lots of trout while a predominantly green one will catch nothing (or vice versa)? No. It means that if orange is the right color, trout will come from a little further away, or maybe from a little deeper; and they will

The classic Grizzly King, with a body of green fur, proved more effective than most other dry flies for me during 1971 in Connecticut. It was my main searching fly.

move more aggressively, arriving sooner (before drag sets in). The green fly will still catch trout that are willing to rise, but under the wrong light it will not *attract* them. Without color intensity it can only look like another possible bit of food (which may or may not be worth the gamble to the fish).

Once, late in October, Gerald Almy and I were on Nelson's Spring Creek. Gerry was fishing the run above the pond, drifting a fly nicely along the far bank and fooling trout periodically. The leaves had all fallen and the grassy banks were dead brown. The mountains behind, with a lot of snow already on their peaks, were a majestic backdrop, but the light came from the weak afternoon sun of winter and there was no natural brightness to color the lower half of the scene. When I started taking photographs, Gerry put on a bright orange knit cap. "Now I know why I see that hat everywhere," I told him. "Do outdoor writers buy them in bulk or do they share the same one?"

Of course, when *Sports Afield* published Gerry's article on spring creeks, that picture was the one they used in a two-page spread. It was obvious why—the orange cap stood out against the drab background, pulling the viewer's eye into the whole scene. It broke up the monotone image.

An intensely colored fly, when it is on fire with sunlight, works the same way. The background is far above the surface, often monotone and sometimes drab, and the bright dry fly rivets attention. The very fact that it's bright separates it from the inanimate flotsam. The color is the triggering characteristic, the part of the fly that fools the trout into believing it is alive from farther away.

Why is the Royal Coachman, and all its variations, effective in so many situations? No one has ever been able to explain why it catches so many trout, but empirical success has made it (especially in the forms of the Royal Wulff and the Royal Trude) the most popular color combination for a fly in our country.

Some boosters claim that it looks like an ant because of its red floss and green knobs of peacock herl. That is a stretch of the imagination that ignores not only all of the other features of the fly that ruin any semblance, such as its hackle, wing, and tail, but also the fact that the fly is used in sizes 14 and larger most of the time—and that is a very big ant.

The Royal Trude, especially on western rivers, has been my most productive dry fly during the decade of the 80s—that speaks to the effectiveness of the pattern under a variety of light conditions.

The doubters dislike it because it's such a bright fly—but they are wrong. It is not bright; it is half-bright. Under most light conditions the Royal Coachman is a fly possessing both dull and bright materials. When the red floss and the coachman brown hackle and tail (which have red accents) are bright under a red-orange light, the green is dull; when the green peacock herl (a vibrant, lively material) is bright under a green light, the red is dull.

This explains the effectiveness of the Royal Coachman. It is not a garish dandy floating down a river. It is a rough simulation of an insect, either a mayfly in upwing variations or a caddisfly in downwing variations, that has touches of brightness that focus attention and attract trout. As well as any fly, it stretches reality without breaking it in most situations on trout streams.

The only time that the Royal Coachman is not particularly effective as an attractor is on an overcast day. When the sky holds high clouds to block the sun, but enough rays escape to light the land in a soft, even glow (a situation photographers call cloudy-bright), every color is intense. The clouds diffuse the sunlight, wiping out shadows and spreading all wavelengths of the spectrum. Both the red and the green materials in the Royal Coachman are suddenly intense. The fly becomes the bright clown that everyone thinks it normally is—and fish are suspicious of it.

The best flies on gray days are not attractors at all. Gray day—gray fly (for me, probably a Gray Wulff). Gray—like white—is a color that reflects all wavelengths of the spectrum evenly. Whereas white reflects 97 percent of the rays, gray only bounces back 18 percent of them (at least a photographer's gray card reflects only 18 percent of the light—other levels of gray reflect different amounts). So, gray materials on a fly mute the gaudy color of diffused light on a cloudy-bright day.

Mixed colors not found in the spectrum, those that really don't have the capacity for tremendous intensity, also keep a fly properly subdued. Brown, for example, is a combination of red, orange, and yellow; add specks of black to a flat, not a fiery brown and normal people call the result mud. Fly fishermen call it a Hare's Ear. A dry Hare's Ear with slate gray duck quill wings is usually effective on a dark day.

Black and White

White, which consists of all colors mixed together, reflects the wavelengths of the spectrum equally. Black, on the other hand, is the absence of color, absorbing all wavelengths (it simply carries the concept of gray to the extreme). These colors are not intense themselves and don't function as exciting attractors the way that spectral colors do, but they provide high contrast that draw trout by making a fly visible from a greater distance.

Black actually provides better contrast than white, which has an amorphous quality, but few aquatic insects are actually black. Even bugs that anglers think are black are really a dark brown—and trout can see the difference. This may explain why trout, in clear water, frequently refuse an all-black fly. It is just too stark.

As part of a fly, however, black *is* valuable in two situations. When a fly is backlit, with the sun directly behind it, the edges on any lighter colors turn fuzzy. The black parts of a fly present a clean, sharp line—and this can be important if trout demand a particular shape (like an ant).

Black also adds to the effectiveness of a fly in low light. When seen against the sky, which is surprisingly bright even at night, black provides the best silhouette. The perfect fly for dark or near dark, therefore, has black wings. The pattern with a touch of white somewhere on the body and black both at the front and the back, tied so that it has some bulk, works because it presents a well-defined target on the water.

White is very seldom a true white. It *is* really white when the light source is evenly balanced, but natural light almost always has some sort of flavor, tilting from blue to red. White reflects all colors equally. So what happens when the light source doesn't have all colors? White takes on a tinge, a bluish one in the shade or a pinkish one at sunset.

There is a time just after sunset—known as dusk—that might also be called the "great shade." On western streams it happens suddenly because the sun drops quickly behind the mountains. It is not dark, but the only source of light are the scattered, bluish rays from the sky.

In our tests with fly colors, the daytime shadows under obstructions and the total shade of dusk produced the same results. Blue, the color that was supposed to work, did only marginally better than the other colors. One fly was successful as an attractor in the shadows, but it had as much white on it as blue. In these situations the combination of good contrast and a tinge of reflected color made a white fly an exceptional fish catcher.

Maybe the fact that white flies work so well in shade explains why this is a magic color for brown trout. More than other species of trout, browns seek overhead cover for holding lies. They feed in open areas, even during the day, but our observations revealed that they often pick foraging spots that have some solid object nearby—whether it is a rock, a log, or even a bit of moss, that casts a shadow.

A Series of Attractor Patterns

Tory Stosich said, "I suppose it'll fry your butt if we work for two or three months and we end up with a Royal Coachman?"

"It would," I laughed. "But it wouldn't surprise me."

Why not start from nothing, with as few preconceptions as possible, and build a new attractor pattern based on what the trout's reactions told us they wanted in a fly? This was our trial-and-error process of design (what Tory calls a "no-brainer"), but in this case the object was not a better imitation. If trout were actually feeding on a hatch of insects, their acceptance or refusal of a fly meant to match the natural was very conclusive. Developing an attractor, in contrast, required testing non-feeding fish—and the observations were much more random.

With imitations we had our probability charts—_Possible_, _Probable_, and _Acceptable_. With attractors, however, all that we had was our understanding of particular fish. Our many studies bred more than familiarity—these trout became individuals, with pet names. Their actions became so patterned, if not completely predictable, that there was no doubt about their normal responses to food items. Impulsive reactions to odd flies—whether triggered by curiosity, playfulness, or voraciousness—also became predictable.

It took longer than two or three months to develop a new type of attractor. The testing took closer to three years.

How different was the new Double Wing fly? From the underwater vantage it appeared more vibrant—not just because of color—than any other standard dry fly design. Why not? Hadn't the years of work on color predisposed us to look at everything on an attractor as a parody of what was right on an imitation, but without losing the essence of life?

Tail: a stub of Sparkle Yarn (lies flat and spreads out on the water.
Tested against: no tail; stub tails of other material (including crystal flash); two, four, and six pieces of fine rubber; a subsurface, dangling tail of marabou; and a mayfly-type tail of split hackle fibers.

The stub tail, whether it was made of Sparkle Yarn, regular wool, or polypropylene, easily outperformed no tail. It didn't make that much difference when a trout viewed the fly from head on, but when the test pattern passed to the side of the fish he saw the movement of the fibers flush on the water. It was the tail's waggling motion even when the fly was drifting naturally that provoked takes.

Tip: floss (white in most versions)
Tested against: no tip

Does a tip seem insignificant? It wasn't, not in our tests, at least. Maybe it worked because the thin band between the bottom wing and the stub tail gave the fly definition (which may explain how the floss center makes the Royal Coachman a better fly). The white color, never out of place in any light, also added contrast on most of the patterns in the series.

Thick, rough body: dubbed Sparkle Yarn (the fibers are very long and shaggy)
Tested against: smooth and fat bodies, smooth and thin bodies (both with many different natural and synthetic materials), and various types of deer and elk hair bodies

The purpose of the thick body wasn't width (that quality was assigned to another feature). Other attractors, such as the Humpy and Irresistible, achieved both width and bulk with a hair body, but those flies were heavy and pressed into the surface film. It was clear from our observations how much the weight of those flies added to the impression of bulk.

In the end, the Double Wing was also a "heavy" fly that landed with a plop and floated very low, but not because the body material weighed a lot. The dubbing suggested bulk more with its roughness than its thickness. The dubbing method, which Polly Rosborough used to form the collar on the Casual Dress nymph, left long, loose fibers to flare on the water.

Bright body
Tested against: dull body, translucent body, no body

Any fly is a different creation, for better or worse, with Sparkle Yarn. No matter how the material is employed, its effect on a fly's performance is great. Yet, except for very frothy water, it is hard to see how the yarn's brightness could hurt an attractor pattern.

On an imitation, where it is often important to mimic the drab aspects of a natural, there are reasons for not using Sparkle Yarn. On an attractor, which trout rise to best when not actively feeding, the silvery reflection of Sparkle Yarn makes a fly like the Double Wing visible from further away. The shaggy, yarn body also gathers a smattering of air bubbles, not holding them as strongly as the Emergent Pupa (which has the overbody acting as a cage).

Sparkle Yarn has been used so widely and successfully by innovative fly tyers on various imitations, such as on dry patterns like Craig Mathews' Sparkle Dun, damp patterns like Robert Ince's Reed Smut, and wet patterns like Dave Whitlock's Squirrel Nymph, that it is hard for me to understand why tyers haven't adapted it to attractors, too. Why haven't there at least been modifications of standard patterns—bastardizations with names like the Sparkle Humpy and the Royal Sparkle?

The bright body pulled trout from further away than the dull body in nearly every situation (except for heavily aerated water). They would streak out to snatch it and then try to turn back like a thief with a loaf of bread.

V-clipped body hackle: clipped top and bottom (long at the sides)
Tested against: full, unclipped hackle, no hackle

The body hackle sticking out at the sides gave the fly width. It wasn't solid width with the impression of depth like the flat carapace of a beetle imitation, but the hackle fibers laid on the water and moved with the current. Their animation produced the illusion of life.

Why was a clipped hackle better than the full, palmered wrap? On a dull fly with no color intensity or brightness, the choice of hackling methods might not have made any difference, but on the finished Double Wing the palmered fibers that circled the shank obscured the color and brightness of the body.

Double wing: bottom wing of colored elk hair (tied in near the back of the fly, just ahead of the body); top wing of white kip tail (extending back over the stub tail)
Tested against: single upwing and single downwing, with different wing materials; no wings at all, wing under the hook instead of on top (sled effect), split wings tied at the sides of the hook (outrigger effect), solid wings (cut and shaped)

The odd wing on the attractor happened by accident. One of the high school helpers, Kelly Reinoehl, was tying the suggested variations. Once he asked, "Upwing or downwing on this next batch?"

I had walked up to the motor home after my turn at diving. "I'll tell you what, we're not bound by any notions, so tie a few that have both an upwing and a downwing on them."

He laughed at the idea, but he tried it. At first, Kelly's sense of proportions were off—the upwing in front so crowded the eye of the hook that his whip finish forced the white kip tail fibers together and back, creating a double downwing.

He held it up, asking "Do we keep it?"

"Let me give it to Graham to fish," I said. "He's moaning already about getting all the turkeys."

We were working over a radio-tagged rainbow called Two Dot. An hour after his last feeding period, when he was still in his holding water but starting to nose around, Graham drifted the pattern with the double wing over him.

The trout was in a position, snug to a ledge with streamy, faster water flowing over his head, where he could watch not only the main tongue but also the slower current to his right. Two Dot was a "comer"—this was what we called a fish who moved forward, angling ahead on the ascent, to take a fly. That was how he worked when he was perched at his feeding station. He fed on natural insects at the beginning of a hatch, or sucked down matching flies, differently in his holding water, however, falling backwards with the currents. The configuration of the tongues forced him to move in such a fashion. Evidently he did not like to rise this way because if he was at all inclined to feed during an emergence, after a few tastes of the natural, he would swim twenty feet over to his feeding water. He would move even for a sparse hatch.

Two Dot was a very difficult fish to catch on any attractor because, unlike during a hatch, there were no naturals floating overhead to prime him. In his holding water, he would tip upwards when he fancied an attractor or a stray bug, but if he didn't make an immediate decision to rise he would keep watching the fly until it drifted out of sight. Seldom would he change his mind and drop backwards for it.

He never moved ahead or out to the side for the two-wing pattern, probably because he wasn't quite ready to start rising. When Graham put a drift directly over him, however, he watched the fly. Tilting up, his fins waving faster, as if he could not bear to lose sight of it, he turned downstream for the pattern at the last moment.

Flaring out over the edges of the other parts, the fly's top wing exploded with reflected light, while the bottom wing of elk hair formed a background that suddenly made the color of the stub tail much more prominent. It was the Double Wing's entire "package," rather than its individual parts, that convinced trout to rise at the final moment.

Hackle: a regular hackle
Tested against: no hackle
     The hackle provided another strong triggering trait near the front of the fly. It was the only feature that added height to the pattern, and leaving it off definitely decreased the percentage of "early decisions" by trout.

The success of these test flies with their prismatic layered wings changed the name of the attractor series. Originally this type of fly was to be called the Agitator (that struck us as catchy). But, with the wing style obviously the oddest component, the name was changed to Prism.

Whenever we mentioned the fly style among ourselves though, we called it neither of these. Tory Stosich, Graham Marsh, or Tom Poole would say, "Hand me one of the Double Wings."

Thus, through common usage and to the detriment of swashbuckling romanticism, we dubbed the fly "Double Wing" (usually said so quickly that the words run together, "dub-ba-win"). There are eleven color variations, each created for a specific type of natural lighting.

The work on the new Double Wing series was as much a study of attractors—and why trout take them—as an attempt to find a better attractor pattern. The whole process was different than searching for a better imitation. One imitation can be better than another because use pertains to a specific situation, selective feeding on an abundant insect species. No attractor can be better than another—only different. Every one will have its moment of success because there are so many reasons that a trout takes a fly.

The Double Wing patterns, however, quickly became important to us because they were so different. The bulky body, white floss tip, and even the V-clipped hackle were not new techniques—many older flies had one of these features—but it was the first time they were put together (each one planned as a contributor to the final fly). The bright tail and body of Sparkle Yarn on an attractor were new, simply because any pattern with Antron or Creslan becomes effective in new situations. They separated the Double Wing from any of the popular attractors. The prismatic result of layering of the over wing, under wing, and the stub tail stood as the biggest deviation from older dry fly styles. Its value was so clear to us in every test against standard downwing flies made of various natural or synthetic materials. Considered as a whole, the Double Wing series was also different because it was the first group of attractors designed to take advantage of the major possibilities of ambient light.

One discovery during our work on the Double Wing series was more than a curious, isolated fact—it provided insights into the whole process of why trout take odd patterns. The reactions of the trout revealed that not all features of a fly, even when every one was designed to attract, attracted in the same way. Some were "pullers"; some were "savers."

The pullers were those features that the trout recognized as odd from a distance. When a fish spotted a pulling characteristic, the attraction was so strong that he could not rise in a normal manner. Instead, he would intercept the fly by moving either forward or laterally.

On the Double Wing the brightness of the Sparkle Yarn, the bulk of the body, the movement of the tail, and the height of the front hackle all pulled trout. The bright body, light reflecting off both the yarn and actual air bubbles, was the strongest attraction (probably because trout could see this effect under the surface, before the fly even entered the window).

The savers were those characteristics that trout saw once the fly was in the window of vision. These features convinced a reluctant fish that the item was worth rising to—even against his better judgement.

The color intensity of the body; the prismatic effect of the top wing, the bottom wing, and the stub tail; the spread of the V-clipped body hackle; and the tip all changed the trout's initial decision about the fly. These features often saved the Double Wing as the pattern was about to drift fruitlessly out of the window. Either the color intensity or the prismatic wing, depending on how the sunlight hit the fly, could be the strongest rescue feature. By happy coincidence the prismatic combination of materials, creating a "hot spot" of color, ended up at the back of the fly where it proved most effective.

To be valuable, any attractor needs to be a saver (under the right conditions, most are) or a puller. The characteristics that save are more important on rough water; those that pull are more important on smooth water. Ideally, a fly would have both, but while saving characteristics are common, the pulling traits, except for the weak attraction of the hackle height, are rare even on popular patterns.

The purpose of the underwater observation was not only to find out where all of the popular styles of flies—imitations as well as attractors—fit in the overall plan of fly selection, but to try out every oddball concoction on the fish. Not surprisingly, most of the creations failed miserably enough, but there were pleasant surprises (such as a drooping marabou tail) that kept the testing procedure interesting.

While testing tails on the Double Wing, one style—made from marabou feathers—performed as well as the Sparkle material (which floats). The marabou didn't float, but that was the secret of its effectiveness. A marabou trailer, dangled under the surface, pulled trout a long way to the new fly. The choice was either the Sparkle tail or the marabou tail, and since the Double Wing already had other "pull" features, the sparkle tail added more to the overall effectiveness of the pattern.

But it seemed a shame to waste such a deadly concept. The marabou tail was incorporated into a new fly for gray days. Everything else about the pattern was high profile: The sprightly way it acted and the somber way it looked were a contrast, but it was named for its appearance instead of its float characteristics.

The Shroud, a pattern made with a wide band of hackle at the front, is very light (the hook is fine wire). The long fibers at the head tilt the front of the pattern up, and if the marabou tail is wetted, either with saliva or a sinking agent, it droops almost straight down. This is a great fly to twitch because the marabou fibers undulate beautifully.

The day came to take Tory Stosich on a float down the river, to let him fish from a moving raft for the first time. It was the chance for him to match his imitations against those attractors like the Royal Wulff, Renegade, and Humpy that he considered inferior.

On the Big Hole that morning my job was rowing. Tory was in the front seat, using his favorite imitation that season, a size 16 Cream Thorax Dun. Meanwhile, Wayne Huft sat in the back, casting a size 16 Royal Wulff. The beginning of the day was rough for Tory, simply because he had never float-fished. The bank moved by so fast that he was constantly trying to cast back upstream to good spots, but they were gone. There was no time to put a half dozen drifts through a pretty piece of water.

He was such a fine fisherman, though, that he quickly mastered the knack of picking the fly up at the end of one drift, glancing ahead while his line was in the air, deciding on the next prime drift, and putting his fly on the right current. It was like a dance step—one, two, three, four—and soon the float settled into that gentle rhythm, two lines swishing and only an occasional hookup breaking the concentration.

It was not a fast day of catching trout on a dry fly, but Wayne and his Royal Wulff steadily pulled ahead in the count. Tory, with unshakeable confidence, never showed the slightest hint of frustration until the end, when the takeout ramp was suddenly there, surprising him. "Well, what's the bad news?"

I tallied my marks. "The Royal Wulff caught fourteen fish and the Thorax Dun five."

R. Valentine Atkinson

Drifting a river suddenly changes the "rules" of fly selection. The fish is generally only going to see a pattern once, so the fly had better be a style that he is going to fall in love with at first sight.

Wayne clapped his shoulder and said, "But you almost had me even on the whitefish, Tory."

Tory stood there, still looking out at the river. "I can't understand it. Ninety percent of the situations we were in, I know that the Thorax Dun was a better fly."

Maybe he was right; maybe he was wrong. It comes down to a matter of mathematical probabilities, and those numbers explain not only "why" to fish attractors but also "how" to fish them. In most situations, an attractor pattern is less likely than a drabber general imitator or searching fly to catch a fish if each is presented to him correctly ten times.

So the probabilities might look like this:

Attractor pattern—10 casts   Drab searching pattern—10 casts
   20% chance of success   30% chance of success

This shows that the drab pattern is clearly the better fly, doesn't it? No (and that was what confused Tory). The percentages, 20 percent for attractors and 30 percent for searchers, can't be divided up evenly over all ten casts.

On the *first* cast, the attractor fly is much more likely than the drab fly to catch a trout. However, it is probably all or nothing with the bright pattern; if the fish doesn't take it the first time, the chances of a strike go down on later casts (it's not like flipping a coin, where the odds of heads or tails remain exactly the same for every toss).

The drab fly is more of a teaser. A trout becomes more interested in it every time it floats over his head (simulating a hatch). This is why the fourth or fifth cast with a searching pattern usually has a better chance of taking a fish than the first.

The attractor excites and the imitation tempts—that is the nature of the beasts. They not only have to be fished at different times, but also with different styles of presentation.

Tory's ordinary style of fishing, a careful stalk and a series of precise presentations over a trout, perfectly fit the drab flies. His techniques don't work as well with attractors, however, where the first chance at a trout is the best. On a float trip, casting from a moving boat, the first chance is the only chance.

That's why attractors are often the best choice for float fishing. The wading angler, to maximize his chances with a bright pattern, has to do almost the same thing as a boat fisherman—show his fly to a different trout every few casts at the most.

In my view, the master at wading and riffle popping with attractors is Dick Fryhover. When he casts he picks the stream apart. He makes a cast or two to one spot, and then a cast or two to another maybe only a foot away, but there's no doubt that each drift is aimed at a specific pocket. If, by chance, there is someone else on the stream, it's usually easy to see the difference in approach between Dick and the other angler. If he is an ordinary fly fisherman, the other person is casting anywhere, his fly drifting haphazardly over "good" water. Even in the best riffle, however, not all of the water is good. Dick always casts somewhere, not anywhere; by putting his dry fly precisely over certain spots as he moves through a riffle, efficiently popping the edges and pockets of quieter water within the turbulence, he gets the most out of an attractor pattern because he's showing it to nearly every trout once or twice—no more, no less.

The main Low Profile attractors in my carrying selection include the Double Wing for riffles, the Wulff for runs, and the Clear Wing Spinner for quiet flats.

Now that my work on a Theory of Attraction is finished, my selection of attractor patterns is set—for the moment. The main low profile flies are Trudes and Double Wings, both with lateral spread, on broken water; Wulffs or other flies with tall features on runs; and the Emergent Sparkle Pupa, Clear Wing Spinner, and Mohawk on quiet water (although the latter is also effective on riffles because of the underwater bulk). All of these flies, and all of the others in my boxes, are not chucked randomly anymore. The colors are matched to the available light for the most intensity. These attractor dry flies are getting used more now that they are no longer a guessing game.

The theory is not complex:

(1) The "color" of the surrounding light affects the intensity of a fly's color. (2) Flies with "intense colors" attract trout (when trout are in a mood to be attracted).

This is the Theory of Attraction for dry flies on running water. In no way does it conflict with the Theory of Imitation. The two fit together nicely, like matching pieces of a cut coin; trout can be in the mood to feed (and then imitation is paramount) or in the mood to experiment (and then attraction *might* tempt a fish).

The theory predicts when a fly of a particular color will be effective as an attractor. There is no opposite to this—the theory doesn't predict when or where a fly of a particular color will fail. A green fly might work fine (for any one of a hundred reasons that have nothing to do with attraction) in the wrong light for producing intensity—it may be working because trout want a dull pattern.

Could someone work out a Theory of Attraction for underwater flies? Probably not for dead-drift methods. The difficulty of the task is reflected in the fact that almost all nymph patterns are imitations, general or specific (seen any red-and-white artificial nymphs around?). The Brassie, the copper fly, and the skinny, orange San Juan Worm come the closest to being attractors, but the Brassie is a ringer for many types of case-building caddisfly larvae with stone houses and the San Juan Worm imitates a widespread, common aquatic worm.

Imitation is creative laziness. With the infinite variables of underwater feeding by trout it may be the only possibility with subsurface, dead-drift presentations. Attraction underwater is feasible only when the fly moves— then motion adds interest by obscuring the identity of the object.

There are plenty of odd-colored dry fly patterns designed for dead-drift presentations, including red-and-white variations. The variables for dry fly selection are much simpler because there is a natural barrier, the surface film, obscuring any pattern.

This might be one of the few firm rules of fly choice: Attraction is possible only when there is something preserving the mystery.

My Fly Box

Low Profile Attractors

Aft Sparkle (14-16)

Double Wing (6-18)
(there is a full series of patterns for matching the colors of natural light—White Double Wing, Cream Double Wing, Gray Double Wing, Orange Double Wing, Lime Double Wing, Royal Double Wing, Midnight Double Wing, Charm Double Wing, Brown Double Wing, Yellow Double Wing, and Pink Lady Double Wing)

Fan Wing Royal Coachman (10-12)

House and Lot (8-18)
(also known as the H & L Variant)

Humpy (8-18)
(the wide body and the flush float make this an excellent "first choice" for searching rough water; color variations include the Blonde Humpy and the Royal Humpy)

Irrisistible (8-16)
(the name has always been spelled this way in fly fishing—correct spelling would be Irresistible; the White Irresistible is my favorite color variation)

Kolzer (10-12)
(the Kolzer Yellow and the Kolzer Orange are tied with fluorescent bodies)

Lady Heather (10-18)

Madame X (8-16)

Mohawk (10-16)
(the Gray Mohawk, Orange Mohawk, Green Mohawk, Golden Yellow Mohawk, and Brown Mohawk are the versions in my box; this promises to be a valuable fly)

Pink Lady (12-16)

Rat-Faced McDougal (12-16)

Renegade (12-16)
(this pattern actually looks very "natural" from underwater; my stock also includes three other Fore & Aft variations—the Knave, Outlaw, and Rascal)

Royal Coachman (12-16)

Shroud (8-10)
(this pattern is actually half low profile and half high profile, but it is the back end, with its dangling marabou tail, that makes the fly effective)

Stimulator (10-14)

Trude (4-20)
(the Lime Trude, Quebec Trude, Rio Grande Trude, and Royal Trude are all important for me)

Ugly Rudamas (12-14)

Wright's Royal (14-16)

Wulff (6-16)
(my favorite Wulff variations are
the Blonde Wulff, Gray Wulff,
Grizzly Wulff, Royal Wulff, Were
Wulff, and White Wulff; none of
these flies are marginal—everyone
of them catches fifteen or more
trout a season for me)

Comments:

Where and how an angler fishes determines what flies he carries to the water. For me the *where* is usually the area around my Montana home. That is not much of a punishment, considering that Deer Lodge has excellent small streams, large rivers, and spring creeks (not to mention ponds and lakes) surrounding it. Many of those waters are rough, bouncing flows.

The *how* for me includes a lot of float fishing on rivers. Presentation from a moving boat means one cast only to a spot. The premium then is on a dry fly that makes a trout react quickly. The pattern also has to be durable and bouyant.

The *where* and the *how* explains why there are so many attractor patterns in my boxes. Maybe if my home base was still Connecticut, such flies, slightly odd in one way or another, might not be as important in my fishing. Maybe if my base was strictly the Pennsylvania limestone waters these patterns would be missing entirely from my stock.

Or, at least, that is the way I use to think. No more. All of our work with odd flies, culminating in a Theory of Attraction, proved to us that attractor patterns can possess enough subtlety for any type of water. The same rules for color, bulk, and shape apply on any streams, but the size of the fly has to be matched to the daily expectations of the fish on smooth water. If trout have been feeding on size 18 mayflies for weeks, an attractor might work spectacularly during non-hatch periods if it also is a size 18.

Attractors are more important for me now than ever. The color of the fly is matched to the color of the ambient light; the shape and silhouette of the fly is matched to the water type. Attractors work best when trout are in a particular mood (receptive to food but not taking insects generally or selectively in a regular rise rhythm from the surface yet).

Flies (with comments)

An* with a pattern indicates that this is one of the flies that is always in my boxes. All of the dry flies in this section, however, are valuable. When my personal tying is up to date, they sit neatly arranged in compartments like a "team" ready for all situations.

Adams

The Adams, one of the most popular dry flies in this country, is a prime example of consistency. It is not a spectacular fly in any sense, not in our observations—it doesn't change a reluctant trout's mind about rising. But when a trout is feeding on a mixture of drift items, he is very likely to accept an Adams as a general representation of an insect.

The Adams is a consistent fly because there is never anything "wrong" in the visual picture; all of the characteristics—the gray body that mutes all colors of light, the broken, impressionistic outline of brown and grizzly hackle, and the familiar upwing shape of many common insects—are easy for the fish to trust as evidence of a safe, edible item. There is no feature on an Adams that triggers curiosity or, its companion feeling, caution.

Hook: 10–18 (standard dry fly)
Tail: grizzly hackle fibers
Body: gray dubbed fur
Wing: two grizzly hackle tips (tied upright)
Hackle: brown and grizzly (mixed together)

Aft Sparkle

Doug O'Looney

Hook: 14–16 (1X fine wire)
Tail: cream hackle fibers (tied split; three fibers on each side)
Aft Hackle: a "woven" hackle of green/olive sparkle yarn
Body: peacock herl
Front Hackle: cream hackle

The rear "hackle" of the fly consists of long fibers of sparkle yarn (the pieces are cut to about the length and thickness of a regular hackle). The tyer combs out the pieces of yarn, spreads them along a dubbing loop, and twists the loop. This hackle is then wound at the rear of the shank.

The sparkle yarn flattens on the water, not covering the hook like the reverse hackling procedure, but the yarn collects air bubbles and these air bubbles hide the hook. The actual material at the back of the fly doesn't obstruct hooking at all.

*Air Head** (see color plate)

Jeff Kienow wrote to me from Idaho, "That new design, the Air Head, is proving to be a fine stonefly pattern on rough streams. Is the purpose of the head the translucency, or does that just add buoyancy? The fly is easy to follow and impossible to sink. A single size 12 Olive Air Head took more than thirty trout for me on Kelly Creek and never even needed redressing. It's not just new; it's a valuable fly in my box."

Cream Air Head
Hook: 8–16 (standard dry fly)
Body: cream mink dubbing (guard hairs left in for a shaggy appearance)
Wing: bleached white elk hair (tied in halfway

down the hook shank; the body dubbed both behind and in front of the wing)
Head: white foam strips (cut six or so thin strips of foam; tie them sticking out over the eye of the hook; pull them back and tie them down in a bullet head; clip a few strips from the bottom, but leave the rest of them as a collar)

Olive Air Head
Hook: 8–16 (standard dry fly)
Body: yellow/olive mink dubbing
Wing: brown elk hair
Head: white foam strips

Brown Air Head
Hook: 8–16 (standard dry fly)
Body: brown mink dubbing
Wing: brown elk hair
Head: white foam strips

My daughter already has a fly named after her, the Lady Heather—the Air Head has no connection to her. My name for it comes from the air-filled, closed cell foam that forms the very buoyant, highly visible head on this pattern.

The color schemes match some important stonefly situations on both eastern and western rivers. The brown version, in size 16, is my favorite for the March Red (*Brachyptera fasciata*) on New England trout streams; this hatch used to occur just before opening day, but with open winter seasons this is often the first significant dry fly activity of the year. The olive version, in sizes 8 and 10, matches one of the great stonefly hatches on western Montana trout rivers, the *Skwala* of the Bitterroot and the lower Clark Fork; it is an abundant insect from mid-March to late-April, but this is a lonely time on these waters, even though the waters run low and clear before the runoff period (the poor locals have only the slurping trout to share the rivers with). The cream version (or as Jeff Kienow calls it, my August Dawn), in appropriate sizes, matches many of the pale species of summer; often these are night emergers and egg layers, but there are

enough stragglers around at dawn to interest trout.

Beacon Beige
Hook: 14–16 (standard dry fly)
Tail: four grizzly hackle fibers
Body: stripped peacock herl
Hackle: grizzly and brown (mixed)

My samples of this dry fly, like many English patterns, are tied with softer rooster hackles than commonly used in this country. This is not unintentional—the feather tips bend and create an impression that is not particularly well defined. Many English anglers who fish chalk streams prefer this style.

Beaverkill Red Fox
The Beaverkill Red Fox has been in my fly box for over thirty years, never catching a lot of fish, but averaging nearly a dozen trout per year over that span as a general searcher.

Hook: 14–16 (standard dry fly)
Tail: ginger hackle fibers
Rib: fine gold tinsel
Body: gray muskrat fur
Rear Hackle: ginger (tied just in front of the body)
Front Hackle: medium blue dun (tied just ahead of the ginger hackle—not mixed in with it)

Bird's Stonefly
There are two kinds of rivers with Salmon Fly hatches: those that are usually muddy when the insects are out and those that are not. In my area the Henry's Fork, Madison, and Big Hole run high but clear. The Yellowstone, Jefferson, and Rock Creek run high and murky. How murky those last three rivers flow depends on the spring runoff. If there is not much snow left in the mountains at Salmon Fly time, even those rivers might run low and clear.

Both kinds of rivers provide good fly fishing. The murky rivers are considered nymph waters by locals. The angler drifts big stonefly nymphs against the banks (where the hatching insects migrate to crawl out). The clear rivers fish well with either nymphs or dry flies, but the egg-laying flights of the Salmon Fly can trigger such incredible surface mayhem that the dry fly possibilities bring most anglers to the West.

The Salmon Fly hatch is not great every year—one out of four is a good average. Too much can happen to spoil the party. The weather might be too hot or too cold; a strong wind might blow (it can make fishing impossible even if the insects and trout are willing); or the insect populations themselves might be poor during any given year. The ideal conditions are warm but not hot afternoons with a mild breeze. This lets the females fly out over the water and crash onto the surface. The females beat their wings in an inefficient swimming stroke, trying to reach the shore. Few do (unless the trout and birds are so glutted from earlier feeding that they do not care anymore).

Hook: 2–6 (up-eye Atlantic salmon dry fly hook—my personal preference, not standard practice)
Body: orange silk floss
Body Hackle: furnace (clipped short; each band wrapped separately, not palmered)
Wing: brown bucktail
Hackle: furnace (lacquered, pressed flat to project at sides only, and trimmed)
Head: orange tying silk

My early purchases from catalogs were usually a mix of a dozen flies, each a different pattern. My package from Dan Bailey's Flies contained a size 4 Bird's Stonefly. Now why anyone would need a Salmon Fly imitation in Connecticut is still a mystery, but it was my daydreaming fly—someday both of us were going to fish in Montana.

Finally, during college, that chance came one year on Rock Creek. The water was not only muddy but flowing over the banks, running in new channels through the fields and woods. Nevertheless, the Salmon Fly adults were careening everywhere, many hitting the stream. Nothing rose to them in the main current.

That wasn't going to stop me from using my Bird's Stonefly. My slap cast, not accomplished by intent but by sloppy form, caught one incredible trout (fourteen to seventeen inch trout were huge to me) after another in the side channels. It wasn't beginner's luck—it was beginner's ineptitude that helped me that day.

It took me a few more seasons to learn that slapping a Bird's Stonefly in the shallows only worked on muddy rivers. The flying naturals, after all, rarely landed near the banks. The same tactic on clear rivers frightened more fish than it caught. My success on dirty rivers during the Salmon Fly hatch never instilled any great love in me for chocolate flows, though.

Bivisible*

Most commercially available Bivisibles are tied wrong. At least they are wrong for an active presentation. The hackles should not be the same length from front to back. That first hackle on the fly has to be longer—then the fly cocks up, lifting the hook free of the water, on every twitch. This is one of those little differences that can make a fly either a killer of a dud.

Hook: 10–18 (2X fine wire)
Tail: hackle fibers
Rear Hackle: rooster hackle of the main color (one very long hackle or two shorter ones)
Front Hackle: white rooster hackle (slightly longer than the rear hackle)

My favorite colors for the rear hackle are black, grizzly, cree, golden badger, brown, blue dun, and pink.

Black Gnat

It looks like no "gnat" on my streams; usually, it is sold in sizes too large to represent a midge. It is simply a good, black searching fly.

Hook: 10–14 (standard dry fly)
Tail: black hackle fibers
Body: black fur (dubbed thick)
Wing: mallard quill (matched sections)
Hackle: black

Black Quill

In my mayfly box this is a specific imitation for *Rhithrogena* hatches all over the country. This insect emerges from the roughest waters early in the season, when the weather is often miserable. The adult dun is usually more important than the emerging nymph to the trout.

Hook: 14–16 (1X fine wire)
Tail: black hackle fibers
Body: stripped peacock quill
Wing: dark mallard quill sections
Hackle: black

Blue Bottle

Hook: 14–20 (1X fine wire)
Tail: black hackle fibers
Tip: gold tinsel
Body: royal blue floss (tapered to a thicker front)
Wing: gray duck quills
Hackle: black

It's strange how this fly will work when seemingly better imitations of black flies won't attract strikes. It is not one of my everyday patterns, and the only sizes always in my fly box are 18 and 20, but it is not a one-time wonder, either. Usually, it comes out at midday for fishing "splash zones."

What are splash zones? Fast water throws spray on the rock faces of eroded cliffs. Adult flies (looking like small house flies) buzz in the shade of these wet overhangs. They concentrate by the thousands in such places on a trout river.

Blue Dun*

On some days impressionistic patterns work best; on others monochromatic patterns are more effective. My guess (and that's all it is) is that the monochromatic patterns present a better contrast against the sky than the broken visual picture of impressionism. Sometimes—and gray days seem to be one of them—that is desirable. The solid gray Blue Dun is a fine fly on overcast days.

Hook: 16–20 (standard dry fly)
Tail: medium blue dun hackle fibers
Body: muskrat fur (dubbed)
Wing: mallard quill sections (matched and upright)
Hackle: medium blue dun

Blue Quill

There are quill-bodied equivalents for many of the fur-bodied flies in my carrying stock. Trout often prefer a Blue Quill over a Blue Dun (or vice versa). Whether the last important food item had a thick body or a thin body seems to determine which pattern is going to fool more fish.

Hook: 14–16 (standard dry fly)
Tail: medium blue dun hackle fibers
Body: stripped peacock quill
Wing: mallard quill sections (matched and upright)
Hackle: medium blue dun

Blue Upright

Hook: 14–16 (standard dry fly)
Tail: light blue dun
Body: stripped peacock quill
Wing: pale gray mallard quill sections (matched

and upright)
Hackle: light blue dun

This is a paler version of the Blue Quill (and this is just about as far as my deference to color goes). The only reason the shade of these flies is so important in my fishing is that they are usually fished on gray days. Trout can certainly stare critically at patterns when the sun isn't shining in their eyes.

Blue Wing Olive*

The best hatches of the *Baetis* duns occur on the nastiest days. The wet and chilly weather keeps them drifting for so long that the major concentration of insects is *on* the surface film, not *in* it. Frequently, a fully hackled imitation performs better than a hackle-less one.

Hook: 16–20 (1X fine wire)
Tail: dark dun hackle fibers
Body: olive fur (dubbed)
Wing: pale blue dun hackle tips
Hackle: dark blue dun

This is such an important fly in my selection because the *Baetis* species emerge three times during the year. On my rivers both the spring and the autumn hatches are major events; occasionally even the summer activity is worth matching.

Bomber

Hook: 8–14 (Atlantic salmon dry fly)
Tail: woodchuck hair
Body Hackle: brown hackle (palmered)
Body: natural gray deer hair (clipped oval; flat on the bottom)
Wing: woodchuck hair (slanting forward over the eye of the hook)

The body has to be trimmed oval, not round, so that the fly will plane on the swing. The properly shaped Bomber slices deeply into the surface, but it doesn't dive underwater.

Bread

My favorite fry imitation for teasing fish is one of the Flex Hook series, named simply Bread for its all white coloration. Like any the the Flex flies, it is meant to have a life of its own on even the gentlest currents. There is no long shank to handicap imitation with a stiff appearance.

The fly also has an unusual balance. The head section floats high; the rear section, with three wood beads on top of the shank, bobs at an angle. This bending movement mimics an injured minnow laying on its side on the surface, flexing its body futilely.

Hook: 6 (Flex Hook)
Front Section—white cork or balsa cylinder
Rear Section—
Back: three wooden beads
Tail: six pieces of 2-pound test Stren blue fluorescent monofilament (short)
Rib: Stren blue fluorescent monofilament
Body: white sparkle yarn (dubbed rough)
Wing: three white marabou wings (at the rear, middle, and front of the shank; very short)
Topping: four long strands of peacock herl
Throat: red marabou fibers

The Bread is one my favorite flies to tie at angling shows. People are curious about any new pattern; someone always asks, "Where do you fish that fly?"

With this one, at least, there is an obvious answer, "You cast your Bread on the waters."

The Reverend Dan Abrams has suggested expanding this theme into a Biblical series. Nymph fishermen will be able to cast the First Stone to very pure strains of trout and bass anglers will be able to cast Pearls before swine (or "hawgs" as we like to call them).

Burr's Bright

Green is the safest fluorescent color. It is still best used with discretion—the Burr's Bright works best for me not during the dawn or evening hours but on very overcast days as a searcher.

Hook: 14–18 (standard dry fly)
Tail: white hackle fibers
Body: fluorescent green wool
Hackle: grizzly

Buzz Ball*

Doug O'Looney

Hook: 10–14 (standard dry fly—the hook is not a fine wire version because this fly can fool some surprisingly large trout)
1st Hackle: medium blue dun (a smaller size than normal for the hook—for a size 10 fly, this hackle would be a size 16; palmer it, then trim to size)
2nd Hackle: orange hackle (a smaller size than normal for the hook; palmer it through the first hackle, then trim to size)
3rd Hackle: grizzly hackle (very long in proportion to the hook size; palmer it the full length of the shank, then clip a V in the top and bottom, leaving the sides long)

The clusters of midges, the mating swarms, are a mass orgy of hundreds of insects. Sometimes they are as large as a man's fist, but my fishing experiences with huge, size 2 Buzz Balls have not been nearly as good as my days with size 10 through 14 patterns.

This is my winter fly. Even on swift rivers such as the Madison and the Yellowstone, trout rise to midges along the edges. They will bust into a cluster with a smashing rise, gulping a mouthful of insects.

Bucktail Caddis

There are four variations for this fly. They are my favorite caddis imitations in the larger sizes.

Dark Bucktail Caddis
Hook: 6–10 (1X stout wire)
Tail: dark mottled deer hair
Body Hackle: golden yellow hackle (palmered over the whole body)
Body: golden yellow fur (dubbed)
Wing: dark mottled deer hair

Light Bucktail Caddis
Hook: 6–10 (1 X stout wire)
Tail: light tan deer hair
Body Hackle: light ginger hackle (palmered over the whole body)
Body: light yellow fur (dubbed)
Wing: light tan elk hair

Orange Bucktail Caddis (a Kevin Toman variation)
Hook: 6–10 (standard dry fly)
Body: bright orange fur (dubbed)
Body Hackle: dark ginger hackle (tied in hackle tip first and palmered over the entire body)
Wing: dark speckled deer hair
Head Hackle: dark ginger hackle
Head: brown fur

The Orange Bucktail Caddis is a specific match for the Giant Orange Sedge (*Dicosmoecus*) that is a major autumn insect on rich rivers throughout the Northwest.

Peacock Bucktail Caddis (another Kevin Toman pattern)
Hook: 6–10 (standard dry fly)
Body: peacock herl
Body Hackle: brown (palmered over the entire body)
Wing: light speckled deer hair
Head: peacock herl

Captive Dun (a Rene Harrop fly)
Hook: 14–20 (standard dry fly)
Tail: marabou fibers
Body: dubbed fur (pale yellow and olive are favorite colors)
Hackle: grizzly (short)
Spike: grizzly hackle fibers

A good place to fish any stillborn imitation is in the foamy backwaters and eddies after a hatch. During an emergence trout cannot differentiate between normally struggling insects and permanently trapped unfortunates. The stillborns (a term popularized by Doug Swisher and Carl Richards in *Fly Fishing Strategies*) get mired in the scum of the backwaters. The trout move into these areas after the hatch fades and sip the dead or dying emergents. This aftermath feeding period is usually the best chance of the day to catch a very large fish on a small fly.

Carmichael's Indispensable

The great Jackson Hole fly tyer, Bob Carmichael, should never be forgotten for his contributions to the "western" style of fly tying. Jack Dennis, in *Western Trout Fly Tying Manual* (Vol. 1), wrote that he was "considered by many to be the greatest fly fisherman ever to fish Yellowstone Park.

"Bob Carmichael and his friend, Roy Donelly, collaborated in developing great western patterns. His shop stocked various eastern patterns adapted to the West. Every fly either had a western touch, or it was a new pattern designed strictly for this area. Among these were the Whitcraft, Carmichael's Indispensable, Donelly Dark Variant, Dry Spruce Fly, Hackle Tip Blue Dun, and Western Black Gnat."

The Whitcraft and Carmichael's Indispensable are regular flies in my boxes.

Hook: 12–16 (standard dry fly)
Tail: several moose body hairs
Rear Body: yellow floss
Front Body: pink wool
Wing: two wide grizzly hackle tips
Hackle: brown and grizzly mixed (tied bushier, in western fashion)

The Carmichael's Indispensable is an Adams variation, but the pink on the body makes it a better fly for attracting trout (not surprisingly, it seems especially potent for the beautiful cutthroat of the Snake River).

Carrottop

In my box the Carrottop, a Jack Gartside creation, is not an imitation of a drowned or spent mayfly like other parachute patterns. In larger sizes it is a searcher on smooth waters (especially where a riffle empties into a pool).

Hook: 14–18 (standard dry fly)
Tail: split moose body fibers
Body: olive fur or synthetic dubbing (poly recommended)
Wing: a clump of deep orange deer or elk hair (tied upright)
Hackle: grizzly (tied sparse)

It is hard to tell what Jack Gartside is more famous for in the fly fishing community, being an exquisite fly tyer or being the only person in the world with his life style. Few match him for creativity in pattern innovation.

Car Top Caddis

Hook: 18–20 (up-eye hook, standard weight)
Thread: color matches the color of the body hair
Body and Wing: a clump of deer hair (the stubs are layed along the shank and wrapped down lengthwise; the tips of the clump form the wing)

No one who ties as beautifully as Darwin Atkin should be practical as well. The fact that his Car Top Caddis is so simple to tie makes it one of my favorites in small sizes. The color variations in my box are dark gray, olive, cream, and brown.

Cicada

This giant insect is very cyclical, building to population peaks, but there is a smattering of adults any year.

Hook: 4 (standard dry fly; once the Flex Hook is available in these sizes, it will be ideal for this imitation)
Body Hackle: olive grizzly (palmered densely; clipped)
Body: black polycelon foam
Legs: white rubber (knotted double legs)
Under Wing: fox squirrel tail (sparse)
Over Wing: crow feather (flat over the under wing)
Head: dark brown mink (dubbed roughly with guard hairs left long)

I saw that smattering of insects on the Green River in Utah. On the desert tailwater fishery below Flaming Gorge Reservoir even an occasional cicada splatting on the surface brought an explosive attack, usually by more than one trout.

I intend to be ready for that peak—it will be worth waiting for.

Clear Wing Spinner* (see color plate)

The wings of clear Antron are an exaggeration, brighter and larger even than the translucent, bubble-coated wings of the spent mayfly. That great visibility is a major advantage for both fish and fisherman when the surface is cluttered with dying, egg-laying females.

My best day with a *Tricorythodes* spinner fall in the East was on Pennsylvania's Tulpehocken Creek. The insects were quite a bit smaller than western Trikes, sizes 22 and 24 versus sizes 18 and 20, but from twenty-five feet away even the tiniest Clear Wing Spinner stood out like a sparkler in the dark among the naturals.

It was a good day for comparisons, too. Everyone else on the stream was using either hackle-wing spinners, which did poorly, or poly-wing spinners, which did well. There were a lot of nice twelve to seventeen inch rainbow and brown trout sipping spent insects and the Clear Wing Spinner took these fish with wonderful consistency.

Hook: 8–22 (1X fine wire)
Tail: two hackle fibers (tied split)
Body: synthetic seal's fur substitute (black, rust, cream, olive, pale gray, reddish orange, and dark brown color versions)
Wing: clear Sparkle Yarn (tied spent at the sides; an alternative can be tied with one wing cocked up)

The fisherman should study the natural against the light to accurately match the body color. One of our western *Tricorythodes* species, for example, has an olive tint. It isn't the solid black seen on most imitations. The eggs often influence the color of the female's abdomen.

Close Carpet

Hook: 12–16 (standard dry fly)
Tail: deer hair
Body: deer hair (spun and clipped)
Wing: a fan of deer hair (in the Compara Dun style)
Hackle: sparkle yarn (form a dubbing loop; twist the fibers of yarn into a "hackle")

Two new and effective patterns, the Sparkle Dun and the Close Carpet, both utilize the Compara Dun winging style. The tyer then adds an element of brightness to create a different mayfly imitation.

The Close Carpet, developed by George Close on the Wolf River (Wisconsin), puts that brightness up front. The yarn hackle makes trout focus on this pattern as it enters the window—it is a pulling trait.

Compara Dun*

Hook: 14–22 (2X fine wire)
Tail: hackle fibers or deer hair (tied split)

Body: synthetic or natural fur (dubbed)
Wing: deer hair (from the face area)

My boxes contain the full series of Compara Duns from *Hatches*: White/White, Pale Gray/Cream, Cream/Yellow, Pale Gray/Yellowish Olive, Slate/Olive, Gray/Yellowish Gray, Dark Gray/Brown, Pale Gray/Black. The body color, the first part of each name, is much more critical than the wing color.

If this selection is complete, fresh flies nestled in my box in a full range of sizes, it will cover most mayfly hatches anywhere in the country. The style resembles the nymph-dun (the insect's body still flush on the surface film). The Compara Dun series matches species up to size 14 for me (the choice for larger duns is the Mess series).

A big advantage of this style is its visibility—a Compara Dun can be used even on riffles. This reflects the background of the fly (Al Caucci and Bob Nastasi refined the rough-water Haystack, an old standard on the Ausable River in New York, into a mayfly imitation for slow waters and fussy trout).

Cone

Doug O'Looney

Hook: 6–14 (standard dry fly)
Tail: white sparkle yarn (a short, sparse tuft)
Back: foam
Body: synthetic seal's fur (dubbed)
Rear Hackle: rooster (swept backwards)

Front Hackle: light colored soft hackle fibers (swept backwards)

There are three color variations: Vanilla Cone—cream body and light ginger hackle; Chocolate Cone—brown body and coachman brown hackle; and Pistachio Cone—olive body and cree hackle.

The Cone is the mirror image of the Mess. The Mess worked so well with the hackle flared forward that it seemed worthwhile to test a fly with the hackle flared back. They both had the brightness of the foam overlapping the body.

The Cone clearly resembles an emerging insect. The swept back hackle fibers portrays the tangle of legs, wings, and old nymphal shuck. Unlike the Halo Emerger, though, the Cone does not hang down in the water. The bouyant foam keeps this fly perpendicular on the surface. That stretched-out position imitates the hatching nymphs of very large mayflies slightly better than even the Halo Emerger pattern.

Cork Bug

At one time these simple cork flies were very popular in Pennsylvania.

Hook: 14–16 (standard dry fly)
Body: a shaped piece of cork (painted any color)

Cork Bugs still catch trout for me all over the country. The colors in my box include any possible match for a terrestrial, and some combinations (pink with green dots) probably not found in any natural.

Cow Dung
Hook: 8–12 (standard dry fly)
Tail: brown hackle fibers
Body: dark olive fur (dubbed)
Wing: dark gray duck quill sections (tied upright)
Hackle: brown

The original dressing calls for a gold tinsel tag, but that feature hurts the fly's chances on overcast days—that is when it is a good searcher.

Cream Variant

Hook: 12–16 (4X fine wire)
Tail: dark cream hackle fibers
Body: hackle quill (from a cream feather)
Hackle: dark cream hackle fibers (tied oversize)

One way to overcome the problem of imitating very large mayflies is to use a high-riding fly. The profile of the pattern obscures details of the imitation.

This is exactly how Art Flick used the Cream Variant (specifically matching *Potomanthus distinctus*).

Creature*

Doug O'Looney

Hook: 2–8 (up-eye, dry Atlantic salmon hook)
Foundation: yarn (wrap the hook shank with yarn; soak the yarn in glue)
Flotation: balsa (a piece the length of the shank; cut slot along bottom of balsa; bind it onto top of hook shank with tying thread)
Skin: a long, thin slice of rabbit skin with hair on (put glue on underside of skin and wrap it around shank; brown, gray, and tan are favorite colors)

The Creature, which can resemble a mouse, a vole, or a baby muskrat in various colors, wobbles on the retrieve. That movement is probably caused by the water flowing unevenly over and through the hair. A fly crafted of smooth, hard materials does not react that way. The trout show a strong preference for any fly on the surface that swims in such an awkward manner.

This pattern is not just for large fish. A size 8 Creature excites a lot of ambitious trout, many in the ten to fourteen inch range. Of course, in a jumbo version, especially at dawn or dusk, it catches mostly the large hunters in a river. It can be used as a prime chunk with a slow, steady retrieve, or as a locator with a fast, erratic retrieve.

My largest trout on the Creature was an eight pound brown from a small (and very short) spring creek in the Deer Lodge valley. The entire stream is only 300 yards long, popping up as a seep among a complex of ponds. There is a culvert where water drops from a pond into the stream, and the resident brute in that churn pool cannot resist the urge to belt a Creature swimming across the current. The same fish has taken the fly three times (my partner has been a different person on each occasion—Robert Ince, Jennifer Koenig, or Sampson Myers).

Cross Special*

Hook: 10–20 (standard dry fly)
Tail: light blue dun hackle fibers
Body: grayish-white fox fur (dubbed)
Wing: drake wood duck (or dyed substitute; the feathers come from flank of the duck)
Hackle: light blue dun

Can anyone from the Catskills tell me which mayfly this pattern is meant to imitate? The Cross Special still has a smattering of fans throughout the East, but in the 1950s it was much more popular commercially (Harry and Elsie Darbee produced a lot of them).

It is my "pale" searcher. The Cross Special and the Gray Coughlin (dark searcher) are my main searching flies. One of these comes out first when trout are rising to a hodgepodge of insects. The choice reflects the broadest of mayfly generalities—light and dark.

Crowe Beetle*

Hook: 10–16 (standard dry fly)
Back: black deer hair (pulled forward and tied down in the front; leave stubs over hook eye)
Legs: black deer hair (three fibers on each side)
Body: peacock herl (often this pattern has a fur body)

My opinions, based on underwater observation, are very clear about the "show them something different" theory of fishing a hatch. Showing a feeding trout a brightly colored attractor is pretty much a waste of time on a stream with a sophisticated population of risers.

The key word is attractor. It is possible to break a hatch by imitating another food form. There are only a few patterns, however, that have that much power over trout. The ones that can make fish take something that looks entirely different than what they are feeding on represent regular items in the trout's diet.

There are two flies that are very good at breaking a hatch—a Crowe Beetle and an Emergent Sparkle Pupa. Patterns mimicking a food item that trout do not see consistently (for example, grasshoppers) do not make good hatch breakers. Trout can be sipping mayflies, but they will disrupt that rhythm sometimes to rush forward and take a beetle or a caddis pupa imitation. This is common not just on freestone rivers, but on fussy fisheries such as the Henry's Fork, Firehole, and Silver Creek.

Cul de Canard

There are no "miracle" flies, but there are materials that, while not miraculous, prove particularly exciting to fish in the right situations. Those materials end up being used again and again in a variety of patterns, sometimes in ways that enhance the peculiar characteristic and sometimes in ways that diminish it. Those flies that waste the attractiveness of the material fade away.

Underwater observations not only confirm that some natural and synthetic materials produce a special appearance, but that they all seem to fall into one of the major groups of attractiveness. The groups we identified for dry flies (and there may be more) include variegation, water repellence, translucence, and reflectance. The most popular fly tying materials possess one or more of these traits. Hare's ear dubbing is variegated; peacock herl is not only variegated, with an irridescent shimmer, but also reflective. Horse hair, in the finest examples, is translucent; seal's fur is not only translucent but also water repellent.

The French fly, the Cul de Canard, depends on the water repellent nature of the soft, downy feathers from the rump of a wild duck. These feathers surround the uropygial, or preen, gland and become saturated with the oily liquid the duck uses to waterproof its feathers.

The fly has to be tied with the untreated, naturally oily feathers. The Cul de Canard (or Duck's Rump) is a delicate pattern. A fresh fly floats lightly, but once it is soaked or slimed by a fish it becomes hard to keep on the surface. After a few outings the fly loses the water repellent oils and its effectiveness. It cannot be rehabilitated with natural or synthetic floatants.

The duck's rump feathers are used in a number of tying styles. Wherever the fibers touch the surface of the stream they gather air bubbles because of the water repellent oils. That special ability makes the Cul de Canard effective on the toughest waters for the fussiest trout (the popularity of the fly, not only in France but all over the Continent, suggests that it is worthwhile in spite of its delicate nature).

One style of the Cul de Canard, the soft rump feather wound as a hackle, trimmed, and reinforced with a stiff rooster feather, graduated quickly from experimental fly to hatch matcher in my boxes. It worked during any heavy mayfly emergences, probably as a nymph-dun hybrid, when the imitation had to be better than the real insect at attracting attention.

The Gray/Olive Cul de Canard is one color variation. The pattern can be tied in other combinations:

Hook: 12–18 (2X fine wire)
Tail: gray hackle fibers
Body: olive dubbing
Hackle: duck's rump feather and dark blue dun rooster feather (wound together, but the first few turns of the rooster hackle actually start behind the softer duck feather)

There were four size 18 Cul de Canard flies in my box one morning on Hot Creek (California). The trout wanted nothing else during the *Baetis* hatch, but each fish drowned and ruined the pattern that caught him. Four flies; four fine trout—that was my tally for the day.

Daddy Long Legs

Doug O'Looney

Richard Walker, the creator of this fly, in his *Fly Dressing Innovations*, mentions the Daddy Long Legs for moving water, "floated down without drag in river fishing."

This English pattern imitates the adult cranefly. It is very popular on reservoirs in the United Kingdom; even for me it is much more of a stillwater pattern than a river fly (and has been ever since Robert Ince introduced me to it).

It has not caught a lot of fish for me on streams, but the ones it has fooled have been large. A Skating Spider imitates an active cranefly; a Daddy Long Legs imitates a downed one. Both flies are valuable on rivers with large populations of these insects.

Hook: 8–12 (1X long shank)
Body: pale cinnamon turkey fibers
Wing: two badger rooster hackles (slanting back over the body; divided)
Legs: eight pheasant tail fibers (knotted in two places; trailing to the rear)
Hackle: pale ginger grizzly

Dancing Caddis (simplified version)

Ken Thompson

The four main color variations cover 90 percent of the caddis situations.

Brown and Yellow Dancing Caddis
Hook: 8–10 (up-eyed, Atlantic salmon dry fly hook)
Body: yellow fur (with a brownish tinge)
Wing: speckled brown deer or elk hair
Hackle: light brown (clipped flat on the bottom)

Brown and Green Dancing Caddis
Hook: 8–10 (up-eyed, Atlantic salmon dry fly hook)
Body: olive brown fur
Wing: speckled brown deer or elk hair
Hackle: cree (clipped flat on the bottom)

Dark Gray Dancing Caddis
Hook: 8–10 (up-eyed, Atlantic salmon dry fly hook)
Body: gray and brown fur (mixed)
Wing: dark gray deer or elk hair
Hackle: bronze blue dun (clipped flat on the bottom)

Ginger Dancing Caddis
Hook: 8–10 (up-eyed, Atlantic salmon dry fly hook)
Body: cream fur
Wing: light brown deer or elk hair
Hackle: ginger (clipped flat on the bottom)

The problem with a Dancing Caddis on the original Swedish Dry Fly Hook was that it was too easy to tie wrong. The hair wing had to be forced down at an angle so that it didn't envelope the hook point—if it did it turned the fly into the ultimate catch and release toy. The angler would not hook even one out of ten striking trout.

The secret with any upside-down hook is to strike slowly, anyway, allowing the fish time to close his mouth and turn downwards. A trout usually doesn't grab a surface fly. He sucks in water, letting the artificial or natural ride into his mouth, and then shuts his jaws and expels the water through his gills. The normally timed strike pulls the fly out of the trout's still open mouth.

This premature strike is not so bad with a regular fly. The hook, hanging down, usually sets solidly in the lower jaw. What happens is that the water surface is skimming over the top of the teeth and lip anyway and the hook, down in the water, snags the bone.

There's a greater distance, however, between the water surface and the top jaw. An upside-down hook, with the strike, slides on the water right out of the trout's mouth. It touches nothing if the jaws are still open.

The simplified Dancing Caddis is tied on an up-eyed, fine wire Atlantic salmon hook only in sizes 8 and 10. This pattern cannot be tied wrong—the wing of deer or elk hair sits flat, well below the hook point. The aerodynamics of the wing still make the fly land upside-down. The original advantages of the design,

A trout sucks in dry flies, letting them ride a column of water into his mouth. A premature strike often pulls a regular hook into the lower lip (see A), but the upside down hook, far below the upper lip, simply rides the water back out (see B).

a fly that provides the proper silhouette whether it is drifting dead or twitching actively on the surface, are intact.

The fisherman still has to strike slowly. Instead of simply saying, "God save the Queen," before setting the hook, he should bless the entire Royal Family.

Dark Cahill

All of the Catskill dry flies in my box imitate a number of different mayflies. The Dark Cahill, for example, works very well during the western Gray Drake hatch (*Siphlonurus occidentalis*). Maybe the finer details are not quite so critical on a fly that rides high on the water.

Hook: 12–18 (1X fine wire)
Tail: dark ginger hackle fibers
Body: muskrat fur (dubbed)
Wing: lemon wood duck flank (upright)
Hackle: dark ginger

Dark Hendrickson

Hook: 12–18 (1X fine wire)
Tail: medium bronze dun hackle fibers
Body: muskrat fur (dubbed)
Wing: lemon wood duck fibers (upright; divided)
Hackle: medium bronze dun

This Catskill dry fly that is not one of my favorites for matching any specific mayfly, but there are times on overcast days when it works better than more specific imitations even during a hatch.

Dark Montreal

Hook: 8–12 (1X fine wire)
Tail: scarlet hackle fibers
Rib: gold tinsel
Body: claret floss
Hackle: scarlet

David Beyer wrote me, "The Dark Montreal is still a good fly for Maine fishing, but it's not specifically a brook trout pattern anymore (my experiences agree with yours on that). When a red fly will work at all, it will catch brown trout, rainbow trout or even landlocked salmon."

Dave's Hopper

Hook: 6–10 (3X long shank)
Tail: red deer hair fibers
Body Hackle: brown (palmered)
Body: yellow yarn (small loop left dangling off the back)
Underwing: yellow kip tail
Overwing: two turkey wing quill sections (tent-fashion over back; lacquered)
Head: natural deer hair (spun; clipped to shape)

No angler needs all of the popular grasshopper imitations in his box. He can choose from among the similar styles; for example, the Dave's Hopper and the Gartside Hopper are both fine patterns. They layer on enough material to create the impression of bulk (and the natural is a bulky insect).

Deer Hair Hornet

Hook: 12–14 (standard dry fly)
Body: yellow and black deer hair (alternating bands; spun and clipped)
Wing: clear Antron

This is a better floating alternative to the McGinty as a bee imitation.

Deer Hair Wooly*

Hook: 8–12 (standard dry fly)
Body: natural gray deer hair
Hackle: brown (palmered through the deer hair)

The 1984 season was an interesting one for dry fly fishing. The Royal Trude, which almost always ends up as my top dry fly for numbers of trout caught, sank all the way to fourth on the list. The Deer Hair Wooly edged ahead of it into third place.

Obviously, the Deer Hair Wooly was not being used as a caterpillar imitation. Often, on smooth, gliding runs, with trout holding a few feet deep, it pulled fish up all day long with the dive technique. But it wasn't limited to that situation—it became a general fly for me, the palmered hackle bristling under the surface apparently an important characteristic (as any feature breaking through the film is on a dry fly) for attracting reluctant fish.

Delta Wing

The slightest twitch makes the flat hackle-tip wings of this Larry Solomon fly squeeze together. This spasmodic flexing mimics the struggle of certain "feeble" caddisflies perfectly.

The caddisfly females that struggle weakly after depositing their eggs are the ones that carry a visible, gelatinous ball at the end of the abdomen. The release of this egg packet is so explosive that the act damages the insect. The females often collapse on the water and drift with the current.

Hook: 14–20 (1X fine wire)
Body: light olive mink fur
Wing: two gray hen hackle tips (tied flat)
Hackle: brown rooster hackle

This fly can tied in any combination of colors. For an eastern river, such as the Beaverkill, the Delta Wing should be carried in sizes and colors to imitate the *Brachycentrus* Grannom (or Shad Fly), with greyish brown wings and a bright olive body in size 14, and the *Chimarra* Black Sedge, with black wings and an olive-brown body in size 18.

Devil Bug
Hook: 8–10 (2X stout wire)

Tail: deer hair tips (an extension of the deer hair back)
Body: olive sparkle yarn (dubbed)
Back: natural gray deer hair

The Devil Bug is a very old pattern that has gone through numerous changes. This version (by Gary Borger) has a body of dubbed sparkle yarn. On slow waters this is a beneficial change. The fly is a deadly imitation of active, running caddisflies on stillwater habitats (not within the scope of this book).

There are "travellers," usually the larger caddisfly species, on slow moving sections of rivers, also. Do caddisflies run on riffles? No, a broken meniscus is not thick enough to support them. So, the tactic of pulling a dry fly that makes a clean, V-wake on the surface film (such as a Devil Bug) works best on flat water. For rougher water a lower riding fly, one that cuts through the chop like a swimmer, provides a better target.

Double Caterpillar

The macrame cord connecting the hooks is very strong, but at the same time this poly material is flexible enough to allow movement. This is a good imitation for larger caterpillars.

Hook: 12–16 (two standard dry fly hooks)
Connector: white macrame cord (color with a waterproof marker)
Rib: green thread (wrapped on each body)
Body Hackle: grizzly (palmered separately on each body; clipped short)
Body: foam (tied down by the rib on each body; color with a waterproof marker)

Double Trike
One September morning Gary Saindon found that he could hook Missouri River trout well enough on the regular Clear Wing Trico imitation, but he was having trouble landing these strong fish on a size 20 fly and a 6X tippet. There was nothing unusual about losing most

of the trout—most anglers do have problems controlling the rainbows (especially because after one or two jumps these fish dive into the weeds).

Hook: 14–16 (1X fine wire)
Tail: two hackle fibers (split)
Abdomen: pale gray fur (dubbed)
Thorax: olive and black fur (mixed and dubbed; the thicker thorax extends from just behind the rear wing all the way to the front)
Wing: two sets of clear Antron or Creslan wings

Later that day Gary set up his fly tying equipment on the picnic tables at the Craig Access. He imitated two Trico spinners by putting two sets of wings on one fly. The pattern was larger than normal, a size 16.

The Double Trike did not do as well for me as the regular spinner on individual fish (those very selective loners), but it did fool trout that were slurping in pods. The bigger hook and heavier leader tippet allowed me to land a greater percentage of those fish.

Double Wing (see color plate)

This series of flies is designed to match the different possiblities of ambient light. The way they float, very flush on the surface film, makes them strong attractors on broken water.

The hook for all patterns, in sizes 6 through 18, is a standard dry fly wire.

Gary Borger uses the Devil Bug on the rich lakes of Vermejo Park in New Mexico. He catches trout by creating a wake that mimics the "run" of the large Travelling Sedges (Banksiola crotchi).

*White Double Wing**
Tail: white sparkle yarn (combed-out stub)
Tip: white floss
Rear Wing: white elk hair
Body Hackle: silver badger (palmered; clipped flat top and bottom)
Body: white sparkle yarn (dubbed rough)
Front Wing: white kip tail
Hackle: grizzly

Use in the shade or at dusk as an attractor, or on a brown trout stream anytime as a searcher.

Cream Double Wing
Tail: cream sparkle yarn (combed-out stub)
Tip: white floss
Rear Wing: pale yellow elk hair
Body Hackle: ginger (palmered; clipped flat top and bottom)
Body: cream sparkle yarn (dubbed rough)
Front Wing: white kip tail
Hackle: grizzly

This variation is a little better than a White Double Wing when terrestrial moths are common.

*Gray Double Wing**
Tail: dark gray sparkle yarn (combed-out stub)
Tip: white floss
Rear Wing: rust elk hair
Body Hackle: cree (palmered; clipped flat top and bottom)
Body: dark gray sparkle yarn (dubbed rough)
Front Wing: white kip tail
Hackle: grizzly

This is a dark fly for cloudy days.

*Orange Double Wing**
Tail: burnt orange sparkle yarn (combed-out stub)
Tip: white floss
Rear Wing: brown elk hair
Body Hackle: brown (palmered; clipped flat top and bottom)

Body: burnt orange sparkle yarn (dubbed rough)
Front Wing: white kip tail
Hackle: grizzly

Use this color scheme at sunrise and sunset and during the autumn.

*Lime Double Wing**
Tail: lime green sparkle yarn (combed-out stub)
Tip: white floss
Rear Wing: lime green elk hair
Body Hackle: olive grizzly (palmered; clipped flat top and bottom)
Body: lime green sparkle yarn (dubbed rough)
Front Wing: white kip tail
Hackle: grizzly

Use this fly at midday, or anytime on heavily wooded streams when the leaves are green.

Royal Double Wing
Tail: green sparkle yarn (combed-out stub)
Tip: red floss
Rear Wing: brown elk hair
Body Hackle: coachman brown (palmered; clipped flat top and bottom)
Body: peacock herl
Front Wing: white kip tail
Hackle: coachman brown

This pattern is an all-around attractor; like its namesake, it is meant to be half-bright under most conditions.

Midnight Double Wing
Tail: black sparkle yarn (combed-out stub)
Tip: white floss
Rear Wing: black elk hair
Body Hackle: black (palmered; clipped flat top and bottom)
Body: black sparkle yarn (dubbed rough)
Front Wing: white kip tail
Hackle: grizzly

This is a night fly, and it is also good anytime the water is stained.

Charm Double Wing
Tail: silver sparkle yarn (combed-out stub)
Tip: yellow floss
Rear Wing: pale gray elk hair
Body Hackle: bright medium blue (palmered; clipped flat top and bottom)
Body: silver sparkle yarn (dubbed rough)
Front Wing: white kip tail
Hackle: grizzly

It is worth trying as a desperation attractor at midday; some adventurous soul might try it on Atlantic salmon.

Brown Double Wing
Tail: brown sparkle yarn (combed-out stub)
Tip: white floss
Rear Wing: tan elk hair
Body Hackle: furnace (palmered; clipped flat top and bottom)
Body: hare's ear fur and brown sparkle yarn (dubbed rough)
Front Wing: white kip tail
Hackle: grizzly

This is an attractor because of brightness and shape, but not because of color; it is also an afternoon and evening fly for those times when red and orange draw splashy misses)

Yellow Double Wing
Tail: yellow sparkle yarn (combed-out stub)
Tip: white floss
Rear Wing: pale yellow elk hair
Body Hackle: golden badger (palmered; clipped flat top and bottom)
Body: yellow sparkle yarn (dubbed rough)
Front Wing: white kip tail
Hackle: grizzly

Try this variation when there a lot of bright-bodied yellow insects around the stream, during rain storms, and at mid-morning and mid-afternoon.

Pink Lady Double Wing*
Tail: pink sparkle yarn (combed-out stub)
Tip: white floss
Rear Wing: gray elk hair
Body Hackle: dark ginger (palmered; clipped flat top and bottom)
Body: pink sparkle yarn (dubbed rough)
Front Wing: white kip tail
Hackle: dark ginger

The body on this variation is a warm color, not a hot one like red; it is a fly for early morning and late afternoon—maybe because pink is part white, the color inspires much less suspicion than some others.

It is very important that the angler stop fishing and just study the light (the same way a photographer would) before choosing a Double Wing. He should consider variables such as shade, cloud cover, reflected light, and the angle of the direct rays.

Dumpy Butt

Doug O'Looney

The Dumpy Butt is actually an entire series of very innovative imitations—there are mayfly, caddisfly, and damselfly patterns featured in Chuck and Sharon Tryon's new book, *Figuring Out Flies*. This original design creates an effective silhouette on the surface.

Chuck wrote about his pattern: "Like Ed Hewitt's Skater, Dumpy Butt dries are constructed to ride gravity's way with the hook bend hanging vertically beneath the surface. All dressing materials are lashed to the forward half of the shank. The bodies are stripped hackle-stem butts *projecting vertically from the top of the shank."*

The emphasis in the quote is mine. It is that projecting material laying flat on the water, simulating the slender body and two tails of a mayfly perfectly, that make this fly different from other "hanging" flies. Patterns like the old English Mole Fly (or the newer Occasion) float with the hook down, but they lack the sharp silhouette of an insect's body—those flies, as a result, are impressionistic searchers instead of imitations. The Dumpy Butt is a superb fly for matching the hatch.

Hook: 14–16 (standard dry fly)
Projecting Body: stripped hackle stem butt (dyed the appropriate color; hackle fibers at the end of the butt lacquered and trimmed to simulate tails—tie in at right angle to hook shank)
Hackle: rooster (wound normally; any suitable color can be used to match an insect)
Wing: white kip tail (a spike tied straight out over eye)

Any vertical fly, including a Skating Spider, should be tied to the tippet with an Improved Turle Knot (it comes out the bottom of the hook eye) or a Duncan Loop. These knots allow such patterns to land properly and drift correctly on the water.

Dun Variant
Hook: 12–16 (4X fine wire)
Tail: dark blue dun hackle fibers
Body: quill of a brown hackle
Hackle: dark blue dun (oversize)

The properly tied Variant sits so high on the water, with only hackle tips and tail touching, that it does not have to move to simulate movement. It imitates mayfly duns that not only drift for a while, but also kick and fuss, making preliminary jumps before actually flying off.

Elk Hair Caddis*

A current list of the best selling dry flies includes only one pattern developed in the last fifteen years—Al Troth's Elk Hair Caddis. It has spread across the country with incredible speed since the early 1980s. The fly combines visibility, durability, and buoyancy in the downwing form; not coincidentally, its popularity has grown along with the increasing awareness of caddisflies by American fly fishermen.

Hook: 12–18 (standard dry fly)
Hackle: brown hackle (palmered through the body)
Body: hare's ear mask fur (dubbed)
Wing: tan elk hair
Head: stubs of the elk hair wing

Dave Beronio gave me an interesting perspective on the Elk Hair Caddis: "The pattern is still evolving in California. For example, on the Truckee River an orange-bodied variation is popular and on the Sacramento River a Caddis Variant, an Elk Hair with the wing tied more upright and wrapped more around the fly, is important."

The Elk Hair Caddis is valuable as a general searching pattern, but as local tyers adapt it to specific insects it will serve also as an imitation in more and more situations (mainly for egg-laying adults). The body, hackle, and wing colors can be changed to suit any caddisfly.

Emergent Sparkle Pupa*

Doug O'Looney

Tyers frequently ask me why the underbody dubbing of the Sparkle Pupa is a mix of rabbit fur and Antron yarn. Why not just make it a 100 percent Antron?

It galls me to have to stand there like a dummy and say, "I don't know."

Remember, the Sparkle Pupa was developed through underwater observation. That process, as Tory Stosich reminds me, was—and is—a "no brainer," a trial-and-error method for discovering exactly what the trout want in a matching fly. The Sparkle Pupa has an underbody of mixed fur and Antron because that version fooled more trout than a pattern with a pure Antron underbody. It was never necessary to stew about the reason.

Tom Rosenbauer, in "Nymph-design Heresies," a fine article in the June 1989 *Fly Fisherman Magazine*, possibly pinpointed the reason. He wrote about emerging mayflies, but the same theory applies to other aquatic insects:

"Let me show you why (matching flies) *shouldn't* be translucent. Have you ever looked at the surface of the water after a heavy hatch? After a hatch, just a casual glance at the water reveals clumps of shed skins of the hatching flies, left behind like Clark Kent's clothing in a phone booth. These empty skins, or shucks, as they have come to be known, are translucent, especially when held alongside a drifting mayfly nymph that hasn't hatched yet. But a *live* mayfly nymph is *opaque*.

"During the height of a hatch, trout take nymphs just under the surface or in the surface film. Fish that cannot tell the difference between an empty, translucent shuck and the real nymph are weeded out by natural selection. Trout *must select against* translucent flies."

In our experiments the trout were telling us by their actions that an imitation of a caddisfly or a midge needed the brightness, the reflectiveness, of Sparkle Yarn, but to keep the outline of the fly from disappearing entirely, it also needed substance, provided not just by opacity but by the natural proof of color.

That empty shuck of the caddisfly or the midge is not just translucent—it is almost transparent. Translucence with color poses no problem for the fish, the diffused color that matches the live insect adding strongly to the appeal, but without the color of the fur the all-Antron pattern just looks like an empty skin filled with air bubbles.

Four main color variations cover 90 percent of the caddisfly hatches in North America (my book, *Caddisflies*, contains a full set of patterns).

Brown and Yellow Emergent Sparkle Pupa
Hook: 4–22 (standard dry fly)
Underbody: half russet Sparkle Yarn and half brown fur (mixed and dubbed)
Overbody: russet Sparkle Yarn
Wing: light speckled deer hair
Head: brown fur

Brown and Bright Green Emergent Sparkle Pupa
Hook: 4–22 (standard dry fly)
Underbody: one third olive Sparkle Yarn and two-thirds bright green acryllic craft fur (mixed and dubbed)
Overbody: medium olive Sparkle Yarn
Wing: dark speckled deer hair
Head: brown fur

Dark Gray Emergent Sparkle Pupa
Hook: 4–22 (standard dry fly)
Underbody: half gray fur and half dark brown Sparkle Yarn (mixed and dubbed)
Overbody: gray Sparkle Yarn
Wing: dark gray deer hair
Head: dark gray fur

Ginger Emergent Sparkle Pupa
Hook: 4–22 (standard dry fly)
Underbody: half cream fur and half amber Sparkle Yarn (mixed and dubbed)
Wing: light brown deer hair
Head: cream fur

My roommate in college, Lynn Blackwell, would listen to my rantings and say calmly, "If you want to understand the world, you have to understand physics."

I couldn't see any air bubbles in the caddisflies emerging from the aquariums in our science laboratory. I thought that this was enough evidence for me to deny reports of air within the pupal sheath by entomologists or even discredit photographs of actual, bright insects.

There were two ways for me to understand what the trout were seeing with caddisflies—study physics (the easy way) or look at emergers from the trout's perspective (the hard way). That "hard way" led me into scuba diving (it was futile sticking my head under an aquarium).

Physics explains why peering *sideways* into an aquarium is not an accurate method of observation. The light source, either outdoors with a real stream or indoors with a glass tank, is above the water. The rays entering the water bend, or refract, so that they travel downwards. There are no direct rays from the side; without directs rays hitting a surface (the air bubbles) there is no specular reflection from that angle of view. The only way in water to see specular reflection on a transparent air bubble is from below it (the trout's perspective) or above it.

Scuba diving in rivers confirmed the brightness of an emerging caddisfly. The insect did not carry air bubbles inside the sheath; it inflated the sheath and became a single air bubble. Small, individual bubbles did not become distinguishable until the struggling emerger began to shed the transparent sheath at the surface. The dangling, sausage-like skin hanging off the back of the insect was crammed with them (explaining the trailing strands of Sparkle Yarn on the Emergent Pupa).

There is an amazing color photograph by John Gantner in *Caddisflies* of a *live* caddisfly pupa. The air inside the sheath is startling, distended in the center (possibly because the insect has been removed from the water) and glistening around the legs. The actual legs of an adult caddisfly are drab, but there is nothing drab about those appendages on the pupa.

The Emergent Sparkle Pupa matches the brightness of the natural insect. It is not my place to rave about the fly; other writers and fly fishermen, hopefully more objective, label it a good pattern. It is one of the best innovations to ever come out of our underwater testing.

Fan Wing Royal Coachman

The beautiful white wings enter the trout's window first, as if totally disconnected from any fly. The fan style creates the strongest triggering characteristic of any winging method. There are a lot of drawbacks to fan wings (they are very fragile and they twist the leader), but they are almost worth the trouble.

Hook: 10–12 (standard dry fly)
Tail: golden pheasant tippet fibers
Body: peacock herl (knobs front and rear)
Center Band: red floss
Wing: white breast feathers of a duck (matched; curving outwards)
Hackle: coachman brown

Female Adams

Hook: 12–14 (standard dry fly)
Tail: dark ginger hackle fibers
Egg Sac: yellow fur (dubbed ball; larger in diameter than the body)
Body: gray muskrat fur (dubbed)
Wing: matched mallard quill sections
Hackle: dark ginger

Fly fishermen noticed the prominent egg sac many insects carry as a ball at the tip of the abdomen (caddisfly as well mayfly species). They created not only this pattern but other female variations.

Is the egg sac worth imitating? Absolutely. Forget for a moment whether or not trout look for the eggs on an insect—more importantly, the yellow sac creates a "hot spot" on the fly. Trout key on that bit of bright color no matter where it is on the fly.

Flame Thrower

Doug O'Looney

This fly, with a bit of fluorescence in the hackling, is a Variant style. The middle sizes on the list, the 10 and 12 hooks, are not as important as the larger and the smaller versions in the attractor strategies.

Hook: 6–16 (1X fine wire)
Tail: natural cree hackle fibers
Body: cream seal's fur (synthetic substitute)
Hackle: natural cree hackle; fluorescent orange hackle (wrapped together; tied long—Variant style)

The hot orange hackle is muted by the cree hackle—this reflects my feeling that flourescence should be used with discrimination. It is a high floating attractor pattern for low light situations.

Flex Hopper* (see color plate)

The rear section is always the same for this imitation, but the interchangeable front section can be made of many different materials.

Consider just two alternatives:

1. A head of tightly wound hackle makes the forward half of the fly cock much higher than the rear. This oversize head certainly helps the Flex Hopper look and act a bit unnatural; sometimes that sprightly, dancing front section pulls trout from a little further away.

2. A cork head with a slightly scooped face turns the entire fly into a popper. A tug makes the head burble, a sound that can be as intriguing to trout as it is to bass. The Flex Hopper, with this head, pulls trout from incredible distances.

Balsa or cork in various shapes, closed cell foam (bullet shape with a collar like the Air Head), or deer hair packed loose or tight are other effective alternatives for the head. Any of these materials can be used in any color (for some reason a pink-headed hopper is sometimes a killer). The fly fisherman is free to have fun playing with the Flex design.

Hook: 6 (Flex Hook)
Rear Section:
Tail: cree hackle fibers
Body Hackle: dark ginger hackle (palmered and clipped)
Body: yellowish olive sparkle yarn (dubbed thick; color can be varied to suit naturals)
Legs: two pieces of yellow rubber on each side (knotted)
Under Wing: natural brown bucktail (extends to the end of the tail)
Over Wing: turkey feather (layed flat over the back; extends only to the bend of the hook)

Flex Stone*

The Salmon Fly can be difficult or easy to match—it depends a great deal on *where* the angler happens to be fishing in the hatch. Is he at the head, the middle, or the tail? The head is a fresh section of the rivers for the insects; the fish are seeing the adults for the first time and these trout are usually feeding very aggressively. The middle is the peak of insect abundance; there are so many adults landing on the water that fish soon become glutted by the feast. The tail is a section where there are few, if any, adult insects left; the trout nevertheless remember the Salmon Flies and they gladly slam any stray that lands on the water.

The fisherman needs the best possible imitation for the middle of the hatch. A trout there might take a natural every fifteen minutes or so—he is feeding so sporadically that only the sure meal tempts him. He no longer rushes out when an insect makes that initial splat on the surface.

So what does the angler do? He drifts his fly right over the good spots, not once but many times. When fish no longer react to the plop, and start to show a healthy suspicion of any large fly, the Flex Stone style usually draws significantly more strikes than stiff imitations.

Orange Flex Stone
Hook: 6 (Flex Hook)
Rear Section:
Tail: two off-white rubber strands (tied split)
Body Hackle: coachman brown hackle (palmered over the body and clipped)
Body: orange synthetic seal's fur (dubbed rough)
Legs: six off-white rubber strands (three on each side; not overly long)
Wing: brown elk hair
Front Section:
Head: can be formed of cork, balsa, deer hair, foam, or even a tightly wrapped dark brown hackle

Ginger Flex Stone
Hook: 6 (Flex Hook)
Rear Section:
Tail: two pale yellow rubber strands (split)
Body Hackle: dark ginger hackle (palmered over the body and clipped)
Body: cream synthetic seal's fur (dubbed rough)
Legs: six pale yellow rubber strands (three on each side; not overly long)
Wing: light tan elk hair
Front section:
Head: can be formed of balsa, cork, deer hair, foam, or even a tightly wrapped dark ginger hackle.

The Orange Flex Stone imitates the Salmon Fly (*Pteronarcys californica*). The Ginger Flex Stone matches the huge stonefly that pops out in late July and August on higher elevation rivers; this Giant Western Golden (*Claassenia sabulosa*) is a major hatch in the canyon water of the Yellowstone River in the Park.

Fluttering Stone*
Nevin Stephenson brought his new pattern into the Compleat Fly Fisher one morning. It was so different from other stonefly imitations (which floated flush) that all of the guides wanted samples to try on the Big Hole. Most of us had seen trout take struggling, bouncing female Salmon Flies, but this was the first imitation to match this behavior.

It was a quick success with us, which was not a fair test because it was a friend's pattern. Much more of a tribute was how quickly the Fluttering Stone spread to other rivers. Within two seasons shops and their guides all over the Rocky Mountain were using it as an effective, high-riding alternative to other Salmon Fly imitations.

Orange Fluttering Stone
Hook: 2–6 (1X stout wire)
Body: salmon polypropylene yarn (extended off the back of the hook; do not twist this, comb it out—it only took a few incidents of the twisted body snagging the hook for Nevin to change the body design)
Wing: dark gray elk hair (as long as the body)
Hackle: brown saddle hackle (thickly palmered along the entire hook shank)
Antennae: dyed brown monofilament

Yellow Fluttering Stone
Hook: 6–10 (1X stout wire)
Body: yellow polypropylene yarn
Wing: light elk hair
Hackle: dark ginger saddle hackle
Antennae: dyed gold monofilament

Guides usually create valuable patterns. They are out on the river every day and they see not only specific needs but also practical answers to those needs.

The smaller yellow pattern is used on western rivers to imitate the Golden Stone. Actually, in my selection, it is also a high bouncing, active attractor, not just for trout but for smallmouth bass.

Flying Ant

The Flying Ant pattern in my box is simply a regular foam imitation with a flat wing of clear Antron fibers over the back. The wing is tied heavy, with enough strands of bright material to make the fly very visible on the water to the angler.

Hook: 10–20 (standard dry fly)
Body: foam (brown, red, and black are important colors)
Wing: clear Antron fibers

Foam Terrestrials

The effect of water temperature in determining whether or not trout rise is even more important for terrestrials than for hatches of aquatic insects. Why? There are no preliminaries with terrestrials. When an emergence of aquatic insects begins the nymphs issue from the stream bottom. They tempt even reluctant trout into feeding; from there, once there is a concentration of insects on top, it is an easy step for those trout to move towards the surface. The water temperature does not have to be ideal for trout to rise during a hatch.

A fall of terrestrials is different. Sometimes a blizzard of ants, beetles, or moths hits the surface and nothing except small trout rise to them. If the water temperature is too far from the ideal, either too warm or too cold, the fish are tight on the bottom and not at all curious about food floating overhead.

Foam Ant*

Doug O'Looney

Hook: 10–20 (standard dry fly)
Body: foam (tie the foam to the hook shank, leaving appropriately sized front and rear sections; color with a waterproof marker)

Red, black, and brown are the main colors, but a pattern of untouched white foam is also surprisingly effective at times. The translucense of the foam is especially critical for red ant imitations.

Foam Beetle*

Hook: 8–18 (standard dry fly)
Body: green peacock herl
Body Hackle: olive/grizzly dyed hackle (palmered; clipped flat top and bottom)
Wing: foam (tied down at the head, leaving the back end free; colored black with a waterproof marker)

The free back, instead of one tied down front and rear, makes a more effective beetle imitation.

Foam Inch Worm

Hook: 16 (standard dry fly)
Rib: chartreause floss
Body: foam (cut a round cylinder of foam slightly longer than the hook shank; make a slot on the bottom and slide the foam around the hook shank; color the cylinder green with a waterproof marker).

The green inch worm, once he lowers himself on a silk line, cannot pull himself back up. If his branch happens to be over water, he will end up on surface, dragging until the current snaps the thread.

The angler should hunt for "home trees" during the inch worm season. The insects do not spread out evenly—only one tree in a 100-yard stretch of stream may be heavily infested. The inch worm imitation works much better on fish that are already taking the naturals.

Foam Spider

Hook: 14–16 (standard dry fly)
Legs: 4 pieces of natural deer hair (place brown deer hair about 3/4 of the way up the shank; spin it and trim the ends)
Body: foam (lash down a shaped piece of foam where the deer hair is wrapped; leave a smaller front section and larger rear section; color brown with a waterproof marker)

Mike Lawson has noticed that brown spiders fall off the banks of the Henry's Fork. While floating he also frequently has seen them drifting with the wind, trailing a piece of silk—the spiders dropped onto the middle of the broad river and trout rose avidly to them.

The bodies on these terrestrials are shaped from large-cell, closed foam, a common packing substance. The material used on many flies and sold in specialty shops is a small-cell, closed foam—it is denser and much less translucent. There is no comparison between the two types. The glowing, large-cell variety pulls trout from much further away.

Fur Ant*

Charles Cotton, in his *Instructions How to Angle for Trout and Grayling in a Clear Stream* (appearing as the second part of *The Compleat Angler* in the 1676 fifth edition) described ant patterns, including this one for August: "a dubbing of the black-brown hair of a cow, some red warped in for the tag of his tail, and a dark wing."

A rancher friend stared at me with a cocked eye, "You want to do what with my cow?"

The hair of Montana range cattle does have a rich luster after the frigid days of winter, but in spite of my well-known fussiness about dubbing (rivaling Cotton's fanatiscism) there are some materials that are impractical even for me.

A fine substitute, especially for the red ant, is a dubbing mix of 50% sparkle yarn and 50% mink fur (the mink fur cut up with the guard hairs). The Red Fur Ant is my favorite.

Hook: 14–20 (2X fine wire)
Body: half red sparkle yarn/half cream mink fur (two segments—rear one a bit larger; other colors for matching naturals include brown and black)
Hackle: coachman brown (a few turns wound in the gap between the two body parts)

Gartside Hopper

Hook: 6–10 (2X long shank)
Tail: dark moose body hairs
Body Hackle: furnace hackle (palmered and trimmed at a taper from front to back)
Body: poly yarn (yellow, tan, gray, or olive)
Under Wing: natural brown deer hair fibers
Over Wing: ringneck pheasant back feather (dipped in varnish)
Collar: deer hair fibers (tied in on each side)
Head: deer hair (spun and clipped)

This pheasant hopper became even more popular in the West Yellowstone area after Jack Gartside caught a brown trout of over nine pounds with it in the Gallatin River.

Ginger Quill

Hook: 14–18 (1X fine)
Tail: golden ginger hackle fibers
Body: stripped peacock quill
Wing: mallard quill (matched sections)
Hackle: golden ginger

Quill bodies have always fascinated me. They should not be effective, actually, because they are opaque and dull, but they are an excellent feature on matching flies during many mayfly hatches.

The bodies of some mayflies are so translucent that they become almost transparent. The bodies of male duns, with no eggs to provide a strong undercolor, disappear against a strong light, showing only the weak striping of internal organs.

Standing free of the water, as the body does on a properly tied Catskill style fly, the segmented quill must look very vague to the trout. Maybe that "non-body" is the effect they want to see.

Goddard Caddis*

Hook: 10–14 (standard dry fly)
Body: deer hair (spun and clipped)
Hackle: brown
Antennae: brown hackle stems (stripped)

The strength of this John Goddard and Cliff Henry design is its versatility. The Goddard Caddis provides a good silhouette of an adult caddisfly on the water. It is also a fine fly for plopping just behind the eye of a holding trout or for pulling in a steady path over the flat areas of a stream.

Gray Coughlin*

This pattern is for me what the Adams is for other fly fishermen. It is drab and, tied properly, fairly rough. Nothing about it "attracts" trout. Yet, at the same time, it is almost too general in appearance to be an imitation of anything specific. The way the shaggy hairs of the body and the mixed colors of the hackle break up the outline make it indistinct against any background.

Hook: 10–22 (standard dry fly)
Tail: medium dun hackle fibers
Body: grayish brown Hare's Ear dubbing (guard hairs untrimmed)

Wing: matched sections of slate gray duck quill
Hackle: brown and grizzly hackles (mixed)

Frank van Voorst, getting ready to help me with an experiment on brook trout, asked, "Which drab little 'ugly' are we going to use?"

I flipped through *Flies*, looking for an appropriate dry fly, and came across a listing of ingredients for the Gray Coughlin. "This one."

That experiment in 1974 matched a garish dry fly against a drab dry fly on wild brook trout. For weeks a group of us alternated the dull Gray Coughlin with a bright Scarlet Ibis on the swamp section of Willow Creek.

Were the brook trout on this small Montana stream gullible and reckless? Not on dry flies. They responded to the very bright Scarlet Ibis the same way brown or rainbow trout did (usually with a great deal of suspicion).

The theories about brook trout being susceptible to bright patterns started early in our fly fishing history, with the classic American wet flies. But even then, the brook trout's willingness to attack garish subsurface patterns was not because of any lack of intelligence or discrimination.

The brook trout themselves are "bright," especially at spawning time. They strike garish subsurface patterns avidly probably because of anger—brightly colored flies trigger agonistic behavior because brook trout react that way to their own bright brethren.

My own fishing with wet fly and small streamer patterns indicates that brook trout respond to red, brown trout to butter yellow, and rainbow trout to metallic silver. Each species attacks the fly that mimics its own coloration.

Anger isn't a trait triggered by a dry fly. Unlike a wet fly or a streamer, a floating fly cannot resemble an aggressive fish. Brook trout rise to dry flies as possible food items; both imitations and attractors have to stay within the bounds of possibility to tempt them.

That is why the Gray Coughlin found a spot in my box of searching flies. Within another season, however, it became—and has remained —the number one general drab fly in my selection for all species of trout. With the characteristics of two great patterns, the rough body of the Hare's Ear and the mixed hackle of the Adams, it has excellent precedents working for it.

Gray Fox Variant*

The long grass held a secret; when someone sat down in it the smell of the crushed wild mint would creep over the entire island. It was a small island. It was a good spot to eat our sandwiches every noon on the Big Hole.

The morning had been good fishing for rainbows and browns on the river. A size 14 Gray Fox Variant had worked consistently for me no matter what the trout were doing, succeeding even during a scattered hatch of Pale Morning Duns. A few rising trout wouldn't take the Gray Fox Variant, but there were plenty of less finicky fish.

Paul Dodds laughed and accused me, "You're a chameleon."

"Why?"

"You're always changing. A lot of the time you're a Generalist."

"How could I write about a method of fly selection unless I practiced it. Am I a good Generalist? Do I know the tricks?"

"Apparently," he said.

"Could I be good at something if I didn't enjoy doing it? Not likely. When I say a Generalist is damned that's not meant to be a condemnation. That is just a way of distinguishing it from Empiricism or Naturalism. The other methods try to solve a problem with the right fly, but generalism means finding a way around that problem by various tricks."

"There's nothing wrong with that?"

"Of course not. Focusing on presentation can be as much fun as experimentation or imitation. There is no morality scale. This is fly fishing, not religion."

"Oh," he nodded. "Now I see where you're confused."

Hook: 12–16 (4X fine)
Tail: golden ginger hackle fibers
Body: stem from a dark cream hackle
Hackle: golden ginger, dark ginger, and grizzly (three hackles mixed)

The Gray Fox was one of Art Flick's favorite flies. He was friends with Preston Jennings, the originator, and fished with the author of *A Book of Trout Flies* on the Schoharie River. Art told me why he liked the Gray Fox Variant, "It looks like it belongs on the water, just like an insect, and I really think that trout appreciate that."

Greenwell's Glory

It was fun to return to Vermont's Green River, one of my boyhood favorites, and find it in almost the same condition. The wild brookies and rainbows still took a Greenwell's Glory, too—that fly never performed as well in the Battenkill for me, but they always liked it on the upper water of the tributary.

Hook: 14–18 (standard dry fly)
Tail: ginger hackle fibers
Body: waxed yellow silk
Wing: starling (tied upright)
Hackle: greenwell cock (a feather with a black center and a ginger outside)

Griffith's Gnat
Hook: 18–24 (1X fine)
Body: peacock herl
Hackle: grizzly (palmered)

The smaller sizes match the single insect; in size 18 the palmered hackle is wide enough to represent the fluttering wings of a mating pair on the water.

Grizzly King
Hook: 8–12 (standard dry fly)
Tail: scarlet hackle fibers
Rib: fine gold tinsel

Body: olive fur (dubbed)
Wing: gray mallard quill sections
Hackle: grizzly

This recipe isn't exactly true to the original (which was a wet fly)—it is a dry variation that was sold at the Turf Bar in Missoula in the early 1960s. That connection probably reflects the influence of the legendary Jack Boehme on the dressing.

Hair Spider
Hook: 12–14 (standard dry fly)
Tail: natural deer hair
Body: the butts of the deer hair tail (wrapped with the tying thread)
Hackle: natural deer hair (spun; tips stand at a 90 degree angle from the shank)

This Al Troth variation of the Spider style is valuable anywhere a bouncing fly will excite trout.

Halo Mayfly Emerger* (see color plate)
There was one finely conditioned, nineteen inch resident brown trout in the Pere Marquette (Michigan) that was radio-tagged. He did something no other fish in our observations ever did—he rose to insects *on his way* from his holding spot to his feeding territory. Every other fish simply moved quickly from one place to another. This brown trout left his hold as soon as the mayflies began hatching, swimming in a zig-zag manner to intercept insects. He never took an adult—he fed only on emergers while travelling the twenty-five feet. Once he was settled on the feeding lie he often started sipping duns (but never before).

His activity patterns were predictable enough for us to ask angling friends from around the Midwest to try to catch this fish. No one ever came close to hooking him with another emerger imitation. However, he accepted a Halo Emerger anytime the fly drifted across his path.

Hook: 10–24 (1X fine wire)
Tag: clear Antron (wrapped down the shank)
Tail: marabou fibers
Abdomen: synthetic seal fur (dubbed thin)
Thorax: synthetic seal fur (dubbed thicker than the abdomen)
Halo: large-cell closed foam
Spike: fluorescent orange deer hair (extending out over the eye)
(The main colors for the Halo Emerger are Olive, Brown, and Cream—only the tail, abdomen, and thorax change.)

It was odd watching a trout key like that on some unknown stimulus. The important feature of the fly might well have been the aura of the foam flaps. The fish also focussed on specific naturals. It was impossible for us to tell if his targets were in that critical phase of emergence when there was an aura, but the trout usually passed two or three mayfly nymphs on his way to his chosen victim. He was spotting something on the naturals from surprisingly far away (fortunately, the Halo Emerger possessed that something).

Halo Midge Emerger*

Doug O'Looney

It is not enough with midge pupae for the fly to simply rest partly in and partly under the film. The way it hangs, the back humped up against the surface and the body protruding down, creates a unique shape. Trout rise selectively to that outline.

Dr. J. C. Mottram, not only in *Fly Fishing: Some New Arts and Mysteries* (1915) but in his later *Thoughts on Angling* (1948), wrote about such patterns. He lashed small, wedge-shaped pieces of cork to the hooks, creating the buoyancy that balance the flies in the natural, hanging position.

Large-cell, closed foam provides buoyancy for the Halo Midge Emerger. This material also flares over the edges, creating the aura of the adult's escape hole (this feature is not as important on a midge imitation as it is on a mayfly pattern simply because the former has the brightness of the Sparkle Yarn body, but the foam does add slightly to the visual impact—and the effectiveness—of even the midge pattern).

Hook: 16–28 (1X fine wire)
Rib: fluorescent blue monofilament
Body: ½ sparkle yarn/½ fur (dubbed; naturals may be green, red, black, yellow, brown, purple, pink, or even virtually colorless)
Halo: large-cell, closed foam
Breathing Tube: spike of orange deer hair

The shape of an emerging midge pupa is critical to proper imitation, but it is not the triggering characteristic. The most important aspect of the natural is the quicksilver brightness of the air within the transparent outer sheath. If an air bubble is visible in the emerging insect, it overwhelms every other feature. The matching fly needs the sparkle of Antron or Creslan.

Hare's Ear (dry)

F. M. Halford enjoyed great success for years with the Hare's Ear on his chalk stream fisheries, principally the Itchen, but then, in a pique of intellectual integrity or foolhardy sophistry, depending on one's point of view, he abandoned the fly because this ancient no-hackle did not "cock" like a proper dry fly.

He very well knew what it imitated, writing in *Dry-Fly Fishing in Theory and Practice*:

"Probably, however, the very best fly to use for bulging fish is the *gold-ribbed hare's ear*, and the reason is not far to seek. Put side by side, under a microscope with a low power objective, a nymph of any of the Ephemeridae and an artificial of the above pattern. The most casual observer will at once perceive that projecting from each joint, excepting the last three, of the abdomen of the nymph, there are fin-like appendages. These are called branchiae, and are, in fact, external prolongations of the respiratory organs used for the purpose of extracting from water the air held in solution; and the short hairs of the fur picked out in the body of the artificial bear a very strong resemblance to these branchiae."

Hare's Ear (standard)
Hook: 10–18 (4X fine wire)
Ribbing: fine gold wire (optional)
Body: hare's mask fur (dubbed; picked out shaggier at the thorax)
Wing: slate gray mallard feathers (optional; the wings can be tied full height, half height, as stubs slanting back, or omitted entirely to match the emerging nymph at various stages)

Olive Hare's Ear
Hook: 10–18 (4X fine wire)
Ribbing: fine gold wire (optional)
Body: hare's mask fur dyed olive
Wing: slate gray mallard feathers (optional)

The inside of Eric Peper's fly box looks like the remnants of a hare's mask explosion. His nymphs are segregated into lead-weighted, wire-weighted, and unweighted versions. During a hatch he works the fly at the precise level of insect concentration (where fish are feeding). The Hare's Ear itself, so amorphous, represents in its rough fashion nearly half of the important mayflies and also many caddisflies and stoneflies.

Hemingway Special
Hook: 12–16 (standard dry fly)

Body Hackle: medium blue dun (palmered)
Body: medium olive fur
Underwing: wood duck flank fibers
Wing: mallard wing quill section (single feather tied in a cup over the body; end trimmed in a circle)
Head Base: peacock herl (a few turns right behind the eye)
Hackle: medium blue dun (wrapped over the peacock herl base)

The Hemingway Special (named for Jack Hemingway) is a color variation of the Henryville Special. It is popular in the West, but it is effective anywhere as an imitation for egg-laying caddisfly adults.

Henry's Fork Hopper

Occasionally the wind blows on western rivers. For those days, especially when the combination of breeze and warm air creates ideal grasshopper conditions, a big imitation has to be aerodynamic for accurate placement. This Mike Lawson pattern is streamlined (and this also makes it a good fly for the Skip Cast).

Hook: 4–8 (2 X long)
Body: light elk hair (segmented with the tying thread; extending out over the back of the hook shank)
Underwing: yellow deer or elk hair
Wing: mottled hen pheasant feather (lacquered and tied flat on top)
Legs: knotted ringneck pheasant tail fibers
Head: elk hair (bullet head)

Henryville

This pattern was used on Pennsylvania's historic Brodhead Creek by Hiram Brobst, but the original red body was changed to olive (which, as a caddisfly imitation, makes a bit more sense). It was not until after 1960, however, that the Henryville became the most popular caddis pattern in the country.

Hook: 14–18 (standard dry fly)
Body Hackle: grizzly (trimmed flat on top)
Body: olive floss
Underwing: wood duck fibers (from the flank feathers)
Wing: mallard quill sections (slanted over the body)
Hackle: brown

It was May 12th, about a week after the peak of the early Grannom (*Brachycentrus occidentalis*) on the Yellowstone, but nevertheless for Ken Pope, Jay Gaudreau, and me, the dry fly fishing was extremely good that afternoon. The fish were rising to the insects in a very strange fashion, however—they were not taking naturals from the mixing currents, that interface between the dead flow next to the rocks and the fast water of the open river. Normally, that is the feeding line because drifting insects concentrate on that current edge a little off the bank. Today the trout were sucking down adult caddisflies snug against the rocks, feeding so tight to the bank that their cheeks must have been rubbing the stones.

This would have remained a total mystery. However, in talking about Yellowstone fishing in general, Tom Travis mentioned, "There's something odd that happens on this river because of the wind. The clouds of caddisflies come up off the bank and start to drift out over the water, but then a gust comes and slams them against the rocks. The trout are looking in, not out, and they bump right against the boulders taking the adults."

This same phenomenon must happen on other big rivers with wind and boulder banks or cliffs. The trout will take a good imitation of an active adult, such as a Henryville, as long as it is scraping the stones as it drifts down the river.

Hornberg*

The Hornberg is so valuable because it is a "bi-fly." It is intentionally fished dry and wet on the same cast. The angler, after completing the dead drift portion of the presentation, pulls the Hornberg underwater and retrieves it like a streamer. The pattern actually works more consistently as a wet fly, but the trout it does catch on the surface are often very large.

Hook: 10–16 (3X long shank)
Body: flat silver tinsel
Inside Wing: yellow calf tail hair
Outside Wing: mallard flank feathers
Cheek: jungle cock eyes
Hackle: grizzly and brown (mixed)

The Hornberg is my favorite pattern for high water conditions. Any dry fly stands very little chance in chilly, early season flows, but with the wet/dry presentation the Hornberg works well as a streamer and, surprisingly, still manages to take an occasional fish on the surface.

Housatonic Quill

This fly, which has been in my box ever since my childhood days on the Housatonic, has caught trout for me all over the country. It works best when tied on a light wire hook and fished "high" on the water; kept fresh and perky like this it is very effective on flat water (which the Housatonic has in abundance).

Hook: 12–16 (3X fine wire)
Tail: gray badger hackle fibers
Body: stripped peacock quill (with pronounced light bands)
Wing: speckled wood duck
Hackle: gray badger

House & Lot

Hook: 8–18 (standard dry fly)
Tail: white calf tail fibers
Rear Body: stripped peacock herl
Forward Body: peacock herl
Hackle: furnace

This was Dwight D. Eisenhower's favorite fly. It is also one of mine—the House & Lot (also known as the H & L Variant) is a fine hairwing attractor.

Humpy*

It *is* foolish to try to think like a trout. A diver lays on the stream bottom, his mind empty of ideas, and gazes upwards. He attempts to determine if objects passing overhead are edible. But quickly enough, as that parade continues, he also begins to judge the caloric value of the various items. Would it be worth the effort to rise to a particular insect or fly?

Does the trout calculate caloric expenditure? He does not think in terms of equations, no more than a tennis player running for a ball figures speed and distance, but there must be reflexive judgement involved in the decision to rise or not to rise.

This may explain why the width of the fly acts as a triggering characteristic on imitations and as a pulling trait on attractors. A wide fly is, if nothing else, worth the risk of rising. For a trout, curiosity about an uneaten item is reinforced by the value of that helpless, meaty chunk of food.

A Humpy is a very "wide" pattern, its body at least twice as thick as the thin quill or fur body of a standard dry fly. The fact that it sits low on the water also makes it highly visible, even on a broken surface.

Hook: 8–18 (1X stout wire)
Tail: moose body hair (not as brittle as deer hair; a Humpy minus a tail doesn't sit right on the water)
Body: yellow thread (the tying thread itself is yellow; changing the tying thread changes the color of the body)
Back: natural deer hair
Wing: natural deer hair tips
Hackle: brown and grizzly hackles (wound together)

Jack Dennis states about the Humpy, "At some point the deer hair back of even the best tied Humpy starts to fray, especially after the teeth of a few fish work on it. The hair, cut at different lengths, sticks out like a brush, but this doesn't ruin the fly. Many times, a ragged Humpy works better than a neat one."

Jack Dennis and Charlie Ridenhauer devised a popular variation in the *Royal Humpy*.
Hook: 8–18 (1X stout wire)
Tail: dark moose hair
Body: red thread or floss
Back: light gray natural deer hair
Wing: white calf body hair
Hackle: coachman brown

The *Blonde Humpy* is another standard color version.
Hook: 8–18 (1X stout wire)
Tail: white calf tail fibers
Body: yellow floss
Back: white deer hair
Wing: white calf body hair
Hackle: light ginger

Improved Sofa Pillow
Hook: 2–6 (2X long)
Tail: black goose quills
Body Hackle: furnace saddle hackle (palmered)
Body: rusty orange fur (dubbed thick)
Underwing: medium elk hair
Overwing: red squirrel tail
Hackle: two furnace saddle hackle feathers
Head: deer hair (spun and trimmed)

No one was catching fish on the Big Hole. Guides from all over the state had come in as usual for the Salmon Fly hatch, but they had never seen the river so low. The local outfits at least had the advantage of knowing what the river looked like in August—of course, it wasn't August. It was June and the giant stoneflies were in the air.

Nevin Stephenson stopped his boat and waited for me to pull mine over. "We aren't doing anything," he said.

I shrugged, "Don't look at us."

We stood there for a few minutes, just gazing out over the Big Hole. Nevin said finally, "This is the way it looks in midsummer."

We stared at each other and suddenly we knew that we had been fishing the river wrong. Just like all the other guides we had told our clients to pound big flies into the banks. During a normal Salmon Fly hatch the water would be high and fast, pushing back into the willows. The trout hold there, crowded by the strength of the current. But this wasn't a normal year. The Big Hole was already midsummer low during this drought year. We would never blindly work the banks in August.

When the Big Hole shrinks during the summer it leaves an edge of dried rocks. The large trout drop back to the main channel and the deep holes, rising only for a heavy hatch. Either naturals or imitations have to tease these fish up.

After lunch we pretended it was August. We had our people hit the slots and rocks in the center of the river, covering each spot two or three times. The insects were landing sporadically and the trout were watching for them. They took the flies too like they were chunks of prime meat.

Injured Minnow (or Floating Streamer)
My first experience with this Charley Brooks pattern was on the Beaverhead River. There were only two Injured Minnows in my box, but since nothing much was happening on other flies during our float, it seemed worth the risk of losing them to the willow-choked banks.

The very bouyant fly landed on one of those boils that run with the shoreline on the Beaverhead. The churning current sucked down the Injured Minnow—the fly, with a hollow goose quill for a body, however, resisted the pull. The battle between undertow and bobber-like fly reached equilibrium at about four feet. The Injured Minnow just hung there and wobbled underwater outside the willow roots.

A huge brown trout, maybe eight pounds, slid out from the overhang and simply took the fly. It wasn't that he broke it—there was no run and slam. Apparently the current held the line so tight that the fish could pull the fly right off the tippet. He grasped the Injured Minnow, shook his head once, and popped the six-pound leader easily.

I quickly clipped back the tippet and tied on my second fly. I dropped it on a boil and watched it also settle and wobble four feet down. Another huge brown trout, this one even larger than the first, appeared from the roots. He closed his mouth on the Injured Minnow, shook his head once, and popped the eight-pound leader easily.

This was one of the most pathetic performances in a long, if not particularly illustrious, fly fishing career. "Thank God I don't have any more of those flies," I gasped.

My partners in the raft, Glenn West and Galen Wilkins, were rolling with such hilarity that they risked falling out. My mind was already working on the problem of how to get Kevin Toman to tie more of this complex, time-consuming pattern for me.

Hook: 4–6 (6X long shank)
Body: tip of a large goose quill (scraped clean and slipped over the eye of the hook)
Plug: cork (a small piece glued into the front of the quill)
Wing: natural bucktail
Eye: painted

One way to fish the Injured Minnow is to "walk the dog." This is a special retrieve used by bait casters with stick bait lures. The fly fisherman can do the same thing on quiet backwater and slow pools. He rolls a mend first to the left and then to the right. Even good mends make the fly jerk left or right, pulling it with a criss cross retrieve.

Irresistible

The Irresistible is not going to float high no matter how much hackle is used on it—the deer hair, especially after it wicks up a bit of moisture, is just too heavy. Very few insects

have a body as thick as this fly, certainly not in such a compact package. This bulk attracts trout.

The Irresistible has caught as many large trout for me as any other dry fly. Every year my logs record at least a few twenty inch fish, usually ones that came out of the heavy water for this chunk.

My best day ever with it happened during a float on the Box Canyon of the Henry's Fork. Every fish rolled on the strike, flashing a silver side—never before or since have trout risen in such a consistent manner. What physical law dictated the exact same kind of take from all these fish? Beautiful rainbows captured the fly (and it would have been nice even to see the one that nearly cleared Mike Wheat's reel).

Hook: 8–16 (standard dry fly)
Tail: natural gray deer hair
Body: deer hair (spun and trimmed)
Wing: natural brown deer hair
Hackle: medium blue dun

The all white pattern is my favorite color variation.

White Irresistible
Hook: 8–16 (standard dry fly)
Tail: white calf tail
Body: white deer hair
Wing: white calf tail
Hackle: badger

Japanese Beetle
Hook: 6–10 (standard dry fly)
Hackle: black hackle (wound over the shank; clipped flat top and bottom)
Back: pheasant feather (lacquered)

My favorite sizes for this fly, even now when there are no more hoards of Japanese beetles, are larger than Vincent Marinaro recommended on the Letort. The Japanese Beetle has always been a prospecting pattern for me—with or without naturals.

Jassid*

This is an important terrestrial for me even on the roughest streams. Leafhoppers flop into the water continually but they never travel very far out onto the river. The best way to match these insects is by stalking the banks, moving directly upstream and dropping short casts tight to the grass. The water close to shore is very quiet and trout sip either naturals or imitations.

Hook: 16–20 (2X fine wire)
Body Hackle: black (wound over the entire shank; clipped flat top and bottom)
Wing: jungle cock nail

A stretch of warm days on the Madison made the leafhoppers especially active. They landed on the water in a steady rain of green specks. The fish along the edge, after a few afternoons of this, grew very selective, ignoring even grasshopper and ant imitations. They accepted a size 18 Jassid readily enough, however, and it was no trick with a short-line presentation to get twenty or more hookups a day. These were not small fish, either—one afternoon the tiny Jassid took three rainbows over fifteen-inches.

Joe's Hopper*

This is still my favorite pattern for imitating grasshoppers that have been drifting for awhile. These insects are no longer so prim and proper, even on the surface, and the rougher impression of the Joe's Hopper simulates that bedraggled spectacle.

Hook: 6–12 (2X long shank)
Tail: red hackle fibers
Rib: brown hackle (clipped short)
Body: yellow yarn (a loop dangles off the back)
Wing: mottled turkey quill (tent style)
Hackle: brown and grizzly (mixed)

John Storey*

Hook: 12–16 (2X fine wire)

Body: bronze peacock herl
Wing: a small, whole mallard feather (tied forward sloping)
Hackle: natural dark red cock

John Roberts highly recommends this English pattern, "a fly invented in Yorkshire by a riverkeeper on the river Rye. The advance wing, sloping forward over the eye of the hook, is the key feature. A trout looking for wings as a triggering characteristic is given a good view of the mallard feather as the fly drifts into the window.

"This would certainly be on my list of six dry flies."

The John Storey has quickly become one of my favorite searching flies, also—especially on smooth water.

Jughead*

Hook: 2–6 (3X long shank)
Tail: tan elk hair
Body Hackle: brown saddle hackle (trimmed)
Body: orange polypropylene
Bottom Wing: tan elk hair
Top Wing: red fox squirrel tail fibers
Head: antelope hair (clipped to shape)

The water typically runs high during the Salmon Fly hatch, pushing back into the streamside willows. The water does not slow down until it is far under the branches, curling among the roots. Since the adult stoneflies either fall from the trees onto this water or, after laying eggs out in the river, attempt to swim back to the bank, this is the place to put a fly.

The Jughead is a very aerodynamic design. It bounces nicely with a skip cast. It is worth changing to this Pat Barnes pattern during a float trip, with the boat passing miles of shore and the fisherman popping a fly as close as possible to the bank, whenever there is a long stretch of willow-lined water. The splash of the skip, and the bounce far back under the branches, is even more critical to success on a chilly, damp day—a time when trout are less likely to come charging out after a fly.

Klinkhamen Special
Hook: 14–18 (tied on a light wire, grub hook—the type used for caddisfly larva patterns)
Body: white poly wrapped on the bottom; tan poly lightly dubbed over the top
Thorax: peacock herl
Wing: white poly yarn
Hackle: chestnut cock (tied parachute style around the wing roots)

A parachute fly, tied without a tail on a curved grub hook, becomes an effective emerger. The originator, Dutch angler Hans van Klinken, commented, "the fly is much like an iceberg; it gives best results when 90 percent is under water."

John Roberts wrote glowingly about the Klinkhamen Special in his latest work, *A Guide to River Trout Flies.* John is such a fine angler that his recommendation was enough for me to try the fly. On my first day with it, a May morning on the Delaware River in New York, the new pattern earned its spot in the Emerger Box by fooling the fussy browns of the flats.

Kolzer
The two Kolzer patterns are the most intensely colored attractors in my box—the fluorescent bodies guarantee that distinction. They catch trout when nothing else will; they fail when every other fly will catch trout. For me they are strictly for drifting on rough water at dawn or dusk.

Kolzer Orange
Hook: 10–12 (standard dry fly)
Tail: brown bucktail
Body Hackle: brown
Body: orange fluorescent yarn
Wing: brown bucktail hair
Hackle: brown

Kolzer Yellow
Hook: 10–12 (standard dry fly)
Tail: brown bucktail
Body Hackle: brown
Body: yellow fluorescent yarn
Wing: brown bucktail hair
Hackle: brown

There are no geographical boundaries for these flies—they have caught trout for me from the Lamoille in Vermont to the McCloud in California.

Lady Heather

Doug O'Looney

The Lady Heather, named after my daughter, was devised by simple dogged empiricism as a Trude-type dry fly for gray days. This meant running out to fish various color combinations every time the sky grew overcast. Enough rain fell on me that season to make my hair mildew.

There was nothing bright left on the fly after all that flogging. Even the butt (egg sac) was gray—not bright green or yellow as common sense dictated. The cream body and white wing had that amorphous ability to reflect all colors equally, also. Gray predominated again in the mixed hackle of blue dun and grizzly feathers.

Hook: 10–18 (standard dry fly)
Tail: dark blue dun hackle fibers
Butt: gray muskrat fur (dubbed)

Body: cream fur (wrapped or dubbed; thinner than the butt)
Wing: white calf tail
Hackle: grizzly or dark blue dun (mixed)

Leadwing Coachman*

The Leadwing Coachman is one of those green flies that always seems deadly on canopy streams.

Hook: 10–20 (standard dry fly)
Tail: brown hackle fibers
Body: peacock herl
Wing: gray mallard sections
Hackle: coachman brown

Leckford Professor

Hook: 10–12 (standard dry fly)
Tail: fiery brown hackle fibers
Reverse Hackle: white and fiery brown (use softer hackles; the two hackles are not mixed—the white is wound first and then the fiery brown; the position is not far back on the shank—the tie-in spot should be right above the point of the hook)

The Leckford Professor, according to John Roberts, is the only reverse hackle pattern that even comes close to attracting a wide following in England. It is widely used on the Test (the stream where riverkeeper Ernest Mott developed it).

A successful Letort Cricket

Letort Cricket

Ed Schenk, who actually added the flat turkey wing to the original Letort Hopper, tied this dark variation. He used it very effectively for night fishing, catching many large trout from his Pennsylvania waters.

How many crickets does a trout see in a lifetime? Not many. In all of my stomach samplings, East and West, there have been very few crickets. Nevertheless, the imitation excites trout well enough. The Letort Cricket is especially effective at dusk and dawn, as well as at night, and that is its value for me.

Hook: 4–10 (2X long shank)
Body: black fur (dubbed)
Wing: black crow
Head: black deer hair (spun and trimmed)

Letort Hopper*

The Letort Hopper is, in the words of its creator, Ernest Schwiebert, "a synthesis of other hopper imitations." [quoted from Ted Rogowski's *Crackerbarrel Discourses*]

Hook: 4–10 (2 X long shank)
Body: yellow nylon wool (dubbed)
Wing: turkey wing slips
Head: deer hair

It was a unique combination of the Muddler style head and the wing silhouette of older patterns. Most grasshopper patterns developed afterwards, in flattery through imitation, mimicked the head style.

Light Cahill*

The eastern Light Cahill (*Stenonema canadense*) hatches near the end of the spring and summer blitz of insects. If the summer days are as warm as normal, the adults emerge at dusk; they are almost white duns. The hatches are not heavy on most streams, but it does not take too many of the Cahills to interest trout.

Hook: 10–16 (1X fine wire)
Tail: dark cream hackle fibers
Body: yellowish cream fur (dubbed)
Wing: lemon wood duck fibers
Hackle: dark cream

Anyone who snorkels or scuba dives during a Light Cahill hatch quickly notices the strong color of the light pattern, those series of reverse pimples caused by the weight of the insect pressing on the meniscus. The dun makes deep enough dots for the walls of those impressions to pick up the orange, pink, and red colors of the sunset rays.

The fisherman does not have to worry about imitating the *color* of the light pattern as long as his fly makes as clean an impression as the natural on the surface. It is the walls of the reverse pimples themselves reflecting the light that the diver (or the trout) sees in the film—not any part of the fly. The proper imitation, however, has to cock correctly and touch the water only with the hackle tips.

The light pattern is an important characteristic with many mayflies—trout use it to isolate the natural during the hatch. It is not the exact configuration of the dots that makes this true, but the color of the walls pushing below the surface. The fish see these points of color before they see the actual insect. The imitation cannot be too light (there would be no impression at all) or sloppily overdressed (the buzz of material would shatter the surface).

Light Hendrickson

How many more publicly owned streams will adopt a system of daily fees and assigned beats? It is not a bad way of managing a resource, providing a measure of privacy even on urban trout waters. The income provides protections for fisheries that probably would not exist otherwise.

The low fees are a small price to pay for excellent fly fishing on streams like the Connetquot River on Long Island (New York) or Bullhead Creek in North Carolina.

Hook: 12–18 (1X fine wire)
Tail: medium bronze dun hackle fibers
Body: urine-stained fox belly fur (or, better still, an appropriately colored synthetic substitute)
Wing: lemon wood duck fibers
Hackle: medium bronze dun

There was a surprisingly fine hatch of Hendricksons (all three species in the group, *Ephemerella rotunda*, *Ephemerella invaria*, and the darker *Ephemerella subvaria*) on Bullhead Creek one afternoon. My beat was one of the longer, upper stretches where there aren't as many large fish as there are on the lower pools, but tight against the bank a sizeable rainbow captured every adult mayfly that floated over him. He refused my fly three times, even dropping back with it once; the Hendrickson was mashed and sodden from previous fish, though, and apparently he did not want a half-drowned fly. It was amazing how trustingly he accepted a fresh Hendrickson. The rainbow measured nineteen-inches—locals report that this is not an exceptional fish from this catch-and-release stream.

Little Olive Stonefly

Hook: 14–18 (standard dry fly)
Tag: red tying thread
Body: bright olive dubbing
Wing: fluorescent olive elk hair (select very hollow hair that flares well)
Hackle: grizzly

Both the Little Olive Stonefly (for *Chloraperla*) and the Little Yellow Stonefly (for *Isoperla*) are featured in *Fly Patterns of Yellowstone* by Craig Mathews and John Juracek. These patterns have fluorescent wings, but in the middle of the day (when naturals dance over the water) this feature is not going to be either negative or positive. These are simply durable, buoyant, highly visible patterns that meet a need by providing imitations for two important stoneflies; imitations that are too often missing from western fly selections.

Little Yellow Stonefly

Hook: 14–18 (standard dry fly)
Tag: red tying thread
Body: bright yellow dubbing
Wing: fluorescent yellow elk hair
Hackle: ginger

The *Isoperla* stonefly is commonly known as the Yellow Sally.

Madame X*

Hook: 8–16 (standard dry fly)
Tail: elk hair; a few strands of pearlescent flashabou (optional)
Body: yellow floss
Legs: rubber strands (two on each side)
Under Wing: flat, synthetic sheet (cut to shape)
Over Wing: elk hair
Head: bullet-shaped deer hair

I suppose that I am like most fly fishermen with new patterns. I will buy or tie a half dozen samples of the fly and stick them in the box. If those six flies are lost or worn out, and never do much in the process, they are not replaced. This is not really a fair test.

The Madame X is a pattern with something special. It survives even random judgements simply because on the proper water, riffles and runs, it is going to catch trout. The rubber legs, dangling out at the sides, make it a wonderful Low Profile attractor—fish have a hard time resisting the excitement of movement.

My first experiment with this Doug Swisher fly was on the Frying Pan in Colorado. The Madame X pulled eight trout out of the riffle; it caught over thirty fish that day. It graduated quickly from experiment to standby in my attractor box.

March Brown

Hook: 10–16 (1X fine wire)
Tail: dark ginger hackle fibers
Body: sandy beige fur (dubbed; as Eric Leiser points out in his *Book of Fly Patterns*, "but then,

without a sample, it is a difficult shade to describe.")
Wing: wood duck flank fibers (pick distinctively marked feathers)
Hackle: dark ginger and grizzly (mixed)

There was a fine hatch of March Browns (*Stenonema vicarium*) in Abrams Creek in Tennessee one spring, quite a few weeks earlier than the insects appear in the Catskills. The odd part of the day was that the fish really wanted a classic, hackled fly, not a flush floating pattern, and this hasn't always been my experience with the hatch elsewhere. The duns really fluttered and kicked on this mountain stream.

McGinty

My first trout was caught on a McGinty. The fact that practicality always loses out to nostalgia in my selection means that there will always be room for it.

Hook: 14–18 (3X fine wire)
Tail: red hackle fibers (dyed)
Body: alternating bands of yellow and black chenille
Wing: matched slips from the secondary feather of a mallard; the blue, white tipped feathers are actually called McGinty feathers (tied upright and split)
Hackle: brown

Using the fly in small sizes, especially during rainy weather, makes it a dependable attractor. It doesn't float so much as wallow because of the water-absorbing tendencies of the chenille.

McKenzie

Hook: 8–14 (standard dry fly)
Tail: coastal blacktail deer hair
Body Hackle: grizzly (palmered)
Body: light green floss
Hackle: grizzly

Any fly with a palmered hackle tends to drop to the surface lightly. Some fishermen try to prevent this fluttering effect by using stiffer and shorter tippets on their leaders, but this quest for straight, neat casts is a mistake. The fact that a pattern such as a McKenzie is not aerodynamic is an advantage whenever anglers need long drifts—they can simply let the fly fall naturally with a lot of curls in the leader.

Meloche

Three Meloche dry flies, one in each size, were my first purchase from a catalog (using the money from my paper route). The story of how Gilbert Meloche rushed a sample of the natural mayfly to Dan Bailey, and then went back to the river with Dan's imitation and caught a four-pound, eight-ounce trout, was enough romance for any twelve year old.

Hook: 16–20 (my own stock are tied on 1X fine wire hooks)
Tail: light ginger hackle fibers (the Bailey flies use hair)
Body: tan dubbing
Wing: pale grizzly hackle tips
Hackle: very light ginger

Mess* (see color plate)

The foam back on the Mess has a much different effect than the deer hair back on a Humpy. The deer hair is opaque, adding width to the Humpy—and that is an important component of that fly's attractiveness. The large-cell foam is very translucent, adding an aura of diffused color. On my imitations the underbody of synthetic seal's fur matches the color of the female's eggs and the foam strip, painted with waterproof marker, simulates the general body color.

The odd, cupped hackle, a feature of Buck's original fly, is tied on first. A soft mallard's feather, slightly longer than the rooster feather, and a regular hackle, Variant length, are wrapped normally and then forced forward with the thread. These feathers are not wound tight to the eye—there is actually a small gap of bare shank between the eye and the base of the hackles. The space is left so that there is room for the final whip finish—it is important that the thread doesn't force the flaring hackles backwards.

Hook: 6–12 (1X long shank)
Tail: 4 hackle fibers (split; two on each side)
Back: strip of foam (cut wide enough so that the edges overlap the sides of the body; colored with a waterproof marker)
Body: synthetic seal's fur (dubbed)
Hackle: rooster—with a mallard fronting (forced forward in a cup)

A fisherman walked up to me on the Lehigh River (Pennsylvania) to see my imitation for the Green Drakes (*Ephemera guttulata*) that were emerging. I showed it to him and said, "It's a Mess."

"That's obvious," he nodded, "but what is it called?"

In just a few years the Mess has become a special pattern with my testers. It turns the toughest hatches to imitate—those large may-flies—into consistent, if not easy, fishing. The fly mimics the size and wing height of these big insects without the clumsiness of other styles.

The main color combinations, with the first word referring to the rooster hackle and the second one referring to the body dubbing, are White/White, Medium Gray/Lime, Cream/Lime,

Medium Gray/Orange, Cream/Orange, Dark Gray/Brown, Slate/Olive, Gray/Yellowish Gray, Pale Gray/Yellowish Olive, and Pale Gray/Black. The colors can be altered to match any mayfly dun; the egg colors especially vary from species to species.

*Mink Wing Caddis**
Hook: 10–12 (3X fine wire)
Body: fur (dubbed; color matches the natural)
Wing: mink guard hairs (very long)
Hackle: high quality rooster

This is a variation of Leonard Wright's Fluttering Caddis—that pattern featured a wing of hard-to-find hackle fibers (found on one part of the neck).

*Mohawk** (see color plate)
Dave Whitlock was next to me at the fly tying tables during the 1986 Federation of Fly Fishermen Conclave. My fifteen-year-old daughter, Heather, who has been tying since she was four, stepped up behind us. Dave held up one of his deer hair bass bugs and asked her, "Did your Dad ever teach you to tie anything like this?"

The nice part about raising a child, from teething pains to boy friends, is that a father knows it will be worth it; he knows that she will always be his number one booster. "Not likely," Heather said, fascinated by that bass bug. "He can't tie anything that beautiful."

Dave spent the next hour showing her how to make special tools and teaching her tricks for creating deer hair miracles—and that was only the start of the binge. She came home with every possible color of deer and elk hair. She went down to the fly tying room and within the week created the Mohawk.

Hook: 10–14 (standard dry fly)
Glue: dab the shank with a strong glue just before applying every pack of deer or elk hair
Rear Body: tightly packed deer or elk hair

(covers two-thirds of the shank; stacked and clipped so that it comes up in a blocky V-shaped wedge on top of the shank—favorite colors are natural gray, orange, green, golden yellow, and brown)

Front Body: tightly packed white deer or elk hair (goes up close to the eye; stacked and clipped so that it comes up in a blocky *V*-shaped wedge on top of the shank)

Hackle: white or cream rooster hackle (very long and very soft; the feathers are the large, webby hackles that are normally worthless for dry flies)

Naturally, my daughter insisted on fishing with this flight of imagination. She began making fine catches with the Mohawk immediately. The new pattern, in spite of its strange appearance, earned its reputation quickly enough in her hands. She also tied up packs of Mohawks for our fly fishing friends around the world and let them test the fly on their home waters.

A year later the scuba diving team studied the pattern. They noted not just the "rush rise," the same distinctive way that trout took many large terrestrial naturals and imitations, but the fact that trout turned and hunted for the Mohawk as it drifted in its top heavy, wobbling manner.

Mosquito

Adult mosquitoes are not even rare items in a trout's diet. However, this fly, with its mayfly silhouette, proves valuable as a nondescript searching pattern with good contrast.

Hook: 10–12 (standard dry fly)
Tail: grizzly hackle fibers
Body: black and white moose mane fibers (wrapped together to create striped effect)
Hackle: grizzly

Muddler (dry)*

One simple change makes this a much better dry fly. A body of dubbed fur (any color)

instead of the gold tinsel increases the sure strikes, eliminating most of those last moment refusals. The metallic flash, much more appropriate for minnow imitations, ruins the Muddler's appeal especially during a dead drift presentation.

Hook: 2–16 (3X long shank)
Tail: brown mottled turkey quill (matched slips)
Body: flat gold tinsel (an alternative material, dubbed fur, turns this pattern into a more effective general searcher)
Bottom Wing: fox squirrel tail hair
Top Wing: brown mottled turkey quill
Head: deer hair (spun and trimmed)

Nymph Hopper

Hook: 14–16 (standard dry fly)
Body: rabbit fur (dubbed halfway up the shank; color to match natural)
Wing: natural gray deer hair (separated into two bunches—one out to each side)
Head: rabbit fur (dubbed thicker than the body)

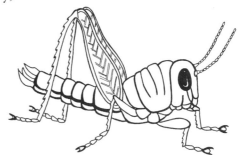

The small, immature grasshoppers are worth imitating early in the season.

If a large grasshopper imitation works in the West early in the season, it is probably because the trout believes that the pattern is a stonefly. There is a gap, however, between the end of the big stoneflies and the beginning of the excellent grasshopper fishing.

The Nymph Hopper fills that gap—and this Gerald Almy pattern is not just for small fish. The same trout that react suspiciously to a full-sized imitation rush out to take the more realistic fly. There is a two to three week period when the Nymph Hopper is my favorite terrestrial; it varies from area to area, but the clue is always the tiny naturals bumbling along the stream.

Occasion (see color plate)
Hook: 14–16 (standard dry fly)
Half Body: red floss (wrapped only over the upper half of the shank)
Hackle: one cree feather and two cream feathers
Spike: the cream hackle tips of the two regular cream hackles (these two "wings," coming straight out over the eye of the hook, stand straight up in the air because the fly floats flush on the head hackle)

The Occasion, with no tail, hangs down into the water.

There is no tail. That is a key factor in the dressing. The back of the long shank hook sinks, leaving the buzz of hackle on the surface. This fly style, oddly enough, is not an imitation of anything—at least, it isn't the greatest fly during mayfly or caddisfly hatches—but it is a fine searching fly, working best when trout are in the mood to investigate such a disheveled oddball.

These are my variations, but the "hanging" type of flies are found in other cultures. The English have their Mole Fly and the French have their Pont-Audemer.

Also, see the Tantrum, the color mate for this style.

Olive Quill
Hook: 14–16 (2X fine wire)
Tail: medium olive hackle fibers
Body: stripped peacock quill
Wing: dark mallard quill sections (upright)
Hackle: medium olive

The Olive Quill is my favorite imitation for the smaller Green Drakes on western streams— *Ephemerella doddsi* and *Ephemerella flavinea* are two major hatches, but there are a number of other species in the genus that are similar in form and habit. All together they create a daily "memory" for trout of gray-winged, olive-bodied mayflies. They emerge in the riffle sections from June through August. The high riding imitation proves better than flush patterns during most of the hatch (my formula is to use an olive Mess for the first ten minutes and the Olive Quill for the duration).

Orange Asher
Hook: 12–16 (standard dry fly)
Tail: dark grizzly fibers
Body Hackle: dark grizzly (palmered)
Rib: gold tinsel
Body: orange floss

This pattern has quite a bit of color showing through the hackle. That makes it different than a Bivisible; it is even more of an attractor. It can fished fresh, riding high on its hackle tips, or bedraggled, half awash in the film.

Orange Quill
Now here is an interesting tribute to empiricism. This pattern is still popular in England

as a match for their Blue Winged Olive (not the same mayfy genus as our Blue Winged Olive), even though the insect looks nothing like the Orange Quill.

G. E. M. Skues, who raised the fly to its present status as an imitation, wrote in *The Way of a Trout with a Fly,* "It may be asked why the Orange Quill is taken at night for the blue-winged olive. I answer frankly, I don't know. I only know that it is. I discovered it by accident in the early nineties, and it was a lucky accident, for it has been worth many a good fish to me."

Hook: 16–18 (1X fine wire)
Tail: orange hackle fibers
Body: stripped quill dyed pale orange
Wing: rusty-dun hackle points
Hackle: orange

In England the popular sizes are 12 and 14. My flies are size 16 and 18 for matching the smaller, evening mayfly hatches of summer. The Orange Quill has always been surprisingly effective at dusk on the Big Hole, from the middle water at the Abutment Pool all the way down to the Red Cliff section.

It was my own empirical experiences with the Orange Quill that made me put some orange on every evening imitation. This apparent contradiction created some frustration. My evening insect collections would go into a bottle for later viewing; they wouldn't get looked at until the following noon. All of the insects appeared so greenish or grayish in the daylight.

Queen of the Waters
Hook: 8–12 (standard dry fly)
Tail: golden ginger hackle fibers
Body Hackle: golden ginger (palmered)
Body: orange floss
Wing: mallard quill sections (upright)
Hackle: golden ginger

The Queen of the Waters through the years always caught a smattering of trout for me—

enough to stay in my box. The King of the Waters, tied to the same style but with a strong red coloration, never did fool many trout for me. There were other red patterns that filled that niche. Eventually, in a rather messy divorce, the King was dropped from my selection.

Pale Evening Dun
Hook: 14–20 (1X fine wire)
Tail: honey hackle fibers and pale blue dun hackle fibers (mixed)
Body: pale green fur (dubbed)
Wing: gray mallard fibers
Hackle: honey rooster and pale blue dun rooster (mixed)

After college in Montana, work took me back to Connecticut for a few years. My job was at the state training school in Southbury. Our rented house was on the Little River, not a great trout stream but an enjoyable one. For great streams there were surprising rivers all around the area. Within a short drive the choices included the Amawalk in New York, or in Connecticut, the Housatonic or Yantic.

Still, my favorite fishing spot was the East Fork of the Croton in New York. A short walk from Old Route 22 took me into a watershed so primitive and so rich that there wasn't much chance to miss Montana rivers. Every June the Pale Evening Duns (*Ephemerella dorothea*) popped all over the stream, trout rising in the runs, riffles, and pools. Not all of these fish were normal eastern sizes—a hackled Pale Evening Dun, a Charley Fox pattern, caught three brown trout over seventeen-inches one season for me.

Parachute
In my selection parachute flies imitate drowned mayfly adults. They also mimic spent mayfly egglayers reasonably well.

Adams Parachute*
Hook: 12–18 (standard dry fly)

Tail: grizzly hackle fibers
Body: gray fur (dubbed)
Wing: white kip tail (a single post)
Hackle: brown and grizzly (two hackles mixed)

I actually fish this fly more than a regular Adams.

Blue Wing Olive Parachute*
Hook: 16–20 (standard dry fly)
Tail: dark blue dun hackle fibers
Body: dark olive fur
Wing: white kip tail (a single post)
Hackle: dark blue dun

The *Baetis* duns do drift a very long way on damp days. Many of them drown in any patch of rough water.

Light Cahill Parachute*
Hook: 14–24 (standard dry fly)
Tail: cream hackle fibers
Body: cream fur
Wing: white kip tail (a single post)
Hackle: cream

Mahogany Parachute
Hook: 12–16 (standard dry fly)
Tail: brown hackle fibers
Body: mahogany brown dubbing
Wing: white kip tail (a single post)
Hackle: grizzly hackle dyed brown

The rich brown coloration of the Mahogany Parachute makes it especially valuable during the Brown Drake (*Ephemera simulans*) hatch.

Pale Morning Dun Parachute
Hook: 16–18 (standard dry fly)
Tail: pale blue dun hackle fibers (tied split)
Body: gray and yellow mixed dubbing
Hackle: pale blue dun
Wing: white kip tail

Ken Pope works a river differently than most guides. "A raft, where the fisherman is sitting down, isn't like a drift boat. We don't have to be forty feet out from the bank. We can work twenty feet away without spooking fish.

The Pale Morning Dun Parachute is a practical choice at that distance, even in sizes 16 and 18. When it is fished accurately, very tight to the bank, it catches large numbers of trout. When fish sip all day on Pale Morning Duns, from late July to August, it's my favorite fly on the South Fork of the Snake."

Od course, even with a normal wading and stalking approach, it is a valuable pattern during the Pale Morning Dun hatch (*Ephemerella inermis*) on western rivers.

Para Spin
Hook: 18–22 (standard dry fly)
Tail: pale blue dun (extremely long)
Body: black fur
Wing: pale gray synthetic yarn (single post; touch it with a drop of glue to make it solid)
Hackle: grizzly

This Bob Jacklin pattern specifically represents the spent *Tricorythodes* spinner. The advantage of this fly (as with any parachute) is the high visibility of the upright post. At the same time, the circle of hackle on the water is not a bad representation of the insect's outspread wings.

Parkany Deer Hair Caddis
Hook: 12–16 (standard dry fly hook)
Body: light brown deer body hair (spun and clipped to shape)
Wing: mottled brown deer hair tips
Head: deer body hair (the stubs of the wing hair are clipped flat on the top and bottom and left flared out at the sides to act as outriggers)

This is both a durable and an effective general fly, but for me it has a very specific moment. It is not unusual for me to spot a trout, change to a Parkany Deer Hair Caddis, and after either taking or not taking that particular fish put the fly back in the box.

It is an ideal pattern for the Reaction Method. The compact design makes it easy to cast accurately and it lands with a delicious plop. It is my specialty fly for trout hanging near the surface.

Pheasant Tail*

This is a great G. E. M. Skues pattern. In *The Way of a Trout with a Fly* he recommended it as a mayfly spinner imitation, "not of an evening only that the spinner is a taking fly. It is often a tender memory to the morning trout, and a fish found feeding before the general rise begins is usually taking spinners, and is very accessible to the temptation of a good imitation."

Hook: 14–20 (3X fine wire)
Tail: honey dun hackle fibers (only three)
Rib: fine gold wire (for the purpose of rein-

IN MEMORY OF G. E. M. SKUES
WHO FISHED THESE WATERS FROM 1883-1938
A MAN WHO HAD A WAY WITH A TROUT

forcing the pheasant herl; the wire, buried in the body, is nearly invisible)
Body: three or four strands of herl from the ruddy part of the center feather of a cock pheasant's tail
Wing: golden dun hackle fibers

The Pheasant Tail certainly works as a spinner imitation, presenting the right silhouette on the surface. For me, however, the fly is more of a searcher. The mottled pheasant tail herl is one of those naturally variegated materials that gives trout sufficient excuse to rise.

Robert Ince

On August 9, 1980, Keith Skues (center), the grandnephew of G. E. M. Skues, paid tribute to his famous relative during the Skues Memorial Ceremony on the Abbotts Barton fishery.

Picket Pin

The Picket Pin is a "bi" fly—it can be fished wet or dry. Either way it is a fine representation of the larger, green-bodied stoneflies.

Hook: 8–12 (2X long shank)
Body Hackle: brown (palmered)
Body: peacock herl (wrapped to make a full body)
Wing: gray squirrel tail
Head: peacock herl

This fly was originated in Missoula (Montana) by the legendary Jack Boehme. He operated a small tackle and fly business in a cramped corner of the Turf Bar and Grill. When he died the section stayed there, but the sales withered away from lack of attention. His corner deteriorated into a dusty clutter.

During college Stan Bradshaw and I worked at the Turf. Stan tended bar and I sold packaged liquor. In our spare moments we straightened out the tackle section, restocked the fly bins, and talked to fisherman. The sales figures grew steadily and the owner of the Turf decided to keep the section.

We both had to leave our jobs after a year. The fishing section withered again and the owner closed it, carting away Jack Boehme's casting trophies, homemade fly tying equipment, and fly displays (large boards with the original patterns, fascinating dries and wets, mounted and named) to the dump.

Stan or I could have had all of that history just by asking for it. Everyone tells us that we were idiots. Neither one of us denies it.

Pink Lady*

The autumn is possibly the best dry fly fishing of the year, even better than the magic, hatch months of late spring and early summer. It is a special season not because of the abundance of insects but because of the lack of them.

The dearth of aquatic food for the trout is especially evident underwater. Compare a kick sampling in the spring, when the screen is cluttered with nymphs of all shapes and sizes, to one in the fall, when the large nymphs are mainly species with more than a one year life-cycle, such as *Pteronarcys* stoneflies, and the rest of the nymphs are the tiny hatchlings of the earlier emergences of the season.

There is a cycle of abundance in the nymph population:

Spring—This is a time, just before and during major hatches, when the nymphs of so many species are not only at full growth but also very vulnerable. There is a period when the nymphs get active just before emerging.

The dry fly fisherman has to constantly wonder, when he doesn't see rises, if the fish are too preoccupied with underwater feeding to care about surface items. There are those seemingly perfect days when the dry fly fishing turns out disappointing—they happen more at this time than during any other season of the year.

Summer—Not all of the nymphs are gone. There are enough aquatic hatches continuing through the summer to keep the mature nymphs drifting, but not so many that fish can ignore everything else. Fish feed steadily as long as water temperatures don't climb too high.

The terrestrials—beetles, grasshoppers, ants, and leafhoppers—begin raining on the water steadily, forcing trout to be aware of the surface. Even without hatches, a dry fly produces as a searching pattern.

Fall—The surplus of nymphs is gone. Nevertheless, trout are following a biological imperative to add fat reserves for the coming winter. The fish, more at this season than at any other, seek food instead of waiting for it. Their aggressiveness helps overcome their innate wariness of attractor flies.

Hook: 12–16 (1X fine wire)
Tail: ginger hackle fibers
Rib: gold tinsel
Body: pink floss
Wing: light slate duck quill (matched sections)
Hackle: ginger rooster hackle

George LaBranche's Pink Lady works better for me in the autumn than any other season. With the gold tinsel rib it becomes, in my lexicon, a strong attractor. All of the other features, including the pink floss body, are not particularly unnatural. When that floss becomes wet it turns a darker shade, not unlike the deep reddish glow of many mayflies.

For years I experimented with LaBranche's creating-a-hatch strategy. The results were spotty, never more so than when the fly was the Pink Lady. That pattern really was too strong of an attractor for the method (the best fly was a Gray Fox Variant).

Poly Caddis*
Hook: 8–16 (standard dry fly)
Body: polypropylene
Wing: polypropylene (cut and tied down so that the stubs show)

With a sharp tug it dives, pulling a stream of air bubbles after it. And then it pops back to the surface. This Gary Borger fly, in any appropriate color scheme, is one of the best designs for the deadly Dive technique.

Quill Gordon*
Larry Duckwall generously ties my Quill Gordons for me. Any attempts of mine would look so clumsy next to his Catskill dries that he has to do them all. He achieves perfection by practicing Elsie and Harry Darbee's philosophy of tying.

He explained this to me, "Elsie was the one who taught me how to tie flies. She said that the way to be consistent was not by spending a lot of time on each fly, primping and fussing with it, but by doing hundreds of the same pattern. Tie enough of them and the proportions and techniques became automatic."

Hook: 12–18 (1X fine wire)
Tail: dark blue dun hackle fibers
Body: stripped peacock quill (varnished)

Wing: lemon wood duck fibers
Hackle: dark blue dun

Rat-Faced McDougal
Hook: 8–16 (standard dry fly)
Tail: dark ginger hackle
Body: carabou hair (spun and trimmed)
Wing: grizzly hackle tips
Hackle: dark ginger

The hair-bodied pattern is almost the embodiment of an idea that failed for imitations. The concept of everything—tail, body, and hackle—being tied bushy on an attractor, however, is valid. The style is too exaggerated to simulate any aquatic insect, but it represents a hearty serving of meat to a trout (maybe the chunkiness reflects the fact that the original hair-bodied fly was created for bass, a fish that really appreciates a substantial teaser).

Red Quill
Here is one of the great marvels of selectivity. The females of *Ephemerella subvaria* emerge from one riffle and the males from another. The mystery is that the male and female vary only in body color, but trout want a specific pattern for each sex.

Art Flick wrote in his *Streamside Guide*, "When it is considered that the only difference in the dressing of the two flies is in the body, it is hard to understand this selectivity. Often I have been unable to raise fish to a Red Quill (imitating the male), changed to a Hendrickson (imitating the female), and had good luck. To prove the point, I have again changed to the Red Quill, have not been able to raise another fish, and have again gone back to a Hendrickson, and again caught fish. Those trout fishermen who contend that fish cannot distinguish color and are not selective on a hatch would have a hard time explaining away the above conditions."

Roy Steenrod's Hendrickson has a body of pink fur from a red fox vixen; Art Flick's Red

Quill has a body of reddish-brown hackle quill (this is the first fly to use a stripped feather quill as a body material). The Red Quill, in my experiences with *Ephemerella subvaria*, is critical for imitating the male dun.

Hook: 14–18 (1X fine wire)
Tail: blue dun hackle fibers
Body: stripped quill of a Rhode Island Red cock feather (well-soaked in warm water before wrapping)
Wing: mandarin or wood duck drake flank feather
Hackle: blue dun

Reed Smut

Doug O'Looney

Hook: 20–26 (2X fine wire)
Body: fur (peacock is used on the Peacock Reed Smut; the body is tied only on the forward half of the hook shank)
Wing: clear Antron fibers
Hackle: soft hen hackle (one turn)

These little specks of fluff in the fly box are very simple flies for imitating adult midges awash in the film. Main color variations for this Robert Ince pattern are the Black Reed Smut, Olive Reed Smut, Peacock Reed Smut, Gray Reed Smut, and Red Reed Smut.

Renegade

The Renegade didn't look like an attractor to us; trout didn't respond to it much like an attractor, either. Especially when the fly drifted directly towards the diver, presenting a frontal view, it mimicked an insect better than many imitations.

The upper half of the front hackle resembled an upright wing; the bottom half resting on the surface film looked like legs (admittedly too many). That rear hackle, viewed from underneath, gave a surprisingly strong impression of an insect's abdomen moving on the water. At first glance the Renegade passed as a mayfly to both diver and trout.

To prove that this illusion wasn't so far-fetched, my friends frequently used Fore & Aft style dry flies during mayfly hatches. The patterns were not spectacular imitations (probably because the silhouette was wrong enough during the confirmation process to create doubts), but they worked as well as many other styles.

The only part that lends any attractive powers to the Renegade is the peacock body. High quality peacock strands always provide their own magic; the irridescent herl is designed for a spectacular display of color on the male bird and it shows the same alluring mix of green and gold to the fish.

The temptation is to put the Renegade with the searcher/general patterns instead of with the attractors. However, many of the best styles—Wulff and Trude especially—are also "gentle" attractors. These flies are not that unusual in silhouette or bulk.

Hook: 12–16 (standard dry fly)
Rear Hackle: brown
Body: peacock herl
Front Hackle: white
Tip: gold tinsel

There are three Dixon Renner variations that do not have any exciting material for the body. They are probably searchers.

Knave
Hook: 12–16 (standard dry fly)
Rear Hackle: cream

Body: brown fur (dubbed)
Front Hackle: cream
Tip: gold tinsel

Outlaw
Hook: 12–16 (standard dry fly)
Rear Hackle: silver badger
Body: black fur (dubbed)
Front Hackle: silver badger
Tip: silver tinsel

Rascal
Hook: 12–16 (standard dry fly)
Rear Hackle: brown and grizzly (mixed)
Body: pale yellow fur (dubbed)
Front Hackle: cream and grizzly (mixed)
Tip: silver tinsel

Royal Coachman
Hook: 12–16 (standard dry fly)
Tail: brown hackle fibers
Body: peacock herl (knobs front and rear)
Center Band: red floss
Wing: white duck quill
Hackle: coachman brown

The standard Royal Coachman, not quite as bulky as a Royal Wulff, draws more solid strikes than its hairwing cousin on gentler waters.

Shroud* (see color plate)
Hook: 8–10 (3 X fine wire)
Tail: red marabou fibers
Body: gray mink fur (dubbed, with the guard hairs, in a very "bristly" body about half way up the hook shank)
Hackle: blue dun (three feathers with the dull side forward; covering the forward half of the shank)

The marabou tail, hanging down behind the fly, "swims" everytime the Shroud is twitched. The pattern otherwise rides high, sliding easily on the surface.

In our observations of attractors, the dangling tail was a tremendous trait for pulling trout a long distance. The fly even drew fish from far under the bankside brush. These brown trout were in a phase of the feeding/resting cycle when they were not supposed to be that curious.

Skating Spider*
Dragging a Skating Spider randomly over the stream isn't the effective way to work it. This fly is an active attractor, but trout still need to be teased into chasing it. The best cast drops at a 45 degree angle downstream, instead of straight across stream—that way the belly in the line is much smaller when the fly begins hopping currents. That first movement, the Spider cocking up suddenly on hackle tips and stuttering in a series of preliminary hops, excites trout more than the sweeping arc of a dragging fly. The trick is to plan the drift so that the initial motion occurs over good water (for a Spider "good" usually means at least a few feet of depth).

Hook: 8–16 (5X short shank)
Hackle: oversized silver badger, blue dun, brown, grizzly, or dyed orange grizzly (at least three sizes larger than normal; a size 16 hook would have a regular size 12 hackle)

Owen Coburn, following an exchange of letters, wrote to me, "I disagree with your belief that Spiders are only for large rivers. They can be tweaked and danced on even the smallest streams. You're right, though, that trout can really bounce after a moving Spider and put on a show on big waters."

They can be used as imitations of very large mayflies (it was one of our favorites for the eastern Green Drake), but even on low, clear rivers with nothing happening, they usually stir up some action. It always surprises me how few anglers fish Skating Spiders. There isn't any fly that is more fun when trout are in a mood to chase something.

Slider*
Hook: 10–16 (2X fine wire)
Body: stripped quill from a brown hackle (lacquered; the body should not absorb any water)
Wing: deer hair (downwing)
Face: deer hair (cut to shape and glued flat with a clear bonding cement)

Motion on the surface grabs the attention of any underwater observer. To a human a skating fly makes a clearly visible commotion, but that movement is probably even more obvious to a trout. James Fenner, a Ph.D. physicist, writes in his article, "Angling Optics: The Fish, Fisher, and Fly," in the Spring 1990 issue of *Trout Magazine*, "some creatures, including fish, have a unique way of recognizing motion: Research has shown the rainbow trout possess receptor cells in the retina sensitive to various types of motion, cells the human eye apparently lacks.

"Trout also have unique nerve cells which recognize objects entering their visual field for the first time. These special cells merely alert the fish of an intruder, whether an angler, a predator or a possible food item."

The fact that nature has equipped fish with special eye cells for detecting and recognizing motion indicates how important such movement is in the underwater environment. Trout need to spot movement in order to escape predators and locate food. At the instant of recognition the trout must distinguish between opportunity and danger.

It is that duality—opportunity and danger—that makes repetition an important factor in active, dry fly presentations. During the first pass the fly might be a threat, but once the size, direction, and speed of the intrusive object are established the danger diminishes and gives way to opportunity.

Snow Stone
Hook: 16–20 (1X fine wire)
Tail: two slips of gray duck quill (split; short)

Egg Sac: olive synthetic seal's fur (dubbed into a thicker ball)
Body: very dark brown mink fur (dubbed rough—with guard hairs)
Wing: black calf tail hair
Hackle: black and white (the white consists of a few turns at the front)

The white hackle at the front is for greater visibility—the feature never seems to bother the trout on imitations. The Winter Stonefly (*Capnia* sp.) of western rivers are small insects. The adults crawl on the snowbanks and they are such weak flyers that they continually end up on the surface. Fish rise to them selectively in the clear winter flows of the lower Clark Fork and the Bitterroot.

Sparkle Dun

Doug O'Looney

Craig Mathews, creator of the Sparkle Dun, handed me an entire set of new flies to test one evening at the Bitterroot River Lodge. Many of them featured Z-lon, a bright colored nylon. There was the X series, featuring the X Caddis, X Midge Adult, and X Midge Pupa, as well as the Sparkle Dun.

Craig has a wonderful advantage in innovating new flies. He runs a large guiding service out of his fly shop in West Yellowstone. His guides can give a pattern more hours on the water in one week than a single fisherman could in a full season—and be assured that such crusty individualists as guides would let him know if one of his creations failed to catch trout. His innovations are tested so thoroughly that they are proven by the time the public hears about them.

Hook: 14–16 (standard dry fly; undoubtedly effective in smaller sizes, also—14 and 16 were the sizes in my tests with this new concept)
Trailing Shuck: Z-lon or sparkle poly
Body: natural or synthetic fur (dubbed)
Wing: deer hair

(Colors match the natural—the same set as the Compara Dun makes a fine starting point for a selection: White, Pale Gray/Cream, Cream/Yellow, Pale Gray/Yellowish Olive, Slate/Olive, Gray/Yellowish Gray, Dark Gray/Brown, Pale Gray/Black.)

The addition of the sparkling shuck to the Compara Dun style makes this one of those special flies—it is an imitation and an attractor at the same time. The bright trailer on the fly more than likely serves as a saving feature, making a trout come after the Sparkle Dun at the last moment.

Spent Partridge Caddis*

In various sizes and colors this Mike and Sheralee Lawson pattern can imitate many different egg-laying caddisflies, but it is used mostly for two abundant species on the Henry's Fork—the Little Western Weedy-Water Sedge (*Amiocentrus aspilus*) and the Grannom

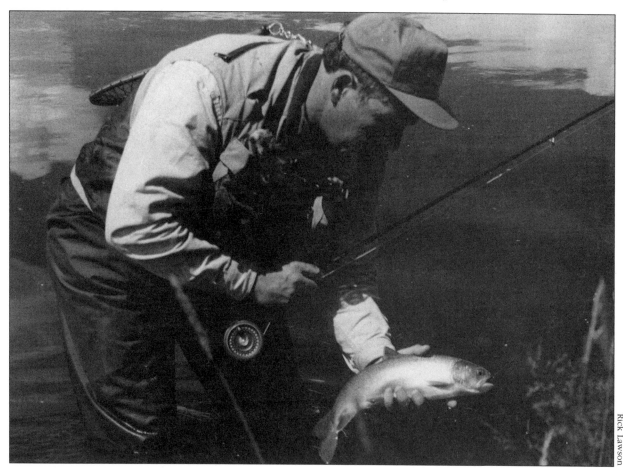

Rick Lawson

Mike Lawson believes that there have been greater populations of caddisflies on the Henry's Fork since the high water discharges from Island Park Reservoir in the mid-80s. One possible reason is that the added flow flushed some of the silt from the Railroad Ranch section, creating better habitat for the caddisfly larvae.

(*Brachycentrus americanus*). Both of these insects belong to the family Brachycentridae. The females in this group carry their eggs in a prominent ball at the tip of the abdomen. When they drop that egg packet, the force of the escaping gasses injures or kills the insects. These caddisflies fall flush on the surface and, for the most part, ride quietly.

Hook: 16–24 (standard dry fly)
Body: olive fur (dubbed)
Wing: mottled fibers of a partridge feather
Hackle: brown (wound over the head; can be clipped flat top and bottom)
Head: peacock herl

A packet of eggs from a Weedy-Water Sedge female hatched into larvae and grew quite well in my aquarium. They pupated and emerged, flying up into the netting. These twenty-seven adult survivors demonstrated a surprising range of colors. The wings varied from medium to dark mottling. The bodies, obviously different for males and females, still showed quite a bit of difference within each sex, ranging through almost every shade of green.

This hatch, along with other aquarium broods of various mayflies and caddisflies, explains my indifference to exact color in imitation. Even among brothers and sisters there is a range of colors. It is more important for an imitation to match the float characteristics (as the Spent Partridge Caddis does for dead or dying egg-layers) exactly—there is a margin of error for color, size, and even silhouette.

Spruce Moth

I confessed to Ellis Tupper as we drove along the Gallatin, "This really isn't my favorite dry fly river. It just spits out a lot of 8- to 12-inch fish."

Above Spanish Creek there was an incredible infestation of Spruce Moths. That afternoon the pests were landing all over the surface. The matching fly fooled trout after trout, but these fish were 13- to 18-inch rainbows and browns. There were none of those small trout that always seemed so common on the Gallatin.

The first thought that crossed my mind was that I must have been fishing my dry flies very poorly all of those years never to see a decent fish. Quickly enough, I dismissed that ridiculous notion.

I told Ellis, "It's amazing how big these trout have grown since I was here last time."

"When was that?"

"Three days ago."

"It's a miracle, if you ask me."

Hook: 12–14 (standard dry fly)
Body: cream/tan mink fur (dubbed thick and rough, with the guard hairs left in the mix)
Wing: light elk hair flared flat over the back
Head: spun light elk hair (clipped round)

The populations of terrestrial spruce moths are cyclical. Sometimes they disappear from a forest; then the infestation grows until it hits a three year peak. That is when the telephone lines buzz in the West and dry fly fanatics concentrate on the hot areas for six to eight weeks. There is no better surface action than the Spruce Moth "hatch"—not when these moths, which have no reason to be on the water, litter the surface.

Stimulator

Hook: 10–14 (2X fine wire)
Tail: elk hair
Body Hackle: furnace (palmered)
Body: 1/2 sparkle yarn/1/2 rabbit fur (mixed and dubbed; yellow, orange, or olive)
Wing: elk hair
Hackle: grizzly (wound over the head)
Head: amber goat (dubbed)

This very practical Randall Kaufmann fly can match either stoneflies or grasshoppers—that makes it a valuable searcher most of the season.

Stopper

Hook: 8–12 (standard dry fly)
Body: yellow polycelon
Underwing: golden pheasant tippet strands
Wing: deer hair (from a whitetail deer)
Head: deer hair stubs (the butts of the wing trimmed close)

I find myself using this stonefly/grasshopper hybrid of Nick Nicklas, a simple, buoyant pattern, either to imitate the smaller stoneflies or the smaller grasshoppers of early summer on the high gradient, bouncing streams.

Anyone who wants to see a variety of fine stonefly hatches, by the way, and not just the few major species of large rivers, should fish the smaller creeks of the Rocky Mountain region.

Tantrum

Hook: 14–16 (standard dry fly)
Half Body: green floss (wrapped over only the upper half of the shank)
Hackle: one light blue dun feather and two grizzly feathers
Spike: the grizzly hackle tips of the two regular grizzly hackles (these two "wings," coming straight out over the eye of the hook, stand straight up in the air because the fly floats flush on the head hackle)

This is the color mate of the Occasion. Under warm, reddish-orange light, trout tend to rise to the Occasion, but in greenish-blue light it might be wiser to throw a Tantrum.

Trude

These flies became my favorite attractors through simple experience. If nothing specific was happening, it was time to experiment. Trudes were frequently the fly type that caught trout. Pretty soon they weren't the third or fourth pattern out of the box but the first one.

Lime Trude*

Hook: 4–20 (standard dry fly)
Body Hackle: dark ginger (palmered and clipped)
Body: lime floss
Wing: white calf tail hair
Hackle: brown

The One Fly Contest, a charity event created by Jack Dennis, makes the angler pick a single fly at the beginning of the day. Then, even if the pattern is ineffective during the float down Wyoming's Snake River, the fisherman has to stay with his choice. Also, if the angler loses or breaks his one fly, he is finished for the day. Points are awarded for the number and size of trout caught by each fisherman.

This contest, with twenty teams of four anglers each, generates a great amount of empirical data every year. What if the results were analyzed? Shouldn't they fit the theories (at least for the dry fly) on pattern choice?

Here is an analysis:

1. Most of the actual fishing is done from a moving boat. The fish see the fly once.

Choice: an attractor instead of an imitation because of the float fishing.

2. The water type is split between flat runs and broken riffles, but riffles seem to constitute the prime holding water.

Choice: the importance of broken water points to a downwing pattern instead of an upwing fly.

3. The hours of fishing are restricted; very early morning and evening are eliminated—also, the event is held during the summer.

Choice: the ambient light during the midday fishing hours has a lot of green in it—this means that the attractor fly should have a lot of green.

The best dry fly then should be a green, downwing attractor.

The best dry fly over the years has been a Lime Trude. The runner-up has been an Olive Stimulator. They both fit the profile; not coincidentally, these patterns have been the favorites of the winning teams from the West Bank Anglers fly shop in Jackson.

Interestingly, in the 1989 One Fly Contest, George Anderson chose a nymph. This was not without risks—it would be a lot easier to snag and lose a sunken fly (ending the angler's fishing for the day). George not only didn't lose his George's Brown Stone, he single-handedly outscored whole teams, leading the Simms Company group to the championship.

Quebec Trude
Hook: 4–20 (standard dry fly)
Tail: scarlet hackle fibers
Rib: gold tinsel
Body: green fur (dubbed)
Wing: gray squirrel hair
Hackle: brown

Rio Grande Trude
Hook: 4–20 (standard dry fly)
Tail: golden pheasant tippet fibers
Body: black chenille
Wing: white calf tail hair
Hackle: brown

Colorado angler Dick O'Connor made this fly famous. He stalked the large spawning fish that ran up out of the reservoirs into the South Platte. He used the Rio Grande Trude both as a wet and a dry fly, aggravating a particular trout until he swatted the pattern.

*Royal Trude**
Hook: 4–20 (standard dry fly)
Tail: coachman brown hackle fibers
Body: peacock herl (knobs front and rear)
Center Band: red floss
Wing: white calf tail hair
Hackle: coachman brown

From 1980 through 1985 the Royal Trude caught an average of nearly three hundred trout per season for me. It was the top pattern every year except 1984. No other fly averaged more than seventy-five fish a year during that span. The total for the Royal Trude was built with a number of thirty and forty fish days (and it doesn't take too many of those). The results showed my faith in the fly as an attractor.

In recent years patterns such as the Emergent Sparkle Pupa, the Clear Wing Spinner and, just lately, the Mohawk have become important not just as imitations but as attractors, also. Their catches rob from the totals for the Royal Trude, balancing the numbers for the top five flies each season, but the Trude is still the best overall attractor in my box.

Turkey Wing Caddis

The Turkey Wing, by Ron Zaworsky, is a generic fly for me, matching the brown-winged caddisflies of late spring and summer. The presence of so many similar adults constantly around the stream makes this a good searching fly (as are many of the adult caddisfly imitations in my box).

Hook: 16–20 (1X fine wire)
Body: brown fur
Wing: brown mottled turkey (cut to shape)
Hackle: brown

Ugly Rudamas

Gary LaFontaine

Hook: 12–14 (standard dry fly)
Tail: elk hair; a few strands of pearlescent flashabou
Body: pearlescent flashabou (wrapped)
Under Wing: synthetic sheet (flat over the body; cut to shape)
Over Wing: elk hair
Head: bullet style elk hair

This John Foust fly is already a standard on the Bitterroot (Montana) and it is spreading fast to other western regions. Its popularity is not only due to the fact that every fisherman wants a pattern named Ugly Rudamas in his box—it is a very good rough water fly. The hair wing spreads very wide; overall the pattern is a bright puppy.

Walker's Red Sedge

Hook: 14–16 (3X fine wire; upeye)
Butt: fluorescent orange wool or silk
Body: pheasant tail fibers (wrapped)
Wing: brown hackle fibers (tied long)
Hackle: brown

The Mink Wing Caddis is my favorite skittering sedge for larger flies. This Richard Walker pattern, actually an older fly than the nearly identical American design for a fluttering caddis, is a lighter pattern—and it is my preferred fly in sizes 14 and 16.

Whitcraft

Hook: 12–16 (standard dry fly)
Tail: brown hackle fibers
Body: stripped peacock quill
Wing: grizzly hackle tips
Hackle: brown and grizzly hackles

This is another Bob Carmichael pattern. It is almost an Adams Quill, but in the original, museum samples that I have seen the hackles are as long as classic variants.

White Deer Hair Moth

Doug O'Looney

Hook: 8–12 (1X stout wire)
Body Hackle: cream hackle (palmered and clipped)
Rib: green thread
Body: white foam (cut a slit in a strip of foam; slide the strip over the hook shank and bind down with the green thread rib)
Wing: bleached white elk hair (heavy; split to each side by the head dubbing)
Head: cream mink fur (dubbed rough, bristling with the guard hairs; figure-8 the thread through the hair wing)

There is a cycle on dark nights. Until a little after dusk a trout feeds on whatever insects—caddisfly, stonefly, or mayfly—that might be hatching. Usually, there is a lull in surface activity once it gets dark. The rod cells, the light receptors of a trout's eyes (as well as ours), take a while to adjust. This doesn't mean that a fish stops feeding—it means that other senses besides the eyes helps him locate food. The angler can still get rises by slapping his fly on the water. A large, bulky moth pattern generally works best until after midnight. From 1 A.M. to 4 A.M. a minnow fly, worked in the shallows, catches more and larger trout (cripples such as the Bread, Creature, and Injured Minnow are good choices). Near dawn the insect imitations become effective again.

White Miller

This upwing pattern has correlations in nature—it can look like certain active moths or like very pale mayflies. Its most valuable feature, however, is its visibility to both angler and trout.

Hook: 10–14 (standard dry fly)
Tail: white hackle fibers
Body: white fur (dubbed)
Wing: white duck quill sections
Hackle: white

Wickham's Fancy
Hook: 14–16 (standard dry fly)
Tail: brown hackle fibers
Body: gold tinsel
Wing: slate gray duck quill (matched and divided sections)
Hackle: brown (palmered with wide spacing over the body; wrapped heavier at the wing)

The Wickham's Fancy, with its tinsel body, performs best on bright, sunny afternoons. Even then it draws an annoying number of flash misses, but that makes it a good "locator."

The same pattern, minus the palmered hackle over the tinsel body, did poorly in all underwater comparisons with the original recipe. It was that visual confusion of the hackle fibers that kept the unnatural looking tinsel from stretching reality beyond the breaking point of the trout's sensibilities on the real Wickham's Fancy.

Woodruff
The white hackle tip wings make this searcher more visible than most of the other olive-bodied flies in my general box. That bit of practicality helps it keep a place in the selection.

Hook: 12–14 (standard dry fly)
Tail: brown hackle fibers
Body: olive fur (dubbed)
Wing: white hackle tips
Hackle: brown

Wright's Royal
Hook: 14–16 (standard dry fly)
Rear Body: peacock herl
Front Body: red floss
Wing: light elk hair
Base: peacock herl (this herl is wound in front of the elk hair wing; the hackle is wound over the herl)
Hackle: brown

This effective variation of the Royal color scheme is popular on the Big Hole. This pattern, designed by Phil Wright to look more like a terrestrial in overall shape, is generally used in smaller sizes, 14 and 16, on the river.

Wulff
Jack Dennis, who ties Wulff patterns down to size 24, insists that these flies don't have to be attractors. "Wulffs can be tied in any colors. Mine usually have white wings, for good visibility, but the variations can match any mayfly. Pale Morning Duns, Blue Wing Olives, or even Trico duns—I tie Wulffs for all these hatches. I have a buoyant, hairwing style that works better on riffles than other fly types."

For me a standard Wulff usually is an attractor. The hackle, pushed below the surface, makes a somewhat bedraggled picture for the trout, but the wings present a very sharp outline above the meniscus. The overall silhouette is not too far away from the generalized mayfly shape. My way of using a Wulff is not that much different from Jack's ideas on imitation. A Wulff is one of the first flies out of my box because it is one of the most believable attractors (or, in other words, it stretches reality only a little).

Blonde Wulff*
Hook: 6–16 (standard dry fly)
Tail: light tan deer hair
Body: tan dubbing
Wing: bleached ginger deer hair
Hackle: ginger

The Blonde Wulff, by matching the Spruce Moth, caught more trout for me than any other dry fly during 1984. The terrestrial moths, suicidal around water, were falling on the surface for most of the summer on Rock Creek. They would land on the stream, get their wings wet, and, after a brief struggle, drown.

The rainbows and browns were ignoring the lifeless insects, although there were more of those on the currents, and taking the struggling insects. The trout clearly preferred the upwing Blonde Wulff to downwing flies during the frenzy. It was not until later in the evening, when fresh victims stopped plopping onto the water, that they shifted attention to flat insects (and matching flies).

*Gray Wulff**
Hook: 6–16 (standard dry fly)
Tail: brown calf tail hair
Body: gray muskrat fur (dubbed)
Wing: brown calf tail hair
Hackle: medium blue dun

I am sure that if I counted catches only on overcast days, the Gray Wulff would be my leading dry fly. It is so consistent in diffused light.

Grizzly Wulff
Hook: 6–16 (standard dry fly)
Tail: dark brown calf tail hair
Body: yellow floss
Wing: dark brown calf tail hair
Hackle: brown and grizzly (mixed)

Royal Wulff
Hook: 6–16 (standard dry fly)
Tail: brown calf tail hair
Body: peacock herl (knobs front and rear)
Center Band: red floss
Wing: white calf tail hair
Hackle: coachman brown

*Were Wulff**
Hook: 6–16 (standard dry fly)
Tail: brown bucktail hair

Body: hare's ear (dubbed)
Wing: white calf tail hair
Hackle: brown and grizzly (mixed)

Bill Blackburn was handing flies to our client, Ron Ballantyne, and naming them, "Royal Wulff, Gray Wulff, Blonde Wulff, and ...," and Bill said nothing because the new fly had no name.

"What's this one," Ron asked, "a Were Wulff?"

Our adaptation suddenly wasn't an orphan anymore. It had been no great feat of creativity for us to concoct a different color scheme for the Wulff style, but from our guiding we knew that this particular variation was badly needed on the Big Hole. We had sat at the tying table the night before tossing suggestions back and forth as each part of the fly went on the hook.

The fly had a great lineage, with an Adams for a mother and a Hare's Ear for a father. It performed up to expectations, giving us a rough, brown, and impressionistic Wulff with white wings. All colors were muted—attraction came from the more substantial silhouette of the style.

White Wulff
Hook: 6–16 (standard dry fly)
Tail: white calf tail hair
Body: cream fur (dubbed)
Wing: white calf tail hair
Hackle: light badger

Yankee
Hook: 16–18 (2X fine wire)
Tail: white hackle fibers
Rib: flat silver tinsel
Body: dark fur synthetic dubbing
Hackle: scarlet

Every angler needs a fly as farfetched as the Yankee in his box. This is one of those patterns to put on when the fishing is so fast that "anything" will catch trout. Those moments of easy catches are actually good learning opportunities—the angler keeps changing flies, looking for a concoction that will *not* work, and when he finds the breaking point in credibility, he has discovered something about the sensibilities of trout.

However, the Yankee has had plenty of solid moments for me. It is one of the oddball flies that was tested during Solunar Periods, and in that situation and others when trout were very aggressive it occasionally proved more effective than more realistic patterns. As an "exciter" it is better in the smaller sizes; also, the ones in my box are tied on 2X fine hooks so that they ride lightly on the surface film. The combination of red and blue (from opposite ends of the spectrum) means that it always going to be a bright fly, but it is acceptable to all species of trout in water broken enough to obscure the incongruities.

Stub Wing Bucktail

(Note: this is not a dry fly, but the dressing is included because the pattern is mentioned in the book to illustrate a point about imitation.)

The Stub Wing Bucktail is based on the concept of the "rear eye." The exaggerated eye is placed at the bend of the hook. The simple fact that trout strike the tail of this imitation instead of the head increases the percentage of hookups by roughly 30 percent.

This trick can be (and should be) adapted to any trout streamer, bass bug, Atlantic salmon fly, or saltwater pattern. Almost any technique for creating eyes, including plastic doll eyes and jungle cock feathers, can be shifted to the rear of the hook.

Hook: 2–10 (up-eyed, Atlantic salmon hook)
Tail: white sparkle yarn (combed out/clipped)
Eye: painted on the built up black tying thread
Rib: blue fluorescent Stren line
Body: off white sparkle yarn (wrapped; brushed or picked out to make it fuzzy)
Joint/Trailer: red wool yarn (the trailer is a combed out stub of yarn on the underside of the hook; the joint is a wrap of the same red wool)

Rear Wing: white marabou (short, stub wing)
Front Wing: white marabou (short, stub wing)
Throat: eight long strands of blue fluorescent Stren line
Topping: long strands of green flashabou

There are many parts to this fly, but each one of them is sparsely layered. Everything adds to the vibrancy of the Stub Wing design. The fluorescent blue Stren spinning line, for example, is a "magical" material on a subsurface fly—normal colors can't attract fish the way that it does. The elements of attraction and imitation don't have to be nearly as subtle as with a dry fly (different rules apply underwater).

Is my selection biased? Of course it is. Someone who lives in New York, or in Oregon, is going to have different preferences simply because of his proximity to the local fly fishing culture. My choices reflect my association with many of the great fly tyers of the Rocky Mountain region.

Just because someone's favorite imitation or attractor didn't make *my* list doesn't mean that it is unworthy. It is just not part of my experience. By the same measure, though, good flies work anywhere—and on appropriate water types my selection should cover the major dry fly problems anywhere.

On some days fly choice doesn't matter—either any dry fly will work or no dry fly will work. This selection gives me more than enough possibilities on those days when fly choice does make a difference in my chances. Pattern selection by any method is a game and the game is fun.

Observing Trout

The difference between scuba diving and snorkeling is that with an air supply a person can join and stay among feeding trout. Snorkeling is also a tremendous amount of fun, providing a fisherman a safe peek at the river world, but scuba equipment allows the diver to become a part of that world.

All photographs underwater are taken at very close range (lenses are wide angle). It is not hard, after an acclimation period, for a diver to stay within three feet of rising trout. He can see not only the fish but also the food items that the fish is picking from the currents.

If he is trained as an observer as well as a diver, a person can accurately study trout behavior. He settles on the bottom in a feeding area as slowly as

Dan Abrams

possible. The best spots for observation are deep, slack areas next to a heavy current (the Abutment Pool on the Big Hole, a dining room for roughly a hundred trout, is perfect).

The flow that is good holding water for the diver, the quiet cushion right among the rocks, is also good for trout. At first, when he noses among them, he disturbs the school—the line of fish waves like a flag in the wind as it moves over. Some skittish fish flush to deeper water (rainbows) or cover (browns). After approximately seven minutes the trout nervously edge back into an area; occasionally, a particularly bold individual, especially if the diver is exactly in his spot, will rush towards the human intruder in a display of agonistic behavior (none have ever nipped me). After approximately twelve minutes the trout resume feeding naturally; nevertheless, they are aware of the diver. After approximately seventeen minutes they start using the diver for cover.

The sport of scuba diving does not require any great physical talents, but the neophyte needs qualified instruction. Most cities have not only certified teachers but also scuba diving clubs (when we were filming the *Tying and Fishing Caddisflies* on Utah's Green River, a group of more than fifty divers were swimming the stretch from the dam down to Little Hole—it looked like fun).

Comments

My manuscripts go through one extra step—at least, it is "extra" for fly fishing books. All scientific works are reviewed by authorities in the given field for errors and inaccuracies. A book such as The Dry Fly, *with its controlled research, ends up halfway between art and science. To guarantee the validity of the scientific statements (and this effort straddles a number of disciplines), it has to be read by qualified people.*

The readers for *The Dry Fly* were:

William Vessie, M.D.
A great deal of "A State of Mind" (Chapter 3), depended upon my assessment of the human brain (and comparisons with the development of the trout's brain). That information had to be checked by a medical expert.

Eric Peper
Eric Peper (former head of the Field & Stream Book Club) is one of the few people with an equal grounding in eastern, midwestern, and western fly fishing. His knowledge of the literature, and a lifetime of testing the theories and flies in those books, made him uniquely qualified to judge the ideas (which jump so freely between East and West) in this book.

James Fenner, Ph.D.
Physics is not my field. The information on the properties of light in "A Theory of Attraction" (Chapter 10) had to be reviewed thoroughly by an expert.

Robert Ince
Both Robert Ince and John Roberts read the manuscript to make certain that my assumptions about fly fishing in the United Kingdom were correct (and often they weren't; have no doubt that there is a different and fascinating fly fishing culture in the United Kingdom).

John Roberts

John Roberts is also a fine historian, a careful researcher who goes to the source for the origins of patterns. His books, such as *To Rise a Trout* (published in this country by Stoeger Press) include flies from around the world.

Paul Bach, Ph.D.

Paul Bach, a practicing psychologist, reviewed the comments scattered throughout the text about selective feeding (a basic stimulus/response activity) and the psychological interpolations of "A State of Mind" (Chapter 3).

All of these men are also fly fishermen. All of them read the entire manuscript, not just their particular areas of special interest, and scribbled comments on the pages. They weren't expected to be "rubber stamps"—praise and agreement (although it feels good) wouldn't make *The Dry Fly* a better book. Their questions and their contradictions made me clarify (and sometimes change) my ideas.

Dr. William Vessie, my fishing partner in Deer Lodge, was involved throughout the writing of *The Dry Fly* in the discussions about theories. At the least, his ideas should have been recorded for later transcription. Unfortunately they were not and excellent material was lost.

All of the written comments by the other five readers couldn't be incorporated into the main text. Much of it is humorous; most of it contains further insights. In some instances, the questions demanded greater explanation by me.

These comments are too good to throw away—here are some of them (and my responses and comments in italics).

John Roberts

On Chapter 1 (Why Flies Fail)
When I wrote, ". . . as the English say, 'get the color,'" John noted in the margin, "This Englishmen has never heard it."

My reference comes from Dry Fly Fishing in Theory and Practice *by F. M. Halford. "Fish generally rise best at the commencement of the hatch of a particular fly on any day, and this is accounted for in two ways—first, because they, like other living things, are more hungry and keen at the commencement of their meal; secondly, because, although, as before said, it is questionable whether they are ever as particular to mere question of shade in the artificial fly as the fisherman is, they have not quite got the color in the earliest portion of the hatch, and hence are not quite so critical as to the pattern of artificial as later on," he wrote.*

On Chapter 2 (Why Anglers Fail)
John writes, "Dare I disagree with Harry Ramsay? He might be wrong! Surely trout do not 'always know you're there.' Wild fish on some of my streams never feed if they are aware of an angler. Most disappear at a shadow. On these streams, those that have risen to the fly have never known about the angler. On one such wild trout stream it is very common for guests not to catch anything at all, simply because when trout have become aware of a presence (however slight) they do not feed—most disappear for half an hour.

"P.S. I remember your advice to me on *To Rise a Trout*, 'Never say always or never!.'"

Oh, sure, throw my own advice back up into my face. That makes it tough for me to deny the truth of John's comment (and there's a lot of truth in it).

It took me twenty years to totally agree with Harry Ramsay. It wasn't until I was underwater, watching fish, that I could see the small signs of nervousness. The trout may not have been aware of the angler, per se, but as soon as the commotion of presenting the fly began he was certainly aware of an intrusion. The reason he didn't stop feeding is because he wasn't sure if this intrusion constituted a danger to him.

This brings up another point (which John touches on). Trout in heavily fished streams become used to the intrusion of anglers and are much easier to approach. Wild trout in untouched waters can be the spookiest targets for the angler (requiring extreme stealth).

On Chapter 4 (The Empiricist in Us All)
John wrote across the top of the first page, "Now I know why my fly box looks the way it does! I'm an empirical generalist with a leaning towards naturalism."

This is John's wonderful wit coming out, but he's also absolutely right. Don't most of us fit his definition?

On Chapter 6 (Imitation through a Fun Glass)
John asked about the title of the chapter, "I didn't understand the significance of the title. Is it a U.S.A. concept, or a subtle joke that I've missed completely?"

When we were children, our families would take my cousins and me up to Riverside Park in Agawam, Massachusetts. This amusement park had a fun house filled with warped mirrors—they would make people look thin and tall, or fat and squat. They always fascinated me.

On Chapter 6 (Imitation through a Fun Glass)
"You've given no consideration to the USD series of John Goddard and Brian Clarke. Surely they merit inclusion. *To me* they are the best imitation of a mayfly dun.

"They're crap to tie, crap to cast, but they are superb imitations. I find them impossibly difficult to tie neatly, and casting into a breeze with them is as about as successful as peeing into a force 6 gale."

Here the issue of practicality comes up. Another problem with the USD series is that the flies hook poorly. No matter how good a pattern is as an imitation, it won't be popularly accepted if it's not easy to tie and fish.

On Chapter 9 (Unnatural Acts)
John commented on moving the dry fly, "There are not many 'restrictive' fisheries left in England—and all of those are on southern chalk streams. Ninety-nine percent of the U.K. trout rivers allow active and downstream dry fly tactics."

On Chapter 10 (A Theory of Attraction)
John wondered about the pressure waves for the Mohawk, "A dry fly is static, not moving like a Muddler. Can a floating fly give out *detectable* pressure waves? This might be stretching belief. You're right that it will be extremely difficult to prove. I have grave doubts."

John is so diplomatic. My other readers just scrawl "Bull feathers!" across the page when they have grave doubts.

Obviously, I have doubts about trout being able to sense the pressure waves of the Mohawk, also. But remember, most of the fly is under the surface, pressed down by the top-heavy weight of of the deer hair.

I called Wayne Hadley, a biologist, and explained the problem to him. He suggested a possible experiment. There is an instrument named a hydrophone that will record underwater vibrations. It could be used to record the "sounds" of the Mohawk as it drifts and rocks; then these sounds could be played to trout (with no fly present). If they respond to the recording, the pressure waves are detectable.

Now, this opens up all sorts of possibilities for testing flies. No matter what happens with the Mohawk, the hydrophone procedure is going to be a major part of one of my future books on streamers and bucktails (the imitations will "sound" like the corresponding naturals).

On Chapter 10 (A Theory of Attraction)
John commented, "Most flies evolve or happen by chance, or are a tying fluke which is discovered to work. The Double Wing was *designed* to work after all the factors were analysed and stream-tested. Has *any* fly ever been examined so closely?"

There were more than twenty-eight hours of scuba work on the Double Wing. It really doesn't take very long to determine whether a "whole" fly is good or bad, but it took time to test each component of the Double Wing separately.

The Double Wing is a "good" fly, as determined by the testing, but as a fly design it doesn't overwhelm me with its genius. It is as a series, each pattern suited to particular conditions of natural light, that the concept is valuable.

Paul Bach

On Chapter 2 (Why Anglers Fail)
Paul commented on the word *micro-drag*, "I've never liked this term. Microwaves, micrometers—now microdrag, microcaddis, and microshot. How about 'drift distortion' or 'drift resistance?'"

On Chapter 3 (A State of Mind)
Paul, noting the work of neuropsychologist James DeBus (and the surgical procedures on trout), wrote, "Initiative is a fine verb; perhaps a bad noun. Brainstem lesions tend to diminish exploratory behavior and vigilance (curiosity), but they also result in impaired complex motor coordination, so that the trout would be less adept at initiating the complex set of motor events necessary in the pursuit of food."

On Chapter 7 (A Grasshopper Study)
Paul wrote about one of his grasshopper experiences, confirming the value of a sunken grasshopper imitation, "This past August I was fishing the Stillwater River with a good friend who grew up on it. The creek is primarily one to three feet deep riffles at that time of year and grasshoppers were in abundance on the land. The turbulent riffles made a natural float difficult and we took few fish. As dusk drew on, and as we drank a few beers, our casting became sloppier and we started taking trout. Why? A bit of observation indicated that we were letting the fly get washed under and the trout took the fly one to six inches submerged—where they usually saw them. No hopper, live or imitation, could float long on those riffles, so they sunk, where the trout ate them. That night I devised a submerged hopper pattern. We took fish all morning the next day."

Robert Ince

On Chapter 1 (Why Flies Fail)
Robert used one of our friends, Paul Brown, as an example of an angler on the Henry's Fork who doesn't diminish wing size when selecting a smaller body, "Paul uses parachute hackle and a 'bunch wing' of hair or feather fibers. It's quite high, often higher than the natural—his size 18 may have the wing of a size 16 or larger."

On Chapter 2 (Why Anglers Fail)
There was a circle around my sentence, "The average nymph fisherman now is better than at any time in fly fishing history."

Robert wrote, "Over here (the U.K.), I'd agree with that statement on stillwaters but not on rivers.

"Sure, there are more fly fishermen, but I seldom see what I would call skilled nymph fishermen—I seldom see good 'dry fly' fishermen—no watercraft!"

On Chapter 2 (Why Anglers Fail)
Robert refers in his notes to big trout that we have caught on our trips together. He mentions a five and a half pound brown trout (a beatifully colored fish) that we "hunted"—and he caught amid a lot of whooping and hollering—on a spring creek in the Deer Lodge valley, "Gary, remember us on that side channel near the Hog Hole? Lying down in the dirt, really taking the trouble to conceal ourselves? That was stalking!"

On Chapter 3 (A State of Mind)
"Surprised you haven't mentioned the Daddy Long Legs, *the* most effective imitation for craneflies. Trout find them irresistible—you caught a nice, seven pound brown trout on this pattern on the Hog Hole in 1981."

The Hog Hole is a pond. There are points of reference between what works in stillwaters and what works in running waters, but there are great differences in fly selection. Why? The trout generally move for their food in ponds and lakes; instead of a searcher the fish is a hunter.

My intent throughout The Dry Fly *has been to avoid confronting the problems—dry or wet—of stillwaters (they will be left to a future work,* Stillwater Tactics*). There is a wonderful body of modern literature in England covering ponds, lakes, and reservoirs, with writers such as Steve Parton, Bob Church, Peter Gathercole, Brian Clarke, John Goddard, Alan Pearson, Taff Price, and C. F. Walker, that stillwater fly fishermen over here can learn from.*

The Daddy, by the way, has caught trout for me on good cranefly rivers—one morning it took four trout, all in a span of fifteen minutes, on the Beaverhead. On that performance alone it has earned a spot in my running water selection (and it is listed in the Fly Pattern list).

On Chapter 3 (A State of Mind)
Robert added to my observation on the Clark Fork ("trout don't stay in the same lies, not for a lifetime, not for a season, not even for a month"): "Sometimes, not even for a day. I watched a nice brown (1 $^3/_4$ lbs.) move to several lies (within thirty yards) in one day this year."

On Chapter 8 (Large Trout with Finesse)
Robert, an excellent fish spotter, noted on shelf tailers, "These fish are *very* difficult to spot *until* they start to feed. I find that the color of the shelf feeders and the color of the gravel matches on my rivers. By standing still and looking *into* (not at) the water, I can see them.

"I take a lot of trout from those areas. It requires a stealthy approach; and I catch 90% of them on emergent patterns and 10% on terrestrial patterns."

In my opinion, the trick to spotting trout is "standing still and looking"—instead of walking and glancing over the water.

James Fenner

On Chapter 1 (Why Flies Fail)
James has done a lot of observations on insects from below, "The wings of many mayflies, seen edge-on by trout, may not be discerned at all—I had trouble seeing them from under water."

Do I agree? It is certainly possible that the wings are more visible on some mayfly species than on others.

On Chapter 6 (Imitation through a Fun Glass)
James added after the section on the Stub Wing Bucktail, "Atlantic salmon flies with jungle cock in the wings may also have been developed to get more solid strikes. The same may be true of short-shank streamers, often used in saltwater."

On Chapter 6 (Imitation through a Fun Glass)
Circling my comments about Thorax Duns being "ultimately too good," James wrote, "You can, however, tie 'pseudo-thorax duns' (as I do), which are *not* such perfect imitations—they merely float better."

On Chapter 7 (A Grasshopper Study)
James commented, "I use the skip cast for all flies fished under overhangs, unless a drift from above will cover the water. Skipping a grasshopper is harder than skipping a beetle or an ant, though!"

Actually, the right *grasshopper pattern skips easily enough, but it has to be a tie, such as a Letort Hopper, that isn't too air resistant (beetle patterns or ant patterns usually are compact creations).*

On Chapter 10 (A Theory of Attraction)
On flourescent flies, James added some historical perspective, "Herter's work indicated that flourescent flies were better ⅓ of the time, worse ⅓ of the time, and made no difference the rest of the time. He did *not* say *why* they proved better or worse."

On Chapter 10 (A Theory of Attraction)
James explained why colors are compared with heat, "The 'warm' and 'cool' terms come from psychology—we associate red and orange with fire (warm) and blue with ice (cool)."

Eric Peper

On Chapter 1 (Why Flies Fail)
Eric commented on the sequence of acceptance and refusal during a rise, "In a conversation with Al Caucci and Bob Nastasi, we discussed the fact that the larger the trout, the more likely he is to 'consummate' the take and, by corollary, the less likely he is to refuse.

"Our theory is that this is tied directly to the 'energy out versus energy in' equation. Once he starts, a large trout is committed."

Here is an example of the "energy equation" that Eric is referring to (from Challenge of the Trout):

$$\frac{Abundance\ of\ food\ item\ \times\ Bulk\ of\ food\ item}{Difficulty\ of\ capture} = \begin{array}{c} Energy\ spent \\ per\ calorie \\ consumed \end{array}$$

It can be expressed in different ways, but the point is that a trout must take in more calories than he expends during the process of feeding. Different hatches actually have different caloric value (professional studies have shown, for example, that trout can grow to nine inches on a diet of midges, to eleven inches on a diet of mayflies, to fourteen inches on a diet of caddisflies, and to nineteen inches on a diet of Pteronarcys *stoneflies—beyond that in running water they need "meat" as at least part of their diet).*

On Chapter 2 (Why Anglers Fail)
"Personally, I don't think that you can become a good fly fisherman unless, and until, you have fished bait *in small streams.*"

On Chapter 2 (Why Anglers Fail)
Eric circled my paragraph about lashing a sugar cube as a disappearing "sinker" onto the leader and wrote in the margin, "I used an Alka Seltzer."

There would be fewer headaches that way.

On Chapter 2 (Why Anglers Fail)

Eric made an important point on timing an approach, "My own experience is that actively feeding trout (trout that have been on the feed for awhile) are less likely to 'spook' than trout that have just begun to feed on the hatch.

On the other hand, sloppy wading or casting will *definitely* keep a trout from starting to rise. Even *careful* casting will, if it's done too early in the hatch."

Stalking a good fish? Let him settle into his feeding routine before trying to approaching him.

On Chapter 2 (Why Anglers Fail)

Eric is an excellent "hunter" of rising trout, so it probably isn't a surprise that he had a lot of comments on Chapter 2, "Suggest to the reader, 'Think about what makes you aware of someone on the stream with you. Chances are that it's either motion or glare. Think about the number of times you have seen glare flashing off a rod.'"

I would just add, "Or off a reel, or a watch band, or a metallic trinket on the angler's vest."

On Chapter 2 (Why Anglers Fail)

"Advances in tackle design have made 'fine and far off' a realistic 'populist' strategy—albeit an ineffective one for wild trout. The problem is, *it works* often enough on stocked trout in 'No Kill' areas.

"Remember, fifteen year ago, you couldn't find a nine foot rod for a number four or five line very easily. I wouldn't lay the prevalence of long distance presentations totally on the legacy of spin fishing."

On Chapter 2 (Why Anglers Fail)

Eric wrote at the end of the chapter, "A critical component of all this information is how close can you get to a feeding, wild trout? I've been within two feet of wild browns on both the Madison and the Delaware. Several times, I've spent over a half hour studying feeding, wild rainbows from ten feet on the Henry's Fork. Interestingly, I've gone on to catch these fish, too.

"I think that the fly fisherman needs to understand that not only can he get this close, *but also* that the fish will come this close to him. I have had big, wild browns on the Delaware almost accost me because they were concentrating so hard on feeding up a 'dun line.'"

Often, I've stood dead still in calm water and let a good fish feed into close range, where he could be dapped (or close to it.)

On Chapter 3 (A State of Mind)
"This is great stuff (although I suspect that you'll get some arguments). I think that you could avoid some conflict with the ethologists if you'd say at the outset that all the trout's behavior (as is man's) can be related directly to its basic overriding reason for being: to propagate *its* own kind, individually—not just the species. (I've got this in personal correspondence with Robert Bachman)."

This is included for all of those ethologists out there.

On Chapter 4 (The Empiricist is Us All)
Eric mentioned another way that empirical knowledge (with a good background in entomology) could be put to use, "What about empiricism applied to water type? It 'looks like' *Isonychia* water. Or, it looks like there should be *Baetis* in here."

Any aquatic entomologist worth his collecting bottles, on a strange stream, could, without touching the water or sampling the fauna, make an excellent profile of the mayflies in that water. Fly fishermen, by learning to judge variables such as bottom type and richness, can do the same thing empirically on the rivers in their home region.

On Chapter 6 (Imitation through a Fun Glass)
Eric noted about the observation that trout are not as selective at the start of a hatch, "My own experience on this is not consistent. On some hatches, yes; the start yields some reduction in selectivity. Good examples of this are *Baetis* and the Quill Gordon.

On other hatches, I've found that trout are tough from the very start—most notably the Trikes and the Hendricksons."

On Chapter 6 (Imitation through a Fun Glass)
Eric added to the observation that in broken, riffle water "nymphs transform quickly into adults." He wrote, "Wind on flat water may have the same effect—the broken surface might allow a faster escape."

On Chapter 8 (Larger Trout with Finesse)
After my opening description of tactics for large trout, Eric suggested, "Trophy methods can be compared to trapshooting, where the key to becoming an

expert is to have total preoccupation with the present instant.

"It's the only sport I know where stupidity is a virtue."

When I say things like that, I get into trouble. That doesn't mean that I don't love it.

On Chapter 8 (Larger Trout with Finesse)
Eric wrote about shelf tailers, "My experiences in general with these kinds of fish include: one, they like *very* slow water (five inches per second), two, they *do* take adults, but they prefer emergers, especially early in the hatch, and three, they are 'lane' selective, but not pattern selective once the feed is underway. My experiences on the Delaware, the Madison, and the Beaverkill have been consistent."

I find shelf tailers in slightly faster water, but they are always behind some sort of minor obstruction (a slightly larger rock on the pea gravel) that keeps them out of the current.

On Chapter 8 (Large Trout with Finesse)
Eric also noted on these shelf areas, "Many nymphs move into the shallower areas just prior to hatching. This also increases the concentration of food on the shelves."

On Chapter 9 (Unnatural Acts)
In the discussion of the twitch (when and where), Eric wrote, "You may be amused to learn that Vince Marinaro did this (I saw him do it and talked with him about it) during super dense evening hatches. He twitched his imitation primarily so that he (not the fish) could tell the fly from the naturals. The hatch was *Ephoron leukon* on the Yellow Breeches."

Amused? Don't tell anyone in Pennsylvania about this.

On Chapter 10 (A Theory of Attraction)
Eric is a colorist [also see next comment]; not surprisingly, this is the type of fly fisherman who has the background of experiences to compare against the theory of color attraction, "I love this! The effect of light—not only on flies but on lies that trout choose—has been one of my prepossessions for years.

"There's probably another whole book here!

"This is probably why even prescribed patterns vary in color from area to area, and stream to stream. The 'Sulphur' patterns are one of my favorites for this. I used to tie one for the Willow, in Wisconsin, with orange ostrich herl in it."

On Chapter 10 (A Theory of Attraction)
Eric gave his recipe for the body color of the Pale Morning Dun, "My 'mix' for this is a 'pukey' chartreuse—heavy on yellow (65%), with bright olive and a touch of cream."

_____

One suggestion from the readers was not incorporated into the final version. Each one marked the text, underlining sections for italics. The problem was that, with each of them choosing different spots, half the book would have ended up in squiggly type.

The reader is welcome to pick out his own points of emphasis and highlight them accordingly.

Sources for
Materials and Accessories

These are not advertisements. This information is included to save readers the trouble of calling or writing about items and services mentioned in the text of The Dry Fly.

Solunar Periods

For those anglers who want to follow Solunar periods, contact Hannon's Lunar Calculator/Moon Clock at Tern Corporation, 9259 Park Boulevard North, Seminole, Florida 33543.

Ralph Manns has compared Hannon's Lunar Calculator, Knight's Solunar Tables, and Action Graph. He found that the major and minor periods correlated closely on all three of them. Anyone who is researching scientific literature and wants a list of appropriate papers on the subject (and copies of those papers) can hire the services of **Fishing Information Services**. Write to Ralph Manns, Fishing Information Services, 8800 Silver Arrow Court, Austin, Texas 78759.

Feathers for hackling the Cul de Canard

These are the long, downy feathers surrounding the preen gland of a wild duck. The Cul de Canard, very popular in Europe, is beginning to appear in our fly fishing catalogs (Orvis). The actual feathers for tying the fly are distributed wholesale by **Umpqua Feather Merchants** (and local shops can stock it through them).

Sparkle Yarn

My first two books, *Challenge of the Trout* and *Caddisflies*, sent readers into knitting shops looking for Sparkle Yarn. They didn't find it.

There is no such thing as "sparkle yarn." This is a generic name that I made up to cover all of the brands of bright yarns (all with similar and acceptable properties for the Sparkle Pupa series).

Antron is a DuPont nylon; Creslan is an American Cyanamid orlon. They both achieve reflectance by having fibers with flat sides (the fibers can be three- or four-sided). Also, both materials resist felting, or, in our terms, dubbing (the fibers resist clumping into a sodden lump even in water)—and this allows them to gather air bubbles.

Fly shops carry cards of these bright yarns, and for the normal fly tyer this is the most economical way to purchase the various colors. Anyone who wants a supply for more than one lifetime can go to his mass market retail outlet (such as KMart) and purchase a skein of Ultra-Aire, Puff, Caress, or Dazzle-Aire knitting yarn.

Clear Antron

Clear Antron (rather than the mix of clear and dyed fibers found in knitting yarn) is recommended for the Clear Wing Spinner. It is available is some shops and catalogs, but not in all of them.

Normally, that would be good enough, but Antron comes in many forms. Many of those variations do not possess the properties that make the fibers resist matting. The tyer needs the clear, crinkly fibers mixed in the knitting yarn.

White sparkle yarn is not a bad substitute for the clear Antron. The real fanatic tyer, who wants the pure effect, can also separate the clear filaments from the colored ones in knitting yarn.

The best source of clear Antron is Jack Mickievicz (the man purchased a carding machine and train carload of the material): **Jack's Tackle**, RD 1 Box 196, Galeton, PA 16922.

Flex Hooks

The situation with the Flex Hooks (designed for imitations of large insects and for bass bugs) demonstrates what happens when "amateurs" create or promote products. The word amateur fits me—fly fishing in not my occupation. It is my hobby.

The design on the hook is finished; the prototypes have been tested (exact dimensions are listed in the text). People with much more business sense than me will be manufacturing and distributing the hooks soon.

My choice as producer of the Flex Hook was **Tiemco**. The consistently high quality of all of their hooks was the deciding factor (and the extensive distribution system of **Umpqua Feather Merchants** was also an important consideration).

They manufacture the front section of the hook separately. The tolerances are matched exactly to the TMC 800 B (size 8) straight eye hook. This TMC 800 B, a wide gap design perfect for all of the Flex Hook patterns, is the rear section.

R. Valentine Atkinson (photographer)

Collectors who desire photographs for framing can contact Valentine directly for his splendid black and white and color prints at 1263 6th Avenue, San Francisco, California 94122.

Gretchen Grayum (illustrator)
Gretchen's original art works and the original illustrations from *The Dry Fly* can be purchased directly from her. Write to 813 9th Avenue, Helena, Montana 59601.

Polycelon/Ethafoam/Polyurethane Large-Cell Foam
In fly fishing shops and catalogs these products are often lumped under the name "foam" (Orvis uses the term Fly Foam). The fly tyer can be sure that the material is suitable for creating the halo, or aura, on flies by holding it up to the light. The edge of the foam should be translucent.

David Halblom, who has a background in the industry, tells me that my favorite foam (a common packing material available in sheets) is a large-cell, closed-cell polyurethane.

River Rap Audio Tapes
These are wonderful listening; each one is unique. The tapes are currently available on the Madison River (with Craig Mathews), Henry's Fork (with Mike Lawson), Yellowstone River in Yellowstone Park (with Bob Jacklin), Yellowstone River in Montana (with John Bailey), Housatonic River (with Dale Spartas), Beaverkill River (with Eric Peper), Margaree River (with Joe Garman), and Wolf River (with Wayne Anderson). They are available from **Greycliff Publishing Company**, Box 1273, Helena, Montana 59624.

Video tapes (and fly tying instructions for my patterns)
The Dry Fly does not contain photo sequences or illustration sequences for tying the new patterns. Why not? My experience with *Caddisflies* was that possibly one tyer in ten could learn how to tie the patterns from sequences.

But any good tyer could learn to make an acceptable replica by watching a video. The visual medium simply does a better job at teaching the intricate steps in fly tying. So why waste valuable paper? Each medium—video, audio, and print—is the best at certain things.

"Tying and Fishing Caddisflies," which shows the patterns from *Caddisflies*, and "Tying and Fishing Attractors," which shows many of the flies featured in this book (including the Double Wing), are available from Jack Dennis at **Snake River Books**, P.O. Box 286, Jackson, Wyoming 83001.

Speaking
My speaking dates are limited (remember my amateur status). But escaping Deer Lodge and discovering the real world is a lot of fun for me. Engagements in warm climates during the dead of winter are especially appreciated.

Much of my speaking consists of weekend seminars with my friends, Jack Dennis and Mike Lawson. Our group goes by the catchy name of **The Travelling Fly Fishermen**. Contact Snake River Books (address above) or call 1-800-522-5755 for a schedule of events.

My individual speaking dates can be arranged through the **Book Cellar**, P.O. Box 166, Deer Lodge, Montana 59722 (telephone 406-846-3876).

Original Fly Patterns

Approved versions of my patterns are available through Umpqua Feather Merchants. This company does not sell directly to individuals, but they supply fly shops around the country.

Umpqua has exclusive rights to any of my flies that they see fit to produce, but some of the newer patterns or more exotic patterns (with insufficient commercial demand) are not available through them.

All of my patterns are available to individuals through **Private Label Flies** (same address as the Book Cellar). These include flies produced by Umpqua in Sri Lanka and India and flies produced locally specifically for Private Label Flies.

My own tying is restricted to flies that are given away—none of these are for sale. There is a boom at the moment in collecting flies by well known tyers. It is always an honor to be asked to sell my personal efforts, but the demand is too great for me to meet (and they are really pretty scraggly creations, anyway).

Caddisflies

This book continues to sell amazingly well even after ten years in print. It is available to fly fishing shops and book stores through **Lyons and Burford**, Publishers, 31 West 21 Street, New York, New York 10010.

Challenge of the Trout

Greycliff Publishing Company owns the rights to *Challenge of the Trout* (my first book). It will be reprinted in a revised edition in 1992.

Book Cellar newsletter

Many of the stories in *The Dry Fly* originally appeared in the Book Cellar newsletter. The response to that material convinced me to break the tradition of totally humorless writing in fly fishing how-to books.

The lack of laughter in almost all fly fishing literature seemed totally at odds with the excitement and joy of actual fly fishing trips (none of mine end up being all that solemn). Nobody needs to tell me that such frivolity is going to bother some readers.

Those who enjoy such an approach can write to the Book Cellar (address above) for future newletters.

Postscript

In the House of Commons, during a particularly bitter debate, William Gladstone shouted at his opponent, "You, Sir, will die either on the gallows or of venereal disease."

Benjamin Disraeli, without the slightest pause, responded, "That, Sir, depends on whether I embrace your morals or your mistress."

A fly fisherman, with his limitless choices, accumulates experience and knowledge, but just like a politician he must quickly embrace a philosophy for powering the opinions acquired from that experience. A dry fly fisherman, especially, better be certain about what he embraces because his failures will be more absolute. The gallows or venereal disease? No, the consequences more likely would be maddening refusals from rising trout or lonely floats over blank water.

It is easy to spot the beginner on the stream. He is the one changing flies every few minutes, not with any plan for choosing but out of desperation, trying to stumble onto an answer when he has no idea of what the question is. He is also the fellow asking everyone, "What fly are you using?" This is the way we all were in the beginning.

The dry fly has always required more faith than other methods.

A dry fly purist, except maybe on the richest of spring creeks, should not be a rigid imitationist. Strict imitation requires a keen sense of observation but only a minimum of imagination. The purist often wonders if a nymph, wet fly or streamer would be catching more trout than his dry fly—he needs to hope for the triumphs of attraction.

My own fishing includes nymph, wet fly, and streamer tactics. The thought of being a purist never appealed to me; instead, my philosophy embraces a preference, sometimes to the point of being illogical, for the dry fly. It recognizes when other methods may be superior.

I like a quote from John Gierach's *A View From Rat Lake*:

I had determined that the answer was the small *Callibaetis* nymph, the one with the ostrich herl along the abdomen to mimic the gills. It's what I was catching my few fish on. Gary, incidently, had determined the answer to be the dry fly and that's how he was catching his. There was a time when things like that were great mysteries to me, but lately it's become clear: he got them on dry flies because that's how he wanted to do it.

John was also fishing a nymph because "he wanted to." One of his trout on a nymph that week was an eight-pound rainbow. Do you know what I remember from that trip? Seldom, while actually fishing, did either one of us ask what fly the other was using. It didn't matter; neither one of us was going to frantically tie on the "killer" fly that the other was fishing with because we knew for sure what we wanted to catch trout on.

Each method of fly fishing has its prime moments. The effectiveness of nymph imitations is linked to behavioral drift; the naturals reach peak levels of abundance at different times of the day. Trout feed, sometimes selectively, on the predominant form in the currents. The classic wet fly is not a "quaint but impractical" method of fly fishing; it is usually the best tactic for imitating egg-laying insects, both those that fall helpless and drown and those that actively swim. The streamer works surprisingly well during hatches, especially for larger trout at dawn and dusk; of course, it's also a proven way of teasing aggressive, spawning trout into striking.

My observations in western rivers show roughly how much time trout spend feeding on insects at each level of a trout stream:

Surface—10 percent (adult insects on top of the surface film)
Just below the surface—10 percent (emergers or drowned adults hanging on the bottom of the film)
Drift level—60 percent (nymphs swept along just above the bottom, in that mixing zone between the calm water among the rocks and the unobstructed currents above)
Bottom—15 percent (nymphs crawling and swimming in the calm water among the rocks; trout "grub" these insects off the bottom)
Stray feeding at other, random levels—5 percent

This is only the hours that trout spend feeding. They take insects imitated by dry flies or emergers 20 percent of the time, but stomach samplings reveal a different set of percentages—adult and emerging insects make up 35 to 50 percent of the actual diet by item. The discrepancy shows that trout feed more efficiently at the surface. When they can rise regularly, and with unerring accuracy, they take insects faster from the roof of the stream.

This is the secret of the dry fly's effectiveness as a searcher. Trout prefer to rise even when nothing is happening on the surface, because they are naturally adept at it. Any fly on top is a temptation for them.

Why did I study attractor patterns? Not just to catch more trout on the surface, but also to extend the number of hours when a dry fly would work. It wasn't enough to randomly flog with bright flies during those extra hours, though—there had to be a philosophy for making intelligent choices.

I always needed a Theory of Imitation. When those trout rose under my nose on Mill Brook, snubbing my fly and taking naturals, they simply convinced me that for each situation there was one imitation better than any others. Every important trout-stream insect from then on stood as a challenge to me.

I needed a Theory of Attraction for another reason. Without one, there was no difference between the expert casting a Royal Coachman and the neophyte casting the same fly. If I wasn't sure of my fly choice, I'd be one more frantic beginner, no matter how polished or assured my presentation, asking everybody on the stream what they were using and changing flies every few minutes.

The development of a fly fisherman is away from that bumbling behavior. The angler eventually embraces not someone else's philosophy but his own, choosing his own selection of patterns to carry on stream. He studies both sides of the fly fishing coin—imitation and attraction. Then, when his own theories give him confidence, he knows where to start; and, when his first fly fails, which will happen often enough, he knows what area of dry fly theory to try next on the trout. He's then on the verge of becoming an accomplished fly fisherman and not just a lost soul gazing at those mysterious natural and synthetic creations in his fly box.

The Dry Fly
New Angles

Edited by Rob Davidson of Field & Stream
Designed by Bonnie Lambert of Desktop Type
and Glenda Clay Bradshaw of Greycliff
Composed in Garamond on an Apple Macintosh by
Desktop Type
Printed on Finch Opaque (acid-free) by
BookCrafters, Chelsea, Michigan